'Over the past decade two phenomena have come to define the Kurdish conflict: the consolidation of Turkey's surveillance state and the Kurdish movement's harnessing of gender politics. In this charged space between Turkish drones and the compelling figure of the Kurdish female fighter, Latif Tas brings the recent transformations in Kurdish politics into focus. His ethnography is both intimate and critical, with a healthy dose of analytical distance. A must-read for scholars of authoritarian politics and the role of gender in contemporary forms of resistance.'
Mucahit Bilici, Associate Professor of Sociology, John Jay College and CUNY Graduate Center

'Tas walks you through the Kurdish streets while conversing with Kurdish activists, former female PKK fighters, Assyrians, ordinary people and Turkish police. This well-written ethnographic study, devoid of academic jargon, presents a critical approach to the Turkish state and Kurdish political movement. Undoubtedly, this book will be a great source to the interested public and enrich MENA syllabuses in general and Kurdish studies in particular.'
Ekrem Karakoc, Associate Professor, Binghamton University

'Kurds are among America's best friends globally with whom western countries share both values and strategic interests. The dynamic of Kurdish international relations is explored on these pages. *Authoritarianism and Kurdish Alternative Politics* is a "must-read" for faculty, students and followers of the Middle East.'
David L. Phillips, Director, Program on Peace-building and Rights, Institute for the Study of Human Rights, Columbia University

'We constantly need to understand the nature and evolution of authoritarian regimes. We must understand how these regimes disrupt lives and how people react to them. Latif Tas's book contributes to this important endeavour by focusing on Kurds' stories. Tas's approach is direct, aimed at comprehending the everyday struggles of people.'
Antonio De Lauri, Research Professor, Chr. Michelsen Institute (CMI), Norway

'This is a heartfelt cry against the depredations of authoritarian rule and the resulting sufferings of the Kurds past and present. Latif Tas has the keen journalistic sensibilities of someone who, having listened empathetically to anyone and everyone, is able to piece together a compelling story, and who possesses the historical memory to put it all in context.'
Webb Keane, George Herbert Mead Collegiate Professor, University of Michigan

AUTHORITARIANISM AND KURDISH ALTERNATIVE POLITICS

Governmentality, Gender and Justice

Latif Tas

EDINBURGH
University Press

Edinburgh University Press is one of the leading university presses in the UK. We publish academic books and journals in our selected subject areas across the humanities and social sciences, combining cutting-edge scholarship with high editorial and production values to produce academic works of lasting importance. For more information visit our website: edinburghuniversitypress.com

© Latif Tas, 2022

Edinburgh University Press Ltd
The Tun – Holyrood Road
12 (2f) Jackson's Entry
Edinburgh EH8 8PJ

Typeset in 11/15 Adobe Garamond by
IDSUK (DataConnection) Ltd, and
printed and bound by CPI Group (UK) Ltd,
Croydon, CR0 4YY

A CIP record for this book is available from the British Library

ISBN 978 1 4744 5741 5 (hardback)
ISBN 978 1 4744 5744 6 (webready PDF)
ISBN 978 1 4744 5743 9 (epub)

CONTENTS

FIGURES

ACKNOWLEDGEMENTS

The last five years have been unbelievable. It has been a really challenging time on a global, local and personal level. On a global level, authoritarianism and autocracy have become a hot topic around the world, creating a new world order. Progressive and democratic forces and institutions around the world are threatened by these new, destructive forces. On a local level, populism and nationalism have increased, and majoritarian-supported demagogues have introduced themselves as new 'survivors' with their anti-truth, anti-science, anti-ecology, sexist and discriminatory approaches. Fictionalised news media, power-hungry 'intellectuals', mafia bosses and groups of people who seek easy benefits and nepotistic positions become the embodiment of such authority and the integral force of ruling. On a personal level, these new authoritarian approaches have affected the lives of many people, including my colleagues' and my own. I was not able to visit my father to say goodbye to him while he was on his deathbed in 2018, because we had signed the Academics for Peace Petition, asking for the authoritarian Turkish government to stop their violence against civilians and innocent people. Not only myself, but my children were also punished, and not able to travel to see their grandfather for the first and last time. This means authoritarianism does not only punish individuals in the present, but also future generations and extended family members. A civil death is created for anybody who is against the regime.

This book was written during these turbulent times. Despite these global, local and personal limitations and disadvantages, there have been amazing people, institutions and organisations around the world which give us hope for a better future. First, I would like to thank the European Commission for their Marie-Curie Global Award, which allowed me to focus on my research and contributed hugely to the writing of this book. My research received significant funding from the European Union's Horizon 2020 research and innovation programme, under the Marie Sklodowska-Curie grant agreement No. 703201. My research was hosted by SOAS University of London (UK), Syracuse University (US) and the Max Planck Institute for Social Anthropology (Germany). This Marie-Curie Global Award was not just one of the first successes for Kurdish and Turkish studies, it was also the first time in history that SOAS secured this grant. This achievement created an example and opened the way to new successful applications and thinking in Kurdish and Turkish studies.

As a scientist, studying political violence, social movements, authoritarianism, youth, gender, migration, diaspora and social justice, I have been doing ethnographic research in Turkey, Germany, the UK, Iraq and Syria for the last thirteen years and this award helped me to focus my thoughts and research. My institutions in the US, the Maxwell School at Syracuse University, and especially Professor Yuksel Sezgin, have been amazingly helpful, and we shared many discussions before and during the writing of this book. The Director of the Moynihan Institute of Global Affairs, Professor Margaret Hermann, as well as Professor Brian Taylor and Dr Nazanin Shahrokni, with their intellect and friendship, made the Maxwell School at Syracuse unforgettable. In Germany, the Max Planck Institute (MPI) for Social Anthropology has become a home for me; the rich academic environment provided a great platform for endless discussions and opportunities for inspiring and testing new knowledge. The Director, Professor Marie-Claire Foblets, has been always very supportive, offering a welcoming home for me and organising several group workshops which helped sharpen the arguments of this book.

To be a member of the Institute for Advanced Study (IAS), Princeton, was a milestone, and I was very fortunate to be surrounded by many great intellectuals and minds, and to find a rich and serene environment in which to shape this book. The School of Social Science, with the directors Diddier Fassion, Alondra Nelson and Marion Fourcade, and all the other amazing members who took part in the 2019–20 discussions despite the disruption of Covid-19, created an atmosphere of unique knowledge and new science. Personal discussions over lunch meetings or during teatimes allowed me to bring challenging questions to the table and to find creative, exceptional approaches and new outcomes.

Most importantly, this book would not have been possible without contributions from critical Kurdish and Turkish politicians, lawyers, activists and community members. I am indebted to the many Kurdish people in Kurdistan (Turkey, Syria, Iraq, Iran) and the diaspora for their valuable time and insight. I am especially grateful to the Kurdish-led HDP leader Sellahhatin Demirtas, Diyarbakir former co-mayors Gultan Kisanak and Firat Anli, Mardin co-mayor Ferhunde Akyol, former MP and lawyer Ayla Akat and many others, whose honest and real-life accounts helped me to understand the Kurdish struggle in the Middle East and Kurdish alternative politics against authoritarianism in practice.

I would also like to thank the editorial team at Edinburgh University Press, especially the editors for Islamic & Middle Eastern Studies. They have been an extremely supportive team. The comments and suggestions made by the reviewers and my copy-editor polished the text considerably, for which I am also very thankful. Nadje Al-Ali read an early version of chapters and provided valuable comments. Werner Menski's treasured comments and recommendations strengthened the argument of this book tremendously. Zehra Dogan, a well-known Kurdish artist, allowed me to use some of her art work. I am thankful to them. Especially for their great friendship, and mental support I would like to also thank my colleagues Katayoun Alidadi, Kadir Bas, Nusret Cetin, Weysi Dag, Mehmet Kurt, Kathrin Seidel, Engin Sustam, Omer Tekdemir, Mengia Tschalaer and Janine Ubink.

I have not just written this book over the last five years, but I have also been gifted with my four beautiful children, Lukas, Ayla, Leyla and Cyrus during this time. This was another big challenge for myself as an academic, and my life partner Hannah. While many colleagues find it difficult to deal with one child, we manage as a great team, and I cannot express enough my love and gratitude to Hannah for her wonderful support, friendship and love. I have been away from my country and my family for five years and my mother has remained an unrivalled force, even though there are thousands of kilometres between us.

This book is dedicated to my father, Fahrettin Tas, to whom I was not able to say a last goodbye. However, our roots are so deep, deeper than those of any authoritarian regime. None of these regimes can compete with or eliminate such strong roots between us, our children and our kindred.

I hope the arguments of this book and the real-life experiences of Kurdish people under authoritarianism will be an important contribution to increasing awareness and understanding of authoritarian regimes, making possible alternative politics, and helping to eliminate or limit their power. I am confident that the next generations will continue to produce better knowledge, and sow a new, loving, liveable, more peaceful and richer life for themselves and those who come after.

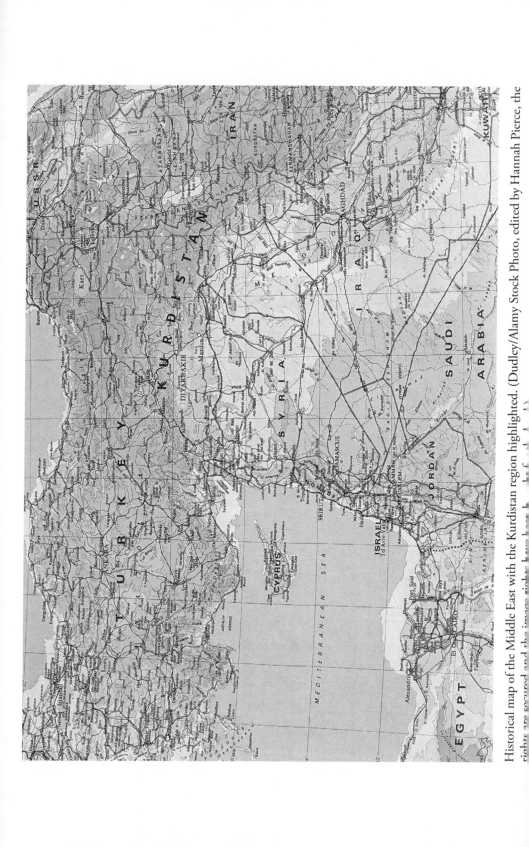

Historical map of the Middle East with the Kurdistan region highlighted. (Dudley/Alamy Stock Photo, edited by Hannah Pierce, the rights are secured and the image rights have been leased for the final book.)

INTRODUCTION

On 12 May 2015, I saw a small police drone camera flying over me, just around 100–150 metres above ground. It was during my visits to the backstreets and local neighbourhoods of Mardin, a border city between Turkey and Syria. I was trying to understand the normal daily life of Kurdish people, their relations with the justice system and politics, but this drone was moving and seemingly following my movements. 'Big Brother' was not just hiding behind police uniform or secret cameras any more, it was very visible, in the air and covering a much larger area than the eyes of the police or the corner camera's static position. It was very unsettling for the local people who were under almost continuous surveillance and followed closely. This new power was far beyond the actions of a traditional police state. Arrest, which had also increased while I was there, was no longer just something physical; it was an emotional and psychological attack that had the effect of changing thinking by forcing you to think about the next step. This perpetual monitoring and controlling of the state structure was not just limiting, recording and intimidating its individual members, but moving beyond that and including anybody who was interacting with any of its citizens or any small groups they deemed suspicious. These surveillance cameras were the additional and advanced eyes, ears, brains and weapons of a government whose aim is absolute control.

Kurdish regions have been in a permanent state of exception and lawlessness of the state forces for decades, but I was surprised that this was so visible around May 2015, when there were so-called peace talks between the Turkish government and representatives of Kurdish guerrilla and political wings. In reality, there was no real peace process, and no talks. The main aim was to disguise the conflict under the so-called peace process, which gave the Turkish regime some time to complete its monopolised authoritarianism among the state's institutions. At the same time, it also gave the Kurdish movement time to postpone their fight with Turkey and focus on liberating space and creating a Kurdish autonomous state in Syria. Playing the game of 'peace' was thus beneficial for both sides. I questioned these peace talks in an article on 9 July 2015, in *Open Democracy* titled 'What kind of peace?' However, even at that time accounts were exaggerated to be 'so-peaceful' or 'progressive' by many academic works and articles.[1]

Visibility of the obvious police and state power was also creating some invisibility or even absence of equality, justice and the right of free movement of the individuals in the region. The police did not just have the power to act freely and flexibly for the administration of the regime and to make verdicts about individuals' lives and actions, but also had the laws and orders of the regime in their hands, with full authority over any enforcement.[2] The fear was visible in every corner of the city and was affecting the minds and actions of Kurdish ethnic and small non-Muslim religious minorities. The question of how plural and complex nations can live together without alienation and marginalisation of certain demographic groups, both free and equal, and both similar and different has been asked by many social scientists. Walzer analysed this in his work on *Spheres of Justice* and suggested the concept of the 'binational state' as a solution.[3] While there is an increase in populism and authoritarianism that receives its power from the dominant national identity

---

[1] See, for example, Gunter 2013; Ensaroglu 2013; Tezcur 2013; Aras and Duman 2014; Philips 2015.

[2] See, ICJ 2016; OHCHR 2016b; Amnesty International 2016c; PEN International 2016. Especially, the International Commission of Jurists (ICJ) and OHCHR Turkey's reports discussed in detail how Turkey's judicial and prosecution process have been totally reshaped according to the needs of the regime. Freedom of expression by media, academics and the general public was restricted for political control. Under Erdoğan's leadership Turkey has introduced new bills which allow the regime to extend its control of the Turkish Court of Cessation, Turkish Council of State, and to watch, hunt and arrest Turkish citizens inside or outside of Turkey.

[3] Walzer 1983.

of a group and its nationalism, how can it be possible to re-create Walzer's 'binational state'? Equally, while there is the problem of religion and discrimination based on religious identity, religion cannot therefore be a solution for a plural nation, not until equal and free space is created for different religious groups, as we know from many examples around the world including, Lebanon, India and Israel.[4]

John Rawls also argued for reasonable pluralism in his work *The Law of People*, where he proposed that 'in public reason comprehensive doctrines of truth or right be replaced by an idea of the politically reasonable addressed to citizens as citizens'.[5] The 'post truth' and 'alternative facts' and 'fact inventing' have become part of authoritarian leaders' new political reasoning and justification for any of their illegitimate actions. For example, after the November 2020 US presidential election, without showing any evidence, President Donald Trump and his supporters claimed that the election was fraudulent and stolen from them. He wrongly claimed that he won the election, and many of his supporters believed him. He refused for weeks to acknowledge defeat and Joe Biden's huge margin win in the democratic election. This and similar examples have created and strengthened an autocratic centric society which does not believe anything beyond what their autocrats say, true or false. Social facts are discussed in great detail in *American Anthropologist* articles by Ho, Cavanaugh and Greenhouse.[6]

In the Kurdish regions of Turkey, the state wanted to be totally in charge in any way possible, under the autocratic rules and the controlled media's alternative-fact-based propaganda machine. For example, hundreds – almost all – Kurdish-elected mayors were removed from the office between 2015 and 2020, and were described as members of terrorist organisations without any proof.[7] Around the same time, according to deputies of the Kurdish-led People's Democratic Party (HDP), in total 16,300 of their party members

---

[4] See, for the discussion of religion and plural society, Rajagopal 2001; Menski 2006 and 2011; Belge 2008; Solanki 2011; Sezgin 2014; Natanel 2016; Scarciglia and Menski 2018; Kokal 2019.

[5] Rawls 1997: 2; 1999: 55.

[6] See, Ho and Cavanaugh 2019; Greenhouse 2019.

[7] See, Human Rights Watch 2020.

were detained and 3,500 of them were jailed. Just between August and December 2019, twenty-four Kurdish elected mayors were removed from office and imprisoned without any conviction.[8] When the Turkish president's spokesperson, Ibrahim Kalin, was questioned by a famous journalist, Tim Sebastian, at the *Deutsche Welle* (*DW*)'s Conflict Zone programme on 28 November 2019, about the removal and imprisonment of Kurdish mayors, Kalin responded that 'they will be convicted'. Sebastian questioned further: 'Since the 2016 coup attempt, 180 media outlets have been forcibly closed, over 220,000 websites blocked. . . . Scores of journalists remained in jail or under travel bans. Hardly a proud record for you, is it?' Kalin's answer was, 'Yes, but [that's what happens] when you're dealing with PKK news outlets spreading propaganda for the terrorist network.' Sebastian pressed him further: 'Your party has sat back and watched countless people's lives ruined while you threw allegations at them that turned out to be false. So what happened to the presumption of innocence? They're just simply taken out of their jobs, removed.' Kalin replied by saying that there is an ongoing judicial process and they would be convicted. Sebastian emphasised that eventually everybody would be charged and that may include Kalin when the next Turkish government comes in.

Kalin's response or lack of response was more telling about how the Turkish regime operates. His response means that, politically, Kurdish politicians and activists were already found guilty and decisions were made even before the judicial process found any single piece of evidence about the so-called 'terror' accusations. There is a presumption of guilt by the mere fact that a person is Kurdish. Kalin was right that they would be convicted according to the autocrat's decision and the judiciary would just blindly follow, as has happened over several decades. This was the reason why some of the arrested persons, for example former co-Mayor of Diyarbakır Gulten Kisanak, and the former leader of HDP, Selahattin Demirtaş have been in prison for almost four years without any conviction. The rights and choices of the people were not taken seriously by the state authorities and there was no democracy at all. This was also clear proof that the rule of law, political and legal justice was working differently here or was not working at all.

[8] See, Home Office 2020.

It is almost impossible to discuss the Kurdish movement's fight against Turkey without recognising their negatively marked space within legal politics in Turkey. Kurds have not been allowed to take part in any meaningful legal politics and cannot argue for their rights. To be in prison or killed have been almost the only two options left for Kurdish political activists grabbed by the state's authorities. After mass arrests, the children and relatives of arrested or dead Kurds found a way to go to the Kurdish mountains, and to join Kurdish guerrilla forces to fight against the state. Eren Keskin, a famous female Kurdish rights defence lawyer, said on 25 September 2020, after her the arrest and that of another eighty-two Kurdish politicians and activists: 'What the voice in me says; "they want us all dead"! This is exactly my feeling . . . Therefore, let's live more and multiply.'

For 'distributive justice' as Michael Walzer discusses, equality and basic democratic values are the main necessity of any legal and political justice,[9] but in Turkey, and many other authoritarian countries, a specific group was receiving an unequal share of (in)justice from that distribution. Judges were not making decisions according to evidence but rather the political will of the sovereign power. There was an arbitrary executive order and a kangaroo-court-style process. The state's authoritarian blatant lawlessness was almost shameless; it could easily be mistaken for a badly written dark comedy. As Diego Cupolo's article in *The Atlantic* argued on 6 May 2018, 'Turkey's dangerous game of "hostage diplomacy"' was not just limited to Turkey, but included foreign nationals as well. The courts co-operated with the authoritarian regime and it became 'normal' to put anyone behind bars if they were critical of the government. As a result, even some judges, including technical judges from the supreme court, public prosecutors, and many lawyers have had to seek asylum abroad.

The state's hegemonic style of government and rejection of a plural society creates endless conflict and division. As a result, the governor-governed relationship is broken. When the society and its political economy are not governed equally, when pluralism is denied for the sake of one group or nation, when there is an absence of justice for some groups and when the state power is very visible in every corner, then resistance, revolt and chronic conflict are

[9] Walzer 1983.

also inevitable. When targeted discrimination is combined with continuous authoritarian rules reinforced by surveillance police and devices, then it usually leaves many with a 'nothing to lose' attitude, creating fearlessness and a total rejection of the state and its authority.

The questions 'Where is Kurdistan?' or 'Who are the Kurds?' have been asked often and answered differently by different groups and power holders. Kurds are indigenous people of the Middle East. They have not created a modern nation state yet, but they also have not surrendered their ambitions to do so and have managed to keep their identity. The terrain in which they live has not been easy for them. While sometimes high mountains create some level of protection, this is no longer relevant or useful against today's modern weapons, especially drones. The terrain has mostly brought problems, risk and trouble for them: they are at the centre of clashing powers, the main trade routes between east and west, north and south, and most importantly, economically and naturally rich lands. Kurds rebelled against the Ottomans when the Ottoman sultans were brutal. They have mounted dozens of rebellions against the Turkish, Iraqi, Syrian and Iranian states, since the foundations of these states are based on authoritarian structures that do not respect ethnic diversity and people's rights to a 'homeland'. Their revolts have been almost always oppressed, but this never stops Kurds from starting another one. While this has made it arduous for them to establish a unitary, independent state, it has also made it difficult for others to occupy and control Kurdish lands under one or multiple powers. While Kurds are divided between themselves and have created multiple and conflicted fronts, an important contributory factor in their unsuccessful attempts, they remain, however, emotionally united against the various occupiers. This makes any political calculation very difficult in Kurdistan and has many unexpected results.

The state's legal discrimination against Kurds or betrayal of Kurds did not just start recently. It has been happening for more than a century and almost every Western power has managed to betray the Kurds at least once since the late nineteenth century. This became obvious with the end of WWI and continues today. During the brutality of WWI, 'for the peace of the world' then American President Wilson established fourteen conditions at the beginning of 1918, which included absolute freedom, democracy and self-determination for national minorities, including Kurds. He also promised that the political independence and territorial integrity of small states and minorities would be protected. His twelfth condition was specifically about the Ottoman Empire, Turks and Kurds. It stated: 'The Turkish portion of the present Ottoman Empire should be assured a secure sovereignty, but the other nationalities which are now under Turkish rule should be assured an undoubted security of life and an absolutely unmolested opportunity of autonomous development.'[10]

Following these conditions, Western powers promised an independent Kurdistan in 1920.[11] However, soon afterwards in 1923, the Kurds were abandoned by English, French and Italian delegates during the Lausanne Agreement with Turkey, in return for the petrol of Kirkuk and Mosul. Turkish diplomats threatened the Western powers and claimed that they would adopt Lenin's Bolshevik ideology if they didn't accept Turkey's wishes and get rid of the ideology of any Kurdish rights or state. They were successful in the diplomatic arena, as they have been in the last four centuries. Nothing much has changed since then.

Later, the Soviet Block made another promise to Iranian Kurds for the Kurdish Republic of Mahabad in 1946, but left them without any protection to be crushed by the Iranian regime a year later. In the 1970s, Iran promised Iraqi Kurds support for independence, but again abandoned them later and opened the way for thousands of Kurds to be killed by the Iraqi regime. Saddam continued his crimes against Kurds and in 1988 used Western-made chemical weapons against them, killing thousands more Kurds in Halabja in March 1988. A few years later, in 1991, the US asked for Kurdish help in its war against Saddam and got what they asked for. A short time after, George W. Bush left the Kurds at the mercy of Saddam and again they had to pay a further heavy price. Only after 2003 did the Iraqi Kurds achieve some level of autonomy – an autonomy which has been under attack from the Iraqi, Iranian and Turkish states ever since.[12] ISIS was the last authoritarian power that did not miss any chance to carry out genocidal acts against Kurds in

---

[10] The US President Woodrow Wilson's 14 points for world peace established on 8 January 1918.

[11] See, Ali 1997.

[12] See, Bozarslan 2014 and 2017.

Syria and Iraq and other small, powerless minorities. Kurds were forced to the front line by the Western powers to defeat ISIS, and again were given many promises, including autonomy. But again, after the Kurds did what they were asked for, they did not get what they were promised. The Kurdistan independence referendum in Iraq in 2017 was not supported by almost all Western powers, even though more than 90 per cent of Kurds voted for their independence. Kurdish autonomy in Syria has been threatened by the Turkish and Syrian authoritarian regimes. Kurds in Turkey don't even have any legal, political and cultural rights and their basic right to life is endangered.

Securing oil and resources and geostrategic concerns have always come before the protection of ethnic minorities and their right to life in the Middle East. Kurdish lands have long been a battle ground between superpowers. It was so between the Persian and Ottoman Empires for centuries, then between the Ottoman, British and French Empires a hundred years ago and currently between the United States and Russia. While global and local powerful nation states try to dominate people's lives and force them to follow their rules and regulations, most power holders have failed to understand or have ignored that central state power is not the only power. Alternative governmentality and challenging politics at regional and local levels have been introduced by different political groups and minorities who aim to limit the total control of the central state's authority and create a foundation for ending the power of existing autocrats. However, a workable solution has not yet been found with regard to the predicaments faced by Kurds in their various ancestral lands.

Kurdish Youths with Kalashnikovs

I did not only visit different neighbourhoods in the centre of Mardin, but I also visited a number of towns, such as Nusaybin and Kiziltepe and many other Kurdish-dominated cities: Diyarbakır, Kars, Batman, Agri and Urfa. I noticed that many people in the Kurdish regions did not trust anything in the state media or politics, true or false. This created a marked disconnection between Turkish and Kurdish societies, and the authoritarian forms of governance were strongly resisted. Instead, alternative politics, spaces and institutions have been created and are being practised by the Kurdish movement's local area representatives. Seeking an alternative state-like structure was not just the result of the current authoritarian regime and its policies, but has been fuelled by centuries of injustice towards Kurds, and the regime's repeated refusal to recognise its national diversity and act fairly and treat them equally. This has resulted in harsh autocratic rules and lie-based propaganda, but such interventions can have a reverse effect. The statutory enforcement of state authority, including judiciary, tax and security, was not followed by many and an alternative authority expanded its power and structure. There was de facto based civil disobedience and alternative ways of governing beneath the surface.

During my field research, I was repeatedly told that the power and role of the youth in shaping and breaking the political situation is unavoidable. I had several meetings with Kurdish street boys and girls, aged between 12 and 20. The question of who the street children are; what kind of role they have; who is organising, giving roles, empowering and protecting them, has been widely discussed. My own observation of Kurdish youth finds Christopher Williams's description closest to what I have seen and understood. Williams asked the same questions and also tried to answer:

> A street child is any boy or girl who has not reached adulthood for whom the street (in the widest sense of the word, including unoccupied dwellings, wasteland, etc.) has become her or his habitual abode and/or source of livelihood and who is inadequately (if at all) protected, supervised or directed by responsible adults.[13]

The notion of hierarchy seems to be very important among the Kurdish youth. The terms *abi, abla* (big brother, big sister) or *Hewal* (friend) are usually used between those of different age, gender, experience and political status. While those who are young and have limited roles or experience call their seniors *abi or abla*, when it comes to different gender, the term *hewal* is usually preferred. They rarely use their official names or surnames for each other. Almost everyone is known under an alias and informal name, but the terms *abi, abla* and *hewal* are used very often, for not referring to their coded name or individuality is a way to put the interest of the group before any individual needs, and also to hide individual identities. While

---

[13] Williams 1993: 832.

hewal equalises the relationship, it also leaves some space between different individuals or genders to develop different, romantic relationships, while *abi* or *abla* block such relationships. These terms were not only used among the youth, but also very often by senior Kurdish politicians, military commanders and activists. Not only was the language of Kurdish youth central to Kurdish politics, but they were also the main forces to decide or change the political direction.

The Kurdish youth were not just in charge of some streets, but also some small neighbourhoods; they formed into small groups and carried light weapons. When I asked them if they did not worry about being seen by the drone cameras, one of them responded: 'When I see them, I just pull my trousers down and piss and then I put my hand up to show them my gesture of pissing is to them. We just laugh at them.' While he made his statement, others, a mixed group of young females and males laughed. I found their language and responses very childish and naïve, highlighting their obliviousness to danger, and the fact that they felt they had nothing to lose; a fearless attitude to what could possibly result in a deadly attack from the state forces. They were very thin and nimble, dressed casually, wearing old sports shoes and jeans and light scarves in Kurdish colours (red, green and yellow), sometimes around their neck but also tied around their wrists and waists. They kept repeating that they were fighting for a normal life, with no threat of death; that their parents and grandparents didn't have any peace, so they wanted to make change for themselves and future generations. I was not even sure if they had had enough, or any, military training before holding their ubiquitous Kalashnikov guns.

They were acting as the de facto police force or militia of the parallel state and creating a new sovereign power against the existing state's power. These youths explained how they were not just resisting and fighting against state forces, but also dealing with socio-economic and judicial processes in their own neighbourhood and were used to implementing the de facto, alternative Kurdish court's decisions. Almost every Kurdish neighbourhood would operate its own de facto courts, as an alternative to the state court. It seemed that most Kurdish people, old and young, male or female, were following their orders and sympathised with them. Resistance and, when necessary, the use of violence against the forces of the authoritarian regime was the only way they thought possible to create equality and be representative of their people. The logic of their military actions, their resistance strategy, was to secure different pockets of their neighbourhood, have them controlled by a small number of people, and eventually to make connections between these pockets, to create a chain of power and eliminate the regime's authority fully from their neighbourhoods, towns and cities.

There was obviously a clash over political, military and judicial sovereignty between the authoritarian regime and the seekers of alternative politics. However, it was not looking realistic as a strategy for grabbing power from the state and regime, especially when taking into consideration the power imbalance, and the difference in levels of logistics and resources. Their only advantage was that they had the direct support of some local people and the sympathy of most. This could only help them to have a sustainable and effective resistance, which may eventually enable the transfer of power. Most of them might be annihilated by the forces of the regime in a short time and they were aware of that. When I questioned if their use of violence and digging of trenches in the middle of towns and cities were justified, and why they put their lives in danger, their response was that their actions of defence were the result of the Turkish regime's brutality and unequal treatment.

May 2015, while I was there, was also the time of the preparations for the 7 June Turkish parliamentary election, when the Kurdish-led HDP would go on to gain huge momentum. However, that momentum and 'peace' were not going to last long. Later, Erdoğan would not recognise the result of that election and put Turkey into more darkness. So it would not be easy for many people to travel to Mardin and many other Kurdish cities due to increasing conflict. There was no space left for Kurds to be part of a democratic and peaceful process, which means the regime was pushing for resistance, violence and war. However, I decided to push my luck, take a risk and visit Mardin as well as other Kurdish cities including Diyarbakır again in September of the same year and witness that revolt, violence and war directly. While the regime's physical destruction and mass arrest was to be introduced under emergency law in many Kurdish cities and towns, society as well as the state was divided. Since then, Turkey has been like a lorry without brakes rolling uncontrollably downhill with a mindless driver.

In this book, I have problematised the triangular relationship between nationalism, justice and gender politics, to argue how this allows authoritarian rulers to stay in power longer and justify their actions for monopolising power. Gendering politics and hierarchy, especially the bodies, minds and collective mobilisation of women, is important for authoritarian rulers as well as for the opposition forces. While women's personal freedom, individuality and societal equality is not guaranteed, or has even been further endangered during conflicts, their personal sacrifices are seen as normal by autocratic regimes and sometimes by opposition movements too. The question is whether the Kurdish movement has changed the role of women within society and politics for the advantage and benefit of women; have Kurdish women become more independent or increased their dependency for the national cause? These are important questions and will be analysed from witnessed, direct observations of ethnographical accounts of Kurdish men and women's daily political activity, behaviour, positionality, actions and dress code. While the numbers of women fighters are increasing among the Kurdish military wings, it is important to see how much this has secured gender equality among political party members and society. While the Kurdish movement in the Middle East seems to be against the hegemonic politics and elite class domination, to see and examine if they are also creating their alternative hegemonic and elite political class among themselves is another important focus of this book.

The Material, Methodology and Structure of the Book

Based on ethnographic research in Turkey, Syria, Iraqi Kurdistan and Kurdish diasporas in Europe, this book tries to answer the following six main interconnected questions: How is authoritarian governmentality built and operated? Is it possible for an authoritarian state to become a democratic state naturally, without violence? How and why is alternative governmentality created? Does alternative governmentality work effectively? How much is alternative governmentality different from the existing authoritarian structure? How much does the role of justice, gender and nationalism play in breaking a state or building a new state and alternative governmentality?

Didier Fassin argued that 'critique, under its multiple forms, is inherent to the anthropological project . . . [which] is more than ever needed in times laden with worrying spectres'.[14] The context of this anthropological and socio-legal research is a fieldwork investigation examining how authoritarianism creates revolt and how alternative governmentality and justice is seen and practised in conflicted environments. The anthropology and politics of state(less) people and their societies have been discussed in several important works, stemming back to *Anthropology and Modern Life* by the early American anthropologist Franz Boas.[15] More recent are studies like *Weapons of the Weak: Everyday Forms of Peasant Resistance* by James C. Scott,[16] *Small Places, Large Issues: An Introduction to Social and Cultural Anthropology* by Thomas H. Eriksen,[17] and *State Formation: Anthropological Perspective* by Christian Krohn-Hansen and Knut G. Nustad,[18] are important foundations. In this book, the examination of the state and understanding the everyday life of regular people are mainly based on direct ethnographical accounts. People's spoken accounts are not just a reflection of the current political climate and life being lived, but also a historical account of how future generations will see the history of our times.

In my previous book, *Legal Pluralism in Action*,[19] I discussed the value and practice of pluralism from the cases of Ottoman Millet Practice[20] and the current UK state perspective. Both cases had soft, flexible and pluralistic approaches where minority practices were welcomed and space was made for them. However, when we look at the centralised, hard or authoritarian state perspective, the picture is different. It would not be wise to argue the existence of pluralism in a visible way, when there is no space or tolerance for different ethnic and religious practices, such as under the Turkish authoritarian regime, where parallel state structures become almost a necessity. Given the limited literature available on alternative justice and governmentality of the Kurds in the Middle East and its diaspora, my book engages with categories of social, legal and political actors, and intends to

---

[14] Fassin 2017: 4.

[15] Boas 1932.

[16] Scott 1985.

[17] Eriksen 1995.

[18] Krohn-Hansen and Nustad 2005.

[19] Tas 2016d.

[20] Tas 2014.

capture the personal experiences and accounts of different Kurdish individuals and communities.

This interdisciplinary and ethnographically grounded book is based on in-depth interviews with Kurdish female and male politicians, mayors, lawyers, former and active guerrillas, the members of youth organisations, activists, alternative court representatives and judges, members of women's organisations, tea shop owners and regular customers, academics, barbers, taxi drivers, the representatives of different religious and ethnic groups, including official state judges, politicians, police officers, academics, lawyers and journalists. The research included all diverse groups of Kurdish society and beyond while discussing this important subject: *Authoritarianism and Kurdish Alternative Politics*. Aside from the qualitative empirical data collected from life stories and oral history accounts, participant observation, case study analysis and focus groups, the book also draws on official reports by governments, state documents, state and non-state court records, white papers, reports by NGOs and multilateral bodies, literature produced by international activists, as well as media reports. The contents of the oral interviews have been analysed with reference to the historical development of state and non-state institutions in the Middle East. Relationships with diaspora communities have also been very important.

Since 2015, I have carried out sixty-two interviews and five focus group discussions in Turkey (Diyarbakır, Mardin, Kars and Istanbul) in addition to carrying out eighty-five interviews and ten focus group discussions with Kurdish community members in Germany and the UK. I have also completed fifty-five interviews with Kurdish people closely connected to the Kurdish political and national movement in Rojava and Iraqi Kurdistan (in total 202 interviews, and fifteen focus group discussions). Due to the ongoing security and political situation in Turkey and Syria in recent years, some of my latest research has taken place with Kurdish women and men, politicians and activists living in the diaspora, including those who have moved recently (Berlin, London and New York), as well as those visiting these cities for professional, political or personal reasons. Additional interviews with these new arrivals helped me to understand the evolving politics of justice, parallel state institutions and governmentality in the Middle East and the diaspora. These interviews have been supplemented with email and telephone conversations/

interviews with women and men living inside Turkey and Syria. In addition, I have directly observed hundreds of de facto court cases in different locations. I was also lucky enough, thanks to Kurdish court judges, to have access to the alternative courts' case files of different cities and towns in Turkey, as well as in Berlin and London. My ethnographic research based on participant observation has allowed me to observe and analyse everyday lives, practices, interactions and tensions between ideology and empirical realities. I received ethical board review approval from SOAS University London for this EU Marie-Curie funded research. The ethical processes were also closely followed by the EU, the funder, and several reports detailed my research challenges and risks. In addition, a detailed report conducted by an external ethics adviser provided assurance of my data and the value of such ethnographical work.

The societal ethical codes and challenges in everyday life have been problematised in this book. As Webb Keane argues, ethics is not just limited to moments of reflection, and moral awareness is more than solitary pondering of dilemmas. Ethical life is intersubjective, and often habitual. The relation of a voice to its speaker varies, and the ethical positions these voices depict have differing relationships to their speakers. Ethical standards and also moral codes also change over time and are not static. Ethics rest on three important foundations: first, second and third person perspectives.[21]

During my fieldwork study in Turkey and Germany, I spent a considerable amount of time in traditional teahouses, which are important places for observing and understanding different communities. I chose different types of tea shops which were dominated and represented by different ethnic and religious groups, such as Kurds, Turks, Alevi and Sunni. These memberships are very important for meaningful connections, unseen and hidden realities. In such places, people spend long hours, use their own languages, exchange information and wealth, gossip about politics and daily life, while building trust and extending networks. They are publicly visible, look to be collective and open, but in practice more takes place than first meets the eye. They have their own hierarchy and code of conduct. Everything may be visible and seem accessible, but they are mainly male-dominated spaces that operate according to unwritten laws and membership criteria.

---

[21] Keane 2015.

As Linda Tuhiwai Smith argues, without decolonising methodologies,[22] it is not possible to establish any new, right and scientific knowledge about the oppressed minorities and indigenous people. It would be only the repetition of the collective memory of imperialism and their intellect machines. Smith argues that:

> many researchers, academics and project workers may see the benefits of their particular research projects as serving a greater good 'for mankind', or serving a specific emancipatory goal for an oppressed community. But belief in the ideal that benefiting mankind is indeed a primary outcome of scientific research is as much a reflection of ideology as it is of academic training. It becomes so taken for granted that many researchers simply assume that they as individuals embody this ideal and are natural representatives of it when they work with other communities. Indigenous peoples across the world have other stories to tell.[23]

Without touching people's lives, walking their streets, using their language, participating in their meetings, festivals, funerals, weddings and observing the look of fear or happiness on their faces and understanding what they feel, it would not be possible to write about oppressed groups and indigenous people. It would be just written from a distance, with the help of already-established knowledge, limited by their censors and borders. It can only be serving the colonisers and oppressors, but not the people of the subject. As Keane states, ethnographic evidence problematises and challenges the established psychological and sociological perspectives of knowledge, which then creates a distinctive ethics of recognition of the truth and human dignity.[24] The aim of this book is to decolonise methodologies, to catch and retell oppressed people's stories from their own language, culture, streets, living spaces, daily practices and experiences of their real-life stories, through their eyes. People's untold, unnoticed and not easily shared powerful stories, views and practices are part of their day-to-day resistance.

Chapter 1 focuses on authoritarian governmentality and the global increase in autocrats' capturing of states, much like hunting octopuses. This

---

[22] Smith 2008.
[23] Smith 2008: 2.
[24] Keane 2015.

chapter will argue how the legal system has been an important instrument at the hand of autocrats, and laws and policies have been created as a corporate set of conditions. This chapter sets up the puzzle of why Foucault's concept of governmentality has its limits, and how authoritarian governmentality is born, functions and fails in the end. The role of media, intellectuals and society in authoritarian governmentality and how authoritarianism cannot be limited to a simple individual power is analysed from the cases and examples. This chapter then moves to introduce a new theory, alternative governmentality, against autocratic rules. The question of how and if any alternative politics against authoritarian governmentality can be different or follow a similar pattern, is argued. The section also critically engages with the Weberian notion of the state, which claims that only the state has a 'monopoly on violence' (*Gewaltmonopol des Staates*) and a monopoly on the legitimate use of physical force within its territory.

Chapter 2 starts with my direct observations of the atmosphere in Turkey just before and during the most recent conflict. I will re-examine my ethnographical account in Mardin just before the conflict in May 2015, and then I will recount my experiences of being caught in a curfew during heavy clashes between the Turkish police and Kurdish youth activists in the Sur district of Diyarbakır in September 2015, when female Kurdish MPs and women's rights activists came to my rescue. The ethnographic account will show how people live a 'normal' day under continuous conflict and authoritarian rules.

Chapter 3 discusses monopolistic nationalism and the decomposing state. The chapter provides a historical context of national sentiment to the current situation in the Kurdish regions in Turkey and also Syria, showing how the politics of gender has played a role for group identity and nationalism. It aims to demonstrate how local justice, alternative governance and new gender roles have been shaped by and, in turn, have shaped the evolution of alternative politics and social structures.

Chapter 4 focuses on the politics of gender. This chapter starts with the account of the Yezidi Kurdish women's tragedy in 2014 at the hands of ISIS religious authoritarianism, when the rest of the world 'discovered' the role and power of the Kurdish women's movement in the Middle East. The chapter explains the links between official rhetoric regarding the role of women in the post-ISIS Middle East and measures implemented to increase women's participation in political processes. It highlights the failure or challenges of these measures in effectively addressing the actual situation of Kurdish women both within Turkey and Syria and in diasporic contexts. The chapter provides a localised and gendered analysis of political transformation and an assessment – beyond mere numbers – of the degree to which women have been able to participate in new Kurdish political, economic, social and legal structures. After analysing the development of the Kurdish women's movement, the chapter continues to analyse what kind of new gender codes and relationships have been introduced by the Kurdish movement. The chapter moves onto the direct account of the day I spent observing the election of members of the Kurdish women's court in Berlin 2017, and discusses the politics of *jineoloji* ('women's science') from that account.

Chapter 5 addresses parallel justice and governmentality. It starts with an official Turkish state judge's account. It analyses how Kurdish de facto judges have practised and negotiated prevailing power relations, illustrating the practice of Kurdish justice before 2000 from a Turkish man's case, and also the development and changes of local courts in Kurdish towns and cities after 2000. The chapter maps out the diverse and varied scene of Kurdish parallel justice procedures and mechanisms. In this context, the gendered demands and activities of key actors and beneficiaries are analysed, and relations, tensions and political rifts beyond the actual court procedure explored. This chapter sheds light on the different obstacles and challenges facing women and men, while also paying attention to ethnic and religious diversities and different believers of the Kurdish movement and the conflict between dogmatic, passive, moderate and liberal critical followers.

Conclusion identifies the main causes and implications of authoritarian regimes, their discriminatory legislations and unjust actions. It underlines the ways in which alternative courts have been instrumentalised to serve competing political agendas and new power structures, while consideration of new gender roles and norms have emerged as key to an alternative governmentality. It discusses how the empirical case study of Kurdish political mobilisation contributes to our wider conceptual understandings of the intersections between alternative justice, new forms of political control, as well as the potential and challenges of trying to create alternative forms of governmentality amongst minorities.

1

AUTHORITARIAN AND ALTERNATIVE GOVERNMENTALITIES

What we learn in time of pestilence: there are more things to admire in men than to despise. (Albert Camus – *The Plague*)

Life is not equal and laws are not always right. Living in times of continuous conflict and war does not provide a life of happiness. It only creates deprivation, sickness, deep scars, misery, destruction, injustice and early death for many, and endless greed and abundance for a few. The foundation of a state is based on the rule of law and justice. Power and control results if a state is able to make and enforce laws, and if those laws are followed and respected by a large group of people. Without these conditions, the state and its institutions, the economy, governmentality, police and power cannot function or even exist.

The first part of this chapter focuses on authoritarian governmentality and the global increase in autocrats' capturing of states, much like hunting octopuses. It critically engages with the Foucauldian type of governmentality, where 'discipline – sovereignty – governmentality'[1] is limited almost only to white and Western liberal states. This chapter will argue how the legal system has been an important instrument in the hands of autocrats, and laws and policies have been created as a corporate set of conditions. The chapter sets up the puzzle of why Foucault's concept of governmentality has its limits and how authoritarian governmentality is born, functions and inevitably fails in the end. The role of the media, intellectuals and society, and how authoritarianism

---

[1] Foucault 1991: 102.

cannot be simply limited to the power and lifetime rule of one individual, is analysed from the cases and examples.

After the discussion of authoritarian governmentality, the chapter introduces a new theory, alternative governmentality, against autocratic rules. The question of how and if any alternative politics against authoritarian governmentality can be different or follow a similar pattern, is argued. The section also engages with the Weberian notion of the state, which claims that only the state has a 'monopoly on violence' (*Gewaltmonopol des Staates*) and a monopoly on the legitimate use of physical force within its territory.[2] Within parallel governmentality a new de facto power, the militia, which supports and implements parallel justice, and collects taxes for the alternative state institutions, suggests that the state no longer has a 'monopoly on violence' and authority. In a de facto way, it is discussed in the practice of the Kurdish political movement in the Middle East which will be the main subject of the following chapters. In addition, this chapter will discuss the borders and boundaries within and between states, and explore how they change and are being challenged over time.

Foucault's Governmentality

When we look at Foucault's conceptualisation of governmentality, power and biopolitics we can see that it is not about the end of sovereignty and the power of the state.[3] For Foucault and many other thinkers, governmentality is the state's different methods, mentalities, practices, arts and regimes of governing.[4] Their studies of governmentality allow us to see how the state combines, arranges and fixes existing power relationships, which are then codified, consolidated and institutionalised for the governmentalisation of the state.[5] However, the main aim of the argument of this book is to move beyond Foucault's and other existing writing on governmentality[6] that does

---

[2] See, Weber 1974, 2014 and 2015; Tilly 1985; Olson 1993; Phelp 2014.

[3] See, Foucault and Gordon 1980; Burchell et al. 1991; Foucault 2000a and 2007; Foucault et al. 2008; Kelly 2014; Martire 2017.

[4] Foucault 2007; Bröckling et al. 2011.

[5] See, Wallerstein 1976; Burchell et al. 1991; Kelly 1994; Cohen and Arato 1994; Rose 1999; Dean 1999; Bratich et al. 2003; O'Malley 2004; Bröckling et al. 2011; Kelly 2014: Tazzioli 2014; Chandler and Richmond 2015.

[6] See, Burchell et al. 1991; Dean 1999; Bratich et al. 2003; Bröckling et al. 2011; Chandler and Richmond 2015.

not focus on collective and conflicting resistance and that does not recognise or study alternative and/or parallel governmentality structures within any given state.

Governmentality is a combination of 'government' and 'rationality'. It describes a rational state and authority by which rules are defined, and designed in advance. Its actions guide, manage, shape, control or affect the people. Theoretically, Foucault's governmentality does not describe absolute and disciplinary sovereign or authoritarian power and rule, but instead the conduct (leading authority) which shares power, includes people and supports plural participation. Foucault's decryption of governmentality is about the art of state government. It is about the Western liberal state and government of the state's indirect rules, calculated strategies, actions and behaviours.[7] Governmentality has been discussed and understood mainly in reference to liberal political economies (regimes) and their rationality.[8] For the liberal state, there are three important elements; trade (wealth), security of the wealth which is created from trade or in other ways, and population (as a customer and also the protector of the state's wealth). These points have been justified and some logical reasons are created by the state for the benefit of the state. Knowingly or unknowingly people devote their working lives for the trade, security and protection of the state's wealth and continuity of its sovereign power.

Foucault argues that 'man remained what he was for Aristotle: a living animal with the additional capacity for a political existence; modern man is an animal whose politics places his existence as a living being into question'.[9] For Foucault, sovereign and disciplinary power, with the help of the new technology of biopolitics, gradually transformed into a 'government of men'. The obedience and loyalty of the public is a crucial element for the salvation of government.[10] In that sense, Foucault follows John Stuart Mill's concept which state that:

> The traditions or customs of other people are the rule of conduct . . . No one's idea of excellence in conduct is that people should do absolutely nothing but copy one another. No one would assert that people ought not to put into

---

[7] Foucault 2000c; Martire 2017.

[8] Foucault 2008.

[9] Foucault 1978: 143.

[10] Foucault 1991 and 2007.

their mode of life, and into the conduct of their concerns, any impress whatever of their own judgment, or of their own individual character.[11]

Mill also recognised that the uniform power of conduct weakens the possibility of resistance.

> The demand that all other people shall resemble ourselves, grows by what it feeds on. If resistance waits till life is reduced nearly to one uniform type, all deviations from that type will come to be considered impious, immoral, even monstrous and contrary to nature. Mankind speedily becomes unable to conceive diversity, when they have been for some time unaccustomed to see it.[12]

Foucault's governmentality is not just limited within Europe, but is claimed to have emerged since the sixteenth century, with the birth of modern European nation states and the influence of their Christian values.[13] He states that 'the history of the pastorate in the West, as a model of the government of men, is inseparable from Christianity.'[14] Foucault did not just see Christianity as the main shaper of European modernisation, he also excluded the fact that other beliefs can practise liberal governmentality under different types of religion. Arguably, the modernisation of Europe did not come about because of Christianity, but the limitation of power and influence of religion. Society moved away from the strong and conservative codes of Christianity and only then did it manage to develop secular laws, rules and modern democracy over religious laws, rules and conservatism. Foucault's limitation or monopolising modern life and liberal governmentality under Christian values also contradict the Durkheimian concept; that every group has different religious dimensions which shape their lives differently.[15] Including Europe, there is no place in the world where there is a totalitarian religion and belief which is followed by all its citizens.

---

[11] Mill 1977: 261–3.
[12] Mill 1977: 275.
[13] Dean 1999; Martire 2017.
[14] Foucault 2007: vii.
[15] Durkheim 2008.

Foucault's claim was more of a political statement rather than one based on any scientific evidence. Foucault's approach also reminds us that some thinkers feel they have to mention religion and God for their public acceptance. Hobbes used God in almost every paragraph of Leviathan for his own security against the pressure and threat from the Church, but if you remove almost every word of God from his work it would not change the meaning of the text. It was for his own protection at a time when the Church was as powerful as today's authoritarian regimes, and could easily punish him severely if he used criticism or didn't show Christianity and God as the main source of his argument.

However, why did Foucault fear to use Christianity as the main influence on the birth of liberal governmentality? He might have been influenced by Durkheim's concept of the connection between religion and Church which stated that 'the idea of religion is inseparable from the idea of a Church'.[16] Foucault replaced the words of religion and Church with the words of government and Christianity and created similar 'inseparable' claims. Throughout history, political leaders as well as some philosophers have used religious accounts, codes and values as a reason to give more meaning to what they try to say or to influence large crowds. On 3 January 1954, just a year before his death, Albert Einstein wrote a letter to philosopher Erik Gutkind after reading his book *Choose Life: The Biblical Call to Revolt* and to respond to those who use a religious source for everything:

> the word God is for me nothing more than the expression and product of human weakness, the Bible a collection of honorable, but still purely primitive, legends which are nevertheless pretty childish. No interpretation, no matter how subtle, can change this for me. For me the Jewish religion like all other religions is an incarnation of the most childish superstition. And the Jewish people to whom I gladly belong, and whose thinking I have a deep affinity for, have no different quality for me than all other people. As far as my experience goes, they are also no better than other human groups, although they are protected from the worst cancers by a lack of power. Otherwise I cannot see anything 'chosen' about them. In general I find it painful that you claim a privileged position and try to defend it by two walls of pride,

16 Durkheim 2008: 46.

an external one as a man and an internal one as a Jew. As a man you claim, so to speak, a dispensation from causality otherwise accepted, as a Jew the privilege of monotheism. But a limited causality is no longer a causality at all, as our wonderful Spinoza recognized with all incision, probably as the first one. And the animistic interpretations of the religions of nature are in principle not annulled by monopolization. With such walls we can only attain a certain self-deception, but our moral efforts are not furthered by them. On the contrary.[17]

Modern governmentality and democracy is not a source of religion, but a move away from religion. The value of religion and its rigid codes and rules are much closer to authoritarianism and conservatism than to liberal governmentality or democracy. As we discuss in the later part of this chapter, governmentality is not something limited to Christianity, modern nation states or Europe, it existed and was practised widely and earlier than Foucault claimed. As Hegel argues, '[w]e are almost led to think that no state or constitution has ever existed, or now exists. We are tempted to suppose that we must now begin and keep on beginning afresh for ever. We are to fancy that the founding of the social order has depended upon present devices and discoveries.'[18]

Governmentalities or the mentality of governing create common belief and response. Government constructs and controls people's beliefs. It rationalises their power with the help of different controlling mechanisms including religion, flags, statues and debt. It has existed since the small communal and tribal structure of human life. Individual and group mentality is knowingly and unknowingly constructed. Unknowingly, as in the way you are born into that way of thinking which has already been created and adopted by your family and community. You find these adopted thought processes normal, even if they are not. Knowingly, with the help of education – from nursery to university – training, indoctrination, economic and social relationships, rules and laws, behaviour, actions intentionally created and shaped for the benefit of the power holder. This can include but is not limited to religion, nation, state and sovereign. Governmentality does not just exist in political ideology or judiciary rules

[17] Einstein 1954a.
[18] Hegel 1991: 3.

which are organised heavily around creating common behaviours, but it is also a driving force of many other important areas, which include religion, medicine, media, the economy and education. While individuality or individual autonomy is lauded by the argument of 'conduct of conducts',[19] in reality all these different power agents are interconnected to shape and control individual actions for the sovereign power. In that sense, individual freedom is not a real freedom, but the people are forced to work, produce, obey, protect and sacrifice their life when it is needed for the sovereign.

Foucault did not publish his work on governmentality during his lifetime. It was mainly based on his *Security, Territory, Population* lectures at the Collège de France in 1978–9, and they were published by others later, after his death.[20] Since the death of Foucault in 1984, there have been many different interpretations, and understanding of governmentality, depends on how one reads and understands his work. Translation of his work into English and probably other languages from French, as Fassin argues, may affect these different meanings of Foucault's work.[21] Foucault also studied governmentality in the latter part of his life. Even in a short period of time, he changed his theory and developed it into new thoughts. While his early work considered subjectivity as externally constituted, later he claimed that one could proactively change one's subjectivity.[22] For example, his early work briefly mentions the possibilities of some resistance to governmentality, but later he went further, detailed a bit more and discussed his understanding of the role of resistance. However, in the last six years of his life he did not publish or develop further his governmentality. Again, Fassin reminds us that although he had enough time to developed his theory, he did not.[23]

Foucault accepts that wherever power exists, resistance is counter-conduct alongside. For him 'each individual can conduct himself, the domain of one's own conduct or behaviour'.[24] However, he refuses the notions of 'revolt',

---

[19] Gordon 1991; Peters et al. 2009.

[20] Burchell et al. 1991.

[21] Fassin 2009.

[22] Rabinow 1997; Foucault 2000a.

[23] Fassin 2009.

[24] Foucault 2007: 94–5.

'disobedience', 'insubordination', 'dissidence' and 'misconduct'.[25] His notion of soft resistance doesn't go beyond individuality and self-resistance against some societal norms, and mostly about how people would like to shape their identity differently.[26] It was more about the individual choice of their subjectivity and relations with power and agency, which could be their family, school, community, peers or workplace. Foucault's study of resistance shows that it is part of the integral component. For him resistance is not against power, but imbricated within it.[27] In addition, both the dominant and resisting powers are fragmented and inconsistent, with each always containing elements of the other.[28] His approach to resistance does not go so far as to give meaningful harm to power holders and authority. Not just individual but what is it about a group's identity and a strong resistance? How this can turn into collective actions to challenge or break authority totally when the authority creates destructive power and actions over the lives of others, was not discussed by Foucault's governmentality.

Giorgio Agamben argued[29] and Didier Fassin[30] also agrees with Agamben's discussion that Foucault 'never oriented his research toward the very sites of modern biopolitics: the concentration camp and the structure of the great totalitarian states'. However, Fassin asks how 'questions of life and – and death – stay out of the picture in Michael Foucault's theory of power and subject'.[31] These are very important gaps in Foucault's work on power and governmentality. While he touches on refugee issues,[32] the transnational

---

[25] Foucault 2007.

[26] See, Martin 1988; Scott 1990; Gal 1995; Tait 2000.

[27] Foucault 1978.

[28] See, Sharp et al. 2000; Raby 2005; Johansson and Lalander 2012.

[29] Agamben 1998:10.

[30] Fassin 2009.

[31] Fassin 2009: 46.

[32] Foucault gave a short speech in 1981 at the UN in Geneva, 'Confronting Governments and their "Human Rights" policies'. Speaking in front of representatives of all member states, he argued that the 'suffering of men' has been ignored by governments. Around the time of his speech, there was the crisis of Vietnamese asylum-seekers in the South China Sea and attacks against them from different power holders, similar to the humanitarian catastrophy we have today in the Aegean Sea between Turkey and Greece, against Syrian refugees. See, Foucault 2000b; Whyte 2012.

and cross-border migration were other important subjects that were not the main attention of Foucault's work.[33] Even though it is not possible to limit Foucault to one discipline or subject and he refused to be identified under one discipline,[34] of course, one still cannot assume that Foucault should have written about all different issues in a detailed and concurred way. He explained in one of his interviews:

> I don't feel that it is necessary to know exactly what I am. The main interest in life and work is to become someone else that you were not in the beginning. If you knew when you began a book what you would say at the end, do you think that you would have the courage to write it? What is true for writing and for a love relationship is true also for life. The game is worthwhile insofar as we don't know what will be the end. My field is the history of thought. Man is a thinking being.[35]

If there is a state where there is continuous conflict and ethnic, religious, racial and class division; if the legal conditions, laws and rules don't apply to everybody equally and justice is discriminating; if the rights of citizenship, economic options, the workplace and wealth are not open to everybody equally; if the government has a culture of corruption and nepotism; if the elections are only symbolic and the ruling elite doesn't change after a certain period of time; if a regime or its leader finds it difficult to follow, or does not have the ability or capacity to think about the conditions of peace, and acts against scientific and factual truth then we cannot begin to talk about a democratic regime, or, as Hobbes stated, 'a well-grounded State',[36] but only an authoritarian regime.

Autocratic Governmentality

Governmentality is not a set of the same or similar rules; there are many different styles of governmentalities that exist according to their management, administration, order, prediction, control and classification of an individual

[33] Fassin 2001 and 2011b.
[34] Foucault 1972.
[35] Foucault 1988: 9–10.
[36] See, Nagel 1975; Hobbes 1985; Nerney 1985.

and their life. Identity, ideology, race, religion, gender, class and geography shape the style of governmentality. It does not exist without exercising rules, laws and power.

Many autocratic leaders and their regimes have been hard at work for years to create monopolised power. They take near-absolute control of the judiciary, media, economy and society, fire and jail dissenters at all levels of society – from labourers, journalists and college students, to teachers, judges and representatives of perfectly legitimate opposition individuals, groups or parties. They play all the monetary cards they have, and stoke the rising ethno-nationalist and religious sentiments by spreading and repeating lies about the groups and minorities they have labelled as the 'enemy' and anyone who is working to protect the rights of these powerless groups. These lies have a large and willing audience and those who don't agree with them are called traitors.

The power to make rules for self-interest helps authoritarian governments to make its own predictions and control other possible predictable outcomes, including, for example, news about elections, economic growth, weather conditions, earthquakes and even a pandemic virus. There are no independent regulatory authorities and no free press to check or question the numbers which are provided by the regimes. They pass laws easily and establish statistics, including the result of elections, economic growth and big disasters, but this do not mean they are accurate. Demonstrations of false efficiency and fabricated statistics are the best propaganda machine for authoritarian regimes. For example, the Chernobyl disaster and Covid-19 are important examples of the manipulation of these types of governmentality, which created global human and natural disasters that were hidden by authoritarian regimes for a long time.

It is now an established fact that in 1986 the Soviet Union hid the extent of the real danger and correct information about the Chernobyl disaster for months, from their own people and the rest of the world.[37] Millions of people in the Soviet Union, Europe and Turkey paid a heavy price, many of them died in a short period of time or got cancer due to the autocratic regime's lies and mismanagement. People were never fully informed to protect themselves and many still live with the effects and illnesses today, often passed on to

---

[37] See, Herbert 1987.

the next generations. In the contaminated Black Sea region, near where the Chernobyl disaster occurred, there are ongoing high birth defects and early-age cancer and death.

Cunning Figures (*Lukavaya Tsifra*) and many other cases are important examples of the manipulation of autocratic regimes.[38] Whereas the autocratic Chinese and Turkish regimes have claimed continuous economic growth over the last decade, the autocratic Soviet regime claimed high growth levels for decades. However, two Soviet economists, Seliunin and Khanin, published an article in 1987 under the title 'Cunning Figures (*Lukavaya Tsifra*)', which argued that between 1928 and 1985 the Soviet Union GDP grew more than ten times slower than the statistics and reports submitted by the authoritarian regime. Many international organisations, including UN, UNESCO, World Bank and WHO need data for institutional assessment which affects the international trade, health, aid, education level, development, conflict assessment, freedom and people's movement, including tourism. Even academic institutions and well-established journals love data, even if is very distorted or fake. The most 'prestigious' academic journal would not publish anything if the research did not include some fancily represented government data, statistics or manipulated surveys, including that of authoritarian governments. These are mostly submitted as evidence of the truth, which is not mostly the case, as the 'Cunning Figures' showed us.

'Diseases like covid-19 are deadlier in non-democracies', ran a headline in *The Economist* on 18 February 2020. The statement came at a time when the authorities in China were deliberately misleading the world about the death tolls of people from coronavirus in their country. Not until almost a month later did the World Health Organization (WHO) label what was occurring a pandemic. By then, three months after the outbreak of the virus, it was already too late for most countries to take strong measures to protect their people from serious illness and death. The WHO had taken Beijing's false reports as fact, ignoring warnings from doctors and scientists around the world – including Li Wenliang, a 34-year-old physician in China who was detained for 'spreading false rumours', 'seriously disrupting social order', and 'putting the public in danger'. He was forced to sign a letter that he was

[38] See, Easterly 2013; Jerven 2013.

'making false comments' and that he had 'severely disturbed the social order'. On 7 February 2020, he lost his life when infected by the virus while he was saving the lives of others. Six weeks after his death, the Chinese authorities apologised to his family for their earlier improper response and treatment, but it was too late for Wenliang and the rest of the world. Dr Wenliang is seen a 'martyr' and 'loved' by many Chinese today and his grave receives a huge number of visitors every day. However, authorities in China have continued to censor information and refuse to collaborate for a global solution. A year of the pandemic, the outbreak was still believed to have begun in the Chinese city of Wuhan. Even after almost a year of global disaster and millions of deaths and widespread economic collapse, Chinese authorities refused to allow the WHO experts to investigate the origins of cause and source of the Covid-19 pandemic in their country. The WHO experts were disappointed by China's denied entry and many have suspected a cover-up.

Two Chinese documentary film makers, Lin Wenhua and Cai Kaihai, documented life throughout lockdown in Wuhan, between January and April 2020. Some parts of this documentary were shown by the BBC on 19 January 2021, titled 'Our World, Wuhan: life after lockdown'. By the end of January 2020, while it was almost the beginning of the outbreak, all hospitals in Wuhan were already packed and there was no space for new patients. Two military hospitals had to be created urgently to answer the demand. However, the demand was bigger than just two hospitals. By the end of February, in the first month of the outbreak of the virus, more than 50,000 people were infected. The lack of state management and help meant that more than 50,000 volunteers, without adequate protection, took action to provide food and medical supplies to help people in most need. Most of these people also exposed themselves to the risk. One of the volunteers was Xia Qiyun, a hairdresser, who gave haircuts to more than 2,000 medical and frontline workers between January and April 2020, during the lockdown – even though he had his own limitations and difficulties. For him, and many other people in Wuhan, their life had changed forever since the first cases of Covid-19 were reported in their city.

The documentary showed how Covid-19 affected the lives of many regular people in real terms, and how Chinese authorities responded publicly. Wang Kui and her mother ran a florist business for weddings and funerals for years, but after nobody was allowed to attend funerals or have proper weddings, she lost her business and started selling fruits and vegetables to be able to continue to look after her family. However, the police did not allow them to do this on the street. Wang Kui said, 'I understand the police because they are doing their job, but they don't understand that we somehow have to survive.' Another factory worker, who lost her job and started doing delivery work for survival, said the factory owners and many other people died and the pandemic did not discriminate between poor and rich. She said, 'rich people of Wuhan have also suffered from the pandemic'. Another resident of Wuhan believed that surviving under harsh conditions, such as the pandemic, 'has made people stronger and more positive'. Within a population of 11 million, a study by researchers at the Chinese Centre for Disease Control and Prevention has shown that during the first quarter of the outbreak, between January and April, Wuhan alone had more than 500,000 Covid cases. This figure is five times higher than the total official number of infected (99,026) announced by the Chinese authorities and submitted to the World Health Organization by 20 January 2020.

Other authoritarian governments around the world have also concealed the truth about how their people have suffered. Many claimed for weeks that they had no cases of Covid-19 in their countries. These claims were against natural and geographical spread. These were the subject of many Twitter and Facebook jokes suggesting that virus was jumping over and bypassing authoritarian regimes. For example, while the countries who have open border policies with Hungary and Turkey had already reported many infected cases and deaths by early March 2020, how could it be possible that the virus was not affecting these two countries, if it was not their 'supergenes' as claimed and boasted by Turkish-regime-supporting media outlet, *Haber Turk* on 10 March 2020? There have been also views from different experts that 'silent' and 'hidden' infection rates are far more widespread and higher than these regimes have claimed.

It is a strange coincidence that once the WHO announced that Covid-19 was a pandemic on 11 March 2020, after the World Health Organization who were listening to claims and waiting approval from Chinese authorities for more than three months, on the same day many autocratic regimes, including Turkey, Hungary and Russia joined the long list of Covid-19 countries by reporting a few cases. After the high number of deaths reported from Western countries, such as Italy, France, Spain, the United Kingdom and the United States, the Chinese authorities must have felt embarrassed by their reported numbers, which they had argued for months to be around 3,200 deaths. While they claimed that they had controlled the virus totally, their numbers suddenly rose sharply on 16 April 2020 when they declared that Covid-19 had killed 4,632 of their people, an almost 50 per cent increase in one day. According to the WHO's statistics, the Chinese authorities, between April 2020 and January 2021, declared fewer than 200 deaths which is an unbelievably low number considering its large population, and a deadly and fast-moving pandemic.

Big Crisis is 'God's Gift' for Autocrats

A big crisis or disaster such as Covid-19 is 'God's gift' for autocrats. They don't miss any opportunity to use such an excuse to expand and deepen their power and authority. Taking full control of a legal system and constitution is the dream of all autocrats. The rest is merely detail when they have this power. They use lawfare to make legally, politically and morally wrong actions 'legal'. Fake becomes truth and truth becomes fake according to the laws of the autocrats.

The Hungarian leader, Victor Orbán, was one of the greatest beneficiaries of the Covid-19 pandemic. He took every opportunity to issue himself the legal right to use the law as a weapon against anybody who disagreed with him. He pushed for the changing of the law at the end of March 2020, sidelined the parliament indefinitely and gave himself unlimited, and monopolised power and authority under his iron fist. The Hungarian parliament, with his party in the majority, voted to suspend its operations, and Orbán has the power indefinitely to extend the country's state of emergency, to rule by decree, and to jail anyone he believes to be spreading 'false' information about the virus. Those emergency powers were officially rescinded in June, but with legislation that codifies many of the new powers Orbán assumed in the preceding months or years. In *The Times*, Oliver Moody wrote on 2 April 2020 that 'Victor Orbán's power grab in Hungary heightens fears of dictatorship in EU'. In the *Daily Telegraph*, Ben Kelly warned on 31 March 2020 that 'if the EU cannot rein in Hungary's dictator Viktor Orbán, it will rot from the inside'. *The Economist* questioned on 25 April 2020 whether 'would-be autocrats are using Covid-19 as an excuse to grab more power' and added specifically for Hungary that 'Mr Orbán has in effect become a dictator – in the heart of Europe.'

Ferenc Falus, Hungary's former medical chief, stated in November 2000 that 'there is virtually a military dictatorship in Hungary'. His statement was part of the 'Covid-19: Hungary's pandemic response' medical report which was prepared by Kata Karáth for *The British Medical Journal* (*BMJ*). Falus explained that 'it's very fitting that even the hospital directors [previously appointed by the government] were not trusted, and thus soldiers and police officers were assigned to them'.[39] The commanders look set to remain in place indefinitely, even after the state of emergency ended in June.

Like the Chinese government, Hungary's maligned single party government, and its leader Orbán did not miss any opportunity to create 'PR' out of their 'fast solutions'. On 20 March, Orbán had ordered the construction of a slick, temporary hospital at the premises of Kiskunhalas prison. Under the slogan 'Europe's most modern mobile epidemic hospital', it was finished in just two and a half weeks, providing 150 beds 'to manage the sudden emergence of great pressure and a significant patient load', explained Zoltan Kovacs, Hungarian secretary of state. However, very bizarrely the facility officially opened only on 1 October. In late March, the government declared that the pandemic would be over before the summer. In April, Orbán announced that the infections would peak exactly on 3 May, and ordered the gradual ease of lockdown measures from that specific day.[40]

While the Orbán government bought around 16,000 ventilators with the aim of winning the ventilators competition against other leaders and countries between March and May, it was estimated that only 2,000 doctors and 2,000 intensive care nurses in the country were able to operate them. Increasing authoritarianism and a crumbling healthcare system has created a brain drain of doctors in Hungary. While between 2010 and 2016 around 5,500 doctors left Hungary to work in different countries, according to the Union of Hungarian Doctors, more than 8,000 medical workers, mainly doctors,

[39] Karáth 2020.
[40] Karáth 2020.

left Hungary's healthcare system in the first half of 2020. All this data and politics stated that securing its long-term authoritarian rule and using the pandemic 'as a gift' for a propaganda machine has been more important for the Hungarian leadership and government than to respond the virus according to scientific advice and its people's needs in real and realistic terms.

In Turkey, Erdoğan had already thanked God for the gift after the 2010 constitutional change and the 2016 military coup, which gave him full power, and left only the lifeless and gutless skin of parliament hanging on his palace wall. A lifeless parliament only functions when it is orchestrated by autocrats. Decisions about war, cross-border operations, amnesty, tax, life or death are decided by a narrow circle. Parliament is only told to pass the orders which have already been decided behind closed doors by the autocrats. There is not much discussion or transparency and parliament becomes a puppet.

Even after this monopolisation of power, Erdoğan did not miss any opportunity to go after the Twitter and Facebook accounts and local media sources who shared any different claims about the virus other than the regime's approach. In that sense China and Hungry followed suit. The Turkish regime also introduced a wider amnesty for prisoners. However, this amnesty mainly allowed murderers, rapists, mafia bosses and people who committed crime for the sake of the state, to be released, and successfully left out all journalists, novelists, Kurdish politicians, activists, liberal businessmen and even many politicians with serious illnesses. These imprisoned, mostly unsentenced critics of the regime are an average of 60 years old, so it creates a huge risk for them to stay in prison. Özgür Deniz Değer, co-chair of the medical chamber of the eastern city of Van, was arrested by police after he criticised the government for not including political prisoners, in an interview on 19 March 2020 that he gave to *Mesopotamia News Agency*.

In Turkey, only the national government had the authority to give any numbers or information about Covid-19 infections and deaths, silencing local authorities such as governors, mayors, doctors and civil organisations. Disbelief over the government's official Covid-19 numbers was widespread among doctors in Turkey. Halis Yerlikaya, a physician at a hospital in the south-eastern province of Diyarbakır told *Reuters* on 19 September 2020, 'the numbers of just one city, or the numbers unveiled by just one or two medical chambers are almost equal to the (official) numbers for the whole country'.

According to *Reuters* (19 September) and *British Medical Journal* (*BMJ*) (29 September), medical experts and doctors who shared local Covid-19 numbers on social media showing huge differences between official calculations and reports from professionals on the ground have faced criminal charges. Many doctors around the country carried out a week-long protest between 13 and 20 September against the government for hiding the truth, and they wore black ribbons to commemorate colleagues lost to the pandemic. One said, 'You can't handle it. We're burning out.' President Recep Erdoğan's coalition partner Devlet Bahçeli, leader of the Nationalist Movement Party, labelled the protest a 'treacherous plot' and called for the Turkish Medical Association to be outlawed and its leadership prosecuted. He tweeted 'The Turkish Medics Association is as dangerous as coronavirus and is disseminating threats. The Medics Association which carries the word "Turkish" in its name should immediately and without delay be shut down.'

Many doctors were being interrogated on suspicion of 'issuing threats regarding health with an aim to create panic and fear among the public' (Article 213 of the Turkish Penal Code). The offence carries a possible prison sentence of between two and four years. The co-chair of Şanlıurfa Medical Chamber, Ömer Melik, and its secretary general, Osman Yüksekyayla, have on more than one occasion been detained and interrogated by police, after posting the number of local cases on the chamber's Twitter account and when the chamber raised concerns over the deaths of health workers and the lack of personal protective equipment. On 10 June 2020, *Human Rights Watch* (*HRW*) released a report and criticised the Turkish government's response to doctors and Covid-19. Hugh Williamson, Europe and Central Asia director at *Human Rights Watch* expressed concern:

> The Turkish authorities criminally investigating medical chamber officials is not only an outrageous attack on free speech but impedes the fight against the deadly Covid-19 pandemic and obstructs their legitimate work . . . Official efforts to discredit and criminalize the association or its provincial affiliates, notably those in the mainly Kurdish southeast and eastern regions, undermines efforts to uphold public health and the right of medical professionals to do their job.

The Turkish Medical Association has long been a target of Erdoğan's government. Its entire central committee was arrested in 2018 after it criticised a Turkish military incursion into Syria. Eleven members, including its chair, Sinan Adıyaman, received prison sentences of twenty months or more. More than 3,300 doctors were forced out of their jobs under a decree promulgated after the 2016 coup. The harsh environment has fuelled an increasing medical brain drain to other countries.[41]

Chinese, Hungarian and Turkish examples show that authoritarianism has created alternative facts, silenced critics and put the government and its leaders' needs before the public. Moral and ethical codes are usually set for the legitimisation of the actions of the ruler. Even if the truth is false it can be accepted as truth if the sovereign says so and his network and majoritarian population support this. This post-truth,[42] is repeated as many times as possible by the media, which is in support of autocrats for its own benefit, or under the direct control of the autocrats. After continuous and repeated listening, watching and reading by the majority of the people, the false is accepted and followed as truth. After this indoctrination, any real truth or opposing ideas are seen as false and unhealthy for 'the unity of the nation', and so are criminalised. The aim is to use all methods to control the public and any information which is given to the public. The aim of this fact making and brainwashing totalitarian discipline is to give continuous living power and sovereignty to autocrats and their governments. Hobbes described this at the beginning of his *De Cive*, 'Man is not fitted for society by nature, but by discipline.'[43]

These examples shows that authoritarian governmentality is dangerous for human and public life, diversity, peace and security. Silencing criticism, faking economic and social factors and statistics is almost always more important to autocrats than to deal with enormous disasters and saving lives. Some of this behaviour of course is not just typical of authoritarian regimes, but it may apply to some democratic regimes where pluralism still exists, where the rule of law is in place, fair and equal elections still in progress, but where there

---

[41] Dyer 2020.

[42] Ho and Cavanaugh 2019; Greenhouse 2019.

[43] Hobbes 1991.

is also a leader who has autocratic wishes, who may use and abuse the state power for their own interests and is desperate to create societal problems and divisions for their autocratic wishes, but only on a premature level.

Donald Trump has been the most prominent example of this tendency – with his defiance of congressional subpoenas, building his wall with Mexico without approbation from lawmakers, and calling any media outlet that criticises him a purveyor of 'fake news'. His absurd claim in March 2020 that the virus was 'under control' hampered the government's response, which led the United States to have one of the worst outbreaks in any place around the world, costing more than 400,000 people's lives during his presidency. In July 2020, the Trump administration launched an effort to discredit the nation's leading infectious disease expert, Anthony Fauci, seemingly because Fauci was more trusted than the president himself – a direct echo of the sort of personality politics that play out under autocrats in other countries around the world.

The invisible pandemic creates enormous indiscriminate effects but at the same time increases social polarisation and alienation between different economic, social and political classes and systems. Which systems have failed, and which have shown some moral resistance or solutions for the right and fair living conditions during this injustice will of course shape the future. As Alondra Nelson argues, societies will be radically different after the pandemic and 'the multifaceted effects of the Covid-19 pandemic are and will be staggering. We are in the midst of a social tumult that will have a far-reaching impact.'[44]

While a democratic style of government can be claimed to be the least dangerous we have so far,[45] we should also note that pluralistic and democratic regimes may have weaknesses which could allow intolerant leaders to turn them into dictatorships.[46] Many Western democratic states are ill-founded. The wealth of the current privileged class is developed at the cost of the poverty, inequality, early death and inherited debt of many others.[47]

[44] Nelson 2020.

[45] See, Przeworski et al. 2000.

[46] See, Moore 1966; Linz and Stepan 1996; Zakaria 1997; Ottaway 2003; Morlino 2006; Svolik 2008; Filali-Ansary and Ahmed 2009; Teorell 2010; Brands and Edel 2019.

[47] Graeber 2011.

Free elections, a free press, freedom of speech, separation of power and rule of law does not mean that all inequalities disappear. Inequalities are justified in many forms and continue for decades, or even centuries for the sake of 'common unity'. Laws are important tools to carry out and justify economic interests. The codes of laws are designed to create, protect and justify wealth and inequality.[48] The grandchildren of the poor still have poor living standards, die young and are vulnerable to disease.[49] The Industrial Revolution developed like the economy of China today – an economy which has grown very fast to the benefit of the state and capitalist ruling class, but the large majority of working class have paid a heavy price.[50] The state and ruling class have become wealthy but that wealth has not been shared with the people. This inequality continues, while the state and also a small minority of the rich hold the maximum wealth. It is like a building which is growing very fast, but almost 70–80 per cent of it is not well structured and has weak foundations. Such a building would not be very strong or survive long, and even a little wind would be enough to shake it or destroy it, as is the case with today's democracies.

The justice system in most Western democratic countries is not much different from the medical system in the US: expensive, complicated, takes a long time to resolve any issues, and only privileged groups can enjoy it fully and use it for their own benefit. Most lawyers and legal practitioners are gatekeepers of the code of inequality. Like authoritarian leaders, lawyers also pick and choose the rules for their own client's benefit and needs even if it is not right. Legal education also produces this kind of legal practitioner. The result of this kind of uncritical legal education is that it creates problems more than it finds solutions. Legal practitioners are also often as greedy as some medical doctors and medical institutions in the US. A small case can take years and cost an individual thousands of pounds before they even see the judge, and they have to fill in and sign many documents without much understanding, similar to the medical system in the US where a huge premium has to be paid for insurance before going through the door of a medical centre. These

---

[48] Pistor 2019; Al-Dahdah and Corduneanu-Huci 2016.

[49] See, Garret 1994 and 2001; Kim et al. 2001; Leon and Walt 2001; Fassin 2007; Chakrabati 2013; Lavinas 2013 and 2017.

[50] See, Schumpeter 1943; Rueschemeyer et al. 1992.

are not just problems with lawyers or doctors, but the fundamental problem of a modern nation state and its education and management. Most Western countries would claim that they have a better legal, medical and democratic system, but their example is not perfect and is built on unequal societal division. In addition, on some level, in most Western democratic countries, sexism, racism, ethnic and religious segregation, and violence against powerless minorities still continues and is seen as normal by a large part of society.

Autocrats and their narrow circles use all these flaws of democracy as their pathway to power. They pitch 'great' populist and nationalistic promises to people. Then after coming into power, they burn all bridges including the rule of law, freedom of speech, free media and take control of all the different institutions of the state. In the end, they eradicate democracy totally.[51] Some of the worst tyrants started their political career by claiming to end colonisation, disenchanted justice systems, slavery, discrimination, economic and social inequalities and create an equal and fair society for all. Some autocrats who committed unforgivable crimes were not originally recognised as dictators, and were even given the Nobel Peace Prize. For example, Aung San Suu Kyi from Myanmar won the 1991 Nobel Peace Prize, however under her de facto leadership and active support, hundreds of thousands of Rohinga Muslims from Myanmar faced genocide and fled to neighbouring Bangladesh due to an army crackdown.[52] Ethiopian Prime Minister Abid Ahmed

---

[51] See, Schedler 2006; Levitsky and Way 2010; Onis 2015; Özbudun 2015; Esen and Gumuscu 2016; Somer 2016; Bieber 2018; Cianetti et al. 2018; Yilmaz and Bashirov 2018; Luhrmann and Lindberg 2019.

[52] In November 2015 Aung San Suu Kyi led the National League for Democracy (NLD) to a landslide victory in Myanmar's first openly contested election for almost twenty-five years. However, the Myanmar constitution forbids Suu Kyi from becoming president because she has children who are foreign nationals. But she was widely, internally and internationally seen as de facto leader. Her official title was state counsellor. After the Rohingya genocide, according to the BBC News on 6 November 2020, Suu Kyi described the generals in her cabinet as 'rather sweet' in August 2018. Derek Mitchell, former US Ambassador to Myanmar, explained in the same coverage of BBC News that 'The story of Aung San Suu Kyi is as much about us as it is about her. She may not have changed. She may have been consistent and we just didn't know the full complexity of who she is. We have to be mindful that we shouldn't endow people with some iconic image beyond which is human.' However, her continuous pleasing was not enough for the 'rather sweet' generals, and they removed and detained her and her party members from power on 1 February 2021 by bloody military coup.

was also given the Nobel Peace Prize in 2019. However, he did not hesitate to use his military power against the local government of the Tigray region in November 2020, which caused tens of thousands of people to be trapped and face starvation, migration and death.

When dictators discover that to deliver promises of 'peace', 'a better economy' and 'equal justice for all' requires heavy-duty work and the possible political risk of losing power, they seek and find an easier way – a way where it is possible to not keep any promises, to give nothing back to the people but take everything from them, whatever they have, with the help of cheap and empty nationalism, religious fundamentalism and military forces. They ask people to die for their political aims if they want to be rich, and millions have followed these leaders, and died for them. Meanwhile, they have increased their own wealth and created an elite circle, while leaving millions of others in poverty.

While charitable hand-out dependency-type policies, nepotism, ignorance, lies, cheap and nationalistic TV programmes, and religion keep the masses following the autocrats; oppression, violence, imprisonment and death is their weapon against any opposition. From the examples of the Soviet Union to Russia, Iran to Hungary, China to Libya, Turkey to Egypt, Marx was wrong to claim that 'the dictatorship will be temporary and short-lived' and would take on democratic forms later.[53] Marx's assumption that the working class or proletariat dictatorship would be different from other forms of dictatorship, including the elite or monarchies has also been proven wrong from many lived examples.[54]

Elections and Autocracy

There are many democratically elected leaders, such as Hitler from Germany, Mussolini from Italy, Orbán from Hungary and Erdoğan from Turkey, who later destroyed free elections, rule of law, free press, free protests and democratic society and built authoritarian regimes instead. They create a fully dependent and corporate judiciary system. These autocrats melt their large numbers of supporters into one shape of individuality, turn them into bullets against any

[53] Marx 1978: 546.
[54] Marx 1978: 590.

opposition groups or voices, and use that power to turn the country into an iron-fisted autocratic regime. In the end, regimes lose their checks and balances, as does the human immune system, and cannot easily find internal solutions against their own destruction and might need to find a new, counter iron-fisted power to eliminate the existing one. This problem is not just limited to the existing authoritarian regimes and their societies to resolve, but the most secure societies and governments may also turn into an authoritarian structure if they don't take responsibility before the disease of authoritarianism catches them too. Levitsky and Way explained that:

> in the form of patronage jobs, pork-barrel spending, clientelist social policies, and privileged access to media and finance exists in all democracies. In democracies, however, these advantages do not seriously undermine the opposition's capacity to compete. When incumbent manipulation of state institutions and resources is so excessive and one-sided that it seriously limits political competition, it is incompatible with democracy.[55]

Even if there is still some competition as Levitsky and Way claimed, or it would right to say that it is more an act of competition, it is mainly used for bringing international investments into the country. In reality these should be considered full authoritarian regimes, probably even more dishonest and dangerous than the actual totalitarian regimes. The act of electoral competition is just for the international image of autocrats, but internally they do the same as what shameless dictators do. Instead of showing the result of the election as 97 per cent, as happened in Egypt under Sissi, they show around 50 per cent, as Erdoğan has followed. Like totalitarian regimes, they also practise and control economic resources, media and the law which indicates that they are not much different from each other. Levitsky and Way agreed that:

> three aspects of an uneven playing field are of particular importance: access to resources, media, and the law . . . Access to resources is uneven when incumbents use the state to create and maintain resource disparities that seriously hinder the opposition's ability to compete . . . Incumbents also may use the state to monopolize access to private-sector finance. Governing parties may

[55] Levitsky and Way 2010: 5–6.

use discretionary control over credit, licenses, state contracts, and other resources to enrich themselves . . . the state controls all television and most – if not all – radio broadcasting. Although independent newspapers and magazines may circulate freely, they generally reach only a small urban elite . . . in many competitive authoritarian regimes, incumbents pack judiciaries, electoral commissions, and other nominally independent arbiters and manipulate them via blackmail, bribery and/or intimidation. As a result, legal and other state agencies that are designed to act as referees rule systematically in favor of incumbents.[56]

On 7 December 2018, the title in *The Washington Post* argued, 'democracies slide into authoritarianism', and a one-man run – charismatic, populist and liar – authoritarianism is increasing.[57] In the early 2000s, there was hope that the 46 per cent of democratic, open society would go up. However, by 2020 this had decreased to 39 per cent, instead of increasing. Democratically elected governments find it difficult to deal with the power of populist authoritarianism, whose lies are easily challenged by free media and strong opposition. However, hardly anybody is able to check, challenge or question the fake numbers of authoritarian regimes.[58] Critics will find themselves in jail the following day if they dare to ask a wrong question. Their people start believing and supporting their lies as truth. They lose the ability to even differentiate between them. Democratic regimes have to care for all people, including those who hate them, criticise them and never vote for them. This is the only way they can be re-elected. However, authoritarian regimes act according to their own majoritarian needs. They usually leave out the real numbers of the minority for the sake of unitarity and the benefit of their own majoritarian group. These excluded groups, for example immigrants in the Western context, small and powerless religious or ethnic minorities in the Middle East and Asia, progressive democrats in the context of Latin American, are important punchbags for populist authoritarian regimes. They put all economic, social

---

[56] Levitsky and Way 2010: 10–12.

[57] According to the Freedom House index, 2019 was the fourteenth consecutive year of the decline of global democracy and freedom. Aside from the Freedom House 2018 and 2019 index for data of authoritarianism and democracy around the world, see also, Plattner 2015.

[58] Wright 2008; Wright and Escribà-Folch 2012.

and political blame on these people. Without creating these internal enemies, authoritarian regimes cannot survive.

There are different types of dictatorship, including military dictatorship, totalitarian or absolutist dictatorship, competitive or electoral dictatorship, hybrid dictatorship, majoritarian dictatorship, monarchies, single-party dictatorship and constitutional dictatorship.[59] However, their governmental style, the control of wealth, power and population, the claim of 'God-given power' or to be 'messiah' are common among all of them. To make differences between them and to claim that one is better than another is a problem. It does not make much difference when power is grabbed by military coup, election or family inheritance, and held indefinitely. In the end the dictatorship controls every area of an individual's private and societal life and decides what is law and what is not, what is true and what is false.

A normal, well-grounded democratic regime creates an open society which builds a flexible, pluralistic and balanced power-sharing type of government, where elections, rule of law and wealth include almost each and every citizen, where the rules and constitution are not changed very often and the judiciary is not shaped according to the need of rulers. The system includes and respects the rights of all diverse groups. People have the option to decide who is in power after each term. It is normal that political parties and leaders are changed often when they don't deliver their promises. The flexibility, multiplicity and tolerance of this type of pluralistic state structure is the actual power of its longevity. The possibility of internal or external conflicts are much lower compared with other regimes. Local government is strong and different languages, cultures, laws and values are in practice. Social and economic diversity and statistics are clear even if they go against the government's plan. On one side we have these inclusive open societies, but on the other side we have centralised and exclusivist authoritarianism which only knows how to censor, manipulate, fabricate and kill. According to different studies, only in the twentieth century, more than 128 million people were

---

[59] For different type of authoritarianism, see, for example, Friedrich and Brzezinski 1956; Huntington 1968; Linz 2000; Diamond 2002; Schedler 2006; Brownlee 2007; Gandhi 2008; Levitsky and Way 2010; Bunce and Wolchik 2010; Ezrow and Frantz 2011; Wahman et al. 2013.

killed by their own authoritarian regimes (62 million by Soviet, 35 million by Chinese, 21 million by Nazi regimes alone, 10 million by others, including Turkish, Iraqi and Serbian regimes). These regimes have more than three times the possibility of committing internal and external genocides.[60] Their exclusivity and narrow base of governmentality is the main reason for many internal and external conflicts.

Authoritarian governmentality is like a virus; it can spread very quickly and infect weak democracies. Even the most advanced democratic regimes are not safe against authoritarian lies, fabricated statistics and nationalist populism. Autocrats turn the government of law into the government of lawlessness. Their increase in number is evidence of the crisis of humanity. They create destruction ethically, morally, legally and politically. Populism, empty slogans, nationalism, racism, egotistical selfishness and idiocy are the main traits of authoritarian governmentality. They might resolve one or two issues fast and efficiently by force and base all their politics around this 'positiveness', but they mainly bring hatred, conflict, divisions, blood and tears to the people and eventually the state and society become gangrenous. They are not much different from a pandemic virus and create a similar outbreak and level of contagion. It is a global problem even if it appears locally.

Dictators don't respect borders and boundaries. Borders, restrictions and oceans do not stop the influence of populist authoritarianism, much like a pandemic virus. Sooner or later, it will influence large populations and different geographies. The style, structure and popularity of such authoritarianism influences other societies to adopt it without thinking. The rise of authoritarianism and its circles means the decline of all types of freedom. Naivety, ignorance, selfishness and bad habits may not only create, spread and cause an epidemic virus to become a problem for everybody, but they may also provide a breeding ground for authoritarian regimes to grow and become a potentially uncurable political disease.

Even the most advanced democratic regimes are not completely safe and some of their leaders may have elements of totalitarianism and turn their countries into autocratic regimes. Molly Ball in her September 2016 article in

---

[60] See, Rummel 1994; Glover 2000; Power 2002; Gellately and Kiernan 2003; Weitz 2003; Rieff 2005; Meister 2010.

the *Atlantic*, and Roger Berkowitz in his August 2017 article in the *Deutsche Welle* (*DW*), both gave the example of Trump as an authoritarian leader. He used similar methods and tactics as autocrats. Authoritarian leaders spread the fear first, using 'terror', 'migrants', 'refugees', 'border controls', 'foreign viruses' as threats. It is the easiest, cheapest thing to make people to fear these.

Populist autocratically minded leaders tell the masses that they have a way to end their fear, to transfer their fears to others, to make others scared of them. To put up walls, to get rid of some groups of people, to have more flags, to create a pure nation, are the only solutions they bring. Even their open solutions or suggestions do not end the fear but only transfer the fear from one to another. The conflict must increase and become legally justifiable for the transfer of fear. A person under continuous fear even can cuddle a shark for a quick solution or ask for help from their enemies without thinking of the next step. Spreading fear causes the masses to make to make decisions without thinking clearly when looking for a quick solution. Worried people are turned into uncritical masses, they start listening, taking, following and obeying more and more what a cult, populist leader suggests for their warriors. This is one of the first signs of the birth of an autocratic leader and the foundation of their regime. After losing their judgement, moral values, humanity and individuality, the hypnotised minds of people become open to anything under the command of their leader.

Examples and practices around the world show that allowing one or a few autocrats to stay in power for a long time might not just influence local but also global politics. It is just a matter of time. The leadership style of Bolsonaro in Brazil and Trump in the United States shows that the recent authoritarian pandemic has already crossed the Atlantic. In the same way that oceans are not strong enough barriers to stop viruses, they are also not strong enough to stop the influence of authoritarianism. It is a political viral illness and it doesn't just affect the enemies of dictators, but it eventually contaminates everybody, including the supporters of the dictators. Not many can escape such a virus if it is not stopped, controlled or destroyed while it is still manageable. Local challenge is not enough, there should also be global challenge.

New modern technology is controlled and works for the benefit of autocratic regimes. Autocrats set the limits and control almost all information.

Twitter, Facebook, WhatsApp and Google cannot function in any authoritarian countries without permission and co-operation, otherwise the platforms are blocked until they agree to serve fully and comply. These regimes and their autocrats destroy the multiple and independent voices of media and free speech and create multiple channels but with one voice. They benefit from advanced technology to create a powerful, mono-voice media for their own propaganda. With the help of the new digital surveillance technology, mass monitoring systems, the control and power of governments over its citizens has increased. While in democratic regimes, citizens also have the power to use advanced technologies, to observe, check, criticise and contribute to the policies and actions of their governments, this is not possible in authoritarian regimes and any simple criticism by a journalist or even a regular citizen is harshly punished.

From the practices of many authoritarian surveillance governments, the space for the inclusion and participation of the people is very limited. Surveillance technology becomes a right hand of power for the autocrats and their government. With the help of visible and invisible drones not only cities are watched, but individuals are also followed and detailed information is collected about them. Naturalisation or even annihilation can take place if an individual, group or community are seen to be dangerous. Even a peaceful protest can be seen as risky by the regime. It is very easy for them to oppress peaceful resistance, as we have seen from many examples around the world, from the Gezi Movement in Turkey, many Iranian street protests over decades and the summer 2020 Black Lives Matter protests in the US against Trumpian institutional injustices. Peaceful protests, due to their harmless nature, give the opportunity of training and the exercising of power to autocrats. It mostly works in favour of the autocratic regimes but rarely results in any meaningful change. The authoritarianism increases after such protests. Dictators not only increase their technology and invest in more powerful and cleverer drones for oppressing people and such protests, but they also hire thousands or even millions (depending on the size of the population) of faithful followers and henchman, and send them to each neighbourhood to get information about the activities of every individual, day and night. The foot soldiers of dictators do not just monitor the public, but they closely watch journalists, academics, young and ambitious community and local leaders, and students who may be critical of autocrats and share some real facts with the public. Another important role of these aides is to create fabricated stories against real facts and make sure that the public believe their alternative facts rather than the real statistics and truth.[61]

With this help, the autocrat decides what the truth is and what it is not with the direct support of new social media, surveillance technologies, the armed forces, financial institutions and their network of unquestioning allegiances, who are not just the direct or indirect beneficiary of the totalitarian government and their actions, but also are part of the body of the regime itself. There are different versions of the truth depending on how you look, see and estimate things. First, the truth is usually very fragile and may not always want to be heard. For example, if a person has cancer, this is the truth, but rather than hearing every bad thing about their illness they may prefer to hear some possible positive options, to give them hope that they might live longer than expected. Second, the truth is also usually a contested, local and temporary subject. For example, if the weather is −20 today, it might be right for a specific location, but not for everywhere, and also it does not mean that it will be the same tomorrow or even 30 minutes later. Third, the truth has many different sides. For example, the government forces and a rebel group have a battle. Government forces lose ten of their members; the other side, the rebel group loses nine. The government might just give the death of the enemy as a successful operation without mentioning their losses. This does not mean that the government is lying but it is just not disclosing the full information. These methods may be used by different governments, competitive groups, including democratic ones but it does not mean they are fake.

The fake is imitation, non-real and a copy. It is knowingly and fraudulently created for the purpose of giving an advantage to somebody, to establish anti-truth against the real truth. The fake is not just human-made. In nature, for example, many birds create a fake nest to protect their actual nest. However, political anti-truth and fraud is not as innocent as a little bird's own defence system against predators. Autocrats represent those predators and not the birds. Hannah Arendt once wrote how the most successful totalitarian leaders of the twentieth century used lies to erode all truth and instil in their

---

[61] See, Kakutani (2018); Ho and Cavanaugh 2019; Greenhouse 2019.

followers 'a mixture of gullibility and cynicism'.[62] Ministers of public enlightenment and propaganda, and the spokespeople of leaders are more important than, for example, the finance or foreign minister for autocratic regimes. For example, Hitler's Minister of Propaganda, Joseph Goebbels, attacked any critics of the regime, especially leftish and Jewish critical writers and academics were discredited in the eyes of the public. One of the main roles of Goebbels was to create an atmosphere of continuous fear in Germany which allowed the Nazi youth and security officers to commit any crime against these critics, and at the same time to make sure that the public continuously supported and justified their atrocities against them or, according to their definition, 'enemies' of the regime. American ambassador William E. Dodd described Goebbels as Hitler's 'first lieutenant', ranking even above the Nazi military leader, Goering. Dodd stated that Goebbels 'has combined all the newspapers, radio, publications and art activities in Germany into one vast propaganda machine'.[63]

Lies are very important for the mobility of support for the dictators. One of the main aims of authoritarian governments is not to eliminate their opponents first, but to capture their supporters fully, body and mind, and their every movement, and to make them fully dependent on the regime. After this, it is be much easier for autocrats to eliminate their opponents. Losing control of their life makes people lean towards the stronger camp for their survival and benefit. An 'us' and 'them' mentality becomes very visible. People are no longer represented according to their education, ability or skills, but their dress code, the shape and style of their moustache or haircut, the flag they carry, the finger or hand sign they show, the headscarf they wear, the likes or dislikes they have on social media. Without 'others' the 'us' cannot be created. Even if the existing enemy is being annihilated, a new one must be invented soon to ensure the survival of the authoritarian regime. Like Frankenstein, they live with blood. Even opposition groups may try to follow the regime's policies for survival reasons but it does not change much. Once they are labelled as 'terrorists', 'parasites', 'dangerous', 'infidel' and 'enemies' by the autocratic circles then it is the beginning of the end for such groups.

[62] Arendt 1951.
[63] Irving 1996: 171.

Fake news and lie-based propaganda are used for the elimination of 'others'. As long as autocrats have the control of their camp of people then they don't give up. Once all their enemies are eliminated then the new enemy will be selected from their own camp from the less committed, or from a different ethnic, religious or colour background. Almost everyone will have their turn to be described as an 'enemy' as long as the regime continues.

Justice and Judges in Autocracy

Laws are the most important and also the most dangerous political weapon of autocrats. They use laws to achieve their aims, and especially they change the legal system for their personal needs by appointing similar-minded judges, reshaping and occupying the judiciary, updating laws and regulations, and thereby violating the basic rights of all other individuals. With these new 'rights' those of individuals or groups can no longer be guaranteed. What would be described as criminal under a democratic regime becomes normal, and normality becomes criminal after such changes. In a fair society, as Robert Nozick explains, 'Individuals have rights, and there are things no person or group may do to them (without violating their rights). So strong and far-reaching are these rights that they raise the question of what, if anything the state and official may do.'[64]

Autocrats don't follow basic human and international laws or rights, use monopoly of violence by law against their opponents, and make sure that, as Kim Lane Scheppele argues, they have a legal system which covers and legitimises all their actions: 'they are often following a script using tactics that they borrow from each other'.[65] Politicisation of the legal systems[66] and controlling of laws and judges are the most important steps for autocrats. After the monopoly of law and violence under the regime, the public also shows admiration for the criminal mafia bosses who collaborate with the autocrats.[67]

---

[64] Nozick 1974.

[65] Scheppele 2018: 545.

[66] Ferejohn 2002.

[67] For example, a video created on 13 May 2021 by Sedat Peker, an organised crime leader and mafia boss from Turkey, was watched on YouTube by more than 3.5 million Turkish people in just one day. His 29 May video was watched more than 10 million times in just ten hours. In total, his eight videos in May were watched by more than 100 million people.

Without controlling the judiciary fully and monopolising this power, it is not possible for autocrats to establish a full authoritarian regime. Control of the elections, press, wealth, society, minorities and security forces becomes an easy process after capturing the judiciary and making laws in their own interest. Once the right of the monopoly of laws is given to one person, the rest face lawlessness. As Ergun Özbudun explained:

> The status and functions of the judiciary have always been among the most hotly debated issues in Turkish politics. At the centre of the debate are the composition and powers of the Constitutional Court and of the High Council Judges and Public Prosecutors (*Hâkimler ve Savcılar Yüksek Kurulu, HSYK*). Both were the subject of radical change in the constitutional amendment of 2010, adopted by the Justice and Development Party (*Adalet ve Kalkınma Partisi, AKP*) majority in parliament and approved by a mandatory referendum with a 58 percent majority. The changes regarding the HSYK were among the most controversial points in the amendment package that involved changes in 24 articles. In general, these changes were welcomed not only by AKP supporters, but also a majority of independent liberal democrats and major European institutions such as the European Union (EU), the Council of Europe and the Venice Commission.[68]

This was the deadly and decisive dagger to the heart of the already limping Turkish democracy. It opened up the road for the creation of a one-man dictatorship. The support of the public and intellectuals also gave the new rules full legitimacy. The rearranged legal system gave autocrats full reign to blame others with the help of false reasoning, to attack powerless minorities and to deprive the lives of the people with their ill-conceived policies. There would no longer be any laws or judges to stand in their way. People who support autocrats also turn against innocent and powerless groups. Without independent courts and free and equal legal protection, there is no hiding the fact that there will be ethnic and racial crimes, occupation, destruction, institutionalised and weaponised rape, and breaches of basic human rights against the quietest or weakest groups. The belief that authoritarian regimes can be removed by normal elections has been a delusion of some liberal intellectuals

[68] Özbudun 2015: 45.

for decades. Once autocrats are in office and have full power and control of the judiciary, they will never leave, unless there is an equal or stronger force to challenge them.

Laws become a set of rules which only prevent others from challenging or criticising the autocrats. The names of individuals, leaders or states may change but their actions have remained mostly the same; the strong against the weak, with the help of the laws of dictators. From this perspective, the basic human values of respecting and protecting each other have not much developed. This may be evidence of the fact that since primitive times, hunting has only become more sophisticated and much more destructive.

As Didier Fassin discussed in his article, 'Another Politics of Life is Possible', 'the problem of what is life – or more simply what we should understand here by this word – is complex'.[69] If you are not part of the mafia-style political gang, if you prefer to stay independent, then it won't be possible for you to even find a space and carry out your life and work – as Walter Benjamin stated – the 'simple fact of living'.[70] If you are a member of the inner circle of autocrats, who don't hesitate to increase their oppression against non-members for their own benefit, then you will be the puppet master of other people's lives, wealth and even their future. These are the ethics and moral values of these tyrants and their supporters. These tyrants, according to their own laws, punish others under claims of 'terrorism' but describe themselves as the 'defenders of human beings', 'God's gifts', 'peace makers' and 'peace keepers'.

During the 1950s, when a rich class was booming under the umbrella of American nationalism, when the laissez-faire type of capitalism, power and materiality was allowing a small elite to shape the people's minds and beliefs, Wright Mills wrote *The Power Elite*. He stated:

> They spread into various commanding circles of the institutions of power. One promising son enters upon a high governmental career – perhaps the State Department; his first cousin is in due course elevated to a high executive place in the headquarters of a corporation; his uncle has already ascended to

[69] Fassin 2009.
[70] Benjamin 1978.

naval command; and a brother of the first cousin is about to become the president of a leading college. And, of course, there is the family law firm, whose partners keep in close touch with outlying members and with the problems they face.[71]

Under authoritarian regimes, justice is not impartial, objective, equal, fair, reasonable, natural and non-partisan. The rules, their limits and division of resources are decided by the authority. It is a truism that the justice system only acts as the right hand of the authority in charge and justifies its actions. The autocrats' infinite power depends on the control of infinite justice. The line between justice and vengeance is very thin. Many authoritarian and populist governments past and present do not easily welcome the real meaning of justice, human needs, objectivity, democracy, equality or freedom unless it helps their authority and governmentality. Enduring freedom means freedom for them to do whatever they like. Fairness and justice are limited. If right and wrong are decided by an authority, if this authority is above everything including the law, then the concept of doing the right thing, in the right way, for the right reasons can be very problematic and wrong.[72] People will rush to answer the demands of the autocrats, but their demands only increase. While the power of autocrats increases, the rights of ordinary people shrink. As Jacob Burckhardt stated, 'They are all what we are not.'[73]

With the help of new advanced technology, the police and the intelligence services also become the eyes, ears, hand, legs, heart and brain of autocrats. There is an interdependency between them over wealth, power and ruling. While almost all daily activities are controlled under such regimes, new technology was created for the benefit of the regime rather than for the people. For example, with the use of technology which allows people to be spied on without their knowledge, to help the police by showing how they think, what they write, what they like and dislike, where they are or what they will attend. People do the job of the police against themselves. The information which is circulated by people, with other people, including their family members, is then used against them by the prosecutors of authoritarian

[71] Mills 1956: 69.
[72] Pettit 1997; Laborde 2008.
[73] Burckhardt 1943: 303.

regime. This self-censorship destroys any independent thoughts even before they come to mind. The result is a society with no independent thought, a society that doesn't ask questions, and is afraid to say or write anything. People are even imprisoned for their thoughts. While under democratic rules and rulers these human rights are seen as normal, part of freedom of thought and speech, and protected under law; under authoritarian regimes, these individuals can be tracked easily and their 'personal' information can be used against them as documented evidence. For example, if somebody criticises the regime on Twitter or Facebook and circulates it to their network then this is seen by autocrats as destroying the peace of society and an act of terrorism, and the individuals concerned almost always face prosecution and are punished. Equally, anybody who likes or shares these critical comments, can also be described as a supporter of terrorism and they are possibly convicted too. One innocent message may put many critical minds and independent thinkers behind bars.

Economics of Autocracy

Under an authoritarian government that uses surveillance, a new wealth and class are created around sovereign power. Under autocrats, the poor usually become poorer and the rich become richer.[74] Typically the existence and size of the middle class creates some balance under democratic governments but it disappears under autocratic regimes. Autocrats make sure that economic power and wealth stays in the hands of only the chosen elite who are very close to the ruler. The wealth is important to their family and kin. Controlling the economy and wealth is more important than increasing the wealth and living conditions of the people. Dictators are the richest people in the world, not the founder of Amazon, Jeff Bezos, or Microsoft founders, Bill Gates and Warren Buffett. For example, according to the March 2020 'richest people in the world' list in the American business magazine, *Forbes*, Bezos had $113 billion, Bill Gates $96 billion, and Warren Buffett $67 billion, because they mainly structure their businesses in regulated entities, pay taxes and disclose information about their wealth. However, dictators don't pay tax – they collect tax. In addition, they openly give and receive bribes on an almost daily

---

[74] See, Kim et al. 2001; Leon and Walt 2001; Lavinas 2013 and 2017.

basis. Economic activities cannot function under their authority unless the companies pay additional commission. They control the full economy. The head of one of the biggest automotive companies in Turkey told me in 2015:

> When we open a new factory in Kocaeli, we have to invite President Erdoğan. It is unwritten rule. If we didn't invite him, we would be punished harshly and we would not be allowed to carry on our business. So when we invite him for his 2 hour ceremony, which usually turns into his own propaganda, then we have to pay more than 3 million US dollars to his people for his attendance. If we want to be part of this power circle, do business and continue our life in a normal way under his rule, then we cannot escape without paying.

Erdoğan comes from a poor family background and could not even afford to pay for his children to go to private primary and secondary schools during his time as mayor of Istanbul (1994–8). However, in 2004, after just two years in power, when he was prime minister, the US Embassy in Ankara reported to Washington that Erdoğan had at least eight Swiss bank accounts. Later, in December 2013, a secret phone conversation between him and his son, Bilal, become public and revealed that he had a billion dollars in cash just at home. People were complaining and joking that he had built a gargantuan palace for himself with 1,000 rooms. However, he himself corrected the number of rooms, with the information that it was in fact 1,150, not 1,000! After this palace, which broke records for its size, he built a few other palaces in different parts of Turkey, worth more than 2 billion US dollars in total, joining leaders like Saddam Hussein and Muammer Gaddafi, who were also showing off their luxurious properties. Erdoğan didn't stop there. *Deutsche Welle* (*DW*) reported on 15 September 2018 and the *Financial Times* provided analysis on 17 February 2020 that in 2018 Erdoğan put all the state wealth into a fund, which was then around 40 billion US dollars, took full control of it, and also legally appointed himself as the head of the state wealth fund.

Erdoğan is not alone and he followed the same path as many other dictators. Most dictators steal not small, but huge, amounts of money from their people. For example, according to a report submitted to the United Nations Security Council in 2015, the Yemeni dictator Ali Abdullah Saleh, who subjected his country to endless conflict and starvation, had 68.3 billion US dollars. While the people of Yemen were dying of hunger, Saleh enjoyed his life without any punishment. Indonesian military dictator, Suharto, who was responsible for the execution of more than a million people in the 1960s and 70s, stole 35 billion US dollars from his subjects. According to a report in *The Washington Times*, Hosni Mubarak of Egypt stole and made a 70 billion US dollar fortune. In 2017, the financier and CEO of Hermitage Capital Management, Bill Browder, told the Senate Judiciary Committee under oath that the Russian president, Vladimir Putin, was estimated to have 200 billion US dollars. Exiled Russian banker, Sergei Pugachev, told *The Guardian* during an interview on 28 July 2015 that 'everything that belongs to the territory of the Russian Federation Putin considers to be his. Any attempt to calculate [Putin's wealth] won't succeed. He is the richest person in the world until he leaves power.' According to a *Forbes* article on 8 November 2011, and several others news outlets, the Libyan dictator, Muammar Gaddafi was worth 200 billion US dollars in 2011, when his oppressive power and laws turned Libya into a country of endless divisions and wars. In 2011, after the downfall of Gaddafi, the US alone seized 30 billion dollars of his family fortune, Canada froze 2.4 billion dollars, Austria controlled 1.7 billion dollars and the UK government also seized another 1 billion US dollars. The King of Saudi Arabia and his family are also estimated to have around 14 trillion US dollars. Some of these dictators have personal wealth greater than that of their whole country. They own the country's GDP and they can be easily described as owning the country as long as they rule it.

Under autocratic regimes, there is no such thing as public money. The central bank of the country operates like the autocrats' own bank account. They don't feel the need to give anything back to the people, but they expect people to continue to pay them. Controlling wealth is very important for the discipline and management of the masses. Autocrats create dependency with their hand-out style propagandistic distribution of power. For example, during the Covid-19 pandemic, many democratic countries such as the UK, Germany, Belgium and even the United States provided additional financial support for their people and affected businesses in March–April 2020. The UK government offered to pay 80 per cent of salaries of all working people, up to 2,500 British pounds. The United States Congress passed more than a 2-trillion-dollar relief package for people and affected businesses. Germany, Belgium and many other European countries offered similar compensation.

However, in Turkey, Erdoğan ordered people to pay donations to the state during this difficult time. Money collected from people's donations was then given as handouts in the city centres where thousands of desperate people gathered to collect this money. So that the public would notice that it was coming from Erdoğan, 1,000 Turkish lira (144 US dollars) was given with his signature. It was a very risky way for people to receive aid as it could easily spread infection. However, the propaganda was considered to be more important than people's lives. In addition, any local authorities who tried to collect some donations and help their local areas were given a final warning before their bank accounts were frozen and the collected money was transferred to the central authority to ensure the donations were also monopolised. Moreover, despite the fact that much of the personal protective equipment (PPE) was manufactured locally, most people in Turkey found it difficult to get any support, or to find any medical supplies and masks. The authoritarian regime did not miss the opportunity to step up 'medical mask diplomacy' and fill planes to send to Italy, Spain, the United Kingdom and many other countries for their own legitimacy, display of power and to show international support.

If internal dependency and the distribution of wealth is not enough, an autocratic regime extends its reach internationally, to steal or seize the wealth of others, and to circulate this new wealth within its own networks, thereby increasing their support and rendering the autocrats almost untouchable. Max Weber described this as running the state like a set of enterprises.[75] Autocratic governmentality and expansionist wishes are interlinked. Autocratic leaders cannot survive without wars and expansionism. In order to remain firmly in power for a long time, internal control and warring against minorities, while transferring their wealth and resources to their supporters, may not be enough for the power and governmentality of autocratic regimes. The international propaganda and sources are as important as internal. In 1940, under the command of Goebbels, minister of propaganda, the Nazi regime was broadcasting in more than twenty-two foreign languages, including Arabic, Gaelic and different Afrikaans languages. The English-language broadcast section was huge, targeting the working classes and anti-colonial movements. The anti-plutocratic nature of the war was one of the main emphases of the

[75] Weber 1927.

news bulletin. Goebbels reported to Hitler that 'fifty-four percent of the "little people" in England admitted tuning in to his propaganda'.[76]

Autocratic regimes almost always find a reason to legitimise their actions when they need to.[77] After the concept of terrorism which has been heavily used to justify many governmental actions, especially at the end of the twentieth and the beginning of the twenty-first centuries, the new strategies of 'safe zones', 'creating walls', 'stopping migrants and refugees', 'foreign viruses' and 'pandemics' are also shaping the new world order and creating a foundation for the autocratic regimes and leaders who have colonialist and expansionist wishes. We have observed over the last three decades how the concept of terrorism has worked perfectly to justify the extraordinary actions of aggressive and autocratic states.[78] The new strategies are expected to serve for similar purposes.

The twentieth century was the century of genocides and this evil continues.[79] Crimes are committed against minorities and weaker sections of society, while the autocrats stay in power. Evil regimes with their immoral reasoning, rule of government and administration have simply taken on different forms. Just because a few ill-informed politicians, activists or 'social scientists' are talking about 'post-colonisation' or a 'multicultural world', it does not mean that the end of colonisation is in sight. Tolerance is not yet possible in many parts of the world. Many social scientists who work on this subject almost always confine themselves to Western colonisation and imperialism, and blindly ignore and rarely mention local predators, who have been equally as destructive.[80] Local autocrats and their expansionism have just used cleverer disguises. Ottoman expansionism and slavery have affected minorities on three different continents. This has happened not only in Turkey, but Kurdish land and people in Syria and Iraq have been under Turkish military control, as well as half of Cyprus since 1974, under the guise of 'peace operation' and

---

[76] Irving 1996.

[77] Tas 2019.

[78] See, Feldman and Ticktin 2010; Fassin and Pandolfi 2010; French 2011; Cubukcu 2018.

[79] See, Ignatieff 2001; Ophir 2005.

[80] See, Varisco's *Reading Orientalism: Said and the Unsaid* (2007). It is an important study for a detailed discussion of how some intellectuals analyse differences between East and West or how they see the Orient.

'Turkishness'. Authoritarian Turkish regimes rule, and nobody dares to take Turkey out of these places. Northern Cyprus has become a haven for the black economy of Turkey,[81] and Northern Syria and Iraqi Kurdistan are in the process of serving in a similar role as they served the Ottomans for centuries. Like Turkey, many other expansionist authoritarian regimes, whose survival and wealth rely on and thrive only by seizing the resources and the lives of others, have continued to colonise. The cycle of colonisation and invasion persists, so that the wealth and continued existence of one group comes at the expense of the wealth and extinction of another.

As with the old style of colonisation, the old type of mercenary also continues to ensure the power of autocrats. Turkish authoritarian governments have used Kurdish village guards against Kurds in Turkey for decades. Since the Syrian war started in 2011, according to an article in *The Independent* newspaper on 7 February 2018, Turkey has trained and armed former Al Qaida and ISIS members, Salafists, bounty and booty hunters, looters, and all types of jihadist mercenaries.[82] Most of these were selected from Syrian refugees who were forced to join by the Turkish state, for its own current colonisation plans.

It is no secret; the Turkish authoritarian regime under Erdoğan has done this very openly, in front of the rest of the world. Syrians killed other Syrians for Erdoğan's power, as did some Kurdish village guards. This is nothing new. The Ottomans created ruthless armed forces, Janissaries, from different minority groups, especially kidnapped or press-ganged Christian boys, and these were tactics and war strategies learned from the Romans and Christian crusaders. The families of those kidnapped were killed, their land occupied, their young sons forced to convert to Islam and their young daughters forced

---

[81] See, Jensehaugen 2016.

[82] See also Bolton 2020. John Bolton, US President Donald Trump's former national security adviser, revealed in his book, titled *The Room Where It Happened* that Erdoğan's Turkey did not see ISIS as a real threat but only focused on stopping any Kurdish autonomy or political rights. According to Bolton's direct account, while the US knew about this, they prioritised their relationship with Turkey and Erdoğan's demands were vindicated, but not those of the Kurds, who were fighting against ISIS for the US and many other Western powers. There was a close mindset between Trump and Erdoğan regarding policies in the Middle East, Turkey, Kurds, the judiciary and the use of authoritarian power.

to be part of Ottoman sultanates or the harems of some general. After long military training these boys turned into ruthless killers and were sent out as guards of Ottoman borders and ordered to destroy their own kin whenever necessary for the state. The trained and armed so-called 'Free Syrian Army' or later newly named 'Syrian National Army' do not differ much from these Janissaries. They too are sent to kill their local neighbours and kinship networks in the name of jihad. However, this jihad serves no one well apart from autocratic leaders and their expansionist states. Erdoğan tweeted in Arabic during the October 2019 operation against Syrian Kurds, 'I kiss the foreheads of all the hero members of the Muhammadian army' who were entering Syria, and invading Kurdish land.[83]

Powerful states do not usually use their own people and resources for wars against others. The British used Indians against Indians, Arabs against Arabs, South Africans against South Africans. Irish people were divided and killed each other for over a hundred years for Britain's gain. France did similar things in North Africa, and Spain and Portugal created empires and ruled vast lands and stole the resources of others. Today Saudis use Yemenis against Yemenis for their own benefit. Iran takes a similar approach, making some Yeminis killing machines against other Yemenis, again for its own benefit. Afghanis killed Afghanis first for Russia in the 1980s, and in recent decades for the US. Libyans are slaughtering Libyans for others. Turkey first used ISIS against Kurds. After ISIS was defeated by the Kurds, Turkey changed the uniforms of the surviving ISIS members, mixed them up with some other Syrian and Turkish fighters, renamed them the 'National Syrian Army', and reused them against the Kurds and any regimes they disliked or any land they wished to benefit from, including Syria, Libya and Nagorny Karabakh. All these actions remind us of Adam Smith's work titled *The Theory of Moral Sentiments*, which started with this opening paragraph:

How SELFISH so ever man may be supposed, there are evidently some principles in his nature, which interest him in the fortunes of others, and render their happiness necessary to him, though he derives nothing from it, except the pleasure of seeing it. Of this kind is pity or compassion, the emotion we

---

[83] Tas 2019.

feel for the misery of others, when we either see it, or are made to conceive it in a very lively manner. That we often derive sorrow from the sorrows of others, is a matter of fact too obvious to require any instances to prove it; for this sentiment, like all the other original passions of human nature, is by no means confined to the virtuous or the humane, though they perhaps may feel it with the most exquisite sensibility. The greatest ruffian, the most hardened violator of the laws of society, is not altogether without it.[84]

In the animal world, small animals are prey for a big or powerful animal. Animals of course also invade; the notorious parasite, the cuckoo bird, takes over the nest of its host by laying identical-looking eggs, which when hatched proceed to kill all the host's chicks. This covert mimicry is not as faceless an invasion as that presided over by tyrannies, but it is not so different in the human world. It does not only happen between states, but also within a state, between different institutions or even individuals. Many people in their own corner can be brutal and act as colonisers and autocrats. This has not just been the problem of far right, fundamentalists and their divisive and destructive politics in the modern world, but many from the left wing have also proved themselves to be tyrants, as we know from the examples of Stalinism and Maoism. All these have committed unforgivable crimes and genocides, and they have all also claimed to be 'socialist' at some level.

Media and the Society of Autocracy

After the fall of Hitler, we witnessed many dictators of a similar mind in power. The new millennium started with a new hope; especially after the fall of Saddam Hussain in 2003 many were hopeful that Middle Eastern societies wouldn't easily allow dictators, or brazenly authoritarian politicians, to gain power again.[85] But the rise of Erdoğan, Assad and Sisi suggested a short collective memory of what had so recently gone down in Iraq. Or, for that matter, of what went down in Turkey at the end of the Ottoman Empire. Erdoğan's autocratic rule, political tactics and expansionist visions are frighteningly reminiscent of the rule of the 'three Pashas' – Cemal, Talat

---

[84] Smith 1759.
[85] Tazzioli 2014; Akcali 2016; Szmolka 2017; Kirdis 2019.

and Enver – the dictators who brought the Empire to collapse, masterminded the Armenian genocide, and created enormous lasting damage in the region.

The current power of the media and channels of propaganda is huge, compared with how it was in the 1940s. For example, the current Erdogan authoritarian regime in Turkey, employs thousands of people from the youth branch of their party, AKP (Justice and Development Party), led by some 'intellectuals' just to fabricate fake news and attack dissenters. They are paid a full salary from the public budget. As the *International Press Institute* (*IPI*) on 13 September 2016 and an article in *The Guardian* by Maeve Shearlaw on 1 November 2016 both highlighted, the propaganda and media soldiers of the authoritarian regime use threats of physical violence, sexual abuse, and al types of smear campaigns against known or unknown public figures, journalists and academics who are critical of Erdogan and his regime. The language of gendered insults is used a lot by these trolls: 'slut', 'whore', 'loose', 'easy', 'wild', 'bitch', 'prostitute', 'frigid', 'traitor lovers', 'mistress' or 'concubine' are used quite regularly for critics, female journalist and academics. 'Traitors', 'terrorists', 'terrorist supporters', 'enemy agents', 'infidels' (*kafir*), 'parasite', 'gay', 'half man', 'spy', 'foreign seed', 'bastard', 'asshole', 'dog', 'donkey', 'pig' are used for male critics. The social media accounts of many critical voices were hacked, the content deleted and this message posted instead: 'I apologise to our honourable president to whom I was unfair and attacking all this time with my libels and insults . . . I apologise to all the martyrs and the Turkish nation for the support I gave to the terrorists.' The worse the trolls are, the more their message can affect the wider society and silence people, making them more submissive. Multiple insults or rumours are eventually understood as facts, and similarly facts become trivial and received like rumours.

Most horrifyingly, Twitter and the Stanford Internet Observatory announced on 11 June 2020 that supporters of the Turkish, Chinese and Russian regimes had created thousands of fake accounts, sending millions of tweets as narrative manipulation and to intimidate the opposition and critics. Twitter identified more than 7,000 Turkish troll accounts, managed by the Turkish AKP government, which sent more than 37 million tweets from fake accounts. All accounts were created on the same day with similar usernames. There were also 'retweet rings' where the trolls and fake personalities retweet each other to amplify a message in support of the government or to insult and threaten critics. Twitter stated that they shared data with the Australian Strategic Policy Institute and Stanford Internet Observatory. According to the information, Twitter discovered in early 2020 that the Turkish network of accounts was co-ordinated using 'inauthentic activity' which demonstrated strong support for President Erdoğan. This army of trolls attacked any voices critical of Ankara's ruling party and its autocrats, including journalists and academics, especially criticising HDP, the opposition Kurdish-led political party, which the Twitter users accused of 'terrorism'. It was also stated that these trolls played an important role for the regime's public support, the results of elections and Turkish army operations in Kurdish towns and cities in Turkey, Northern Syria (Rojava) and Kurdistan in Iraq.

These insults and labelling move faster than an epidemic virus. Before any real imprisonment or killing, the labelling usually takes place as a way to make the punishment justifiable. Most critics – academics, lawyers and journalists, murdered in Turkey in recent decades – were labelled 'traitors' or 'terrorists' before any actual crime was committed against them. For example, the Turkish-Armenian journalist and editor-in-chief of the Agos newspaper, Hrant Dink, was assassinated in 2007, and Kurdish lawyer and human rights activist, Tahir Elçi, was shot down in 2015 – both paid the price with their life after such labelling. According to a statement made by the International Press Institute (IPI) on 13 September 2016, Ogun Samast, the murderer of Dink, defended himself in court in 2011, stating: 'I am not guilty. The headlines that portrayed Dink as if he was a traitor were guilty . . . Where are the people who have brought me to this process? I did not know what Agos was.'

Once morally and legally forbidden crimes against innocent people become legal, the voices of critics are equated with criminality and their punishment becomes justifiable by the authorities. Then mob mentality takes over and the killing of others evokes hysterical pleasure. They lose the ability to think or consider the consequences, as headless chickens move around without any sense of direction. They blindly follow their leader and turn against anything or anybody who is out of favour. They might even know that their leader is lying, but they don't care anymore, and they may even describe this as a sign of their leader's great intelligence. The lies of their leader become almost the only truth for them. Even their religious beliefs are shaped by those of their leader. Everybody takes leave of their senses in such an environment. Nobody trusts anybody. They talk in whispers, while covering their mouth with their hand. Not only critics but also the supporters of the dictators distrust each other. Everybody becomes an enemy and society is turned upside down. Autocrats become untouchable messiahs, while people turn on each other. This is the main aim of autocrats, to create distrust so that people are living a half life. As Arendt said:

> the totalitarian mass leaders based their propaganda on the correct psychological assumption that, under such conditions, one could make people believe the most fantastic statements one day, and trust that if the next day they were given irrefutable proof of their falsehood, they would take refuge in cynicism; instead of deserting the leaders who had lied to them, they would protest that they had known all along that the statement was a lie and would admire the leaders for their superior tactical cleverness . . . Believe everything and nothing, think that everything was possible and that nothing was true.[86]

Attacks on women, and narrowing down their roles to those of 'child bearer' and 'housekeeper' is common amongst almost all authoritarian regimes. For them society can only be redesigned and controlled by gender division and regulation. It is seen as a territory which must be occupied first. Without the control of the body, mind, sexuality and freedom, it would not be possible for autocrats to take full authority and establish the codes and conduct of every part of people's lives, including the bedroom.

Authoritarianism is like an uncurable cancer when it takes full control of its victims. It not only turns human life into an arid desert, but the natural world too. While human lives and values are shaped and homogenised for the regime, nature is also destroyed as resources are used carelessly without scientific understanding or engagement. Autocrats have no understanding or regard for the future. Their vision is limited to their own existence and therefore they feel the need to control and use all resources for their own benefit. People's lives become miserable while nature becomes treeless, lifeless and degraded. Some migratory birds even bypass the sky over autocratic territories, because their space and resources have been taken and destroyed.

---

[86] Arendt 1951.

After the successful elimination of any critical voices, taking control of natural life and resources, occupying and oppressing gender sexuality by adapting the law, people start living a life of trauma. During such times, autocrats see themselves, and are seen by their followers, as messiahs. Since the establishment of the modern nation state and its sovereign power, autocrats are feared and revered almost as divine beings. People look for saviours, or messiahs, especially when things do not go well for them. It is no surprise that orders from the autocrat are followed as if they were orders from God. The ruler is seen a prophet or a shepherd and the people are seen the flock.[87]

The construction of national sentiment around autocratic power is not just limited to or organised by the population within the state borders, but includes the diasporic communities as well.[88] For example, national, oral culture and education, not just within Turkey but in large parts of the diaspora, embody a severe antipathy and distrust of the Kurds, Armenians and Jews. The research I have carried out –involving interviews with many Turkish and Kurdish individuals in Turkey, Germany and the UK over the course of twelve years – has made this very clear. Scores of Turkish children are still raised by Kemal Atatürk's dictum that 'one Turk is worth the entire world', and taught that everyone else – including Turkish citizens who don't primarily identify as Turkish – are their enemies. The Kurdish people are perceived as the closest, weakest and most visible of such enemies at the present time, especially after the decline of Armenian and Jewish populations in Turkey. Predictably, a significant number of Kurds, in Turkey and beyond, have internalised this culture – becoming afraid to claim that they are Kurdish, or even hating their Kurdish-ness. At the extreme end of the spectrum, many Turkish elders, even in modern and contemporary times, have told their children and grandchildren that 'There might be some good Kurds, who identify as Turks rather than Kurds – but in general, Kurds are dark, bad and have a tail.' This, preposterous as it sounds, is not fiction. The parallel with certain propaganda in pre-Holocaust Europe should be obvious. Many Turkish individuals interviewed – in Turkish cities as well as Berlin and London – shared that at least one of their relatives or neighbours had told them that Kurds are dark, bad and have tails. While I was at a conference

---

[87] Gordon 1991.

[88] See, Ciçekli 2003; Barry 2006; Leblang 2017; Adamson 2019; Dag 2021.

in Germany in October 2016, a well-known Turkish scholar (whose name I must withhold to protect him) admitted in his presentation that it took him a very long time to realise that 'Kurds can also be normal human beings' [*sic*], and that, as a child, he and his Turkish friends bullied their Kurdish schoolmates and tried to pull their trousers down, to see if the story often repeated by the elders in their families was true, and Kurds in fact had tails.

These pre-existing, ethno-nationalist and discriminative cultural traditions have clearly facilitated autocrats' rise to power and their autocratic governmentality. Dictatorships feed on tribalism and fear. Media takeover and elimination of real political opposition have served their intended purpose effectively. Public 'debate' in Turkey or many similar regimes is a blur of government-friendly indoctrination and fear-mongering. And the supposedly democratic 'multi-party' system in Turkey is looking more like that of the Ba'athist Iraqi regime every day – certainly when it comes to attitudes and policies regarding small minorities. All but one of the remaining opposition parties in the parliament – e.g. the Republican People's Party (CHP), the Nationalist Movement (MHP) and the Good Party (IYI) – supported operations against Kurdish people in Turkey, the invasion of north-east Syria, 'Operation Peace Spring' in 2019, just like they supported the previous invasion, 'Operation Olive Branch', in early 2018. Religious leaders all over Turkey have joined the support, together with scores of university presidents, heads of corporations, bar associations, government funded non-governmental organisations (NGOs), as well as the majority of voting members of the public – at least according to official domestic polls. For example, the head of the Turkish Union of Bar Associations, President Metin Feyzioglu, levelled some criticisms at Erdoğan during 2013–14. On one occasion, on 10 May 2014, when Erdoğan was prime minister, Erdoğan showed no tolerance for Feyzioglu's very light criticism and left the state's official judiciary annual gala. Later, Feyzioglu worked very hard and gradually regained favour with Erdoğan as a way to keep his position and Erdoğan's support. During the October 2019 Turkish occupation in Kurdish land in Syria, he went to the Turkish-Syrian border and showed his full support for the Turkish invasion and their jihadist proxy army. Feyzioglu did not just stop there but also argued during his press meeting on 12 October 2019 that 'to kill civilians is not against international laws and it is the state's legitimate right, if it is necessary'. Moreover, during his talk at the Carnegie

Endowment, just after the 2016 military coup in Turkey, he also claimed that 'There is no torture in Turkey, none.' Even civilian people were not defended by the only legitimate organisation, the bar association, which should objectively defend anyone, even criminals, but this group can also change its position when it comes to the people who are seen as the 'enemy' of the state.

The second example is that the chairman of the Contemporary Art Fair in Istanbul, Ali Güreli, sent an email to the fair's international mailing list on 14 October 2019, which fully supported Erdoğan's war on Kurds, repeated Erdoğan's claims for his reasoning and asked his members and those on the mailing list to follow him as well. However, this time the international community remained united against Erdoğan's authoritarianism and their supporters. His message was seen as very nationalistic and racist by many international, non-Turkish members and artists. Many of them refused to collaborate with such an organisation. This sharp criticism pushed Gureli to update his position for his company's benefit and he sent another email on 18 October 2019 stating that his first message was 'entirely inappropriate', and he preferred to 'remain outside of any political situation or debate', but he still did not issue an apology. Erdoğan followed a similar approach when the world stood against him and he agreed to a ceasefire with the United States and Russia, and stopped his aggression against Syrian Kurds at the end of October 2019, but only temporarily. However, his tactic of taking a step back for the purpose of taking two steps forward in the future, when the conditions are favourable again, has not only been used by the Ottomans, but also by many other authoritarian regimes. Like Gureli, Erdoğan did not apologise or even acknowledge the crimes, aggression and danger he inflicted. Apologies and confession are not part of the culture of authoritarian leaders.

The third example is that of the Turkish Nobel Laureate Aziz Sancar's continuous love and support for Erdoğan. Not many international media outlets criticised his actions or were even surprised by his support, but several Turkish newspapers, including *Haberturk* on 8 October 2016 and *Yenisafak* on 28 April 2018, argued how Sancar wished a long life for Erdoğan's rule and that God protect Erdoğan and Turkey equally. Sancar was not working or living in Turkey when he made his comments. One cannot assume that he was simply afraid of Erdoğan and was practising *taqiyya*. While he was living under a more pluralistic and democratic regime in the US, he was supporting an oppressive, dictatorial regime for the people of Turkey. I observed a similar approach among many Turkish migrants and some intellectuals in Germany, Belgium and the UK, when I asked which political party they support in their host countries and also in Turkey. Most of them support one of the social democratic parties, including Green in their host countries for their own security, citizenship, language rights, equality and especially freedom. However, at the same time, most of them voted for Erdoğan's Justice and Development Party, and also the nationalist front party in Turkey which was the total opposite of their choice in their host countries. Most people would expect to hear a more progressive approach from a Nobel Laureate and academic than from Turkish guest-workers and their children. This example also shows that dictators are not supported by one specific group, but by different classes, educational backgrounds and gender. Feyzioglu, Gureli and Sancar are not alone. This has happened in the past and continues at the present time. These examples show that Turkey has built an authoritarian and culture of obedience, and 'ethical' values which influence almost all parts of society. As Webb Keane says, 'ethics is something each society creates on its own . . .'[89]

'Intellectuals' of Autocracy

Dictators aren't made in a day. Nor are they 'self-made'. They gain their power with the support of the public, media and intellectuals, of course; those in the corporate class who are the direct or indirect beneficiaries of the dictator's actions. Ethical, moral and intellectual conditions are not same for everybody who calls themselves or sees themselves as an intellectual. Not all intellectuals are successful and become a public figure as a result of unique, original work. Some achieve success because they are a friend or supporter of one of the dictators. Some positions are bestowed upon their family – as with ruling families, power is monopolised and controlled by certain families, classes and groups. It is not easy to break this chain. Some intellectuals have a strong collaboration with autocrats and occupy all positions, and they are often seen on TV and in newspapers, commenting on almost everything from sociology to literature, history to biology, East to West, elections to the economy, while portraying themselves as 'public intellectuals'.

As long as what they say benefits the dictators then they will continue to appear and be seen by the public as the most important 'intellectual'

---

[89] Keane 2015: 3, 6.

authority across many fields. However, in reality the success of many of these so-called 'intellectuals' is merely the result of their being a 'yes-sir' or 'yes-ma'am' gofer who agrees with every action and joke which is made by their leaders.[90] For example, when 1,228 national and international academics signed a petition criticising Erdoğan's authoritarianism in January 2016,[91] 10,000 Turkish national 'academics' and 'intellectuals' signed another petition at the same time, in support of Erdoğan and his authoritarian actions. They were part of the system and of course they did not want the system to be criticised. Interestingly, several of them wrote to me and questioned my criticism and signature against Erdoğan's regime, and even told me that to be part of the same social media, e.g. Facebook or Twitter, or taking part in the same conference or workshop might endanger their work, movements and position in Turkey. They were part of the team who created the Iron Curtain, they were the 'captive minds' as described by Czeslaw Milosz. They did not want anyone to create a hole in that curtain. They legitimised slavery and prison conditions for everybody. Milosz explained that when people say

> something is white when one thinks it is black, to smile inwardly when one is outwardly solemn, to hate when one manifests love, to know when one pretends not to know, and thus to play one's adversary for a fool – these actions lead one to prize one's own cunning above all else.[92]

However, 'intellectuals' don't do this for the purpose of *taqiyya*[93] or *Ketman*[94] as a way of surviving under the regime, as Milosz claims, but they voluntarily

---

[90] See, Arendt 1951; Milosz 1955; McCormick and MacInnes 1962.

[91] Vatansever 2020.

[92] Milosz 1955: 255.

[93] After the end of the Muslim empire in Spain, and the re-establishment of the authority of Christian forces, some Muslim religious leaders established fatwas and encouraged their believers to perform *taqiyya* in order to survive, and not to be slaughtered by the Christian army; in other words, not to show that they were Muslim in public, but to practise their religion in private. Throughout history, small, powerless ethnic and religious groups who have been threatened by the authority in power have acted in a similar way.

[94] *Ketman* or *Kitman* is the Persian word which has a similar meaning to *taqiyya*. Shias minorities used *Kitman* for a long time to survive under the Sunni Muslim majority. It is a mental defence for individuals and groups for contradictions or collaborations with the system.

and knowingly act as autocrats' diplomats and creators while they are beneficiaries of the autocratic system. The relationship is symbiotic, without an authoritarian system these 'intellectuals' can't survive or excel, without them the autocrats have no longevity and cannot monopolise power.

It is not just the 'intellectual confusion' as Marx states,[95] it is also the deliberate collaboration of some intellectuals. Even if they have any disagreements or disbelief in the system, we do not know about it until later, when they have benefited from it. For their own greediness, fear, short-sightedness, tribalism or ideological belief they are part of the system, as are the autocrats themselves. While many others take a risk, resist, lose their life or escape, these collaborators stay very close to the system. One can easily claim that they are different after the collapse of the system. This is also their tactic to escape from any blame. When there is a new leader or regime, like political chameleons they quickly adopt a new guise. Tyrannies and their 'intellectuals' equally create and protect the system, while crushing the opportunity for any opposition to survive. One of the main roles of 'intellectuals' in autocratic regimes is to rationalise the irrational behaviour and of autocrats. They orchestrate the system to create a monophonic intellect for the benefit of autocratic regimes. During the most chaotic times, especially, their silence is support for the autocracy. Antonio De Lauri described in his article, 'Bourgeois Knowledge', how they take the shape of state bureaucrats.[96]

Joan Wallach Scott's question of whether real academic freedom can survive in such an environment becomes more important than ever.[97] Academic freedom is a moral and societal matter rather a than legal one. The work of an academic might not always be completely sincere but it is at least searching for truth and a better society. Academic freedom might only affect a small part of the population but the result of that freedom will affect the larger part of society, and open or close the gate to a better or worse future. Scott reminds us that academic freedom is the ethical practice and civility of the system and indicatesthe level of freedom. She rightly points out that academic freedom becomes more important and suppressed when disciplinary authority starts

[95] Marx 1978.
[96] De Lauri 2014.
[97] Scott 2019.

to oppress. She states that 'regulatory and enabling authority . . . can suppress innovative thinking in the name of defending immutable standards'.[98]

An authoritarian regime should not be understood as a person or a regime of a few people; there are huge groups which are interconnected which allows the system to thrive again. People forget very quickly the disaster these regimes brought and they start to dream of one party and one-man rule again. Intellectuals and the media play their part in the re-creation of tyrannies, and present them as a 'solution' or an 'efficient' regime. For example, Thomas Friedman openly wrote in *The New York Times* on 8 September 2009 about his love for and championing of the Chinese autocracy. Friedman is not alone. Armin Rosen discussed in *The Atlantic*, on 10 January 2013, the position of Columbia professor and Millennium Villages Project founder, Jeffrey Sachs, and how he praised some African dictators such as Paul Kegane of Rwanda. Sachs justified the ruling style of dictators and claimed:

> In my mind, it's no accident that from Senegal to Afghanistan, that belt of more than 10,000 miles is really a belt of a lot of conflict. It's a belt of a lot of hunger and the worst poverty in the world, and unless we have a development model that goes along with the politics and security we'll never resolve these conflict conditions.

Internal and external colonisation and authoritarian regimes have been the main causes of suffering around the world and continuous conflicts. As long as authoritarian regimes are polished nicely, advertised as a solution and their opposition is not supported, then the belt of conflict, hunger and migration will only get longer and wider.

The education system and many educators are the driving force of any regime. They play a very important role in shaping society and youth according to the needs of authoritarian leaders. Without them the system cannot develop or survive. They are the bond between power holders and the people. The autocrats' supporters do not just come from right wing or religious fundamentalist backgrounds. As Slavoj Žižek explained to *The Independent* newspaper on 22 October 2019, many so-called leftist 'intellectuals', 'journalists' and 'academics' have also made their career out of

[98] Scott 2009.

supporting authoritarian regimes and their leaders. A time of conflict is when you see people's masks slip, and how the regime in power distorts the truth.[99] It is when you can recognise who the real intellectuals are.

Some 'intellectuals', while claiming to be critical of an autocrat, knowingly or unknowingly also support the regime's policies. Several recent 'academic' publications show us that even critical Turkish scholars call Kurdistan the 'Turkish eastern region', similar to the regime's description. This travesty of knowledge and false evidence becomes more important than factual, original and critical knowledge during such a time. Very strangely, such publications and their announcements are circulated widely and are awarded by different academic organisations or conferences, who are also directly or indirectly in support of such regimes and their policies. Many so-called 'intellectuals' support dictators – that is, until they get a position outside their country, away from the autocrats, where some of them may then start making some mild criticisms of their home regime as a way of playing at being 'democrats' and opening the way for themselves to join the ranks of genuine international and progressive intellectuals.

To be an intellectual is to take a risk, to be critical and to fight for the truth, even if you have to face hard criticism and lose your position and prospects. This alone will make life worth living. As Fassin states, '[t]he politics of life, then, is not only a question of governmentality and technologies, but also of meaning and values'.[100] Nietzsche also argued that the will to truth requires a capacity for critique.[101] The only alternative is a meaningless and empty life for intellectuals, while their actions have a tremendously damaging impact on the life of others. This is what happens when some intellecuals restructure the truth in the interests of evil.

Critical poets, painters, writers, academics, journalists and their work are observed very closely by autocratic regimes and their agents. These are seen as the most dangerous people by autocrats, even more powerful than an atomic bomb. They keep the autocrats on their guard, because they share the truth with the people and find holes in the system. It is one of the reasons that the

[99] Foucault 2000d; Weir 2008.
[100] Fassin 2009.
[101] Nietzsche 2007.

Turkish authoritarian regime has levelled charges against some critical academics and Nobel Laureate Orhan Pamuk; the Chinese regime has seen Nobel Prize winner Liu Xiaobo as the enemy of state; and the Saudi regime killed Jamal Khashoggi in their own consulate in Istanbul. Ex-US President Trump's anger against any critical journalists arose for the same reason. For authoritarian regimes and their institutions, the scientific truth is not important as long as it does not serve their needs. The Greek philosopher, Plato, wrote:

> The society we have described can never grow into a reality or see the light of day, and there will be no end to the troubles of states . . . till philosophers become kings in this world, or till those we now call kings and rulers really and truly become philosophers, and political power and philosophy thus come into the same hands . . . for it is not easy to see that there is no other road to real happiness either for society or for the individual.[102]

For Plato the worst rulers are the jokers, comedians and showmen who don't take anything seriously, lie and fake stories easily and can even find humour in the destruction and culling of life and nature.

The People's Autocracy

People create autocrats. They support them on their way to controlling all institutions. Autocrats establish new laws and orders in the name of 'the people', and many people submissively follow these new orders. If any strong public opposition had arisen before the genocide took place in Auschwitz, Halabja, Bosnia, Rwanda, the Cambodian Killing Fields, Tamil Land, Sinjar Mountain, then we would not have had to talk about all these serious crimes against humanity, and we would not call the twentieth and twenty-first century the centuries of genocide. When a country or government no longer has any dissenting voices, it is in a position to successfully eliminate a variety of critics and to bring the whole of society under the regime's single umbrella of nationalism and/or religious fundamentalism. This creates a new evil in a scorpion-like suicidal action, beginning with weak minorities, then spreading to the state itself and eventually the whole body politic.

---

[102] Plato 1906.

Voting in elections is not a means of self-expression. It is not a test of purity. It does not necessarily indicate that you agree with or like the person you vote for. Voting is based on different criteria, including which candidate you think will do the best for the people by supporting an open society, freedom, health and prosperity, and creating a safe environment. However, rather than choosing progressive, altruistic and intelligent leaders, the people have mostly voted for killers.

The people are the creators of these dangerous tyrannies, even though some studies argue the opposite. Social science has also failed to deal with the problem of the corrupted public which is directly or indirectly responsible for giving power to tyrannies. Most of them are the beneficiaries of actions which take place against innocent people. Instead of being a 'rescuer', they prefer to take the side of the perpetrators and be one of the beneficiaries of those crimes.[103]

The benefit does not always take material form, but to be a member brings with it the artificial self-importance of being involved in a crime they believe will benefit them and their future generations. The documentary, *The Act of Killing*, based on Indonesia has shown us how society continues to show no remorse for mass killings.[104] We need to acknowledge the truth that the role of the public in Indonesia is not unique. It is an example from just one of the autocratic regimes. If the public do not recognise and acknowledge the evil actions of the past, if they forget or forgive them then they empower those of the present and pave the way for future disasters. If society has the capability and resources but have failed to act, then they become the silent supporters of that perpetrator's actions. Robert Meister reminds us that 'past evil cannot be repeated unless it is forgotten – and what happens next will necessarily be different if, but only if, it reminds us that we have turned away from the past'.[105]

---

[103] Meister 2010.

[104] *The Act of Killing* is about Indonesian mass killing and societal involvement in 1960s. The director of the documentary, Joshua Oppenheimer, asked the perpetrators and their children and grandchildren to reflect on their feelings in front of the camera. While many did not show much regret during the recording, later when the film was shown in Yogyakarta, according to *The Guardian* articles on 20 June 2013 and also 5 March 2014, many people went to the streets to celebrate the killings, but to protest against the documentary.

[105] Meister 2010: x.

Not to stand against a morally damaging action can simply afford an opportunity for another tyrant to seize power. The increase and repetition of evil is like a snowball effect. Hannah Arendt discussed this in detail in her several works,[106] but especially in *Eichmann in Jerusalem. A Report on the Banality of Evil.* We lack a common measurement that can embrace both great evil and the sheer banality of people who have chosen to take the side of evil. Yet they commit these crimes together.[107] Most common people who support tyrants are ready to do anything for him or her just to be part of that regime, and to become a beneficiary of the regime's crimes.

To learn of past evil is more important than to learn about victory in war. The truth is that not many wars bring victory, only disaster. The only war which might be necessary is the war which prevents evil and which may bring some level of victory to humankind. Yet there was much domestic and international silence during Hitler's rise to power, until it was too late. Milosevic slaughtered almost a million Bosnians before the world acted. Saddam carried out his many crimes, including a clear genocide against the Kurds, in full view of the world and with the support of his witless public. It was already too late to stop these dictators.

The level of societal racism and nationalism increases almost everywhere, but this has been exacerbated and ramped up to its highest level in recent years. People, even so-called educated people who had the opportunity to be educated at the best universities, come out in support of the authoritarian regimes and their actions. For example, the Oxford University Turkish Society, joined by twenty-one other Turkish student societies in the UK from different universities, issued a statement on 16 October 2019 in support of the Turkish invasion of Kurdish-controlled north-eastern Syria. One of the reasons for this blinkered patriotism and support is that individuals often benefit from the regime. Many of them receive a scholarship to study abroad from the regime in the first place, with the further promise of a government position. De Lauri discussed the case of Italy, which has many similarities with Turkey and other patronage systems, where the nature of education is such that it has become nepotistic and exclusivist.[108]

---

[106] Arendt 1951, 1964 and 1971.
[107] Arendt 1992.
[108] De Lauri 2014.

Public support is the main driver of many authoritarian sovereignties and their governmental style, which creates a huge threat not just to stability and peace internally, but also to the rest of the world. For example, there is hardly any group or publicly known individual left in Turkey who can openly be critical about what is happening. Even unknown individuals who send a critical tweet or Facebook message are arrested and tortured by the forces of the regime, if they are not discovered and punished by their neighbours first.

The media is not just silent, but it is gleefully engaging in the war, celebrating the government's crimes with unqualified lack of restraint. There is hardly any opposing view or discussion. The stories of failed 'heroes' are covering the whole media either in the form of news or as part of hours-long Turkish soap operas. These very simplistic, emotive, brainwashing propagandist TV programmes portray dictators as a giant 'unbeatable' 'messiah' in every household. Even people's leisure time offers a racist and nationalist propaganda opportunity for the dictators. Many people spend hours a day watching these bloodthirsty soap operas and mafia programmes, which create fictionalised truths. There is a competition between different TV series and directors as to who can please autocrats the most and get state funding and support.[109] For example, in 2012, just after controlling the judiciary, there was a simple soap opera that did not completely follow Erdoğan's guidelines. He threatened the actors, producers and also the TV station with punishment by law. He used his self-made laws as a weapon. In the Turkish city of Kutahya on 25 November 2012, he stated in a speech which was published by almost all newspapers and TV channels that day, and also the following days:

> I know our ancestors very well. The one portrayed in the soap operas, 'Magnificent Century', doesn't show Solomon the Lawmaker accurately. We do not have such ancestry. We don't recognise such a Sultan Solomon. His life wasn't like the one represented in the show. He passed 30 years of his life on horseback fighting for the nation. I condemn the screenwriters, directors of the series and the owner of the TV station. No one has the right to mess with our national values. And although we have warned those concerned about this issue, we also expect the judiciary to give the right decision. There cannot be such an approach. As a nation, we must give the legal response they deserve, teach the lesson to be taught to the ones who twist the values of this nation.

[109] See, for example, Tugal 2009; White 2013; Cetin 2014 and 2015; Tunc 2018; Cevik 2019.

Erdoğan's intolerance of the performing arts and call for such harsh punishment is evidence of his totalitarian rule, which strives to control everything and decide what is right or wrong. Controlling the individual, the family and also society are most important for ensuring continuity of power for autocrats. Once they see any hole in the controlling mechanism, any disobedience or criticism, they jump fast to close it before allowing it to get any wider. After Erdoğan's criticism and threats, not only did his almost fully monopolised media attack the producers of the programme, but also his conservative followers started attacking the programme. A short time after the threat from Erdoğan and his supporters, the producer of the programme changed the setting of the soap opera, following Erdoğan's suggestion. The actresses, especially, were put into a more conservative form of setting, which fulfilled the needs of the autocrat and his mob, and Solomon started spending more time on horseback in battle, rather than frolicking with his harems. Aside from the sociocultural uniformity of the production, the historical presentation had to follow the current authoritarian rules.[110] This is not just a problem for the Turkish media and public; many other authoritarian regimes have also shaped public awareness and encouraged the spread of nationalist sentiments in similar ways.[111]

There has been no apology, acknowledgement or paid compensation for the crimes committed by the Ottomans against Armenia, France against Algeria, Britain against Kenya, America against Vietnam, and Iraq, Turkey and Syria against Kurds, even though there has been a massive amount of irrefutable evidence that they committed crimes against humanity and killed huge numbers of civilians. The lack of remorse does not just open the way for similar actions to be repeated, but also the criminal history of the past is rewritten by the present autocrats, their subjects and intellectual supporters. Marx already pointed out this problem of rewriting history and stated:

> History is nothing but the succession of the separate generations, each of which exploits the materials, the capital funds, the productive forces handed down to it by all preceding generations, and thus, on the one hand, continues

[110] See, Arsan and Yıldırım 2014.

[111] See, Mankekar 1999; Rajagopal 2001; Allen 2002; Abu-Lughod 2005; Salamandra 2005; Porto 2011.

the traditional activity in completely changed circumstances and, on the other, modifies the old circumstances with a completely changed activity.[112]

Passively and actively, as Foucault[113] argued in his lectures at the Collège de France, people have been sucked into and take sides with the sovereign power. Any small resistance from a few liberal voices, any protest or criticism from a small group of intellectuals, is immediately punished with imprisonment, unemployment, and the restriction of any prospects, including working and travelling. The public and intellectual supporters of dictators with their narrow mindset and selective and monopolised media sources support all the restrictions and oppression. Albert Einstein rightly criticised the danger of narrow-mindedness:

> Somebody who only reads newspapers and at best books of contemporary authors looks to me like an extremely near-sighted person who scorns eyeglasses. He is completely dependent on the prejudices and fashions of his times, since he never gets to see or hear anything else. And what a person thinks on his own without being stimulated by the thoughts and experiences of other people is even in the best case rather paltry and monotonous. There are only a few enlightened people with a lucid mind and style and with good taste within a century.[114]

Great thinkers, from ancient times to the present day, from Plato to Descartes to Bertrand Russell and David Hume, have all questioned human behaviour and whether people are rational or irrational animals. For example, as Russell debated in his work, *Unpopular Essays*, 'It has been said that man is an animal. All my life I have been searching for evidence which could support this.' In modern times, the fact that repeated crimes resulting from the collaboration of people and their autocrats have not yet come to trial shows that human behaviour is more irrational than rational. The people are responsible for the growth of tyrannies and also for their own destruction. Without their own people, Erdoğan, Saddam, Milosevic and Hitler would not have taken power and destroyed the lives of others. People may not be directly

[112] Marx 1978: 172.
[113] See, Burchell et al. 1991; Foucault 2007; Bröckling et al. 2011.
[114] Einstein 1954b: 64–5.

responsible, as their leaders are, however, they are directly or indirectly the beneficiary of the crime itself. Foucault may be not wrong in claiming that 'society must be defended' but not all societies are innocent; some have blood on their hands and other societies should be protected from them. Human violence is not just a thing of the past, it is very much in the present, and is being carried into the future.

Alternative Governmentality

When democracy is replaced by autocratic constitutionalism, and there is little room for the basic political and juridical principles of equality and fairness, and when the government, media, financial institutions and justice systems only serve the regime and its autocrats, then an alternative government emerges through necessity. Alternative governmentality cannot be defined as a sub-institution; it works parallel to and independently against the institutional structure and practice of the authoritarian and centralistic state. Creating an alternative judiciary and governmentality is one of the most effective ways to reduce the power of the authoritarian state, to develop a new state within a state and to establish the authority and institutions of the parallel state as a de facto way to bring an end to brutal autocrats and their regimes.

'What we learn in time of pestilence: there are more things to admire in men than to despise' said Albert Camus in his masterpiece, *The Plague*.[115] People are not only the creators of religions, beliefs, pandemic viruses and autocrats, they are also destroyers of such creations, and able to replace them with new ideas, rules, rulers, solutions and cures. While the majority of societies may be hypnotised and in denial of reality under an authoritarian regime, some are more resilient and able to resist the brainwashing tactics of autocrats and look for a solution. It has almost become the normal under colonialism and authoritarian regimes for arbitrary justice or injustices to be used against such resisters.

After the war in the Philippines against Spain, US President William McKinley expressed his authority on 21 December 1898:

Finally, it should be the earnest and paramount aim of the military administration to win the confidence, respect, and affection of the inhabitants

[115] Camus 1991: 308.

of the Philippines by assuring them in every possible way that full measure of individual rights and liberties which is the heritage of free people, and by proving to them that the mission of the United States is one of benevolent assimilation, substituting the mild sway of justice and right for arbitrary rule.[116]

Foucault addressed some important questions related to historical transformation, the exercise of power, public policies, regulations, laws, and how domination and exlusive power create serious social problems – as well as the role of magistrates in these processes.[117] However, he did not provide any meaningful solution beyond the state's structure. As Charles Tilly argued, without organisation, mobilisation and collective action, real change, especially against authoritarian regimes, is not possible.[118] We have observed from many examples around the world, for example in China, Egypt, Venezuela, Iran and Turkey, that Tilly's suggestions may not be enough and that such countries can be oppressed easily as long as the regimes control the police, army, media, wealth, and especially the judiciary and taxes.

The question is how we deal with authoritarian governmentality, how we can bring it down or limit its power in a meaningful way. The answer is not simple and there is no single answer, but many. Creating an alternative governmentality with parallel political and legal institutions is one of the important possible solutions. As we discussed at the beginning of this chapter, authoritarianism starts with the full control of the judiciary. An end to – or limitation of – power should start in the same way, to take away power over the judiciary. The power of authoritarian regimes with control over the legal system can be eliminated by creating an alternative court and justice system beyond the nation state with the help of autonomous individuals who have not been fully dependent on the authoritarian structure. This may be

---

[116] Instructions to General E. S. Otis (21 December 1898), in the United States Adjutant General's Office; correspondence relating to the war with Spain and conditions growing out of same (Washington, DC: Government Printing Office, 1902), p. 859.

[117] Foucault 2000a and 2003.

[118] Tilly 1977.

[119] About the domination of power, see, for example, Beisner 1968; Pettit 1997 and 2001; Bohman 2004; Markell 2008; Laborde 2010; Bachvarova 2013.

more effective than any street protests. To have a large number of critical people who are following alternative rules, rather than those of the autocrat, is the boldest and most effective tool. This will help to limit the domination of autocratic power over deprived people. As long as one group dominates another and people are threatened by the rules, with no capacity to challenge the authorities, then the existing power will continue.

Freedom can only be obtained if the domination of autocratic power is broken with the help of a group to create alternative jurisdiction and power.[119] Philip Pettit argues in his work on the power structure between *imperium* (state) and *dominium* (private ownership) that while *imperium* holds the power of jurisdiction, the *dominium* involves the right of ownership where the control is arbitrary.[120] Patchen Markell highlighted that 'while the state may – indeed, must – use its imperium to combat the domination that arises from particular configurations of private dominium, this use of state power has to be limited and controlled'.[121]

The justice and court of an authoritarian regime, like wealth, is central-ised, held by few and serves in favour of a small circle, but oppresses the large majority of people. However, parallel justice has many advantages. First, it is not centralised, but delegated locally and works autonomously. Second, it is not run by state appointees, but created by seekers of alternative politics, volunteers and members of informal networks. Third, it is open to everybody, less discriminative and, most importantly, an accessible, fast and economical process. Fourth, it forces parties to collaborate with each other and also with the process itself, instead of competing and fighting to win. Fifth, it solves problems, follows procedures, imposes punishments, deals with fines and taxes, involves policing and monitoring, and implements the rules without the autocratic regime's knowledge or involvement.

The aim of alternative politics is to create autonomous and state-like alter-native institutions, including a justice system, alternative militias, economic and tax structures, all of which are essential to alternative governmentality. Providing justice, creating alternative political and economic power, and con-trolling and regulating the lives of a large group of people are all important

---

[120] Pettit 1997.
[121] Markell 2008: 24.

mechanisms for a parallel state structure and governmentality.[122] Alternative politics have complemented and increased public support for the creation and practice of alternative governmentality. Alternative governmentality siphons power from official state authorities and institutions at both the local and transnational levels, and this new power configuration affects the lives and choices of the people.

The Weberian notion of national state borders has its limits.[123] Many states aim 'to distinguish between members and unacceptable residents of the territory – through regulation of the internal boundaries leading to citizenship and legal residence'.[124] In response, others, or unacceptable residents, also create an alternative authority which is not just limited to state borders but moves beyond and across states and challenges the security,[125] economy[126] and sovereignty[127] of multiple centralistic and autocratic states at the same time. This new parallel and borderless state structure shapes the attitude, as well as the political, legal and economic choices of a large number of internal and transnational people who find it difficult to obtain a place and peace for themselves under the authoritarian and centralistic state(s). Of course, having control over the lives and the desperate choices of people also creates new divisions, conflicts and an increase in many different radicalisations within and between states, internally and globally.[128] This, in the end, will open the way for many conflicted and competing governmentalities in one space, but it may also open the way for a better, humanitarian and well-structured democratic state, and most importantly to end or seriously weaken the power of autocracy. We have already observed this happening in large parts of the Middle East, and many other regions over the last decades.

Fair and democratic elections are not possible without a strong alternative authority. As discussed earlier, the police and the armed forces also take

---

[122] See, Skolnick 1966; Habermas 1994; Simon 1994; Lundy and McGovern 2008; Akcali 2016; Busse 2017; Jongerden 2017; Szmolka 2017.

[123] See, Weber 1958, 1974, 2014 and 2015.

[124] Waldinger and Fitzgerald 2004.

[125] See, Andreas and Snyder 2000; Rudolph 2006; Fassin 2011b; Zartman 2017.

[126] Hanson and Spilimbergo 1999.

[127] See, Hansen and Stepputat 2005; De Genova and Peutz 2010; De Lauri 2019.

[128] See, Arendt 1958; Agamben 1998; Bauman 2004; Fassin 2009; Akcali 2016.

the side of autocrats and assimilate into the system until they see that it has lost its legitimacy and power. The use of violence by the existing official state is permitted not only by local, but also by international laws, even if that state is authoritarian and brutal. For this reason, the alternative government first needs to create its own forces and gain legitimacy among its people and abroad. It should show that it has alternative military forces, institutions, ideas, agendas, programmes, rules, courts and that it can respond to the needs and demands of the people. Justice is the first requirement of the people. Once they have their rights, and justice, they willingly pay their taxes. When the new, progressive and open system takes effect and stands as an alternative power, then the existing official regime becomes disabled, without the ability to enforce the rules and collect taxes.

Alternative governmentality is about the undermining of the existing central power by transferring the role and power of the judicial system and the economy obtaining internal and international support, and creating a new administration alongside the old one. While the existing regime might continue to wield its power for a while, the alternative one will gain authority and establish itself in a de facto way. This will bleed the autocratic system and reduce the power of the judiciary. When the economic and financial conflicts, criminal cases, family problems and business conflicts bypass the state and find alternative solutions, authoritarian regimes cannot survive for long.

The Catholic Church in the sixteenth and seventeenth centuries is a good example of this. Alternative governmentality was introduced with the Reformation after centuries of cruelty and oppression under the Catholic Church. It was an authoritarian and oppressive governmentality with continuous control over people's minds and lives. This monopoly of power had to be broken. People stopped going to the Catholic Church for solutions to their problems and also stopped paying any tax or donations. While the Catholic Church survived, its authority and wealth were reduced and new states and authorities were introduced under new churches.[129] The birth of the Protestant Church was a good example of alternative governmentality. Hegel described the broken power of the Catholic Church as a good thing, especially after the long struggle of many people who did not believe in and were unwilling to follow

---

[129] Rawls 2001.

its doctrines.[130] Similar divisions of power happened within Islam, when Sunni authoritarianism started in the early period of Islam. The birth of Shi'ism was the response to Sunni autocratic domination. Alternative mosques, rules and judiciary were created and the powers of Sunnism were also broken and its monopolisation of Islam was challenged.

Without control of the judiciary, wealth and the population, governmentality is not possible. Moreover, the power created by this autocratic ruler is not used for the benefit of the people, but for the benefit of the autocrats and their governmentality. Such power divides the people, as controlling the population and protecting the system is guaranteed only with the help of others. This power might appear very sophisticated and help rule-makers to present themselves as God-given, with special privileges. In reality, the people play the role of God and empower someone else to rule them like a god. Power is the bond between politics and law enforcement that justifies the actions of both sides. Former US Attorney for the Southern District of New York, Preet Bharara, explained in an interview with *The Guardian* on 15 March 2019: '[a] particular person in power doesn't want to be investigated, and wants to get his supporters to doubt the veracity of the result, so he[she]'s undermining people's faith, in a direct way, in the rule of law'.

Leaders in the style of ex-US President Trump would be more upset about an unincorporated justice system than any negative comments from a rich person such as Bill Gates or the owner of Amazon, Facebook or Twitter. It would be easy to punish someone wealthy with a fake court decision or tax penalty if the justice system is fully under the control of the autocrats, but it would not be very easy the other way around. Without holding the power of judiciary, there is not much possibility for full dictatorship. This was made clear after Joe Biden won the 2020 presidential election, when the US Supreme Court refused to hear Trump's fraudulent claims. The judiciary, if and when it is controlled by autocrats, can justify even unjustifiable actions. The judiciary is the brain of any state and is the most powerful weapon of any authority or government. Justice can be used to shape society or create a new one according to an ideology. Justice is the administrative system of the rule

---

[130] Hegel 1991.

and law of a state. It is enduring and ensures the security of any regime. It is even more important and effective than any military power.

Creating laws, constitutions and administering justice was practised by ancient tribal communities in Mesopotamia, Egypt, Greece and elsewhere. Multiple laws and alternative governmentalities were practised from the establishment of Judaism, Christianity and Islam, and during the Roman and Ottoman Empires. This was much before the claim made by Foucault of sixteenth-century Europe. The concept of community, tribe or state does not exist without authority, governmentality, power and justice: they are interconnected.[131] One cannot function fully without the other. Working with each other is necessary for real authority and a sovereign body that legitimises the use of violence against others and prepares rules and laws for its functionality, collects taxes and makes its every action justifiable in the eyes of its own people and outsiders. Creating a social fabric is especially important for the needs of any regime. Without exercising authority over a territory and a reasonable proportion of the population, it would be difficult to talk about governmentality and power in action. Some rulers and intellectuals of modern nation states would claim that 'justice for all' and 'good governance' is something new and belongs to recent centuries or nations. This is inaccurate.

The Code of Hammurabi, which was established by the King Hammurabi of the Babylonian Empire, which included Mesopotamia, established detailed rules. His 282 laws referred to different types of societal roles, rules and punishments, including gender and men versus women.[132] The Code stated, 'Bring about the rule of righteousness in the land, to destroy the wicked and the evil-doers; so that the strong should not harm the weak, so that I should rule ... and enlighten the land, to further the well-being of mankind.'[133] Justice for all was one of the most important elements of Hammurabi's power. He stated, 'Let the oppressed man come and stand before my image as king of righteousness. Let him understand my words and his case, so he will understand what is just and his heart will be glad.'[134] Hammurabi's laws did not just affect different communities, tribes and create the foundation of

---

[131] Clark et al. 2018.
[132] King 2005.
[133] Prince 1904.
[134] Prince 1904.

modern states and their institutions, but it has also influenced morals, rules, orders and different beliefs.

After Mesopotamia, the ancient Greeks also created important rules for their citizens.[135] In ancient Greece (322 BCE), Hyperides declared:

> For men to be happy they must be ruled by the voice of law, not the threats of a man; free men must not be frightened by accusation, only by proof of guilt; and safety of our citizens must not depend on men who flatter their masters and slander our citizens but on our confidence in the law.[136]

The ancients thought 'it characteristic of wild animals to gain power over each other through violence, but that men ought to define what is just by law, persuade each other with reason, and serve both these aims by submitting to the rule of law and being instructed by reason'.[137]

When we apply what we understand from the ancient Mesopotamian and Greek practices to our modern world, for good governance, the laws for well-grounded democracies have the following important basic conditions. (1) law and politics are separate and law should not function or serve as a vehicle or instrument of the sovereign's self-interest. A ruler should assume the position of the servant of the nation rather than 'the boss' or owner of the nation. (2) Legality is not as important as impartiality and equality. Even bad, discriminative, genocidal laws can be made legal if passed by the cabinet of autocrats. This legality does not make such laws right. Moreover, rationality may be also problematic if it is only rational for the sovereign power. (3) The law should apply equally to everyone, not just registered citizens or select individuals. The law should limit and control the actions of politicians and sovereigns as well as the ordinary people, consistently and equally. (4) Officials are held responsible for all their actions. (5) The law is accessible. (6) The laws are easy to understand, clear, predictable and affordable. (7) The laws are fair. (8) No punishment takes place without clear evidence. A person is innocent until proven guilty by clear evidence and facts. (9) Nobody should be accused, detained, arrested, kept in jail or prison before being found guilty by clear

---

[135] See, Cohen 1995; Lanni 2006; Cooper 2007; Harris 2007 and 2013; Hawke 2011.
[136] Harris 2013: 3.
[137] Harris 2013: 3.

evidence. (10) No one should be found guilty according to new laws about their previous actions. (11) Judges are impartial and consistent with the law. (12) The judiciary and judges should be fully independent from the ruler's personal and political needs. Judges should not be influenced by personal relations or bias.

Athenians and Mesopotamians recognised and applied most of these principles thousands of years before our modern democracies. Athenian judges and litigants also acknowledged that trials were primarily a form of feuding behaviour.[138] It was stated that:

> it is not permitted to enact a law directed at an individual unless the same law applies to all Athenians . . . The Athenians put much effort into making the text of laws accessible . . . Officials could not punish someone for an offense not contained in a law passed by the Assembly.[139]

The Athenian legal system had also some weaknesses, unforeseen consequences, but these were mainly about intention to ensure fairness in settlement. In addition, some elites, as today, tried to abuse the judicial system which also opened the way for the development of written law.[140] However, Athenian laws were mainly administered by amateurs and local judges.[141] It would not be wrong to claim that on many levels, Athenians were the first practitioners of 'pure' democracy but also the last.

Ibn Khaldun (1332–1406) wrote and discussed the style of government and its effect in the fourteenth century in his master work, *The Muqaddimah*.[142] He stated at the beginning: 'The nature of civilization. Bedouin and settled life, the achievement of superiority, gainful occupations, ways of making a living, sciences, crafts, and all the other things that affect (civilization). The causes and reasons thereof.'[143] The governmentality of tribes and savage nations, sovereign authority and power, human civilisation, the style of governing and living were

---

[138] Cohen 1995; Lanni 2006.

[139] Harris 2013: 5–9.

[140] Hawke 2011.

[141] Lanni 2006.

[142] Ibn Khaldun 1989.

[143] Ibn Khaldun 1989.

discussed by Ibn Khaldun in detail. Governmental authority was coined by him many centuries before Michael Foucault. He stated:

> the first thing to disappear in a tribe that exercises royal authority, when God wants to deprive the members of that tribe of their royal and governmental authority, is respect for these kinds of people. When a nation is observed to have lost (that respect), it should be realized that (all) the virtues have begun to go, and it can be expected that the royal authority will cease to exist in it. 'If God wants evil to happen to certain people, nothing can turn it back.'[144]

However, Khaldun's work, like that produced by many other non-European intellectuals, was largely ignored, while the much later works by Hobbes and Foucault claimed to be unique. Some other important philosophers also focused on the right of resistance against intolerant regimes. This was one of the main themes of the works of John Locke,[145] Montesquieu,[146] Mill[147] and Marx.[148] When the rules start to serve a select group of people rather than everyone, and when education is created to support this injustice, the result may be a certain unity since restraining the beliefs and choices of the people allows the continuity of power at some level, but eventually it will inevitably fail. Intolerance, discrimination and violence cannot continue without the disruption and failure of authority and power. There are countless examples of leaders who trusted the support of only a select group, and who set people against each other for their own benefit, but in the end faced increasing resistance which made way for the creation of a new or alternative parallel authority.

Alternative governmentality and creating parallel economic, political and judicial power is not something which belongs to the past, it is a very active and contemporary process, connected to local spaces and their links. The notions of 'brotherhood', 'trust', 'loyalty' and 'commitment' are central to alternative governmentality. The parallel authority in charge provides power, protection,

---

[144] Ibn Khaldun 1989: 192.
[145] Locke 1947 and 2010.
[146] Montesquieu 2001.
[147] Mill 1975.
[148] Marx 1978.

justice, opportunity, wealth and prestige to its members. In return, members do not tend to co-operate with the police or engage with official established legal mechanisms but follow a culture of silence, respect and obedience and prefer to deal with issues via their own systems. Roger Ballard in Desh Pardesh (1994) called this 'on their own terms'.[149] This approach encourages dependency, for example, by giving jobs and loans. The net effect is that these parallel structures challenge, to some considerable scale, existing legal mechanisms, creating alternative governmentality and power.[150]

Hawala and alternative banking[151] and money transfers continue to be an important instrument in alternative financing.[152] Non-profit and charity organisations, and small-scale business ventures help to connect the transnational alternative economic activities for fundraising. Hawala is a cheap, reliable money transfer which bypasses the normal bank system. It is not a new system; it has been used since the eighth century. These alternative methods are not only used by small groups against states, but also by some states such as Iran, Afghanistan and Sudan, which have been banned, limited or sanctioned from free trade by the world powers. 'With the US trying to impose ever more vigorous financial sanctions on the other, how on earth else could the bazaar continue to operate without recourse to hawala?' questioned Roger Ballard, one of the scholars who worked on the hawala system for decades, in part of his interview with the *Financial Times* on 14 April 2008. Ballard explained:

> If the US is serious about tracking down the sources of Iranian money that ends up on its shores, it should start by looking no further than New York. It's all a complete hall of mirrors, because hawala is supposed to be a system

---

[149] Ballard 1994.

[150] Moore 1973; Galanter 1981; Shapiro and Alker 1996; Migdal 2001; Holden 2014; Tibi 2014.

[151] Hawala, meaning 'transfer' and also 'trust', is a system which is outside the official banking or money-transfer system and follows Islamic tradition. The money transfer is made by a large network of money brokers, known as hawaladars. The network is connected transnationally and the system is mainly used to transfer money between Western countries, the Middle East and the Indian subcontinent.

[152] See, Passas 1999; Maimbo 2003; Ballard 2005 and 2014.

without records. The best source of data on this is going to be on Wall Street – if money is being sent to Bank of America, where are the records going to be?

Conflicts arising between parties involved in the activities above are often resolved by parallel court judges and non-state legal systems, which renders the alternative creation of a judiciary outside the control and power of the state.[153] The members whose role it is to implement the rule of parallel court judges and make sure that unrecorded businesses continue unchecked are potentially very important in this dynamic and their connection or membership is key to their operation. These alternative financial and judicial systems are resilient and difficult to understand, as they are based on discreet, strong interpersonal relationships. Most alternative practices are highly adaptable to changing conditions, and have seemingly remained 'off the radar'.

To sum up, most authoritarian regimes are organised like criminal gangs who only protect the leader, serve a group and fight against all others. The oppressed ethnic and religious minorities create an alternative way to support themselves, their family, community and identity against autocratic rules, even though some of their methods and tactics may not be different than the ones they are escaping from. As Marx explained, 'The class struggle necessarily leads to the dictatorship of the proletariat, that this dictatorship itself only constitutes the transition to the abolition of all classes and to a classless society . . . The state can be nothing but the revolutionary dictatorship of the proletariat.'[154] Knowingly or unknowingly to be part of alternative economic and legal practices establishes the level of power that the power holder has. If one person refuses to pay tax or to follow the legal system but instead follows an alternative way, this may not harm the whole system. It may not even be noticeable. However, if this one interest becomes many people's interest, if the oppressed population increases and they search for an alternative way, then this passive revolt may cause more damage than any direct war from a powerful enemy.

The following chapters will specifically focus on the structure of the authoritarian Turkish regime and the response and alternative politics from the Kurdish movement.

---

[153] See, Sezgin 2014; Shah et al. 2014; Tas 2016d; Ercanbrack 2015; Kötter et al. 2015; Nash 2017; Rohe 2019.
[154] Marx 1978: 220, 538.

2

MARDIN AND DIYARBAKIR: AN ETHNOGRAPHIC ACCOUNT OF CONFLICT

Home is not the place where someone is born. Home is a place where there is freedom of choice, and freedom of living, equally. Home is a place where someone is protected, pleased and proud. (Kurdish teacher, July 2015)

One sunny day, 11 May 2015, I was in Mardin for my field research. The multiplicity of languages, religions, orders, arts and literature in Mardin creates a rich cultural heritage. The city is currently dominated by Kurds and Arabs, but it used to be inhabited by large Assyrian, Armenian, Yezidi and Jewish communities, although nowadays they have been reduced to a small number. It is easy to recognise signs of their bygone presence that remains in the architecture on every corner of the city.

The old town of Mardin has one main street, an old road that passes through the city centre. It is similar to the Roman town of Matera in the Basilicata region of Italy, but has an earlier history than Basilicata. Some of the architecture in Mardin was not just designed by the Romans, like in Basilicata, but goes much further back in history to Mesopotamia and Assyria, where Kurds find their descendants. The city was one of the most important sites of Mesopotamian civilisation. At more than five thousand years old, Mardin is one of the earliest urban centres in history, where authority, power and social hierarchy were developed and practised. It was the birthplace of many philosophies, religions, political and legal systems, sciences, agricultural and water irrigation technologies, the invention of the wheel, as well as the alphabet and writing.

The old city was built on the hillside and has a different view by day and night. Mardin is well known in the daytime as 'a beauty to just to sit and watch endlessly' for its historical stone houses and architectural design. At night it is famously 'a string of glistening pearls on the neck of a beautiful woman' because of the arrangement of the stepped buildings around the hill and the lights from houses and the main street. The view from the balconies at night gives the impression of being on an island surrounded by dark oceans; this is because there is nothing but a flat uninhabited valley stretching until the fringe of the Syrian border.

I had plenty of time to spare until my first meeting of the day and wanted to take a stroll and absorb the city, observe how the people of this diverse society interact with each other. While I was still in the reception of the hotel, several police cars passed by beeping their horns and I asked the receptionist if there was any problem. She explained, 'It is normal procedure. You should not worry about the visible ones that you see here, but the thousands of them that are under cover so you don't know who is where, that's what makes a problem. Just don't get into politics and the rest will be fine.' I was a bit anxious hearing that the undercover security forces were everywhere, but I could not do much about that now. I thanked her and walked down from my hotel.

Some women dressed in Western-style clothing, young and old, were on the street. Some were alone, entering shops or walking up and down the street, but others were with small children or in the company of another adult. There was also a group of women who were covered in black, from top to toe, accompanied by several other similarly dressed women. Men, especially some older men, were dressed in a very traditional way, wearing local Kurdish *shalwar* (baggy trousers), with large, dark, thick moustaches, balancing tea, cigarettes and rosary beads in their hands while holding intense discussions outside tea shops. Some others, especially young men, casually dressed in jeans and sporty, tight, short-sleeved T-shirts, were smoking and fiddling with their mobile phones. Several other men on the street were clean-shaven and dressed in oversized black trousers and classic-cut jackets, without any tie. They looked like members of the same club, with an unofficial costume. These are typically clothes preferred by conservative, religious people who work for government institutions. They could also have been members of a religious order, of which there are many in Turkey. While I focused on the other side of the road and observed some shops, a few men rushed past me. They had long beards and wore flowing religious gowns. It was difficult not to notice them. My first impression was that the street was almost evenly divided between modern, traditional and religious dress codes. It was an eclectic mix of people, as well as a collection of parallel, non-interacting lives.

Many shop owners were sitting in front of their shops. It didn't look as if much shopping was going on at this time of the day. The front doors of each shop on the main street were uniform in style and the facades well kept. I was informed from a few of the shop owners that the area had recently been redesigned and modernised to present a good image for the tourists. One of them explained, 'They forced us to renew the front of the shop, but the rest of the city is more than 100 years old and has never been touched. Some people still have their toilet outside the back of their house, and some shop toilets are still outside on the back streets.' The different buildings and their varying conditions looked like an old, paralysed person whose face is painted with make-up to look youthful but who cannot act young or barely even move. Another shop owner added, 'When our elected mayors try to do something about our problems, the state calls them terrorists.'

In the year prior to my visit, the elected city mayor's office was won for the first time by the Kurdish-led People's Democratic Party, HDP. They introduced the co-chair system, a man and woman, in an effort to create gender equality and progress in the country's patriarchal politics. The Kurdish co-mayors received a 52 per cent majority vote, which was huge considering that there are several political parties in the country. It was also a huge victory for the Kurds to win in this city against Erdoğan's ruling party with its monopoly of media, financial resources, and police and military support. However, not long after they were elected, the co-mayors faced difficulties and blocks from the governors of the city and different ministries. This prevented them from doing any work for their people, as is common under many other authoritarian regimes.[1]

---

[1] Authoritarian rulers threaten even the most pluralistic societies and democracies around the world, including Brazil (see, Neiburg and Thomaz 2020) and India (see, Kaur and dyuti a 2020).

They were removed by an internal ministry decree and were replaced by the state-appointed officials not long after their election.

One of these co-mayors was a young, 25-year-old Assyrian woman, Februniye Akyol (born and christened as Fabronia Benno). She had to use her official Turkish name, because the cultures, languages and names of Kurdish and Assyrian ethnic and religious minorities are not recognised by the legal and political system of Turkey. They were not allowed to use any different names, letters or languages other than Turkish. I met her twice and managed to interview her while she was still in office. The other co-mayor was a 72-year-old Kurdish veteran politician, Ahmed Turk. They were not just removed from office, but Ahmed Turk was also imprisoned as a member of a 'terrorist organisation' and accused of creating a self-autonomous government in the city. He was released in February 2016 after several months in prison. The Kurdish co-mayors won the local election in 2019 again with a huge majority, 56 per cent of the total vote this time, but shortly afterwards the state repeated a similar process and removed them from office without any evidence.

It was only around 11.30 in the morning but the sun was already very strong and I, as usual, was not dealing with the intense heat very well. I was also a bit tired from the previous night. The city is not far away from the Syrian border and all night I had heard the clashes and the sound of bullets from the Syrian side, the war between Kurdish forces in Rojava and the members of the Islamic State, known worldwide as ISIS. I had not been able to get much sleep. People were anxious here and the name of ISIS had already created fear especially after the systematic rape and genocide they had committed against the Yezidi Kurds. It also created huge anger among Kurds in Turkey who strongly supported the Syrian Kurds against the Turkish government's approach and ISIS.

Aside from this increasing tension and boiling anger, the Turkish side of the border could be described as peaceful. In the two years previous to my visit, between 2013 and 2015, instead of clashes, which have taken place for decades between the Turkish state and Kurdish guerrillas, there were peace talks between Turks and Kurds. However, while the country was supposed to hold a general election on 7 June 2015, the tone of the 'peace talks' had already become more divisive and nationalistic, thanks to President Recep

Tayyip Erdoğan and his governing Justice and Development Party, the AKP. The representative of the HDP and its leader Selahattin Demirtaş (also in prison since November 2016) were blaming the government for helping ISIS and not showing a real appetite for the 'peace'. The state was more concerned about the development of Syrian Kurdish autonomy and did not want any of its own Kurds to seek any rights. The Turkish government worried that the peace process would make space for Kurds in Turkey to ask for autonomy and similar rights to those gained by the Syrian and Iraqi Kurds. I was there to find out how the politics and justice of the country were affecting the daily lives of different minority groups and their expectations from the peace process.

The Silversmith and the Meaning of Peace

All in all, it was quiet on the streets and it did not take me long to walk to the Armenian silversmith's shop. Just around the bottom of the stairs going up to the shop, before entering, I saw a large group of students, aged 10–12, visiting this historical city from a western city of Turkey. They asked me if I could take their photo. I took their photos, we exchanged a few words and then I rushed off for my meeting. I had already been there a few times during my previous field research visits. I was feeling privileged to get to know him. After my arrival the day before, I went to the shop directly but could not talk to him then because he had a few customers in the shop and did not feel comfortable enough to talk. Instead, I just bought a few small silver pieces as presents for my family and friends and left.

The famous silversmith was already working very diligently when I arrived. Unlike yesterday, there was nobody else in the shop. He called the tea boy straightaway and ordered two teas for us without even asking me if I wanted one or not. He gestured to me to sit down and explained, 'I know I promised you yesterday that I would talk, but I am really sorry, I don't have much time today. I've had a big order through from the governor's office to make some presents for their guests. The election is coming and the governor wants to give gifts as usual to encourage people to vote for Erdoğan's party.'

He was complaining that the governor's office had not given him much time for this order and wanted the order turned around in just a few days. He continued: 'It's not fair to expect such a big order to be ready in such a short time. This is not bread; it shouldn't be rushed and made quickly. This is meticulous silver work. These necklaces and bracelets are not just simple, they will be passed down from generation to generation and should be very high quality. I can't lower my standards. Even if they don't care, because it will be given as a present, I do care about the work I do. I respect my work, otherwise how can I claim to be a master of my trade? They don't pay much money for these and usually pay very late, but I still always take great care with each piece.' At which point he sighed, removed his fine-framed working glasses from the permanent indent on the bridge of his nose and continued, 'Anyway, welcome again.'

I promised that I wouldn't take much of his time and explained that I had also arranged another meeting which I had to rush for. The boy had already brought our tea, each with two sugars. It is the usual tradition in this area to serve tea in a small thin-rimmed glass, shaped like a bride's corset, with two sugar cubes. Each time I visit here for research, on average I drink at least ten teas a day. It would not be polite to refuse an offer of tea when you meet someone here.

I asked him about the ongoing so-called peace process and also the upcoming election. He responded, 'Let us talk about silver work. This is more important and more beautiful than politics. The politics here is as usual, nothing has changed and it's just the same – dirty. At the end of the day, whenever you talk about it, it leaves a very bad taste in your mouth.' He kept avoiding talking about the past and present in order to find a way to make some connection with the future, when there could possibly be hope. This was his way of ignoring or avoiding the time already lived and the living for tomorrow. However, I needed to get some information from members of different minority groups here about the peace process, politics and justice system and he was one of the key figures who could tell me about the Armenian community and their past and present life in Mardin. I said, 'I would like to know if you think the so-called peace process and election would bring any justice, peace and equality to this land and your people.' His face suddenly changed. His smile and sense of self disappeared, and was replaced with a look of worry. His body stiffened like someone had put a needle or knife in his ribs.

After a brief silence, he spoke while he nervously and pointlessly rearranged things on his work desk, without looking up: 'Justice! My grandparents never experienced that once during their lifetime. I have stayed silent the whole time but still have not seen any justice in this land either. The peace and colourfulness of this land was lost a long time ago.' Continuous conflict replaced the peace, especially when the butchering Ottoman pashas killed millions of Armenians and many Assyrian, Kurdish and Yezidi people with the aim of creating one single Turkish identity. That action destroyed people's trust and societal equality, and these have not yet been restored. Vast lands from displaced Armenian and Assyrian minority groups were transferred to some of the local Turkish and Kurdish people a hundred years ago, and they have created their fortune from these people. He continued 'Peace with who? And how is it going to be done? I don't think we are anywhere close to any peace in the near future. My only hope is that things do not get any worse than what we have now.'

I mentioned to him that the government was repairing and opening some Armenian churches in different parts of Turkey, for example one in Diyarbakır, the famous Sur Armenian Catholic church, and transferring the rights of some land to Armenian charities. I asked if these were not important steps to help towards healing that historical wound. He looked into my eyes for a moment and then focused again on the piece of silver he was working on and responded, 'Do you think putting two stones on top of each other and praying there is going to make you forgive someone who killed your father, grandfather, grandmother, raped your little sister, took your wife as their wife and stole all your fortune and land? No! I don't think so.'

He was shocked and found it difficult to understand how people could not be aware of the damage to others that had been inflicted by their grandfathers. He went into detail about how some Muslim neighbours had taken action against their own non-Muslim neighbours, acted as state militiasand as voluntary proxies for socio-economic benefit. He continued, 'Many people are still not aware that some of their wealth is coming from others. They even get very angry if anyone mentions this. They tell us that if we are not happy with their country then we should leave. This was and has been our country for centuries. I don't know how now it appears to only belong to a small group of people who know little about the real history of this land.'

He took a sip from his tea, and anxiously looked out of the window, appearing to check in case anyone was in earshot. He then explained that if he did not know me very well, he would not agree to talk to me. He went on and explained, 'I usually don't talk much and try to have a regular day and not be reminded or think of any badness from the past or the present. Thinking and talking is very dangerous in these parts.'

We talked a bit longer, but I did not want to take too much of his time and needed to call a taxi for my next appointment. Lastly, he concluded that

for real peace and justice, real social healing is necessary. There is more than one society in this context. There is the society that is the victim and but there is also the society that has blood on its hands, the criminal. We don't just need political reform or to change a few laws here and there, but we need a societal reform, land reform, cultural reform, wealth reform, gender reform, educational reform and historical reform to really understand the crimes of the past and create a brighter future for all.

The silversmith signalled for his tea boy to call one of the taxi drivers from outside. The tea boy was running around, doing many things. He was skinny, had striking green eyes, and dark curly hair. He only looked around 10–12 years old but was expertly carrying several teas in his hands at the same time. It was a Monday, a normal school day. It was not holiday time and children his age were supposed to be at school, but like hundreds of thousands of other children in this region, he had started working at an early age to help his family. Some of them at this age or a bit older join the city's youth movements or Kurdish guerrilla groups in the fight against the regimes of Turkey and Syria.

A Kurdish Taxi Driver and a Religious Man

There were many people sitting in front of the tea shop, drinking tea and talking over each other. The tea boy spoke to one of them, a man, who was going to be my driver. He quickly left half his tea and rushed to my side. The journey was only three kilometres away, but he seemed very happy to get the job. The driver opened the door for me very gently and welcomed me in. He observed me in the rear-view mirror flitting only his eyes back and forward from the road and then said, 'You don't look like you are from here. I hope you got some nice silver from the silversmith. His work is excellent. We don't have many of these skilful people left around here anymore. But he is stubborn and did not flee to Istanbul or a different country as did many of his kin. Did you buy some of his silver?' 'Not today, but I am aware that his work is very good,' I responded. He repeated his early question again, 'But you are not from here, are you?'

I answered briefly in the hope of no further questions: 'No, I am here just for a short time.' He responded, 'But you don't look like a normal tourist either.' He kept observing me in his mirror and wasn't looking much at the road. The traffic was slow-moving so I did not worry about his driving. After his persistence, I surrendered and out of curiosity asked, 'What does a normal tourist look like?' He took a deep breath and turned his eyes back to check the road a bit while driving down through the hilly town on a narrow road, passing old, historical buildings very slowly and then looked me back at me in his mirror before continuing, 'Anyway, who you are does not matter. Welcome to our beautiful Mardin.'

Now it was my turn; I wanted to learn more from him. I said, 'Thank you. I am an academic, here doing some research and trying to understand the lives of the diverse local people.' I understood already from his dialect that he was Kurdish; anyway, it would be difficult to find a Turkish taxi driver in this city. While Turks are a minority, the majority of them are civil servants in this area.

From my field research I have learned that taxi drivers, barbers and tea sellers are the best people to get information from and hear street-level truths about the life and politics of a place. People with these three occupations spend time with customers one-to-one and they interact and engage with many different people, becoming the hubs of local knowledge. This taxi driver was very talkative. I did not want to miss this opportunity. I asked him about the economic and political situation in the city and added, 'Do you think the ongoing peace process has helped a bit?' He was suddenly not feeling very talkative and seemed uncomfortable answering my questions. 'I hope you are not an agent of the state. They are everywhere,' he blurted out.

After my brief silence, he went on and continued to answer his own questions as well as mine, 'Actually, we don't know who is who anymore. They even created a division between our family members with the help of religion and the ideology of party politics. We used to leave our doors fully open and trust all our neighbours. But today we are even afraid to open our hearts to each other. All doors are locked and all trust has been destroyed.' He took his cigarette packet from his glovebox and asked me if I wanted a cigarette. I thanked him and told him that I didn't smoke. He responded, 'Cigarettes are the only friends we have left. The rest have been alienated from us, become our enemies. Even our neighbours appear to be spying on us for the state. They don't have any reason to spy on us, aside from being Kurds, to speak Kurdish. To be Kurdish is not easy anywhere.'

He then asked, 'Why is it problem to be a Kurd? Do you think we are the problem?' I stayed silent for a bit and then responded provocatively, 'I don't think it is a problem to be a Kurd, but why do you think that way? Don't you have equal rights with the rest of the country?' He looked me again in his rear-view mirror and mumbled, 'Rest of the country? Which country! Turkey? I can see that you are not from here.' He continued, 'In Turkey, the state as well as the Turkish public want us to deny our Kurdishness and origin. They want 20 million Kurds to be fully assimilated into Turkishness. I travel to many cities in this country and once I leave Kurdish regions I appear to be in an absolutely different country. Turks are enjoying everything, and they see themselves as the master of everything. They don't offer any job opportunities and freedom to the Kurds. Many of our young people are left with no other option but to fight against state inequality and join the Kurdish guerrilla fighters.'

It was easy to hear the anger and frustration in his voice. I recalled similar comments I had already heard from other locals. He continued, 'Arrest and torture has become normal for many of us. I have been arrested several times for no reason. Probably for talking too much. But we should be able to talk. They make good roads between our cities and more recently airports, so they have good access for their military vehicles and aircraft. They bought very expensive cameras and drones for watching us. Our skies are full of drones – they are probably flying over us now – but they do not spend money on updating our old drainage and sewage systems. They see how many times we go to the toilet from their drone cameras. Nothing is secret or private here anymore. The money they spend on drones is enough to develop the whole country's drainage system, which I believe is more important than watching people shitting.'

I was not expecting this much openness but when people don't have much to lose, they become fearless. I was aware that Turkey was one of the countries that had invested heavily in drone technology, and armed and advanced surveillance equipment in recent decades.[2] Turkey, under authoritarian regimes, has always been divided into two opposing countries at the same time and continuously in conflict. One is rich, and other is very poor; one is free, and other is very oppressed; the people in one part of the country have the right to do almost anything, but when the people in the other part speak in their mother tongue they are labelled as terrorists.

I learned that the taxi driver was feeding ten people in his household on his daily income. He explained, 'If I don't work one day, then my whole household will go hungry. Six of them are adults, they can work and they want to work, but there is not much work for us here. Three of them are educated. Educated means they have university degrees. They are teachers waiting to be appointed positions, but the state does not offer our people roles locally. Instead, western Turkish people are sent here as teachers with the aim of assimilating and brainwashing our children.

I asked him why he does not move to one of Turkey's big cities where he and other members of his household could more easily find a better job. He gave me a strange look and summarised again the cultural state of the country: 'There is racism against Kurds everywhere in this country. Our land is our honour. We don't leave it and we don't sell it. I have been to different parts of Turkey as a temporary worker for the summer, but always return here at the end of a season.[3] Not only the state police, army and judges, but even the Turkish people we work for treat us worse than dogs. They don't even pay us fully when we finish the work. When we complain to the police, they put us in custody for supposedly damaging the peace and security of society. Law is always one-sided if you are Kurdish. We don't have anybody to complain to. In the end we have to accept what they offer us, which is usually much less than what we agreed in the first place.'

---

[2] For example, the *Financial Times* stated on 8 October 2020, 'Turkey's armed drones bolster Erdoğan's hard-power tactics.' *The Guardian* explained on 27 November 2019 'how UK technology fuelled Turkey's rise to global drone power'. *RUSI Newsbrief* discussed in January 2021 Turkey's rising drone power.

[3] For a brief discussion of Kurdish seasonal workers in Turkey, see also Duruiz 2020.

His testimony and many other Kurdish people's similar accounts showed that Adam Smith's 'invisible hand', and 'laissez-faire' of the state which he discussed in his famous work, *Wealth of Nations*,[4] was very visible here politically and economically. Here, however, there was the taking of discriminative action in a very visible way and letting one side take the law into their own hands against the other with the help of the authorities. The maintenance of justice and honouring a contract with all the people by the state was absent.

We were approaching the end of my journey and I thanked him in Kurdish. He was surprised and but very happy to hear Kurdish words from me and responded to my very first questions: 'The peace process has not shown its face here aside from a few tourists like you who feel a bit more comfortable to come our city. There is an election coming, I don't like elections as often they make things worse in Kurdish lands.'

We were in front of the monastery I wanted to visit. I paid him and in addition gave him a good tip for his openness and trust. Smiling happily, he pointed to the monastery, 'This is one of the treasures which our city has left but they have little tolerance for this place and their people. Assyrians have a similar destiny to us.' I thanked him again for the pleasant journey and talk and left the car.

It was no surprise that many people in this region were questioning their unbearable and unequal life. However, I could never understand why so many so-called intellectuals, journalists, business people and politicians in the same country stay silent, deaf and blind seemingly on purpose. Some of these people are not just silent but have given a lifetime of support to this morphing authoritarian regime. Yet a taxi driver was willing to reflect on the state's injustice and carries on his daily life fearlessly. This must be one of the important signs of hope for any possibility of peace, if it is ever going to happen. Didier Fassin argues that '[t]he politics of life, then, is not only a question of governmentality and technologies, but also of meaning and values'.[5] As Nietzsche rightly argued, the will to truth requires a capacity for critique.[6] From my observations, this capacity was not a matter of wealth or diplomas, but the value and dignity applied to oneself and to others.

[4] Adam Smith 1999.

[5] Fassin 2009: 44.

[6] Nietzsche 2007.

It was almost 2.30 p.m. I was visiting an Assyrian monastery, Dayro d-Mor Hanonyo. It is also known as *Dêra Zehferanê* (Kurdish), and *Deyrülzafaran* (Turkish). Tur Abdin (mountain of the servants of God) is the name of the whole historical area, including the monastery, which was a cultural and religious birthplace and inhabited by Assyrians until the establishment of modern Turkey in 1923. Assyrians, like many other minority groups, enjoyed a certain degree of autonomy under the Ottoman Empire until the late nineteenth century. Later, they also faced persecution, especially genocide in 1915, and many of them were forced to leave or assimilate under Islamic identity. After this, the Assyrian Orthodox Church was moved to Homs first and then Damascus became the new residence from 1959. Some Assyrians still use their original language, Aramaic, and the education at this monastery is also Aramaic.

After touring around a bit, I met with an Assyrian religious man at the monastery. We spoke in the monastery garden, while he proudly pointed out other landmarks and views of the city which could be seen from the grounds. I reminded him of the government's claim to repair and open new churches and increase the happiness of non-Muslim minority groups. He was shocked: 'Happiness! Look around at all this land, to the valley, to the hill and as far beyond as your eyes can see, or not see. All this land once, for a long time, belonged to our people. But now, we are almost imprisoned inside the walls of this church. Everything was taken from us. Our people suffered and were forced to leave. Our numbers are decreasing very fast. Some are moving to Western countries for a better and peaceful life; some others, in order to survive assimilate into Muslim and Turkish culture. The pressure from the state and intolerance against minorities like us from this majoritarian society continues. I am not sure if this church is even going to continue freely to fulfil its historical duty, to serve its people.' We had a long conversation. He also rightly had a pessimistic view about the future of his people, their lands and their different way of life. It was evident that reasonable or even very limited pluralism under liberal democracy were not working in practice here and in the context of these minority groups. They could not be part of that 'reasonableness' – who can and cannot be is decided by the state and sovereign.

A Female Turkish Professor and a Male Police Officer

After I had finished talking with the Assyrian religious man, I walked around and talked with different people who were visiting the church that day. There was a mixed group of men and women, aged between 40 and 70, some in modern dress, some wearing headscarves and others wearing oversized clothes similar to those I described earlier. I chatted with a few of them. I learned that this was a group of academics coming to visit this old city and church for a day from Bursa, a western Turkish city. They were rushing a bit to look around quickly and take a few photos, because their minibus was waiting outside to leave and take them to Urfa, where they were staying the night. This is another Kurdish city close by that they thought was safer to stay in than Mardin. One woman, a professor of economics, blonde, well dressed and in her fifties, expressed her opinion: 'Look, this church is proof that our country and nation are very tolerant. We are allowing this religious minority to practise their beliefs freely and to have their church here without any fear. See, the building also looks very well looked after. It is thanks to our government and our taxpayers' money that these people have this space. We should tell outsiders more and explain how tolerant a society we are. Western powers and media want to divide us and always write things which are not true.' I wanted to listen to her account without any interruption. There would not be much point in reminding her about the problems and discrimination that ethnic and religious minorities have faced, using the many examples I had recently observed and heard directly from the locals. This academic's account was not unique. A large part of Turkish society believes that the state is very tolerant and that people do not appreciate this, but instead create a lot of problems. This example also shows that nationalism, racism and political blindness exists among all genders, education levels and classes, and not something that only the poor, less educated or men display.

I had had a long day and several talks already and was ready to leave the church. I preferred not to take a taxi this time, but instead to walk to the city centre, which was three kilometres away. I was just leaving the church when a police officer outside the main door of the church asked to see my ID. I was worried. It was still 'peaceful times' but I also knew that journalists and academics, especially talking with local people and gathering information, were not welcome around here. I tried to go unnoticed but apparently not carefully enough and they asked for my ID. I did not want to make any difficulties or ask many questions and showed my Turkish ID card. I asked if they were checking everybody's ID.

He cast a sidelong glance at me and said, 'Not everybody's, but you stayed too long and also talked to several people. I would like to know who you are, what you do and why you are here.' This indicated that they were already following me. 'Fine, but why is it a problem to stay so long and talk to people? I am here, visiting this beautiful church. Why do you need my occupation? I am an academic just like that group,' I replied, pointing to the group I had talked to earlier. He did not like my questioning and replied angrily, 'I am the person here who asks the questions, not you. You are also not an academic who belongs to this group.' He pointed to the same group, then shook his head and added, 'I don't understand why you come all the way from London to visit this church. Look, we are taking care of this church very well. The state spends a lot of money for these people. I really don't know why our government doesn't just turn this place into a beautiful mosque for our people. These people live in our country and in our land but are still not happy and complain all the time. Did they complain to you as well?' I responded ironically, 'No, nobody has complained about anything and everybody looks very happy. Do you think people have a problem here?' He was not happy with my sarcastic statement and further questions.

The police officer, who was holding my ID, continued: 'We are a great nation and peaceful country, but these Westerners want to destroy our peace. They send their agents here to do that. Look at what they did in Syria – they destroyed all Muslim countries. I am sure that they want to use these Kurds and Armenians [he was pointing to the city] to divide our beautiful country too. I hope you are not also going to write something bad about us. Have you seen anything bad about us?"

I silently listened to his claims, which many Turkish politicians, state officials, bureaucrats, the majority of Turkish academics and a large part of society also believe and will tell you. He gave my Turkish identity card back and I left. During our conversation, I did not mention that I came from London, but he was obviously aware of my full identity and movements.

In discussions on the normal role of the police, Burchell et al. argued that:

> Life is the object of police: the indispensable, the useful, and the superfluous. That people survive, live, and even do better than just that, is what the police have to ensure. Police 'sees to living': 'the objects which it embraces are in some sense indefinite'. 'The police's true object is man.'[7]

---

[7] Burchell et al. 1991.

This was not exactly what I was observing here. It seemed to me that the police's main priority was not the local people, but the state and its autocrat.

I changed my mind and called a taxi instead of walking to the city centre. The silversmith was right, and I did not trust the smell and climate of the politics there. The atmosphere can become dark and brutal suddenly; easily destroying innocent individuals. In the last four decades more than fifty thousand people have lost their lives and many more remain missing in the Kurdish regions in Turkey and hardly any security officers have been convicted. During the politics of darkness of the 1990s many people were taken away by security forces and never heard from or seen again. This started again in recent years, especially after mid-2015.

Diyarbakır: Kurdish Election Success and After

My last visit to Diyarbakır, a Kurdish majority town in south-eastern Turkey, coincided with the beginning of the most recent overt conflict and violence between the Turkish state and the PKK-Kurdish Workers Party. Shortly after my arrival, following the huge success of the HDP's 13 per cent vote from the June 2015 elections, heavy clashes continued almost twenty-four hours non-stop in Sur, one of the oldest parts of Diyarbakır, inside its 7,000-year-old historical city wall.

In September 2015, while staying in a small hotel in the centre of the Sur district where the main clashes were taking place, I was able to see the famous four-legged minaret which was just fifty metres away and soon became a line of demarcation between both sides. Later, I learned that the area next to the minaret was the place where the head of the Diyarbakır Bar Association, Tahir Elçi, was assassinated, while asking both sides to make peace.

The whole neighbourhood was interconnected by very narrow streets, common for most old towns. The area also created the ideal conditions for street or guerrilla-type fighting, and was a difficult environment for the heavy tanks and modern military tactics of the state. However, the state was ready to destroy large parts of the neighbourhood with heavy weapons and tanks and did not hesitate to shell densely populated urban areas. In addition, airdropped munitions were targeting whole areas, including schools.

There is a long history of curfew in Turkey, and once again, on the third day of my stay, it was introduced by state authorities. Nobody was allowed in or out of Sur. I had been lucky enough to travel around Sur and carry out some interviews with the members of the Women's Academy and youth movement on my first few days. Between 6 September 2015 and 9 March 2016 the state imposed curfew more than sixty times in this specific area alone, ranging from one or two days to indefinite periods.[8]

Sur is a relatively small area but home to around 120,000 people. Most of the population arrived after the 1990s when there was a wave of internal migration, which is one reason most are economically poor. It is a place where almost every household has relatives who joined the PKK or have been in prison; a situation that easily increases the tensions, conflict and strong emotions of everybody who lives nearby. While the conflict continued day and night between the state and militia, ordinary citizens were imprisoned in their houses, unable to meet their basic needs because of the curfew.

From my hotel window I could clearly observe the shooting and random shelling. It reminded me of the live TV coverage of the first Iraq war in 1991. Hotel workers, especially male ones, kept telling me to stay away from doors and windows while they themselves stayed in the main doorways. A woman who worked behind the reception desk was staying away from the main doors and moved to a safe place near an inside door, instructing guests to follow her. After a few warnings from male workers, who were still around the windows, I asked them, 'What are you doing? You are also in danger and staying very close to the outside door!' One of them replied, 'Yes, but we have immunity to state bullets. We witnessed the 1980s and 1990s when shootings and clashes were part of our daily lives, more than bread and butter, and we survived those times. Our minds and bodies have developed a strong resistance to bullets from continuous daily conflict. From time to time, the state reminds us of its existence and rears its ugly head by occupying our streets and our lives.'

I tried to understand what he meant, shocked by his daring manner and attitude. I myself had been working as a journalist during the 1990s and

---

[8] Between 2 December 2015 and 9 March 2016, a 103-day curfew was imposed by the state in Sur. In total, eleven Kurdish cities and forty-nine towns were affected by 314 curfews between 16 August 2015 and 1 June 2018. More than 2 million people suffered directly from continuous curfews. See, Amnesty International 2016a; TİHV 2017 and 2018.

my family had to move to Istanbul from Kars because of the continuing conflict. My father was always warning me not to take part in any activism or dangerous demonstrations, which might easily end in conflict. In Kars, a very diverse city in the north-east part of Turkey, which is described beautifully by Orhan Pamuk in his famous book *Snow*, my father had taken part in many 'peaceful' demonstrations against the state's continued harassment of and brutalism against local people. A few times he survived bullets only by sheer luck. Some of his close friends and neighbours were killed during these 'peaceful' demonstrations.

Meanwhile, in the district of Sur Diyarbakır, I saw a woman trying to grab her young son, around 10–12 years old, and attempting to find a safe place. But the boy was not making it easy for his mother. They were not far away from where I was staying. I could hear them easily. He was shouting *'fasist devlet'* (fascist state); *'diktator Erdoğan'* (dictator Erdoğan); *'biji Kurdistan'* (long live Kurdistan); *'biji Ocalan'* (long live Ocalan). A large number of Kurdish youths – over a thousand – between the ages of 10 to 30, lost their lives during the last overt conflict, between September 2015 and 2017. A *Spiegel* article on 12 February 2016 and OHCHR have also documented that during this period, in Cizre, another majority Kurdish town in south-eastern Turkey, around 300 youths were killed by state forces in one building alone.[9] A Kurdish intellectual stated in June 2016 in Istanbul that:

> Kurdish children and youths are being killed by both the state and the PKK. Children aged 12–15 are given simple guns and without much training are sent to fight with one of the most modern well-equipped armies. The Turkish state, without any hesitation is killing the youth without considering other options. The Kurdish and Turkish public don't question the role of the PKK and the state and continue to talk politics over the bodies of these youths. We should ask why it is that poor people are always the ones who kill and are being killed with the help of the armed forces.

One night, the police station in Sur was attacked by militias. Members of the police force were killed and injured, and security vehicles were destroyed in revenge for what the state had been doing in Sur and other conflicted Kurdish

[9] See, OHCHR 2017.

settlements. Both sides were aiming to score against the other in the competition for power. The militias did not have as many resources or heavy weapons as the state but they did have the support of the majority of local people.

Because of the clashes and continued curfews, I had already been imprisoned in the hotel for two days and was looking for a possible way out. I had already interviewed several male and female members of the Kurdish political movement, including Gultan Kisanak, Firat Anli (both co-mayors of Diyarbakır at that time) and Ayla Akat, a lawyer, activist and former MP. I asked for help from these people to cross police barricades. Several attempts were made but were not very successful. However, on one occasion, a newly elected Kurdish MP from the city of Agri came to my rescue and offered to escort me and a colleague and co-researcher across the barricades. The MP had come to Diyarbakır during the clashes in order to support the resistance of local people and to try to open a way for a peaceful negotiation between state forces and militias. She was accompanied by several journalists and camera people but was stopped several hundred metres away from our hotel and we were asked to walk to the police barricade to meet her. When we arrived, we witnessed tensions between the police officer in charge, who was escorted by dozens of heavily armed security forces and was arguing with the female MP who had come to our rescue. Even though she reminded him several times that she was an MP and the security forces should be more tolerant and respectful to local people, the police officer in charge replied: 'I am the boss here. I give the orders and you obey. I could easily kill you here and my superior would give me a medal to do so. You can go and freely make a complaint against me if you like. I would be happy. I would receive congratulations from my boss, even from the head of the state. They wouldn't even listen to you. Who are you, an MP? You are a terrorists' MP, not a Turkish state MP, definitely not *my* MP.'

She replied that she was recording all this and would question him one day, and added, 'Yes, I am a Kurdish MP, and I am here for my people, to protect my people from you and *your* terrorist state.' She could have easily been killed and be seen by the state as 'an accidental victim of state forces'. Countless times, security forces proudly shared images and videos of how they killed or insulted Kurdish citizens.[10] The death penalty was abolished

---

[10] OHCHR 2017.

in Turkey in 2001 after a long period of pressure from the European Union; however, a huge number of people, especially in Kurdish areas, fear for their lives and some are executed by state forces every year without any court process or even without committing a single crime. The word 'terrorist' can be used as justification for any action by state agents or power holders. For example, Kemal Kurkut was a young university student who joined the Newroz celebrations in Diyarbakır on 21 March 2017. Security forces insisted on searching him, and he stripped off his top while being filmed by many cameras. He was topless and had nothing to hide. He then tried to walk away from the continuous police intimidation, but the police shot him from behind, killing him in front of thousands of people and cameras, as we saw with the brutal murder in George Floyd in Minneapolis in the US. They were both innocent men who were mercilessly killed by the state officers who were motivated and fuelled by racial hatred. In most cases, people have been found innocent, but the first labelling as guilty never goes away and they can never be resuscitated. Many US officials apologised for the death of George Floyd and a jury unanimously convicted Minneapolis police office Derek Chauvin of the murder after the nationwide riots. However, the authoritarian Turkish regime doesn't usually pay any compensation or make apologies for their wrongdoings, even if thousands of people protest, as we observed during and after Kemal's racial killing.

This was not my first trip to Diyarbakır, but it was certainly the most tense and most difficult one. I had been there several times between 2013 and 2015 for my research, especially during the so-called 'peace negotiations' between the Turkish government and the Kurdish national movement, PKK, and witnessed a quieter atmosphere. My experiences of direct conflict and violence in the now largely destroyed Sur district of Diyarbakır provides the backdrop against which I will discuss the more recent failed attempts at peace, and the underlying long history of conflict between the Turkish state and the Kurdish political movement. Conflict and violence have been fuelled by Turkish nationalism and authoritarianism as I will illustrate in the next chapter. At the same time, Kurdish nationalism and the Kurdish political struggle have clearly also contributed to the conflict and violence. However, I will show the relevant ideological and political changes within the PKK-led Kurdish movement, at least in terms of the official rhetoric, moving away from a leftist nationalist movement to one embracing radical democracy with gender-based justice at its centre.

The incidents I experienced and the observations I made during this period of conflict illustrate the nationalistic sentiments on both sides, the lack of accountability of state forces and the vulnerability and precarity that the Kurdish population, even elected MPs, face. In a context where the state is the instigator of violence, able to 'legally' use all types of heavy weapons against a large group of people, it is difficult for this targeted population to feel a sense of belonging and the trust of the state. My own observations during my filed trips to south-eastern Turkey, particularly Diyarbakır, a city I will describe in more detail in the following section, resonate with the wider historical and empirical contexts described in this chapter, which set the scene for the proliferation of alternative politics and localised mechanisms to obtain justice amongst Kurds in Turkey and in the diaspora.

A Pluralistic City

During my visits to Diyarbakır, I used to spend a considerable amount of time in traditional tea houses which are important sites for observing the city's increasing population, diverse culture, and alternative political positions as well as high unemployment rates. While there are increasing numbers of new, modern cafés where mainly young, middle-class people, both female and male, work and socialise, these new trends have not affected the role of traditional tea houses. Almost every corner of the city is occupied by these Kurdish tea houses, which do not only serve cheap tea, but also create ideal spaces to engage in participant observation and interact with people.

For Kurds, the tea house has always been important place where history, culture, art and language are created and preserved. It is a place where community ties and identity are strengthened, where communal networks and business are made, stories are told and passed down to the younger generations, weddings arranged, crimes planned and carried out, and justice delivered. It could almost be seen as a place where the hegemony of the patriarchal system is created and preserved. In contrary to the new modern cafés; these tea houses are male-dominated places. The main spoken language is Kurdish, and if Turkish or other any language is heard, heads are quickly turned to find out where it comes from. It means somebody who is alien to the place is present, which tends to makes the regular customers silent and uneasy.

Without any female presence there is space for men to make sexist jokes. There are a few daily newspapers on the table and people follow the news from them. The TV is on without sound, and Kurdish music is played in the background. Walls of the tea shops, depending on which neighbourhood you are in, carry posters of different Kurdish political and religious figures, artists, politicians and local football teams.

The tea server walks around the tables and serves tea continuously. The teapots don't last long and are quickly replaced. People play games all day, such as backgammon and *okey* (a tile-based game, similar to Rummikub), and argue over politics. If you've missed what is happening in the country or further afield, you can easily get updated on local and national daily news at these tea tables. Disagreements, shouting over people or not listening, and continuing to talk while others try to make a point are all common behaviours over the tables at any tea house. The majority of the city's population might be Kurds, but these tables easily prove that there is heterogeneity of ideas and politics in the city.

The tea cannot be without sugar here and every tea is served with two cubes. It is a tradition, but Turkish President Erdoğan, like many other dictators, even tried to change this centuries-old social tradition. He made a law which stated that tea should be served without sugar. *BBC News* on 26 December 2016 reported that one of the tea-makers was detained for saying, 'I would not serve that man [Erdoğan] a cup of tea.' This comment was seen as 'insulting' the president, which carries a four-year jail term. In this kind of political environment, before any political comment is made at any table, people turn around to check if there are any outsiders, spies or government officials around. If any state official or police officer enters the tea shop then you can observe a sudden silence. It is seen as a violation of their sacred space. The political debate shifts to football, popular culture or harmless gossip until the official leaves, then the debate continues as before.

Another important aspect of these tea shops is showing how the city's economy and people are doing. They can easily give clues to outsiders about the unemployment rate in the city. It was difficult to find an empty table during my visit to the city, when the conflict was raging. War and continuous conflict may work for a few groups of people economically, but it puts many into a situation of poverty, deprivation and desperation. A *Foreign Affairs* article on 23 September 2015 and a *Spiegel* article on 12 February 2016 stated that Kurds, especially young Kurds, are seen as enemies and not equal citizens of the state, and are easily targeted, arrested and displaced by the state forces.

Many people here have nothing to lose. These tea shops can be important for any new groups to attract young people by offering new opportunities. Many PKK and jihadist group headhunters visit these places to recruit members. Importantly, different tea shops might also represent different political views and might be meeting points for specific groups, providing important evidence about the heterogeneity of Diyarbakır and Kurdish society.

There are conservative and Islamist Kurds who mainly vote for Erdoğan's Justice and Development Party (AKP) or any conservative Turkish or Kurdish political party. The Alevi and Yezidi associations and tea shops show close links with the Kurdish-led People's Democratic Party (HDP). In recent years, the HDP and the Kurdish movement has managed to get the support of many conservative and Islamist Kurdish people as well. Many young people from these backgrounds have also joined the PKK. Tribal families and their members are still visible and strong among Kurds, and divided between different political parties and ideologies. There is also a class-based division; while there is an increasing number of capitalist Kurdish business people who are against any conflict in the city and want to take care of their own economic prosperity, on the other hand, there is a huge number of unemployed, economically poor Kurdish young people who do not have much option aside from resistance and to fight against the state.

The political diversity of the majority Kurdish population in Diyarbakır is underlined by the city's long history and contact with multiple civilisations and religions. The historical names of the city are Diyarbakır and Amed, both of which many Kurds continue to use today. However, as with many other Kurdish villages, towns and city names, Diyarbakır was the name officially given by Mustafa Kemal Ataturk, the founder of modern Turkey, during the creation of the new Turkish regime and as part of the standardisation of place names and Turkification programme in 1937.[11] One letter changes the whole

---

[11] Öktem 2008.

meaning. In Kurdish the name 'Diyarbakır' means the city of Bakr (a land of an Arab/Kurdish tribe), while 'Diyarbakır' means a city of copper, a metal the city is rich in.[12] However, more than 3,000 years of the city's history and names were ignored by the new Turkish state and the controlling and reshaping of Diyarbakır's identity has been very important for the Turkish Republic and its authority.[13] Controlling Diyarbakır has meant to indirectly control the Kurdish population, and to keep the country's southern border as well as the whole of Anatolia secure.

Diyarbakır is well known for its historical walls and Hevsel Gardens, which were included in UNESCO's World Heritage List in 2015. After the Great Wall of China, Diyarbakır has the longest and largest wall in the world, and for centuries it protected the city from any outside danger. The Tigris River has been host to many identities and civilisations, including Mesopotamians, Assyrians, Medes, Greeks, Romans, Arabs and Kurds.[14] However, the last four decades of conflict and clashes in the city, between the state forces and the PKK, has overshadowed the city's rich history. Even earlier, the city and the wider region of south-eastern Turkey suffered from underdevelopment while most of the rest of the country was economically and infrastructurally developed and modernised.[15]

While in the 1920s Diyarbakır was ranked the third industrial city in Turkey, in recent decades the unemployment rate has been more than 60 per cent and it is now ranked the sixty-third industrial city. The local economy has not received equal investment from the state since the birth of Turkish Republic. The investment is much less than any other Turkish cities in the west part of the country, while the unemployment rate is twice the country's national average.[16]

The failure of a proper and equal governance by the state turned millions of law-abiding Kurds into disenfranchised citizens within a state to which they do not feel a sense of belonging anymore. Diyarbakır has been at the

---

[12] Ungor 2011.

[13] Dorronsoro 2005.

[14] Donabed 2016.

[15] See, Aydin 1986; Besikci 1992a and 2015; Bozarslan 2002; Watts 2009; Cicek 2017; Yadirgi 2017.

[16] See, Watts 2009; Sarigil 2010; Rumelili and Cakmakli 2017; Cicek 2017; Yadirgi 2017.

centre of the Kurdish political and rebellion movement in recent decades, as it was during many previous ones. Arguably, it has been one of the most politically active cities in the Middle East in recent decades.[17] Diyarbakır has been described by many of my interviewees as an unofficial capital of greater or imagined Kurdistan. One of my interviewees said 'Diyarbakır is Kurdish and Kurds are the Middle East's oldest surviving native nation. They are the indigenous people of Mesopotamia.'

However, before WWI, a third of the city's population were Christian, non-Kurdish and non-Turks. This dramatically changed after the removal of the Armenian population from Turkey during WWI. Until 1960, the city was the size of a small town, with a population of around only 30,000. Later in the 1990s, the city's population increased sharply, especially after the Turkish state's forced migration of the Kurdish population from small villages and towns of Kurdish regions. In total 3,428 Kurdish villages were destroyed and more than 3 million people were displaced by the state between 1990 and 2000 alone, when one of the most intensive wars took place between the state and the PKK guerrilla forces.[18] After this huge internal migration, Diyarbakır's population has jumped to more than 1.5 million people, from just a few hundred thousand in 1990.[19] Almost 75 to 80 per cent of this population are ethnic Kurds.[20]

There is a small number of different minority communities, including Armenians, Assyrians, Yezidis and Arabs, still living in Diyarbakır. The rest are government workers, civil servants, police and soldiers, who are mainly Turks. With the internal migration, years of continuous war has divided the city into separate economic and social groups. While some enjoy prosperity, a new life and technology, the majority live in poverty and find it difficult to get work and make ends meet. Since 2012, after the Syrian uprising and conflict, Diyarbakır has become the host for many new refugees, Kurds, Yezidis, Arabs and Turkmens who escaped from ISIS, Iraqi

[17] See, Dorronsoro 2005; Rumelili and Cakmakli 2017.
[18] See, Yegen 2007; Heper 2007 and 2010; Aslan 2014; Tezcur 2009 and 2014.
[19] See, Kirisci 1998; McDowall 2004.
[20] See, Heper and Sayari 2012.

and Syrian authoritarian regimes. More than a third of Syrian refugees in Turkey were settled by the government in the south-east part of country where predominantly Kurds live.[21]

To summarise, since the establishment of the Turkish Republic in 1923, all majority Kurdish populated towns and cities, and their people, have experienced social, economic and political injustice and collective punishments. This, coupled with successive, right- or left-wing, authoritarian government policies of Turkification and assimilation have not left many options, except a new uprising by Kurds. These ethnographic accounts of life under authoritarian rule and continuous conflict illustrate the lack of accountability of state forces and the vulnerability and precarity faced by the Kurdish population. In a context where the state is the instigator of violence against a large group of people, it is difficult for these targeted populations to feel any attachment to their country.

The next chapter will focus on how nationalism from multiple sides fed conflict and increased the division of a society, and how the body politic is instrumentalised for the purpose of national settlement.

---

[21] The refugees from Syria and other Middle Eastern countries who escaped and fled from war zones and authoritarian regimes were not just used against the Kurdish regions to balance the population and limit the power of Kurdish local authorities by the Erdoğan-led Turkish regime, but they were also very often used against Europe as a bargaining chip, as part of foreign policy strategies. Turkey was paid 6 billion euros to control refugees in Turkey in 2016 by the European Union. However, in late February 2020, when Erdoğan asked European governments to help him militarily and economically for his war and occupation in Syria, Europe refused to follow Erdoğan's wish, and consequently the Turkish authorities opened all its borders to Europe for refugees. The Turkish government even provided buses and packed lunches to hundreds of thousands of desperate refugees, to carry them across Turkey's western border and enable their movement to Europe. It may be the first example of a nation state openly facilitating such a human disaster and using the lives of millions of others for its own survival and desired outcome.

Figure 2.1 A view of the historical Mardin city in 2015. (Author's fieldwork image)

Figure 2.2 A view of the historical Mardin city. It used to be a multicultural, multi-ethnic and multi-religious city but is currently dominated by mosques and a Sunni majority. (Author's fieldwork image)

Figure 2.3 A street view of Mardin which shows plural dress codes still visible. (Author's fieldwork image)

Figure 2.4 A minority religious leader in Mardin. During the interview another two men, possibly undercover servicemen, watched the talk from the wall. (Author's fieldwork image)

Figure 2.5 A view from the city of Diyarbakır. (Author's fieldwork image)

Figure 2.6 A view from the city of Diyarbakır. (Author's fieldwork image)

3

MONOPOLISTIC NATIONALISM AND THE DECOMPOSING STATE

If you imprison me because I ask for an education in my mother tongue, it means you imprison millions of people . . . People, especially those who have money, are escaping from the country every day. The poor have nowhere to go and suffer day after day. You are not going to get rid of us by killing us, and your prosecutors are not going to be able to imprison millions of us by claiming that all of us are terrorists. There is freedom in this country for mafia leaders who say openly that they want to bathe in our blood, but not for people who are asking for justice. (Selahattin Demirtaş, former MP and co-leader of Kurdish-led HDP, January 2019)

On 16 March 1923, Mustafa Kemal spoke to the local merchants in the city of Adana, during a tea party organised for him by Association of the Adana *Türk Ocağı* (Turkish Heart): 'This country belongs to you, it is the land of Turks. This country was, historically speaking, Turkish; hence it is Turkish and will forever remain Turkish.'[1] On 18 September 1930, the Minister of Justice, Mahmut Esad Bozkurt, further clarified what was meant by the new Turkey: 'It is my opinion, my belief that this country in its inner self is Turkish. Whoever is not authentically Turkish has only one single right in the land of Turks and that is to be a servant, a slave.'[2] These statements have been the legal and political practice of the Turkish governments and institutions ever since. Those, like Kurds, who have found it difficult to fit this

---

[1] Toros 1939: 11–26; Ataturk 1997: 120–9.
[2] Parla 1992: 208; Hür 2012; Ergil 2020:4.

mould or have been critical and asked for recognition of their plural identities, as did Demirtaş, have been punished harshly and excluded.

The Turkish state does not publish racial and ethnic statistics officially or correctly. It is illegal to contest this approach. According to the Constitution, all citizens are equal under the law, but only recorded and acknowledged as a 'Turk'. Forcing everyone legally and politically to fit into 'Turkishness', and not recognising any ethnic or racial diversity in Turkey is the backbone of Turkish nationalism. Article 66 of the Turkish Constitution states that 'everyone bound to the Turkish state through the bond of citizenship is a Turk'. Official Turkish nationalism is 'characterised by the denial of the diverse character of the population within Turkey's national borders . . . Since the 1930s, the State adopted several assimilative and nationalising policies, fearful of losing the remnants of the Ottoman Empire.'[3]

Turkish nationalism, with the help of social, economic and cultural roots from the Ottoman Empire, developed a strong assimilative national identity at the beginning of the twentieth century.[4] For Turks, as Sultan Abdulhamid II (1876–1908) stated, 'To strengthen the Turkish nation, we [Turks] need to Turkify all the Kurds everywhere. This is a basic and main point of the strengthening of the Turkish nation.'[5] This political position of the Turkish state and government has not changed much.

During the War of Independence, between 1920 and 1922, Mustafa Kemal Ataturk and his friends took a pluralistic and inclusive approach to nation-building and encouraged the support of different ethnic and religious minorities for the sake of winning the war and healing the nation.[6] During this period, all different groups were welcomed under a 'one party' ideology, *Kuvvai Milliye* (National Unity). People were going to be free to follow their own diverse ways of life as long as they adhered to the aims of Mustafa Kemal and his allies during this period.[7] This temporary 'pluralistic' or 'democratic

---

[3] Cayir 2015: 519–23.

[4] See, Boratav 1998; Navaro-Yashin 2002; Öktem 2004 and 2008; Uzun 2005; Avedian 2012; Pamuk 2019.

[5] Akcura 2010: 54.

[6] See, Hanioglu 2001; Heper 2007; Yanikdag 2014.

[7] See, Ahmad 1993 and 2003; Zurcher 2010; Anderson 2008.

decentralised' ideology gave way for the new Turkish Republic that gained power vis-à-vis the Ottoman Sultanate, which was still in existence in Istanbul. This apparent pluralistic approach sent false signals to the different minorities, including Kurds, and stopped possible uprisings for their rights. At the same time, it signalled to the world the possibility of a democratic regime, which was a refreshing alternative to the old, outdated and autocratic Ottoman system. It was a successful approach, which helped Mustafa Kemal and his supporters to win the independent war, and ended six centuries of Ottoman power.[8]

After the war, Ataturk and his government abandoned their promises of respect for plurality, and followed an authoritarian and centralised ideology instead. Citizens, meanwhile, were encouraged to adopt the dominant Turkish ethnicity and Sunni Islamic identity, and to work under the Kemalist ideology of the Republican People's Party (CHP).[9]

The Turkish political and military elites, with their Islamist and secular elements, considered themselves to be the 'guardians' of the Turkish state, with the right to regulate Turkish democracy and the Constitution by any means, including by military coup or authoritarian leadership.[10] In particular, the military elites from the beginning of the Turkish Republic until the present, 'have not been experiencing any appreciable difficulties in placing themselves in the political life. Unlike its counterparts, the Turkish Army has a considerable amount of political and institutional autonomy, which ultimately leads to an emphasis on its role in guarding the state from "internal enemies".'[11] This strong state tradition was strengthened by several military coups, including those of 1960, 1980 and 2016. These attempted coups aimed to save the state from groups they considered to be 'not-Muslim enough', 'not-Turkish enough', or 'separatists', especially Kurds.[12]

The Turkish state structure relied on having 'strong men' as leaders and a robust Turkish national and Sunni religious identity as the foundation of its ideology. Following in the footsteps of the Ottoman Empire, the tradition of

---

[8] Parla 1992; Yildiz 2001.
[9] See, Rugman 1996; Özcan 2006; Oznur 2009; Yanikdag 2014; Abbas 2016; Polat 2016.
[10] Burak 2011; Özyürek et al. 2018; Bargu 2019.
[11] Burak 2011:143.
[12] Gocek 2015, Tas 2016d.

political autocracy continued under different Turkish leaders, such as Ataturk, Inonu, Menderes, Evren and Erdoğan. Laura Pitel wrote in *The Independent* on 19 January 2016:

> The vision of the modern Turkish republic set forth in 1923 by Mustafa Kemal, known as Ataturk, was based on a narrow ethnic and cultural frame-work . . . Criticising the state or the army or the head of the state (president) is seen as akin to seeking to undermine the country's foundations.

Since the 1950s multiple political parties have existed, but, again, the national 'costume' has been Turkification and Islamism, and almost all political parties and politicians have had to adopt this strict dress code.[13]

Hence, the role of authoritarian and nationalistic rulers, such as Recep Tayyip Erdoğan, are nothing new. They are deeply rooted in the foundation of the Turkish nation state and regime-building.[14] Sunni-based religion, and its institution *Diyanet*, Turkey's Presidency of Religious Affairs, have been important instruments to justify the actions of the state and its autocratic leaders from a religious point of view.[15] For that reason, almost all successive Turkish governments have invested in building new mosques, increasing the *Diyanet*'s budget and paying the salaries of more than 130,000 imams.[16] It is an important example showing how Islam and authoritarianism collaborate and support each other.[17] Abbas and Hakki Yigit also argue that 'religion has been subsumed by secular authoritarian nationalism'.[18] This fluctuating balance between the Turkification of Kemalist secularism and Islamism is supported by the military, state elites, successive governments, civil society organisations and state-sponsored academics, in their attempts to retain power.[19]

---

[13] See, Hanioglu 2001; Kuru 2009; Casier and Jongerden 2010; Turam 2012; Kaya 2014; Abbas 2016; Yegen 2016; Yavuz and Öztürk 2019.

[14] See, Polat 2016: Koukoudakis 2017; Özyürek et al. 2018; Bargu 2019; Christofis 2019; Saeed 2019; Jongerden 2019.

[15] See, Keyman 2007; Gözaydın 2008; Kuru 2009.

[16] See, Abbas 2016; Öztürk 2016; Kurt 2017 and 2019.

[17] See, Fish 2002; Kaya 2014; Abbas 2016; Özyürek et al. 2018; Bargu 2019.

[18] Abbas and Yigit 2014: 16.

[19] Besikci 1990; Bozarslan 2014.

In Turkey, as in the context of other nationalist projects, the ideology of the state has not only been based on the denial, oppression, destruction or assimilation of the rights of different ethnic and religious groups, but has also been explicitly patriarchal.[20] During the 1920s, the Turkish Republic encouraged and promoted one of the most important elements of the building of the modern Turkish nation state and identity with the development of the women's movement.[21] Adopting the Swiss Civil Code in 1926, which recognised women as legal equals of men in some areas, and giving equal votes to men and women in the 1930s, were important policy changes for the sake of the new national identity: middle to upper class, secular and based on Sunni Islam but at the same time 'modern', universalising, with everybody supposedly fitting this new identity. However, the main aim was not to improve or protect gender equality and promote gender-based justice, but to build a Turkish national identity which could gain the support of the 'modernisers'. As several authors have illustrated, the emergence of the Turkish women's movement was directly linked to Kemalism and was explicitly modernist and nationalist. Female doctors, politicians and writers were promoted, and space was even made for them in the air force, as in the example of Sabiha Gokcen.[22]

This gendered dimension didn't stop the state from continuing to be patriarchal, misogynist, masculinist and militarist. As Ayse Gul Altinay[23] has shown in her groundbreaking book, the development of Turkish nationalism and the Turkish state has been based on the development of Turkish militarism which has been gendered. The militarised Turkish nation has historically privileged militarised and authoritarian masculinities while trying to control women's bodies and sexualities. According to a former Turkish minister, interestingly not the Minister of Defence but the Minister of Culture and Art, Istemihan Talay, 'Turks have been known as a military-nation throughout history . . . Turkish military is synonymous with Turkish national identity.'[24] Ataturk stated that 'from ages seven to seventy, women and men

[20] Yuval-Davis 1997; Gocek 2015.

[21] Zihnioglu 2003; Arat 2012.

[22] See, Arat 2010 and 2012; Altinay 2004; Diner and Toktas 2010.

[23] Altinay 2004.

[24] Ozel 2000; in Altinay 2004: 1.

alike, we have been created as soldiers'.[25] A well-known popular belief in Turkey is that 'every Turk is born a soldier' (*her Turk asker dogar*).

Almost all nationalist projects embody the nation as a woman to be protected.[26] Women are seen to be the carriers of the honour of the family and the nation, and they are encouraged to be better wives and mothers, and to give birth to soldiers, who will defend and die for the nation. Conservative and militarist gender norms continue to shape individual identities, the traditional culture of gender roles and relations, as well as political views in Turkey.[27] In many ways women affect and are affected, controlled, perceived, organised by the national and ethnic process in pursuit of nation-building development.[28]

Turkish Authoritarianism

As Öktem[29] has discussed there would be no tolerance for those who did not fit the state's idea of a national identity. In such an environment, freedom, democracy, rule of law and respect for diversity have no value if they are not working for the sake of the state. School textbooks teach a concept of ethno-cultural citizenship and nationalism that does not include or tolerate difference.[30] There is a special article in the Turkish Constitution, Article 299, that protects leaders from criticism and puts them above all others. Under this article any individual that criticises Turkey's political leaders, be it in music, art, literature, the media or academia, can be fined or even imprisoned. Thousands of people have been convicted under this Article during the Erdoğan leadership on trumped-up charges based on fabricated evidence and simple criticism.[31] If the Constitution does not give sufficient power to Turkish political leaders to stamp out such criticism, they can have it amended to suit their needs as we observed during 2010 and 2017 constitutional changes. The resulting intolerance of the 'other' could equally be directed against Turkish or non-Turkish women or men, academics, journalists, writers or

---

[25] Gokcen 1996: 125–6.

[26] Yuval-Davis 1997.

[27] See, Kandiyoti 1991; Çağlayan 2007.

[28] See, Yuval-Davis and Anthias 1989; Yuval Davis 1997 and 2003; Al-Ali and Pratt 2011.

[29] Öktem 2004.

[30] See, Ersanlı-Behar 1992; Gokalp 2007; Bargu 2019.

[31] See, Özbudun 2014; Vatansever 2020.

any intellectuals that supported the others' rights. This could even include well-known Turkish intellectuals and writers, for example Nazim Hikmet and Orhan Pamuk, if they criticised the state's monopolistic national identity. Judicial strategies and methods are used to punish any voice against autocrats and also discourage any future rivals.[32] Turkey's first Nobel laureate, novelist Orhan Pamuk told *The Times* newspaper on 26 January 2016:

> There is something depressingly cyclical in Turkey's slide into authoritarianism. In 1980 the military carried out a bloody coup d'état in which more than 600,000 people were detained, including some of the country's leading politicians. When these politicians eventually returned to power . . ., they did not improve free speech, they only improved their own conditions. Not very different from Erdoğan, actually.

In 2015 alone, 160 media outlets, mainly independent and Kurdish-language ones, including JINHA – one of the few world's news agencies run entirely by women for women – were shut down. More than 130 journalists were detained, including the famous human rights lawyer and journalist Eren Keskin. The Committee to Protect Journalists stated on 13 December 2018 that Turkey is 'the world's most frequent jailer of journalists'. They faced terrorism charges because of their criticism of the views of the state. This number accounted for more than a third of all imprisoned journalist worldwide. Several independent columnists, writers and human rights defenders who acted as symbolic co-editors for a day with the Kurdish newspaper Özgur Gündem, showing solidarity for the situation in Kurdish regions in Turkey, were also prosecuted for spreading terrorist propaganda.[33] More than 10,000 teachers in Kurdish regions, who were serving in Kurdish-speaking municipalities, lost their jobs and investigations were carried out against some of them.

In January 2016, 1,228 academics signed a petition calling for the Turkish government to stop its 'massacre' of the Kurdish people in different districts of Kurdish cities and declared that 'we will not be party to this crime'. After the petition became public at a news conference in Istanbul, on 11 January 2016, the Turkish government, institutions and some members of public started

---

[32] Shen-Bayt 2018.
[33] OHCHR 2017: 16.

criminalising these academics. Erdoğan accused the academics of 'betrayal' of the state, and the Higher Education Council (YÖK) then started an administrative investigation into the signatories. Sedat Peker, a convicted organised crime boss, mafia leader and extreme Turkish nationalist, threatened the academics saying, 'We will make your blood run' and then 'bathe in your blood'.[34] On 14 January 2016, Istanbul prosecutors began to investigate all members of the group for 'making propaganda for a terrorist organisation' under Article 7/2 of the Turkey Anti-Terrorism Act, and 'insulting the Turkish nation' under Article 301 of the penal code.[35] As Judith Butler and Basak Ertur reported in *The Guardian* on 11 December 2017, the state prosecutor claimed that:

(1) In calling for the cessation of violence against the Kurdish people, the signatories are taking sides with the Kurds; (2) the Kurds are regarded as terrorists, so taking sides with them is to ally with terrorism; (3) the call for a peaceful solution involves negotiating with terrorists; (4) a call for negotiation with terrorists constitutes propaganda for a terrorist organisation; (5) a petition to cease violence and enter into negotiation to achieve peace and to comply with national and international laws protecting human rights is nothing more than propaganda for Kurdish violence.

In fact, the petition called for a peaceful solution for the Turkish-Kurdish conflict and asked both sides to stop the violence. The word 'peace' became the code for terrorism propaganda. Many of these academics were detained and most, if not all, lost their posts at their universities as a result. Many of them were subject to travel bans and their passport revoked.[36] With no prospect of employment, these academics in Turkey or academics from Turkey living abroad, have been punished heavily. Most importantly, state authority may purposely have forced many intellectuals to move outside the country instead of putting them in prison. With this approach, the authoritarian regime successfully put a barrier between critical and outspoken academics and the rest of society as a way to eliminate almost all internal critics. In addition, using this method, the authorities managed to avoid international

---

[34] Amnesty International 2016b; Vatansever 2020. After his conflict with Erdoğan's government in May 2021, Sedat Peker apologised to Peace Academics for his previous statement.

[35] Amnesty International 2016a; Vatansever 2020.

[36] Human Rights Watch 2017 and 2018; Vatansever 2020.

criticism for increased imprisonment. 'To love or to leave' has been part of Turkish nationalist discourse. Intellectuals were left with no alternative but to leave if they did not agree with what the government was doing and proposing. As a result, academia and the production of critical and unique information has been severely damaged and limited. In addition, many international scholars who study Turkey and the Kurds, could not enter the country and were unable to carry out research in Turkey after 2016 if they were not complicit with the Turkish regime. These are examples of the blanket style of state punishment. Orhan Pamuk continued, in his interview with *The Times* newspaper on this subject on 26 January 2016:

> The Turkish state is terrorising the whole academic class of this country by targeting more than a thousand professors who recently signed a petition calling for an end to military operations in the southeast . . . These are unacceptable things. You may disagree with the technicalities and rhetoric [of the petition], but you do not have a right to enter the house of a professor at 7 o'clock in the morning as if he's a terrorist . . . All the people who complain – and they're right, and I'm with them – the secular opposition with whom I feel I'm in the same boat, unfortunately when they were in power they were also repressive. The whole national culture of intolerance should change.

The glorification of the past based solely on a Turkish nationalist view of history does nothing to promote social inclusion and cohesion. Instead, it has sharpened ethnic and religious division, particularly amongst Kurds. While such state-sponsored policies may help some ethnic groups to maintain their hegemonic position in society, they exclude others and cause them to live permanently in a sense of statelessness.[37] One national identity ('Turkishness'), one language (Turkish), one religion (Sunni Islam) and one culture (Turkish) is forced on everybody.[38] When a person gains or fails to gain employment or promotion, not because of the skills and experience they possess, but instead as a result of their ethnic or religious background or gender, conflict becomes inevitable, a necessary way of fighting a system which reinforces the advantages or disadvantages of birth.[39] Constant manipulation and persecution has

[37] Tas 2016a, 2016b and 2016c.

[38] Tas 2016d; Gocek 2015.

[39] See, Erkaya 2015.

continued in the name of the state against those groups that have raised their voices against such inequality and discrimination. A Kurdish politician, a former co-Mayor of Diyarbakır, Firat Anli, stated in September 2015:

> We are not just talking about simple discrimination. Kurds make up 20 per cent of Turkey's 77 million population, but they continue to be treated as if they were the subject of a colonial state regime. The Kurdish regions and people have been socially, economically, culturally and politically colonized by Turkey and other neighbouring countries. Those who have criticized this type of colonial state behaviour have been regarded as 'traitors' by almost all Turkish governments and leaders. If Kurds end their resistance to Turkey's undemocratic and discriminative political and legal systems, Turkey will forever be ruled by a totalitarian regime. We are not just fighting for Kurdish rights; we also fight for Turks to have a better, more advanced system.

A former Turkish politician, breaking the silence on the truth and reality of the situation in Turkey, criticised US President Donald Trump for comparing Kurdish groups with ISIS and claiming both to be as dangerous as each other. Tuna Beklevic wrote to *The Washington Post* on 22 October 2019, to explain:

> I am a Turk from Edirne. I have dedicated my life to my country's politics. For several years, I served in President Recep Tayyip Erdoğan's government . . . Erdoğan is consolidating power through violence and repression, at the expense of everyday people . . . Trump says the PKK is worse than ISIS. I say he's wrong . . . I am Turkish. I am a former government official. And I believe that the Kurdistan Workers' Party, the PKK described by President Trump as worse than the Islamic State – is not a terrorist organization.

This former government official is right. The Kurdish resistance movement cannot be compared with ISIS, Al Qaeda or any other similar terrorist groups. They have not used any methods which have been practised by ISIS or similar violent organisations to gain political and economic power. The term used after 9/11 by George W. Bush, 'war on terror', does not include or refer to Kurdish groups' resistance for their basic rights. However, Turkey and many other countries have borrowed Bush's concept, and have been using and misusing this for almost all their actions against Kurdish and similar minority groups who ask for no more than equal rights.

The Kurds have never been regarded as equal citizens of the country, but have instead been marginalised by successive governments who fail to invest properly in their regions for fear that these regions could one day be lost by the state. Continuous conflict has been the main driving force for this type of colonisation. As Edward Said explains, colonialism is an act of geographic violence against indigenous people and their rights.[40] Frantz Fanon, regarding Algeria's struggle for independence from colonial French rule during the 1960s, argued that 'colonialism is not a thinking machine, nor a body endowed with reasoning faculties. It is violence in its natural state, and it will only yield when confronted with greater violence.'[41] The Ottoman Empire and the Turkish state's experience of colonising and ruling Kurdish lands has been the main reason why many Kurdish rebellions have occurred in the twentieth and twenty-first centuries, and why we can observe the development of an alternative Kurdish state structure, increasing violence and nationalism in Turkey and the wider Middle East. Garo Paylan, Kurdish-led HDP MP, shared his thoughts on 1 September 2015:

> A hundred years ago there were Armenians and Assyrians in this geography. My Armenian grandfathers just wanted equality. They wanted to live with their language, their culture and life freely. The state and their authoritarian leaders didn't want that equality. They slaughtered the Armenian, Assyrian and Greek people. They've made this land a wasteland. They promised that 'the Turks and Kurds will be equal', but it did not happen since the establishment of the Republic. Persecution has been going on for a century. All opposition of autocrats has come together in the HDP. Now they're afraid of this union.[42]

---

[40] Said 1993.

[41] Fanon 1963: 61.

[42] After the establishment of 'Kurdish self-rule' of alternative governmentality in different Kurdish town and cities, the HDP MP Garo Paylan together with the HDP Co-Leader Figen Yuksekdag, the Co-Leader of Kurdish Party Kamuran Yuksel, and HDP MPs Pervin Buldan, Saruhan Oruc and Yurdusev Ozsokmenler travelled to the city of Hakkari where there were heavy state operations against the local Kurdish people and youth movement. From Van, where they started their journey, they were stopped several times by security forces who prevented them from entering the city of Hakkari. Figen Yuksekdag, stated during this journey: 'We must take the right to rule ourselves against those who try to rule us, to rule our cities, and lives, our future. This is what the people of Hakkari are doing today.'

The structure of the Turkish state, regardless of which party or political ideology is in power, is totally against the territorial recognition of the 'Kurds' or 'Kurdistan'.[43] Voluntary and – if it is not possible – forced assimilation, including genocidal attempts and forced population movement policies, have been adopted by the state. These policies have been applied by almost all the past Ottoman and Turkish governments since 1850.[44] There is little or no political choice for Kurds to exist as they are. This has created an unequal approach to citizenship by the state towards Kurds and, in turn, weak citizenship connections by Kurds in response to the state.

Kurdish Nationalism

Kurds in the Middle East have been colonial subjects for centuries. Set against a long history of repression and various forms of statelessness, the Kurdish population's insecure relations with the existing nation states (whether Turkey, Iraq, Syria or Iran) means that, depending on where they live, Kurds have become more patriotic or nationalistic as they focus their attention on the establishment of a safe and inhabitable homeland.

Ehmedê Xanî (1650–1707), who wrote the Kurdish national epic poem 'Mem û Zîn', dreamt of a strong Kurdish national identity and the existence of a Kurdish state.[45] He believed that Kurdish leaders should create Kurdish currency and promote Kurdish culture for the purpose of creating a unitary Kurdish identity. He also believed that Kurdish children should learn their own language, which would, in turn, help them to develop a sense of Kurdishness. Xanî wrote: 'The children are our future, they are our hope.'[46] Even at that time Xanî acknowledged a lack of a strong leadership among the Kurds, and he wished for unity amongst them. According to Xanî, if the Kurds had followed one leader, the Turks, Arabs and Persians might have been under Kurdish rule.[47]

Even though Kurds share common myths of origin, language, culture and, most importantly, control over a specific territory – all of which, according to

[43] Tas 2014; Nimni and Aktoprak 2018.
[44] See, Karpat 1982, 2001; Kasaba 2004.
[45] See, Chyet 1991; Van Bruinessen 1992; Ghalib 2011.
[46] Ghalib 2011: 81–98.
[47] Dursun 2013.

Anthony Smith,[48] are necessary for ethnic nationalism – they did not create a common and robust Kurdish political culture, single Kurdish language or currency as dreamed of by Xanî almost 400 years ago. Kurdish nationalism remained, for a long time, at a pre-developmental level, and it is not possible to claim even now that a unitary Kurdish ethnic national identity exists among most Kurds.

Some Kurdish rebellion movements advocating nationalist aims had existed before the PKK, including the Sayyid Ubeydullah of Nehri and Sheikh Said movements of the late nineteenth and early twentieth centuries.[49] However, both followed the Naqshbandi religious school, established by religious clerics with strong tribal connections, and their impact was largely local and short-lived.[50] Both movements, therefore, cannot be described as national movements for the creation of an independent Kurdistan. During the decline of the Ottoman Empire in the 1870s, when many ethnic groups were fighting for their independence and the conditions for rebellion were perfect, the Ubeydullah movement sought to create an autonomous state for the Kurds within the Ottoman Empire, rather than an independent Kurdish state. Ozoglu explained:

> The political and military activities of Kurdish notables in the pre-World War One period were not nationalist; they reflected the desire of powerful Kurdish lineages to consolidate, expand, or recover their regional influence. Kurdish leaders exclusively of landed-notable origin, were mostly members of Ottoman high bureaucracy and as such an integral part of the Ottoman state.[51]

Even if the aim was the creation of a unified political structure, it never materialised. Studies agree that ethnic groups start conflict with the state, especially when they are excluded from state power.[52] Kurds have been excluded from state power not only in recent decades, but since late Ottoman times. The Kurds adopted the idea of self-determination to show their dissatisfaction when

[48] Anthony D. Smith 1999.
[49] See, Safrastian 1948; Jwaideh 2006; Saeed 2014.
[50] See, Olson 1989; Van Bruinessen 1992 and 2000; White 2000; Romano 2006; Saeed 2014.
[51] Ozoglu 2001: 383; Ozoglu 2004.
[52] Cederman et al. 2010.

the autonomy they once had during the Ottoman Empire under the Millet System was reduced.[53] The old pluralistic empire no longer existed, and while many other ethnic minorities including Armenians, Bulgarians and Arabs began to fight for their independence in this new world, the Kurds remained paralysed and asked for something that no longer existed.

For some, having their own Kurdish leadership, to be regarded as equal to Turks under the state's hegemonic identity, or at least to be allowed to speak their language or practise their culture freely, was enough. Many Kurds did not make any significant demands on the empire and, unsurprisingly, it was not difficult for the emerging Turkish state to subsequently destroy their humble expectations and what was left of a nascent sense of 'Kurdishness'. Any remaining sign of Kurdishness was and is still regarded as a significant threat to successive Turkish nationalist governments. A Kurdish academic in Istanbul stated in June 2016:

> Racism and genocidal nationalism have been used against Kurds almost con-
> tinually in the last century by Turkish, Iraqi, Syrian and Iranian regimes. Even
> these states' liberal voices didn't hesitate to assimilate or destroy Kurds. Kurds
> have been seen as border guards or servants of these states by state rulers and
> citizens. They think Kurds do not have their own history, language and cul-
> ture. As long as Kurds obey and follow these countries' rules, flag, language
> and culture, they are welcomed. However, according to these hegemonic
> powers, Kurds should be destroyed if they demand their rights.

Kurds used to be mainly tribal and live in rural communities, easily 'divided and ruled' by hegemonic powers. Women in particular did not enjoy many rights under such an unequal and patriarchal system. Only a small number of Kurds lived in the larger cities before the 1970s, and they usually did manual work (as builders, shoemakers, seasonal workers and labourers) since education was not very common among these groups at the time. Tribalism was very strong.[54] Most of tribal landlords, many whom have been supported politically and militarily by the Turkish state, have played an assimilative 'magnetic' role, creating links between the Turkish state and Kurdish society

---

[53] Tas 2014.

[54] See, Aytar 1992; Van Bruinessen 1992 and 2002.

for a long time. While these tribal leaders benefited economically from state policies, local Kurdish communities lived in extremely deprived conditions. They did what successive Turkish governments wanted them to do, and in most cases, were even ashamed of their Kurdishness. If it benefited the state, they could act like Kurdish nationalists, but locally they separated themselves from other Kurds.[55]

Kurds, especially in Turkey, had to wait until the 1980s for the creation of a unitary Kurdish national movement, when the PKK in Turkey was established to demand the rights of Kurds, including the creation of an independent Kurdish state. Unlike the earlier Kurdish nationalist movements of the late nineteenth and early twentieth centuries, the PKK did not seek to demonstrate how Kurds share many similarities with Turks, Arabs or Persians, or demand equality for Kurds within unequal state political structures in their early years. Instead, the cultural, linguistic, historical and even religious differences of the Kurds became the main force of the PKK's political propaganda. A new Kurdish national identity was introduced, including making imaginary connections with Sumerians, Assyrians and many other ancient civilisations. The myth of Newroz has become a symbol and celebration of Kurds. A 'Kurdification' of nationalism has been promoted during the last four decades.[56]

Key contributions of the PKK movement to the Kurdish nationalist cause are its success at spreading the movement across Turkey to neighbouring countries and different diasporas; and its fight against Kurdish feudal landlords, their weak nationalism and patriarchal rule. Kurds were encouraged by the PKK to abandon their 'victim' identity, and instead be actively proud of their own Kurdish identity. The younger generation in particular has adapted to this new approach, becoming patriots of Kurdish nationalism.[57] They have created a separatist national identity, as in the unification attempts of many others. However, it has not just happened at a cultural level, but more so at a legal and political level.

---

[55] See Yalcin-Heckmann 1991; Aytar 1992; Gokalp 1992; Sahin 1995; Berberoglu 1998; Van Bruinessen 1992 and 2002.

[56] See, Aydin 2005; Aslan 2014; Rudi 2018.

[57] See, Bochenska 2018; Dag 2021.

The PKK initially sought to create an independent state in the 1980s and 1990s. However, after the collapse of the Eastern Bloc, the PKK not only lost important support but also experienced a series of setbacks in the 1990s. Most prominently the arrest of their leader Abdullah Öcalan in 1999 contributed to the growing divisions and internal conflict within the PKK in the early 2000s in a context of changing dynamics in the Middle East. Increasingly, the Kurdish political movement came to understand that creating a unitary Kurdish state was not an easy process and needed to be tackled gradually. For the period of the development of alternative state institutions, not armed conflict but peaceful resolution is believed to be the best option.

After his capture on 15 February 1999, and death sentence (later, after the abolition of death penalty by the Turkish Parliament, converted to life imprisonment), Öcalan took a different approach and put a peaceful solution first and published a new approach, 'Declaration of Democratic Confederativism in Kurdistan'.[58] This, the collection of short essays of a new manifesto, was sent to the European Court of Human Rights as evidence of the Kurdish movement's peaceful approach. Öcalan continued to develop his new ideas and in March 2005, he issued the 'Declaration of Democratic Confederalism in Kurdistan'. He went further and in 2006, he ordered the formation of the 'Truth and Justice Commissions' by the Kurds in the Middle East and different diasporas, which was to be the foundation for the establishment of Kurdish Alternative Courts and Laws and the Social Contract of the Democratic Federalism of Northern Syria. Confederal grass-roots democracy was described as the main aim of the new Kurdish movement. Aside from self-criticism, Öcalan strongly criticised the previous actions of some of his comrades.[59]

Later, Öcalan published the road map of his idea for democratic confederalism or autonomy,[60] which was influenced by the ideas of American eco-anarchist, Murray Bookchin's work on communitarianism and libertarian municipalism and several other important writers, including Seyla Benhabib, Judith Butler, Immanuel Wallerstein, Michel Foucault and

---

[58] Öcalan 1999.
[59] See, Öcalan 2009a; Leezenberg 2016.
[60] See, Öcalan 2009a, 2011a and 2016.

Antonio Gramsci.[61] According to this road map, the old-fashioned nation state structure no longer works and should be replaced with new ecological societies which connect with each other in a loosely communal way. Eventually these small municipalities would form a confederal system and open the way to face-to-face, direct democracy. Democratisation of every aspect of life, especially the judiciary, society and family, including full gender equality has been at the centre of this ideology. New political and societal cultures, citizenship, economic systems, moral and ethical values were introduced within this system. Öcalan's continued prison writings shaped the new policy of the Kurdish movement in the Middle East.

Additionally, and maybe more importantly, I was told by many Kurdish political leaders and PKK's active and former guerrillas that four significant factors have encouraged the PKK to adopt a new policy. Firstly, the result of Turkey's EU negotiation process in 1999 was important for the Kurdish movement to put legal political development before military war.[62] The Kurdish movement created a good relationship with EU countries in the 1990s and early 2000s, but this pro-EU stand started to be questioned from late 2000, especially after the silence of some EU countries about the Turkish harsh political attitude against the Kurds.

Second, the changing of world politics after the 9/11 attacks against the US has affected the PKK directly. Securitisation and the nation state security became the main priority for Western countries. This then affected and sacrificed the ideology of the main slogans of 'liberal democracy' and 'multiculturalism' in the 1990s. Many liberation movements around the world, including the PKK, were listed as 'terrorist' organisations. Due to the increasing pressure from the US, as a way to get the full support of Turkey for its war against 'terrorism' in Afghanistan 2001 and Iraq 2003, many EU countries labelled the PKK as a 'terrorist' organisation.[63] This made any organisations directly or indirectly linked to the PKK, or any individual membership of the PKK, very difficult. They became a main target and were charged under terrorism laws

---

[61] See for the influence of Bookchin (especially 1996, 2005 and 2015) and other important figures on the Kurdish leader's writing (Öcalan 2011a, 2015, 2017a and 2017b).

[62] Ergil 2000; Balci 2015.

[63] Tank 2005.

even in the most liberal Western countries, including Germany and the UK. The world's established powers once again chose national state security over the rights of a minority group. This new world order would open the way for the Sri Lankan government to annihilate Tamils, who had a similar aim to that of the PKK previously, namely to create an independent Tamil state.[64]

Third, the formation of the Kurdistan Regional Government in Iraq in 2003 also encouraged the PKK-led Kurdish movements in Turkey and Syria to implement a new strategy for surviving under the new world order. As part of this strategy and reaction to new realities on the ground, Öcalan and the wider movement shifted from the emphasis on national independence to 'democratic autonomy' and 'democratic confederalism'.[65]

Fourth, conflicts around the world, especially in the Middle East, show that the problem with the concept of a unitary nation state continues. The PKK has also recognised these problems, limitations and crises of the concept of the nation state, and has acknowledged that a unitary nation state ideology can be assimilative and suppressive towards women as well as ethnic and cultural minorities. For these reasons, Kurds in Turkey and Syria, linked to the PKK, have proposed democratic autonomy based on a form of confederalism and autonomy within states where Kurds live.[66]

The uprising in the Middle East and North Africa, especially the Syrian war, from 2011, created an environment for Öcalan's ideology of confederalism and democratic autonomy to spread and be put into practice by the PKK and its sister organisations. Especially after 2015, Kurdish success against ISIS secured a considerable territory in northern Syria (Rojava) which created a perfect stage to test Öcalan's ideology. On the ground, different ethnic and religious groups, women and young people, have been given an active role in local municipal councils and social, political, economic and legal organisations which have been created in their villages, towns and cities. These organisations focus on education, community safety, women's rights and the role of young people, organising everyday life, solving problems, bringing justice and making peace between and within families and communities at the local level, and claiming to do so without much bureaucracy.

[64] Hashim 2013.

[65] Gunter 2004; Goktas 2007.

[66] See, Öcalan 2011a; Jongerden and Akkaya 2011; Akkaya and Jongerden 2013; Leezenberg 2016; Schmidinger 2018; Dinc 2020.

Kurds in Syria are organised under an umbrella organisation called the Movement for a Democratic Society (TEV-DEM), which is made up of six political parties and civil society institutions, including the well-known Democratic Union Party (PYD) and its armed units, the People's Protection Units (YPG) and Women's Protection Units (YPJ). Officially the PYD contests its close connection to the PKK due to pressure from Turkey as well as the criminalisation of the PKK in Western contexts. Aldar Khalil, a member of the Executive Body of the Democratic Society Movement (TEV-DEM), wrote in *Foreign Policy* on 15 May 2017, on the relationship between PYD, PKK and Öcalan:

Modern Kurdish groups can trace their political philosophies to one of two founding figures: Mustapha Barzani and Abdullah Öcalan . . . The influences of these figures and ideas can be seen today. Iraq's Kurdistan Democratic Party (KDP) springs from the Barzani school of thought, and as a result the KRG is ruled by a few, with power and wealth concentrated at the hands of the Barzani family and its friends. Öcalan's school of thought, on the other hand, extends to the PYD, Turkey's pro-Kurdish Peoples' Democratic Party (HDP), and the PKK, as well as other groups in Iraq and Iran. All these groups have implemented Öcalan's ideas differently and pursued different aims, as we interact with different geopolitical players. We don't deny our relationships with all Kurdish parties in the four parts of Kurdistan (spread across present-day Syria, Turkey, Iran, and Iraq), as we don't deny our connection to Öcalan. In fact . . . I am proud to say I have a photo of Öcalan on my desk next to me. Öcalan's views and philosophy are at the core of how we govern the Northern Syrian Federation, or Rojava. And they are why, under our control, northern Syria has become a model – respecting the rights of minority groups and women, and ensuring that individual and collective freedoms are not only protected but empowered. We also don't deny that PKK also traces its school of thought back to Öcalan. However, their implementation of his teachings differs greatly from ours, and their political circumstances do as well. As Kurds, we of course sympathize with our brothers and sisters in Turkey. Many of their towns are divided along our border, partly residing in Turkey and partly in northern Syria. Historically, many Syrian Kurds joined the struggle in Turkey and were martyred there. Equally, some Kurds from Turkey and Iraq came to Syria to join the heroic resistance of Kobani against the Islamic State, and were martyred in Rojava. The PKK offered its help to Kobani, as did the United States.

My fieldwork observations and detailed interviews with the members of the Kurdish movement in Turkey and Syria (PKK and YPG) resonate with the view expressed above. I found that there is a complex relationship between the PKK and the Syrian Kurdish organisation, especially the PYD. Aside from sharing the same ideological roots and recognition of Abdullah Öcalan as leader, there are also organisational connections, including membership overlap, as Aldar Khalil also described in the explanation above.

According to the Kurdish practice of democratic autonomy in Turkey, Syria (Rojava or West Kurdistan) and different diasporas, there is an election for every position which is co-chaired by one woman and one man, who lead councils, municipalities, and branches of diaspora communities. The autonomous women's arm unit of the YPJ and alternative justice system is also created as part of this new structure. These 'autonomous' levels and organisations are linked to each other and follow a pyramid-style connection.

From bottom to top, every level of these organisations has a responsibility to provide reports about their actions to their peers. Within this pyramid-style of organisation, from the lower levels to the higher, there is a rigid hierarchical structure. Any ethnic or religious practice is welcomed, as long as it follows one party ideology. At the top, there is the unchallenged leadership of Öcalan, even though he has been in prison since 1999. This political structure is described as radically democratic. However, like many other radical and rigid forms of governance, including Kemalism in Turkey, the new Kurdish political system has authoritarian elements which push for a dogmatic approach to ideology. From the earlier years until the present day, any opponents of Öcalan's ideology of the PKK, even if it was his brother – Osman Öcalan, have been eliminated.[67]

While the Kurdish movement in Turkey and Syria officially challenges the idea of the nation state,[68] my field research shows that the introduction of the

---

[67] Çürükkaya 1996; Van Bruinessen 2000.

[68] The introduction of the Social Contract of the Democratic Federalism of Northern Syria (Rojava) starts: 'We, peoples of Rojava-northern Syria, including Kurds, Arabs, Syriacs, Assyrians, Turkmen, Armenians, Chechens, Circassians, Muslims, Christians, Yezidis, and the different doctrines and sects, recognize that the nation-state has made Kurdistan, Mesopotamia, and Syria a hub for the chaos happening in the Middle East and has brought problems, serious crises, and agonies for our peoples. The tyrannical nation-state

concept of 'radical democratic autonomy' is also a project of unifying Kurds and initiates a step towards the creation of an independent Kurdish nation state. Within this concept, pluralism within a single political movement is proposed and, so far, has been practised in Rojava, the Kurdish self-autonomous region in Syria since 2012.[69] According to the Rojava constitution (or The Social Contract of the Democratic Federation of Northern Syria, SDF),[70] and leaders of Rojava's statements, different individuals and groups can practise their own cultures, religions and values, and preserve their diversity. Gender-based equality and justice have been central to the practices and organisational structure of the Kurdish movement in Syria and Turkey. However, pluralism, social justice, ecological awareness, women's freedom, emancipation and solidarity can only exist under one political structure and

regime, which has been unfair to the different components of Syrian people, has led the country to destruction and fragmentation of the society fabric. To end this chaotic situation, the democratic federal system is an optimal solution to address the national, social, and historical issues in Syria . . . The democratic federal system of northern Syria adopts, in this contract, the physical and moral values of the Middle East. This document is approved by the free will of all the components of northern Syria and according to the principles of the democratic nation.'

[69] The Rojava de facto self-governance hasn't been internationally recognised. Kurdish self-autonomous administration and forces there are seen as 'terrorist' by Turkish state. However, the NATO forces are there and have operated jointly with Kurdish forces together against ISIS. The quasi-diplomatic meetings between Kurdish representatives in Rojava and the United States and France have taken place. Several other countries, including the United Kingdom have hosted members of the Rojava delegation. Rojava is almost recognised as a parallel state within Syria. In addition, the Belgium Court of Cassation declared on 28 January 2020 that the Kurdish Worker's Party (PKK) is not a terrorist organisation. Belgian federal prosecutors started the case in 2008, accusing the thirty-six suspects linked to the PKK of taking young European Kurds to combat training camps. The Turkish government was very angry over the decision and asked the Belgium government to take steps and change the decision of the Court of Cassation. A press release from the Turkish Foreign Ministry stated: 'We urge [the] Belgian government to take all necessary steps to correct this desperate and contradictory ruling and to continue countering the PKK terrorist organisation in an increasing manner.'

[70] For Social Contract of the Democratic Federalism of Northern Syria, see, <http://vvan-wilgenburg.blogspot.com/2017/03/social-contract-of-democratic.html> (last accessed 31 January 2021). See also Allsopp and van Wilgenburg 2019.

leader, Öcalan. This means that democracy can exist, but only within one party ideology.

While some Kurds favour adopting a plural democratic approach as a way of achieving their political aims, others, including many PKK active and former guerrillas, members of Kurdish diaspora communities in Germany and the UK, many Kurdish politicians and intellectuals, and especially young Kurds, hold strong nationalist views. The PKK and its supporters, like many other political movements, have a public and private image: one adhering to pluralistic values and one that is more nationalist. Most of my respondents would tell me that they were against any nationalism during our first meeting, but at a later stage, especially after a few meetings and conversations, they would share different views with me and act accordingly; for example, by showing strong nationalist sentiments, singing PKK songs, showing the Kurdistan flag and images around their house or shops and expressing their belief in the importance of Kurdish unity and sovereignty. Many of my interviewees argue that the Kurds need to become strong nationalists under one single Kurdish political movement and identity, in the same way that Turkish nationalism has developed, if they are to escape from the hegemony of existing nation states. During our conversations, many of my respondents stated that it was not the time for pluralism, multiple political parties or further divisions, but instead it was the time to create a safe Kurdish authority and state. A Kurdish female activist in Berlin told me in July 2017:

> It is not the time for Kurds to have multiple political ideas or a fragmented opposition; it is time to create a Kurdish state under one umbrella of Kurdishness. Without creating a safe place for Kurds, multiple voices and divisions can only help our enemies and not the Kurds. We have had multiple voices until now and we have gained nothing except further losses. It has cost us more conflict and death. Kurds have lost generations.

In the same vein, a Kurdish lawyer from Istanbul claimed during our interview in June 2016:

> Turkey was ruled by one party until 1950 and still their multiple parties all work for the same aims when it comes to the sake of the state. Divisions so far have weakened Kurds in Turkey, Iraq, Syria and Iran and have stopped

Kurds from forging a national unity. For this reason, our enemies keep telling us to have multiple voices. They know that as long as Kurds are divided and have many small puppets, they can rule us for centuries to come. Kurds need to speak with one voice for their national cause, as other strong nations do.

It is not surprising to see how an increase in nationalism, from both Kurds and Turks, has resulted in more violence and conflict, and vice versa. A study by Sarigil and Karakoc[71] also shows that the failed peace process and intensive conflict after the 2015 June election, when the Kurdish-led HDP won a considerable victory with 13 per cent of the vote, increased the number of Kurds who openly expressed support for Kurdish independence. Simultaneously, promoting 'Islamic brotherhood' or 'Muslim Unity' by the Erdoğan-led authoritarian regime has not let to Kurds abandoning Kurdish ethno-nationalism and the wish for secession.[72] Most Kurds have lost trust in the state due to many reasons. For example, Kurdish areas and Kurdish people have historically been used as laboratories for different authoritarianisms in Turkey. Elections in Turkey, especially in the Kurdish regions, have not been transparent and equal for Kurds. As Levitsky and Way[73] and Levitsky et al.[74] argue, the result of an election is almost always known by the competitive authoritarian regimes; they are not much different from one-party authoritarian regimes, of which there were many around the world before the 1990s. Elections have been only used to back up power and increase the image of populist authoritarian regimes worldwide to portray and claim that there is still competition, which is not the reality. Another aim of the election, under the label of democracy, for these kind of regimes, is to include the masses, to make them part of their autocratic ruling. The election committee and process work under the orders of the authoritarian leaders and regimes. Specifically for the process in the Kurdish areas, as Adar and Turkyilmaz explained in their article in *Open Democracy* on 30 April 2019:

There have been systematic irregularities in elections in Kurdish areas since at least the 1990s; the 10 per cent electoral threshold that has been in place

---

[71] Sarigil and Karakoc 2016.

[72] Gurses 2015; Sarigil and Karakoc 2016; Bilici 2017; Tekdemir 2018.

[73] Levitsky and Way 2010 and 2020.

[74] Levitsky et al. 2020.

since 1983 is also a principle means of blocking Kurdish political representation . . . Those murky or corrupt practices were meant to fix the ballot tally without rejecting the principle that the tally would decide the winner . . . The validity of election outcomes is now dependent on *post hoc certification by ruling elites that the candidate with the most votes is 'fit' for office.*' One early warning of this logic was the appointment of government trustees in many Kurdish cities based on a presidential decree passed on September 1, 2016 in the wake of the July 15 putsch. This move was justified rhetorically by the newly articulated requirement that all officeholders should show 'patriotism' and 'loyalty' to Turkey . . . In the Kurdish heartland – the testing ground for the regime's oppressive measures to undermine the power and conclusiveness of the ballot box – the situation is, to be sure, much worse.[75]

While Kurds have their political spaces and representation severely curtailed, they have continued to experience physical violence, forced displacements and demolition of their housing since the early years of the Turkish Republic. The latest Kurdish uprising in Syria and Turkey after 2014, especially after Kurdish military victories over ISIS in Kobane, opened a new phase for Kurdish nationalism, which was more self-confident than the previous ones. At the beginning of October 2014, thousands of Kurdish youths in Turkey took to the streets to demonstrate against the Turkish state's collaboration with ISIS, when jihadists had already captured almost 90 per cent of Kobani. Fifty of these protesters were killed by state forces in Turkey. However, there were some positive outcomes of this Kurdish youth uprising. First, it opened a way for thousands of Kurdish fighters from Turkey to join Kobane's resistance. Second, it stopped Turkey openly collaborating with ISIS. Third, it even allowed around 200 Kurdish Peshmerga fighters with heavy military equipment, weapons and ammunition to pass Turkey and enter Kobane to help Kurds in Syria. The battle of Kobane against ISIS itself turned into a symbol of Kurdish resistance, sometimes called a 'Kurdish Stalingrad'.[76] This marked a significant change in Kurdish nationalism: from localised and weak nationalism towards a collective, stronger form of nationalism with the help of the mobilisation of the diaspora.[77]

---

[75] Adar and Turkyilmaz 2019.
[76] Abdulla 2016.
[77] Tas 2015.

While international silence against Turkish state oppression and aggressive authoritarian structure towards Kurds continues, Kurds in Syria and Iraq have managed to gain Western support for their war against ISIS, including American air and military ground support which helped them to gain a substantial territory in northern and eastern Syria. Many Kurds from Turkey joined this battle side by side with Syrian Kurds while many Syrian Kurds had also joined the PKK movement since its early days, and have fought against the Turkish army since the 1980s. Many of my interviewees describe how Kurdish nationalists share the aim of creating a place where they can live equally with other ethnic groups and fully enjoy their cultural, political and economic rights – and they do not mind in which country. The PKK is a vehicle to help individuals to achieve this aim, but it is not the actual source of Kurdish nationalism. Many of my interviewees believed that if the PKK fails to achieve the political aims of the Kurds, another group will no doubt replace it, such as TAK (the Kurdistan Falcon Fighters) or Hizbullah (a religious Kurdish movement).

As discussed above, despite some ideological changes, the PKK never abandoned the idea to unify all Kurds in their struggle against the dominant regional powers and create a Kurdish state. One of the senior MPs of the Kurdish-led political party, HDP, told me in March 2019:

> The Kurds need to create their own state. This is the only long-term solution for peace in the Middle East. The PKK and all of us know that it is not easy to create an independent Kurdistan between four states, Turkey, Iran, Iraq and Syria. We cannot just loudly say this every day to give ammunition to our enemies and to make them attack us. Many EU members and the US don't welcome an independent state approach, because they have their own Catalunya, Scotland and North Italy cases. They don't want to open Pandora's box as many secessionists want to find a way for their independence. They want to hear about democratic integration, confederative unity, pluralism and gender equality and we let them hear these very much. However, the national struggle and independent Kurdistan was and is still very strong and the main aim of Kurdish movement in Turkey, Syria and Iraq.

Ideological and tactical changes helped the PKK to make new allies internally, among Kurds, and internationally, especially within Western powers. However Kurdish nationalism has been one of the most important sources of fuel for the PKK's movement from the beginning.[78] While the PKK has demolished the power of traditional families, the movement has also created a tribal style of ideology in which members have to fully obey rules and the ruler. The PKK created a culture of fear, distrust and a mentality of 'the world against us' similar to many other nationalist movements. The 'world' and 'us' was not just describing 'others' and 'Kurds' but Kurds who took the side of the 'others' rather than PKK, including different Kurdish parties, who fully show solidarity and support with the PKK. The policy of 'othering' has been one of the main PKK policies for power, as it was for Kemalism in Turkey between the 1920s and the 1950s. According to several of my interviewees, to be a Kurdish nationalist is not enough, if you are not in support of the PKK, especially Öcalan.

Some of my interviewees have admitted that the 'homogenisation' of the Kurds is not an easy process, even though the loss of young Kurdish women and men in the military struggle has helped to create a wall between 'Kurds' and 'others' (Turks, Arabs and Persians) and has sharpened Kurd-ish national identity. Sacrificing one's life is seen as a way of securing the identity of the Kurdish nation for eternity. For that reason, the memory of people who have fallen during the conflict can help to glorify an ethnic community and nationalism. Glorifying martyrs for the Kurdish cause also encourages others to follow in their footsteps. A Kurdish woman in Istanbul said in November 2015: 'Turks, Arabs and Persians continue to kill Kurds. Many genocides have been carried out against us, but each one makes us stronger than before. This shows that they cannot eradicate the Kurds by killing them. Such actions will only help to unite us, to strengthen our national identity.'

Kurds who argue against the imposition of a one-party ideology worry that this kind of party-based nationalism could easily create deep conflict between different Kurdish groups and in the long term could constitute a barrier to the unification of different Kurdish regions. It may strengthen group nationalism, attract other smaller ethnic groups and help facilitate group mobilisation in the short-term, but in the longer-term, it may also open the door for a more self-destructive form of nationalism.

[78] Olson 1989.

Kurdish Nationalism and Gender

Gender equality is regarded as an important aspect in the new ideology of Kurdish nationalism. The co-chair system, whereby every senior position is chaired jointly by a man and a woman, is practised from the lowest to the highest level of political and military roles. For this reason, the PKK leadership in the Qandil mountains (Iraqi Kurdistan), the PYD and YPG in Syria, the HDP political party in Turkey, and diaspora community organisations in Germany and the UK, all strictly follow this principle and practise co-chair or co-leadership systems, jointly by a man and a woman. According to my interviewees and observations in Turkey and in different diasporas, it is not just Kurdish women that benefit from this practice, space has also been made for minority ethnic groups such as Assyrians, Arabs, Armenians, Turks and Alevis.[79] For the aim of women's empowerment, *jineology* (women's science),[80] was introduced by Öcalan. This new approach was not just for the ideological training of women, but also for the aim of creating gender equality at all levels; dealing with domestic and societal violence; bringing equal and fair justice for all; economic and social equality; abolishment of the centuries-long tradition of 'honour crimes'; and to introduce participatory democracy.[81]

For Öcalan the domestication and discrimination of women was not much different from colonisation, which was seen as the main reason for the majority of internal and external conflicts in the Middle East. He claimed that any solution for Middle Eastern conflict should make the role and equality of women the main focus, as only this could create sustainable peace. Öcalan wrote:

> The extent to which society can be thoroughly transformed is determined by the extent of the transformation attained by women. Similarly, the level of woman's freedom and equality determines the freedom and equality of all sections of society . . . For a democratic nation, women's freedom is of great importance too, as liberated women constitute a liberated society. Liberated

---

[79] Al-Ali and Tas 2017 and 2018a.

[80] Jineology (in Kurdish *jineolojî*), made from the Kurdish words; *jin* (woman) and *lojî*, a derivative from Greek *logos*, meaning 'knowledge' and 'order'.

[81] See, Öcalan 2013; Knapp et al. 2016; Pavičić-Ivelja 2016; Düzgün 2016.

society in turn constitutes a democratic nation. Moreover, the need to reverse the role of man is of revolutionary importance.[82]

There are many reasons why gender-based justice and equality is important for the Kurdish nation-building project.[83] Firstly, large numbers of PKK members, especially the women member of the Kurdish political movement in Turkey, have spoken out increasingly since 2000 that without women's freedom, society cannot be free and conflict cannot be ended.[84] The Kurdish women's movement started to push women's rights and equality as a priority and an essential and permanent policy of the Kurdish movement at all levels. As I will be discussing in greater detail in Chapter 4, gender-based violence against Kurdish women goes back longer and deeper than the conflict with the Turkish state. For example, Ayla Akat, a well-known Kurdish women's rights activist, stated in an interview that a few changes within the constitution could facilitate the end of the ethnic conflict in Turkey; however, gender equality and women's rights cannot be developed with just a few constitutional changes. All of society needs to be changed.[85] Secondly, the Kurdish political movement is making an effort to reach all segments of Kurdish society, to strengthen the Kurdish identity around a 'tolerance for others', including all oppressed identities, especially women, in the attempt to create a distinct social and political identity from 'others', such as Turks, Arabs and Persians. Thirdly, adopting and practising gender equality is an important way of making connections with the rest of the world and to gain international, especially Western, support and sympathy for the Kurdish cause. Fourthly, almost 50 per cent of Kurdish fighters in Turkey and Syria are women and this reality has become part of the discourse on the new Kurdish national identity.

Many Kurdish women that dream of a better, more secure and free life have embraced the Kurdish revolutionary movement. They have moved from

---

[82] Öcalan 2013: 57.

[83] Belge 2008 and 2011; Tas 2016d.

[84] See, Yüksel 2006; Çağlayan 2007; Çaha 2011; Düzgün 2016; Al-Ali and Tas 2017 and 2018a, 2018c; Burç 2019.

[85] The full interview with Ayla Akat was published by *Open Democracy*, available at <https://opendemocracy.net/nadje-al-ali-latif-tas-ayla-akat/kurds-and-turks-are-at-edge-of-cliff> (last accessed 11 March 2017). See, Al-Ali and Tas 2016b.

their traditional family homes to the harsh and dangerous environment of a war zone. This has created a social revolution in Kurdish women's lives. According to former women guerrillas whom I interviewed, in the beginning it was difficult to adopt this new lifestyle, however, after a while it became routine to do all the things that men did in the war. One of these women in Diyarbakır said in May 2015:

> Women's liberation comes at a heavy price. Girls in the war live like men, are armed like men, fight like men, suffer like men and die like men . . .We can be everything; mayors, co-chairs, military leaders and fighters, but we are still not welcomed and do not enjoy life freely as women. Societal barriers continue and even at some level have increased for the female PKK fighters.

While the PKK has fought against patriarchal society and opened the gate for women's rights, this has not stopped the PKK from creating its own style of patriarchy. Strong military structures have affected men's and women's lives within the PKK. An example of which is the fact that women's sex lives remain taboo, and one of my interviewees told me the following slogan: 'Today is for the revolution. Personal needs, including sex, should be postponed for this aim.' This shows that the main aim is not to bring total freedom and equality for women, but as I will illustrate throughout the book with various examples, the movement also uses the body politically to help secure the ideology of the one-party revolution. According to some of my respondents, under the 'moral values' or 'revolutionary cohesion' a strict new type of lifestyle has been introduced for both genders. In addition, to be a female fighter has brought limitations on life, including disappointment, depression, anxiety, rape, injury and death. Another former female guerrilla fighter in London explains:

> Life was difficult for women before the revolution. Damage and deprivation continue during the revolution and it won't be easy after the revolution when depression becomes part of daily life . . . If all this suffering helps to unite Kurds and make their dream a reality, then it is worth it. I hope women won't be forced to go back to their old, unequal, traditional life, which was one of the main reasons why we started this revolution against the patriarchy and the authoritarian state.

The last four decades of wars and conflict in the Middle East has resulted in the death of many Kurdish fighters, male and female. Just during the most recent war against ISIS in northern Syria (2014–19), over 11,000 Kurdish fighters died, and 21,000 fighters were wounded.[86] Many of the active and former Kurdish guerrillas I talked to stressed that almost one third of the recent dead and injured were female fighters. Their armed struggle is seen as a form of self-defence against the state and patriarchy and that they aspire to and envision a time without acute conflict. Unfortunately, the history of peacemaking in the region has been flawed and the strong connection between the state and patriarchy continues.

A History of Conflict and Failed Peace

From the late Ottoman period until the present day, Kurds have created twenty-nine rebellion movements against the state.[87] The Sheikh Said Rebellion in 1925, Mount Ararat in 1930, and the 1938 Dersim rebellions are amongst the most well-known ones. These movements did not stop the denial of Kurdish identity and language by the Turkish state. The PKK, which was founded by Abdullah Öcalan (*Apo* – 'uncle' or 'guardian' is used by his followers), in 1978,[88] has created the longest and most violent war with the Turkish state in comparison with the previous Kurdish rebellions. It may have started with the Marxist-Leninist socialist ideology, but the main aim, as with many previous Kurdish rebellion movements, was to create an independent Kurdistan. Öcalan and his comrades aimed for pan-Kurdish aspiration from the beginning, not just in Turkey, but wherever Kurds live, in Iraq, Syria and Iran.[89]

The PKK-led Kurdish movement faced heavy losses in the 1990s against the Turkish state, but it was also, as Olson explained, 'the biggest challenge to the Turkish state in the 20th century'.[90] Thousands of Kurdish villages, many towns and districts were destroyed by state forces, and millions of people

---

[86] See, Allsopp and van Wilgenburg 2019.

[87] See, Besikci 1992b; Yegen 1996; Ibrahim and Gurbey 2000; Akkaya and Jongerden 2012.

[88] See, Besikci 1992b; McDowall 2004; Özcan 2006; Marcus 2017.

[89] See, Casier 2010; Leezenberg 2016.

[90] Olson 1996: 2.

lost their homes and were forced into exile, especially to Western Europe.[91] Almost every Kurd I have interviewed had a family member, relative or friend who joined the PKK and was killed, jailed, exiled or listed as missing.

Local people in Kurdish regions were almost always caught between two powers; the state and the PKK militias. During the night the militias were in power, visiting villages, receiving food, money or tax and recruiting new male and female members. They punished anybody they thought was collaborating with the state, or who didn't pay their taxes regularly. They also supported anybody who took their side, giving them more power in business and authority over the other side. During the day, in contrast, state forces would visit villages, punishing anybody who willingly or unwillingly hosted militias at their house during the night. Information about incidents was given to both state agents and the PKK militias by some village members, out of fear or to gain some advantage over other villages they thought of as enemies. One aspect that has made the PKK movement different to the previous Kurdish movements is that they were not just there for resistance against the state in the mountains, but also to build a new social, economic, and moral code and a parallel state structure in every village, town and city of Kurdistan in Turkey.

After unsuccessful peace attempts between the Turkish state and the PKK in 1993, 1997 and 2009, the Erdoğan-led Turkish government announced in April 2013 that they would make a historical peace agreement with the Kurds, to end a four-decade-long war.[92] This last peace process was officially announced in 2013 but already secretly started from 2009. Turkish Armed forces, PKK guerrillas and city militias declared a mutually agreed ceasefire which created more than a two-year time period for politicians and civil society members to negotiate. However, as previously, it was a weak peace process from the beginning. There was no international involvement, nor were the negotiations themselves balanced. Messages between the imprisoned PKK leader Abdullah Öcalan and the government were carried by a few selected Kurdish political party members.[93]

---

[91] See, Tas 2016b and 2016d; Baser 2015; Galip 2015; Keles 2015.
[92] Tas 2016b; Toktamış 2019.
[93] Tas 2016b.

Even though it was not a proper peace process, during those two years it felt safe to travel, stay out or even walk around alone in the evening. Yet, many of us could not shake off a sense that it felt a bit like the calm before the storm. Both sides, state forces and local people – especially the organised youth amongst them, the YDG-H, who were visibly acting as alternative forces to the state – were not very friendly to each other. It was a time when both sides brought more weapons into urban areas for possible conflicts, which would inevitably begin. Distrust was very high. Rushing to get more modern weapons and turn cities into arms depots appeared to be more important for the state and the PKK than rushing to make peace. Suspicion and distrust were not only prevalent on both sides but were also rampant against outsiders, especially journalists and academics, as I have already discussed in my introduction.

From March 2015 onwards, the behaviour of both sides during the so-called peace negotiations changed dramatically, with each side taking on a strong nationalistic perspective to monopolise their own power and unify their own camp. In particular, Erdoğan's preference for a one-man rule and attempts to secure his hold on power for many years to come, started to destroy hopes of ending the long-standing conflict between the Turkish state and the Kurdish political movement, and closed any possible doors to peace in one of the Middle East's longest-running conflicts.[94] The legal political Kurdish movement, mainly in the form of the Kurdish-led progressive HDP, had systematically challenged the AKP and Erdoğan in their struggle against authoritarianism.[95] Some of my respondents argued that the co-leader of the HDP, the charismatic Selahattin Demirtaş, sacrificed peace with his challenge to authoritarianism and attempt to appeal to progressive anti-authoritarian Turks. They stated that it was to early to openly challenge Erdoğan before creating a sustainable peace process. Following the HDP's success in the June 2015 elections, the full force of the state began to be felt by Kurdish communities and the political movement, especially after the Kurdish youth movement started to resist in Kurdish majority towns in south-eastern Turkey. Day by day, there was an increase in national discourse on populist politics

[94] Tas 2016b; Gourlay 2017 and 2020.
[95] Tekdemir 2019.

from the election of 7 June 2015 – the rhetoric of violence turned into actual state-legitimised violence, and counter-violence from the local youth trapped the city's population in the escalating conflict. Turkey once again sank deeper into the mire of war with Kurds.

The Kurdish Youth Movement

After the June 2015 elections, any political activities which were critical of the state were banned, HDP centres and their members were targeted, elected mayors, politicians, activists – especially Kurdish youths – were targeted and imprisoned, at the same time as the Kurdish media and the use of Kurdish language were banned as in the 1990s. While the conflict expanded once again from political repression and marginalisation to acute violence, the local Kurdish youth in Kurdish-dominated towns and cities became the most visible resistance against the oppression of the state and its assimilation policies.

The YDG-H (*Yurtsever Devrimci Gençlik Hareket*, or the Patriotic Revolutionary Youth Movement), the PKK's urban youth wing, was formed from local young people in 2013, who socialised at different Kurdish community centres and tea shops with their friends or comrades during the day, but were starting to act as a de facto local armed militia during the night. The formation of the group is relatively recent, but Kurdish youth have been active since the 1990s as part of an emerging Kurdish de facto, alternative state structure. According to my field research findings, the mobilised youths are often children of families who lost their relatives, fathers or mothers and were forced to migrate from their home villages and towns during the 1990s conflict. Because of their background and experiences, they have always been perceived as the enemy by state forces and have also seen state forces as the enemy. As *Middle East Eye* wrote on 16 September 2015, 'While the PKK only conducts guerrilla warfare and are based in the mountains, the YDG-H has taken the combat zone to their home towns and cities.'

Kurdish youth, during the 1990s and early 2000s, followed Palestinian youth methods and first took part in street protests, threw stones, fireworks and Molotov cocktails at the security forces and tried to control the streets.[96]

---

[96] Darici 2013.

The state was only visible with heavily armed police and military vehicles in certain neighbourhoods and cities in Kurdish regions, such as Sur, Cizre and Nusaybin, patrolling mainly town centres without entering some neighbourhoods of these towns. Over the years, intensive clashes between youths and state forces have taken place on specific days, such as Newroz celebrations (21 March), the day of the arrest of Abdullah Öcalan (15 February), the birth of Abdullah Öcalan (4 April), the first attack of the PKK against the Turkish state (15 August) and during the funerals of Kurdish guerrilla forces. These clashes tend to continue for hours and sometimes days and usually end in bloodshed and high numbers of youths being arrested by the police. If such clashes occur in the western part of Turkey, police usually use teargas or rubber bullets, as we saw during the Gezi Movement in 2013, but in the Kurdish regions of south-eastern Turkey, live ammunition and advanced military guns have been used by state forces against stones, fireworks and Molotov cocktails.

In October 2014, the Kurdish youth took over many cities in Kurdish regions of Turkey in solidarity with Kobani where ISIS was advancing. By that time, the youth still did not have guns, as they would have a year later, but only stones. There were heavy clashes with the state forces between 6 and 8 October; stones against the most advanced weapons. It was inevitable that the youths would suffer and around fifty-five of them were killed by state forces.[97] The demonstrations have generally been arranged by local Kurdish authorities and adult men and women attend during the daytime. But in the evenings, when the adults return home, the youths tend to take control of streets and neighbourhoods until the following morning, when they go to work or hang around tea shops with their friends, pursuing their everyday activities and trying to look inconspicuous. Youths usually cover their faces and sometimes their eyes to protect themselves and so as not to be identified by police cameras, which are all pervasive, not only at the ground level but also carried by drones from the air. The masks also help protect against the tear gas which is almost always used during public demonstrations by the

---

[97] See, Aydin-Duzgit et al. 2015. One of the successes of this protest was that it made the world aware of what was going on in Kurdish towns in Syria. The United States started to militarily help Kurds from 20 October 2014. Iraqi Kurdistan also sent them 200 Peshmerga forces with military equipment on 23 October 2014, who went through Turkey as a corridor.

police. One of my interviewees described the use of tear gas and water cannons in the following way: 'It is the starter of the police menu for us today but their actual meal is more bloody if the demonstration continues.' The youths frequently use code names and different clothes during the protests to avoid being recognised by the police and also by possible state agents among themselves. Some of the youths did not remove their face masks during hour-long interviews with me, and used fake names as a way to protect their identities.

The uprisings in the Middle East in 2011, led largely by youths in the various countries, have contributed to the transformation of the Kurdish youth movement. Turkey's operations against the Kurdish movement and the Turkish government's close relations with the Islamic groups left little option for the Kurdish movement but to start trench warfare. The Kurdish youth became much more organised and tried to create safe independent spaces, not just in their own neighbourhoods at night but more broadly in their town and cities, even during the day. Youth activists increasingly started to act under the YDG-H, which later changed its name to Civil Defence Units (YPS). The Kurdish youth movement started to carry weapons, and used tactics as many Syrian Kurds and Arabs did in their own neighbourhoods against the Assad regime. They also learned about different city guerrilla warfare and defence styles from the PKK's well-trained, experienced members.

Some members of the youth groups went to Rojava during the siege of Kobani in 2014–15, fought against ISIS, and gained new urban warfare experience. According to some of my respondents, some military tactics were adopted from the urban warfare of ISIS. The youths created different units of armed forces and improved and expanded their arsenal; they dug deep trenches and built barricades to stop state forces from entering their neighbourhoods and managed to liberate some zones. As part of their urban warfare, they created secret passages between different houses and neighbourhoods. They started to collect taxes and establish alternative justice mechanisms to resolve conflicts in their neighbourhoods and act as an alternative to the state police.

According to some of my respondents, the youth movement is made up of the children of the PKK, which historically has been the main power behind Kurdish political and military mobilisation and grass-roots connections. However, at some stage the youths became powerful enough to act independently and not to take orders, or even sometimes to refuse orders, from the central command of the PKK. The Kurdish young people have not just been an important pressure group amongst the Kurdish public against their family's traditional attitudes but also in relation to their main ideological and military supply power. Some of the militant youth activists joined TAK (Kurdistan Freedom Falcons – *Teyrebazen Azadiya Kurdistan*), another operational city warfare unit, which was formed by the PKK in 2004. TAK sometimes acts independently and has been described as one of the most secretive organisations of the Kurdish militant movement. TAK is also known to have criticised the PKK in the most recent conflict as the PKK has shied away from overt warfare.

From Relative Autonomy to Acute Violence

On my second day in Sur, when I was walking around interviewing members of the Women's Academy, where *jineoloji*, or women's science is taught, they showed me the streets. The PKK's urban youth wing was very visible on almost every corner and it was very obvious that they were in control while I was there. Many walls were painted with slogans; paintings of different Kurdish flags, red, green and yellow; the logo of the Kurdish political party, BDP (*Barış ve Demokrasi Partisi* or Peace and Democracy Party); the logo of the PKK, green flags with a red star against a yellow sun; and its imprisoned leader, Öcalan.

It was almost impossible to pass a street without seeing posters of Öcalan, who has been in prison on an isolated Turkish island, *Imrali*, since February 1999. Alongside Öcalan, many photos and posters of PKK martyrs were on display. The Women's Academy building was displaying photos of Öcalan and Sakine Cansız, a famous female PKK guerrilla who was killed in Paris in 2013 by a Turkish state agent. There were big signs on the wall of the Women's Academy, saying *Jin, Jiyan, Azadi*, which means 'Women, Life, Freedom' in Kurdish. However, it was rather difficult to walk amongst the rubbish and chaos of the streets. One of the members of the Women's Academy, who stayed seven years in the mountains with the PKK, five years in a Turkish prison after her arrest, and five years now out of prison and working here, pointed to the rubbish saying:

> The streets look dirty and messy now because of the state's forces. We used to keep our streets very clean. Our people listened to us and followed our

rules. Then the state forces arrived again and created disorder and mess on our streets. We can look after our city and manage our people's needs much better than the state. We don't need anything from these invaders here. They cannot rule us and tell us how to live. Their laws and authority are dirty just like these streets.

What I saw and understood from our subsequent conversations was that she was really talking about the incompatibility of these two forms of governmentality in a single space. As one of the organisers of the youth movement and also the Women's Academy, she and her friends, as Kurds, saw themselves as the rightful rulers of Kurdish towns and cities and saw the state forces as invaders.

The politics of rubbish is important. It is seen one of the most powerful means of bringing down or raising any regime in a modern state. Erdoğan's rise to power in Turkey started with his promise to clean the dirty streets of Istanbul, which were the result of heavy strikes in early 1990s. After his surprise election victory in 1994, Erdoğan focused on cleaning Istanbul as a priority, and this established his rise to power. He is seen as one of the best rubbish collectors and he has almost always exploited this success before any elections. He keeps reminding the public that if they choose the opposition leftist party then their streets will again be filled with odorous piles of rubbish. These Kurdish Woman Academy members were also aware that people would blame them and punish them for the dirty streets. She was not wrong. Several of Diyarbakır's business people expressed their criticism of Kurdish co-mayors because of uncollected garbage. One of them said: 'I can understand all other problems which might have happened because of the state, but they don't have any excuse for this street mess. This is our space and their only job is to keep this space clean. If rubbish continues like this even my 77-year-old grandmother will raise her voice and rebel against any authority who does not look after our neighbourhood.'

This space was considered to be very important for the survival and continuity of local life and political power. Mona Harb wrote in *Jadaliyya* on 16 February 2017, and also asked several questions relating to how urban neighbourhood spaces were important during and after the 'Arab Uprising', which started in late 2010, early 2011 in Tunisia, and affected many countries, mainly Egypt, Libya, Yemen, Bahrain and Syria:

> How and why does urban space contribute to public action and social movements? What is the relationship between power, space, and resistance? How do different groups utilize space to mobilize and facilitate collective action? Which forces that shape space (physical and technological, as well as social, historical, political, and economic) are combined to guide this action? More broadly, how do specific historical, national policies, and global forces shape cities? How are different inequalities constituted by urban life and how do they reconstitute the city? How do the ordinary practitioners of the city negotiate, navigate, appropriate, resist, and transform urban forms?

Historically, Kurds, from the Ottoman period until the present day, when considering the state authority to be dysfunctional or when they have received unequal treatment from the state, have typically filled these social, political and economic gaps themselves.[98] When central authority fails, the Kurds have created their own leaders and established their own local councils to run their own affairs, as we saw recently in Syria. Less known and documented are the various ways the Kurdish political and legal movement linked to the PKK had tried to establish alternative institutions, mechanisms and processes, especially in Kurdish-majority towns in south-eastern Turkey.

Just after the June 2015 election, many Kurdish mayors and councils followed the DTK's (Kurdish Democratic Society Congress) order to create a self-autonomous structure. Kurdish success in Syria was one of the important encouragements for Turkish Kurds to create similar alternative state models in Turkey. Turkish and Syrian Kurds have become much closer and strongly connected, linguistically and ideologically, and many of them come from the same family background. There was also an assumption that the majority of Kurds in Turkey, like the Syrian Kurds, would take part in this uprising. It was not just a verbal declaration of self-autonomy, but an armed enforcement of it, with armed Kurdish youth militias openly patrolling the streets, and digging trenches to hold off state forces. In Sur, self-governance, as in many other Kurdish towns and districts, was declared

---

[98] McDowall 2004.

in August 2015, just days before one of my field trips to Sur and other Kurdish cities and towns.

From July 2015, the declaration of self-autonomy or parallel state structure only added fuel to the fire of the conflict between Turks and Kurds. The Kurdish alternative education system, armed self-defence militias, independently run health and economic initiatives, alternative courts and justice mechanisms, alternative mosques and imams and tax collectors had already existed in many Kurdish towns and cities in Turkey. However, this was the first time it was openly announced and put into practice. This gave Erdoğan's government ammunition not only to destroy Kurdish villages, which had happened extensively in the 1990s, but this time also main towns and cities.

In contrast to the 1990s, the division of power between competing structures was not only at village level, but was also practised in one of the biggest cities in Turkey – Diyarbakır. Police forces were not just taking control and patrolling the streets during the day, but arresting and killing any suspicious people seen around the conflict zones without discrimination according to their age, class or gender. The state was there with thousands of police, special forces and troops; it took helicopters and tanks to the narrow streets and residential areas and did not hesitate to demolish and destroy historical buildings and the surrounding areas. There was a clear order from the state to 'annihilate' any Kurds who were seen as dangerous or not obeying any rule of the state. On 17 December 2015, *The Guardian* and *Reuters* quoted from Erdoğan's public speech in Konya: 'You will be annihilated in those houses, those buildings, those ditches which you have dug. Our security forces will continue this fight until it has been completely cleansed.'

A *Spiegel* article on 12 February 2016 referred to Turkish government sources which said that 3,100 PKK armed militias and 200 security personnel were killed between August 2015 and February 2016. However, according to the OHCHR report of February 2017, around 800 members of the Turkish armed forces and approximately 1,200 local residents, an unknown number of whom may have been involved in violent or non-violent actions, were killed in six months, between July 2015 and December 2016. According to the same report, 70 per cent of buildings in the Sur district were destroyed. Similar damage was inflicted on many other towns and districts in the Kurdish regions where there was active conflicts. Hundreds of thousands of people were affected by curfews which were introduced by the state almost continually. In the flare up of acute conflict, the dead bodies of young or old people were dragged or left on the streets for days or even weeks. Access to medical care, food and water were prevented and violence against women and young people had become the norm.[99] One of the aims of the Turkish regime, as argued by *Foreign Affairs* on 23 September 2015, was to bring the 'Kurdish population into submission through the use of overwhelming force . . . much like the so-called dirty war in the 1990s that succeeded in degrading the PKK's capacity to conduct guerrilla warfare in the Kurdish countryside'. The state's direct, heavy military operations against Kurds were not just limited to Turkey this time, but went beyond its borders, extending to Rojava in Syria and parts of Iraqi Kurdistan.

Aside from creating more than twenty military bases in Iraqi Kurdistan and routine operations against the PKK camps,[100] a Kurdish canton in Syria, Afrin, was occupied by Turkey at the beginning of 2018, which they called 'Operation Olive Branch.' After the fall of Afrin, according to *The Jerusalem Post* on 3 April 2018, Turkish President Erdoğan stated: 'We marked a comma. God willing, a full stop will come next . . . Now we will continue this process, until we entirely eliminate this corridor, including in Manbij, Ayn al-Arab [Kobani], Tel-Abyad, Ras al-Ayn (Sere Kaniyeh) and Qamishli.' The Afrin canton was a 'missing piece' for Turkey which connected another two de facto Turkish-occupied places: the town of Jarabulus and the Idlib province. The Turkish authorities made it very clear that they didn't have any intention of handing over these occupied lands, including Afrin, to the Syrian regime or Kurdish groups. However, unlike other places, Afrin was a Kurdish town. It had been one of the war-free zones since 2012, which gave space for the Kurdish movement to create and practise their 'democratic autonomy'. It was also a place where the climate was different, much colder than the rest of the Middle East, with mountains, olive trees, rich farmland, roses and green

---

[99] OHCHR 2017.

[100] The Saddam regime ended, but the agreement he made with Turkey is still in place. In 1978, Turkey and Iraq made a deal against Kurds which allowed them to go up to nine miles into each other's territory to pursue Kurdish groups. In 1984, both countries increased these limits to eighteen miles in order to fight and prevent any Kurdish wish of self-determination or independence.

grass. I was very surprised to see this lush, rich land and endless olive trees during my field trip just before the conflict started. I was not surprised when Turkey called this operation 'Olive Tree'. After this, Turkey cut and carried a hundred thousand olive trees into Turkey. Turkey's operation in Turkey, and occupation in Iraqi Kurdistan and Syria continued, and Erdoğan was right that the first one was just a comma. In October 2019, the land between Tel-Abyad and Ras al-Ayn (Sere Kaniyeh) was seized by the Turkish authoritarian regime and its Islamic proxy militias, thousands of people were killed and hundreds of thousands more were forced from their homes.

Decomposing State

As in the 1990s, so during the recent conflict, politicians, lawyers, academics, activists and innocent civilians have faced heavy-handed treatment from state forces.[101] Here, I would like to discuss three well-known cases which, I hope, will help to give a clearer understanding of the state's position against local Kurds and the underlying reasons why Kurdish people generally do not have any trust or sense of belonging, but instead feel the need to construct their own parallel state and institutions.

The first case is Tahir Elçi. He was the head of the Bar Association of Diyarbakır and was shot dead during a daytime press conference in front of Sur's historical four-legged minaret on 28 November 2015. Elçi stated at the conference 'We do not want guns, clashes and operations here', before being shot.[102] These were his last words. Simply trying to tell both sides to stop the conflict and not damage people's lives and historical monuments was somehow seen as support for terrorism by the state authorities. According to the *BBC News* on 28 November 2015, Turkish President Recep Tayyip Erdoğan said 'the incident justified the state's "fight against terrorism"'. This was sufficient justification for his killing and, to date, no security forces have been charged for his death, even though, according to Forensic Architecture's report on 8 February 2019, the police officers who killed him were found to be the only suspects.[103] Many of my interviewees believe that Tahir Elçi was a unique and

---

[101] Gurses 2018.

[102] Forensic Architecture 2019.

[103] Forensic Architecture 2019.

altruistic person, with a strong commitment to human values, asking nothing for himself, instead offering only peaceful words and messages to stop the conflict between both sides. He fought for the rights of many innocent people, civilians who were massacred, displaced, executed in extrajudicial ways, and he won landmark cases at the European Court of Human Rights against Turkey. Hundreds of thousands of Kurdish people, not just from Diyarbakır but also from other Kurdish towns and cities filled the streets of Diyarbakır for his funeral. The state did not show any appetite for any proper investigations and no one, as yet, has ever been charged with his killing.

The second case was Taybet Inan, a 57-year-old mother of eleven children. She was shot dead by state security forces on 19 December 2015, in Silopi, another Diyarbakır district in which heavy clashes were taking place. She was just returning from visiting her neighbours. She was left lying in the street for a whole week. During this time her family tried several ways to communicate with different state departments for help. The Silopi governor and emergency departments told family members to go outside while carrying white flags and they would be able to take her body. Every attempt was made, despite continual shooting from security forces in their direction. Later, OHCHR's February 2017 report stated that, 'carrying a white flag' was meaningless and everybody, including cameramen and journalists were targeted.[104] The security forces would not allow anybody to take her body away. Later, when her brother-in-law went out in the street, again holding a white flag, to take her body, he was shot by security forces. He was badly injured and waited for twenty hours for an ambulance to come. It never arrived and he died. Taybet Inan's husband tried to retrieve her body, he was also seriously wounded. Her son Mehmet Inan said the whole family could have been killed if they had continued to go to rescue his mother's body. According to him, another innocent 11-year-old child was killed on their street alongside his mother, and both were described as terrorists by the state. There were ten bullets in Inan's body. He told the *Evrensel* newspaper on 22 December 2015, 'My mother was 57 years old and mother to eleven children. A child, an 11-year-old boy, was killed by forces on the same street while he was playing. The state claimed they were cleansing the area of terrorists. When did my mum and an 11-year-old child become

[104] OHCHR 2017.

terrorists?' Inan was buried twenty-three days after her death and security forces didn't allow any of her family members to attend her funeral. Later, there was an investigation into Inan's death but no security personnel were charged. Her daughter also made a statement to the same newspaper and on the same day: 'We were not even allowed to bury our mum. Every time I look at that street, I can see my mother's body there. We moved to our village after my mother and uncle died. We couldn't live in that street any more, but when I have to go to town and see that street then it reminds me of everything.'

The third case is not an actual killing, but about not leaving space for any alternative political movements or personalities to exist if they are Kurdish. On 9 September 2015, when I was in Diyarbakır carrying out my fieldwork, the head of the Kurdish political party, Selahattin Demirtaş, tried to travel to another district of Diyarbakır; Cizre. This district also declared a status of self-governance in August 2015, and immediately afterwards faced heavy clashes and curfews. The PKK's armed youth wing dug ditches to prevent state security forces from entering the town and streets. Many injured people couldn't get any medical help and more than twenty people were killed by security forces but could not be buried by their families. Relatives tried to keep bodies cold with iced bottles; some even put them in the freezer of a chicken shop. Water and food supplies were very short. For this reason, the HDP's co-leader, Demirtaş, tried to go to the city on foot, and help people who were in need, but, along with many other politicians, was forcibly prevented from entering the city by security personnel. Ertugrul Kurkcu, a member of the delegation, told BBC journalist Selin Girit on 10 September 2015 that they wanted to prevent state 'atrocities against the civilians. For the last seven days, and for twenty-four hours a day, there has been a curfew in place. I don't think we've seen anything like this even in Gaza. People in Cizre have been living in hell.' Later, in November 2016, Demirtaş and many other Kurdish politicians were imprisoned and have been held without being charged, despite a ruling by the European Court of Human Rights that Turkey must release him. I managed to talk to Demirtaş while he was in London, on 1 November 2016, just three days before his arrest in Turkey. He explained about their political aim:

Our politics are new and different. We are aiming to create an alternative life for our people. Our people don't believe the state and its institutions. It is not possible to make any progress under the current authoritarian regime. Is there any point in following their way and structure? Gezi was a very peaceful demonstration, but the state forces killed many people. Our colleagues, activists and even elderly women have been dragged from their homes and arrested by the state for no reason. I am going back to Turkey tomorrow and probably they will arrest me in front of the world too. Dictators have no shame. But we are not afraid of them. If we are afraid, and do not resist, then they will win. Dictators are cowards and they are even afraid of the people who are close to them. I don't believe that they even sleep peacefully. They have committed many terrible crimes and they should know that many people hate them.

After being in prison for three years, Demirtaş tweeted about his defence and imprisonment on 23 January 2019:

Since 4 November 2016, 2,500 of my political friends have been arrested together with me. I am not only Demirtaş. I am a political representative of millions of people. Six million people voted for me, which is more than the population of many countries in Europe. If you imprison me because I asked for an education in my mother tongue, it means you imprison millions of people. People will be upset . . . There is no hope for rule of law and freedom in Turkey, especially if you are critical of the state. People, especially those who have money, are escaping from the country every day. The poor have nowhere to go and suffer day after day. You are not going to finish us off by killing us, and your prosecutors are not going to be able to imprison millions of us by claiming that all of us are terrorists. There is freedom in this country for mafia leaders who say openly that they want to bathe in our blood, but not for people who are asking for justice.

As we witnessed throughout the 1990s, once again the Turkish state blocked any access for independent investigations into these unlawful killings of civilians, the destruction of private spaces and property, and the forced mass displacement and continuous repression of local Kurdish people. Instead, the state arrested and imprisoned the people who questioned the crimes committed by the state forces. The civil war has escalated since 2015.[105] While the state did not want any international investigations or involvement, it also did

---

[105] Gurses 2018.

not take any measures against these unlawful crimes. On 11 January 2016, Human Rights Watch stated: 'There has been little sign of effective investigations by Turkish prosecutors into civilian deaths and destruction of civilian property.' All these actions were justified for the sake of the survival of the Turkish nation.

There have been countless historical precedents which have paved the way towards a strong nationalism that permits police officers and security forces to commit crimes, to openly declare they will kill an elected MP – even if that MP does not pose any danger to the police officer or others – or even to kill a human rights lawyer in the daytime, in front of the cameras. The reverse can also be true; local people can see a simple government worker in uniform as an enemy, even if that individual doesn't pose a threat.

To sum up, in this chapter, I have focused on the historical and empirical contexts of the conflict between the Turkish state and Kurdish communities and the underlying reasons for the development of Kurdish alternative nation building and governmentality. What should have become apparent through the discussion above is that Turkish nationalism has been part and parcel of the Turkish Republic since its inception. Kurds in Turkey have been systematically marginalised and discriminated against whatever shape and form the government has taken, although one underlying thread for a long time was a modernist secular Kemalist ideology. In more recent decades, there has been a shift to an Islamist government under the AKP and President Erdoğan. Yet even some of the secular and leftist opposition to the increasingly oppressive dictatorship of Erdoğan – that is the secular Republic People's Party (CHP) – has been extremely nationalist and detrimental to Kurdish citizenship and ethnic rights. Instead of recognising Kurdish ethnic and national rights, Turkish leftists have preferred to use the Kurdish movement for their own ideological and power grabbing aims, but have never moved away from Kemalist nationalism and recognising the Kurds beyond 'Turkey's eastern problem'.[106] In the same way that Islamist Sunni Turks try to meld Kurdish identity with 'ummet' ideology, secular left-wing Turks have also submerged Kurdish identity in class solidarity and neither of these movements ever question Turkish hegemonic identity. While the Turkish state has been more willing and open

---

[106] Bozarslan 2012.

to involve and integrate some other ethnic minorities, such as Circassians and Laz people, even the most loyal Kurds are not trusted by the state and are not able to enter important state institutions and positions.

For a long time, Kurds were seen as nobodies, without culture, without language and without civilisation. This historical discrimination has given many Kurds a cause, and a reason to sacrifice their life. It comes as no surprise that many Kurds have joined various resistance movements for the independence, or at least autonomy, of their territory. Although, as this chapter has tried to illustrate, Kurds are not homogeneous and can be found in various political camps, including a Kurdish Islamist movement (Hizbullah) or in support of the AKP. Yet a prevailing feeling of marginalisation, victimisation and distrust of the state has led to a situation where many Kurds support and engage in the undermining of the state by creating alternative legal and political structures.

The next chapter will discuss how Kurdish women in Turkey, Syria and the diaspora have become an increasingly important power, one which almost resulted in independence for the Kurdish political movement and gender equality.

Figure 3.1 The author with Selahattin Demirtas, a former leader of the Kurdish-led political party HDP, just a few days before his arrest in November 2016. (Author's fieldwork image)

Figure 3.2 A painting by Kurdish artist Zehra Dogan depicting the result of the street battles between Kurdish youths and Turkish state forces between 2015 and 2016 in Nusaybin. It symbolises the damage caused to Kurdish living places by the Turkish and Kurdish conflict. The state put its own flags in every corner of the town after the destruction took place with the use of heavy military weapons. (Written image rights have been secured from the artist, Zehra Dogan)

Figure 3.3 The real image of how Turkish heavy war machines destroyed the town of Nusaybin and how authority was re-established, which influenced Zehra Dogan to create her famous painting. The original image was taken by state representatives and the state news agency.

Figure 3.4 Kurdish diaspora mobilisation has been important for the success of the Kurdish political movement. The German city of Cologne is one of the main locations for Kurdish mobilisation in the diaspora. The photo was taken by the author in September 2017, during the Kurdish festival which has taken place there for more than two decades. (Author's fieldwork image)

Figure 3.5 Kurdish events not just in Turkey but also in the diaspora, such as in Germany, are organised under tight security. In this photo, the German police adhere to strict rules and closely follow the events. During this particular festival in September 2017, no drink or food was allowed into the festival area. (Author's fieldwork image)

Figure 3.6 This image was taken during a Kurdish demonstration in Berlin in July 2017, in support of Kurdish resistance against ISIS in Syria. However, the police did not allow any Kurdish images to be shown and as a result conflict arose between demonstrators and police officers. One demonstrator's nose was broken and his blood was spread on a flag which is shown by another demonstrator. (Author's fieldwork image)

4

GENDER, POLITICS AND ALTERNATIVE GOVERNMENTALITY

Kurdish politics should stop prioritising a method which criticises and condemns, and calls on the state for solutions, but instead should directly communicate with the people, and call for their participation in the movement, for them to take responsibility and organise themselves. They cannot wait for salvation anymore, but should take direct initiative. It will be easier to move forward in this way.
(Gultan Kisanak, former MP and Co-Mayor of Diyarbakır, September 2015)

Gultan Kisanak is one of the leading members of the Kurdish women's movement in Turkey and beyond. She was imprisoned in the 1980s and not surprisingly also in 2020, which means that not much has changed in the state's perspective towards Kurds and Kurdish women in over four decades. While Turkish politics have not found any other options aside from silencing the critical voices, the Kurdish women movement has now become one of the most known and supported movements internationally. Kisanak and the Kurdish Women's refusal to surrender, their continuous struggle and insistence on change has been a new era in the history of women, as well as Kurds and wider society in the Middle East. Kurdish women have participated directly in making Kurdish history, re-establishing Kurdish nationalism, and modernising Kurdish and Middle Eastern societies.

It is important to analyse how gender rights and inquiries can be separable from the national aim and struggle. Gendered identity and peace are also important for any post-war justice and reconciliation.[1] The most important

[1] See, Pankhurst 2008; Sahin-Mencutek 2016; Al-Ali and Tas 2017, 2018b.

question is whether gender becomes a 'useful' tool for nationalism and the independent movement,[2] or if the Kurdish movement has revolutionised its earlier absolute and patriarchal stand, and paved a new way for gender equality and pluralism. How much equality in political and everyday life in the private sphere can we see in reality? What kind of codes and conducts have been introduced for different genders which create either new societal inclusion or exclusion? How much do these new roles and attitudes shape solidarity and freedom, or cause individual alienation and exclusion?

This chapter starts with an account of the tragedy of Yezidi Kurdish women in 2014 at the hands of ISIS religious authoritarianism, when the rest of the world 'discovered' the role and power of the Kurdish women's movement in the Middle East. This chapter explains the links between official rhetoric regarding the role of women in the post-ISIS Middle East and the measures implemented to increase women's participation in political processes. It highlights the failure or challenges of these measures in effectively addressing the actual situation of Kurdish women both within Turkey and Syria and in diasporic contexts. The chapter provides a localised and gendered analysis of political transformation and an assessment – beyond mere numbers – of the degree to which women have been able to participate in new Kurdish political, economic, social and legal structures. It highlights how the politics and rights of women have become important and why women have started to differentiate their politics from male-centred needs. After analysing the development of the Kurdish women's movement, the chapter continues to analyse what kind of new codes and gender relationships have been introduced by the Kurdish movement. The chapter will move on to a direct account of the day I spent observing the election of members of the Kurdish women's court in Berlin in 2017, and discuss the politics of *jineoloji* from that account. After a couple of years of intensive field work, which allowed me to establish relations and trust amongst community activists, I was allowed to observe as the only man amongst more than fifty female participants.

On 3 August 2014, Islamic State in Iraq and Syria (ISIS) attacked the Sinjar Mountains, where the majority of the world's Yezidi Kurds live. ISIS attacks against Kurds were not just limited to Yezidis. On 15 August 2014

[2] See, Al-Ali and Tas 2018a, 2018c.

they showed their brutality against powerless Kurds in a small Kurdish town, Kobane, in northern Syria. Both places, the Sinjar Mountains and Kobane, were only defended by a small number of Kurdish fighters, almost half of who were women. However, it was very difficult to prevent the huge number of ISIS crimes against Yezidis in the Sinjar Mountains, where there was only a small number of PKK fighters with very basic weapons.

Yezidi Kurds, like many other small, powerless groups, have faced several different versions of genocide because of their different religious identities throughout history. Yezidi Kurds, who never converted to Islam and preserve their pre-Islamic practices without a holy book but maintain an oral tradition, constitute one of the oldest Middle Eastern societies, but have faced fanatical intolerance and mass extermination. Unlike different Muslim groups (Shias and Sunnis), Christians and Jews in the Middle East, to have no holy book was reason enough for ISIS to commit mass murder and rape against them, wiping out everything that belonged to them: life, cities, holy places. While many men, boys and older women were killed, it was the girls and young women who suffered most at the hands of ISIS. According to Yezidi women and men I interviewed, women and girls (as young as eight) were captured, raped, sold and resold in modern sex slavery markets and online, for as little as twenty dollars. Some of them were sold seven to ten times. Their children were forced to listen behind locked doors as their mothers and sisters were raped and beaten. They were treated like slaves and called 'dirty unbelievers' or 'worshippers of the devil'. Many of these women were killed at the hands of ISIS or during the liberation of cities later and some of them are still missing.[3]

The world watched the ISIS attacks against Yezidi Kurds in the Sinjar Mountains and Kobane for months and did very little. The authoritarian neighbouring regimes, such as Turkey, Iraq and Syria did nothing to stop ISIS attacks or help secure Kurdish women from the hands of ISIS. ISIS occupation and systematic rape continued for more than two years. While these actions and the increasingly precarious situation of the community shocked the world, it also acknowledged the already existing Kurdish women's resistance. Almost every power in the region, as well as globally, exploited these ISIS actions for their own benefit. The Iraqi state was seemingly happy to

---

[3] See also, OHCHR 2016a; Tax 2016; Murad 2017.

publicise these crimes to receive international military and economic support for their own war against ISIS. Turkey was collaborating with ISIS between 2014 and 2016, and providing transport, money, weapons and logistics. The Turkish regime, according to David Philips's article in the journal *Ahval* on 20 May 2019, was running 'the jihadi highway [from the Turkish city of] Sanliurfa to Raqqa, the self-declared caliphate of ISIS'. It used the brutality of ISIS as an excuse to create more military bases around the Sinjar Mountains to prevent the PKK from increasing its power and control. Western power also used ISIS attacks against Yezidis as a way to legitimise its actions in the Middle East and receive internal and international support for their military operations in the following years. The resistance of the PKK's female fighters around Sinjar against ISIS, for the first time in history, legitimised the PKK's actions internationally and gained positive recognition and partnership with the Western powers in the Middle East. The only people that did not benefit, but only suffered, were the local civilian Yezidi Kurds, and around 200 fighters, mainly women, who arrived to help from the Qandil Mountains where the PKK's main camp operates, and who were taking on ISIS with simple Kalashnikovs.

While the Kurdish women's movement has been very active and increased its power gradually, at a heavy cost, over the last four decades, it was the first time the power of Kurdish women had become headlines in the Western media. It was not just a simple news headline, it was sudden 'love affair' or 'tragic drama' type of support to Kurdish women. Instead of focusing on the images of war and its destruction of people's lives and their living places, the image of Kurdish women fighters become more important. From August 2014, not just *The New York Times, The Guardian, Newsweek, Time,* the *Daily Telegraph, The Washington Post, Wall Street Journal,* the BBC, CNN, CNBC and FOX TV, but also fashion and lifestyle magazines such as *Vogue, Elle, Marie Claire, Cosmopolitan* and *Madame* used headlines for the first time for a such a subject in order to report the Kurdish women's battle or their tragic struggle at the hands of ISIS.

Almost all Western media, especially in the US and Europe, romanticised the Kurdish women's armed resistance which had existed since the 1980s when the Kurdish conflict with Turkey started, and was part of the Kurdish resistance in Syria from 2011. The Kurdish women had to wait to be raped or killed by ISIS members during combat to be noticed by the Western media. Kurdish women, like many other women around the world, have been taking part in wars, voluntarily or involuntarily, for decades.[4] A Kurdish female fighter called Aryaa from Rojava, northern Syria, stated, 'Western double standards are not new for us. While they try to take my photo for their news where I'm portrayed as a "hero", on the other hand because of my PKK membership, they criminalise me as a member of terrorist organisation. We are not heroes and not terrorists either. We defend our people, our land and our own life, which is threatened by others who are equipped with advanced Western-made guns.' It was obvious that the attitude to and experience of war was different for the people who were facing battle directly than for those who were looking on from a safe distance, and with different interests at heart.

A *Foreign Policy* headline on 12 September 2014 was 'Meet the Badass Women Fighting the Islamic State'. The *Wall Street Journal* title was 'Kurdish Women Fight on Front Lines Against Islamic State' on 17 October 2014. The British conservative newspaper, the *Daily Telegraph*, claimed that 'Isis fanatics fear being killed by a woman will deprive them of virgins in paradise' on 20 September 2014. Kurdish women's epic journey inspired fashion giants such as H&M to create an outfit and shared this on Twitter with the captions 'peshmerga chic', 'their bravery to be recognised', and 'peshmerga outfit sells in H&M stores' on 7 October 2014 and also 26 February 2015.[5] Kurdish women's stories did not just appear and remain with the newspaper titles, TV discussions or big store outfits, but also became the subject of films. Dozens of films were made locally and internationally; *Girls of the Sun* (Eva Husson), *Resaba* (Mehmet Aktas) and *Girls' War* (Mylene Sauloy), to name just a few.

Warrior Kurdish women have been commodified, and have become part of the popular culture industry of body image, gender politics and objectification, a subject for 'seminar room feminism' to discuss. Western governments have also used them for PR purposes to act against ISIS for their own

---

[4] For example, Algerian women took up arms and joined the resistance against France during the liberation. Women also made up a large part of the Zapatista National Liberation Army, or EZLN movement in Mexico from 1994. For the Algerian women's movement see, Amrane-Minne 1999 and 2007; Turshen 2002; for the Zapatista women's role see, Eber and Kovic 2003; Speed et al. 2006; Klein 2015; Cappelli 2018.

[5] See, Benakay 2016.

policies in the Middle East. This new positive view of Middle Eastern women goes against the well-known Western perspective of women in Islamic societies as 'passive', 'suppressed objects', 'exotic' and 'erotic', and is discussed in more detail by other researchers.[6] However, the 'exotic' and 'product' focus of Western media news stories about Kurdish women is noticeable, in that they have chosen only to pay attention to good-looking, made-up Kurdish female fighters who would agree to pose for the camera.

The Kurdish women's battles in Turkey, Iraq and Syria have not just been against the laws and cultures of those states, but also with their own male-dominated patriarchal culture and societal norms; socially engineered conditions which they have faced almost every day. Patriarchal reproduction traditions and harsh norms have tragically cost the lives of many women who have refused to follow such a culture, or to stay silent against heavy-handed muscular domination. Women's bodies and emotions have been seen to belong to almost everybody – their father, brothers, husband, society, religion, politics, government, autocrats – but themselves. They are described as an 'angel', 'pure', or 'heaven under their feet' when they strictly follow the established family and societal rules and are 'good' mothers and wives for their husband, father and the nation, but once they stand against these rules they are called 'monstrous', 'dishonourable' and 'evil'.

Yezidi Kurds, like many other Middle Eastern communities, have a culture with a very strong 'honour' code. Most girls are not allowed to date before marriage, and marriage within their community is almost always expected to happen. If a Yezidi marries somebody from outside their community then they and their children cannot be seen as Yezidi anymore. The societal code is very strict. In order to be Yezidi, both parents have to be Yezidi. If a Yezidi woman socialises with a Muslim man or marries a non-Yezidi, it means they don't just lose their community connection, but also their life can be in danger from their family members. For example, many years before ISIS arrived, on 2 April 2007, a 17-year-old Yezidi girl, Du'a Khalil Aswad, fell in love with a local Sunni Muslim Kurdish teenage boy, and spent one night with him, away from her family home. Her family and community

[6] See, Said 1993, 1995 and 1997; Ramji 2005; Varisco 2007; Lockman 2009; Rohloff 2012; Kandiyoti et al. 2019.

did not approve of her love and disappearance overnight. A group of around ten men, led by Aswad's uncle and cousins, not only stoned her to death in the main town square of Bashika (between Iraq and the Iraqi Kurdistan border), but also filmed her thirty-minute-long ordeal, celebrated her death and shared her murder video as an example for other Yezidi girls not to make similar a 'mistake.' The film shows that the community elders, local security forces and a crowd of several hundred men were present, watching the lynching as the girl was punched, kicked and stoned with a concrete block to her face. At that time, although people and security forces were present, they did not do anything to stop the brutality. The family of the girl wanted to kill the teenage boy as well, but could not find him.[7] The religious leaders and patriarchal community have taken the side of this 'honour' code and supported the actions of conservative families against their own family members for centuries. There are hundreds of similar crimes against women taking place among Kurds and many other Middle Eastern communities every year.[8] As *The New York Times* wrote on 20 September 2018, ISIS knew about the attitude of the community and repeatedly told the Yezidi girls and women they were holding: 'Listen, even if you manage to escape, there's nowhere for you to go. Your own community will turn their backs on you. Your only option is to now accept your life, convert to Islam, and basically become an integrated member of the Islamic State.'

Many of the Yezidi women who were ISIS captives, or who managed to escape, did not want to live anymore, at least with their family and community. Many of them tried to kill themselves because of the shame, community pressure and the ancient 'honour' code. *Resaba*, a film made by Mehmet Aktas focuses on this societal issue. When it was shown for the first time in Berlin in 2017, I was there to follow the event. A large number of conservative Yezidis, mainly men, attacked the cinema and the film director because they did not want the film to be shown. They described the film as 'ISIS propaganda'. It was not ISIS propaganda at all. While it was heavily criticising the ISIS brutality, the film main subject was the 'honour' code and the families' approach to this code. Some other Yezidis, mainly women, who were aware of this

---

[7] See, Amnesty International 2007.
[8] See, Ranharter and Stansfield 2016.

societal code and also suffered from family and societal pressures, raised their voices during the incident, and supported the film and the director against the mobs of the protesters. The leader of attackers was shouting in Kurdish: 'Yezidis are not Kurds. Yezidis are not Muslim. All Muslims, including Kurds betrayed us. We speak Kurdish but we don't want to describe ourselves as Kurds anymore. We are not Kurds.' One of the Yezidi women stood up in her seat and shouted back at the group, directeing her words at the leader: 'Don't you feel shame? You speak Kurdish and you claim that you are not Kurds. Who are you to decide that Yezidis are not Kurds? I am Yezidi. I am Kurdish. I am a woman and supporting this film. You and ISIS are of the same mind. All of you are the enemies of women. You are against any change. Kurdish women went to Sinjar. They fight for you. They save you. But you escaped to the diaspora for your own safety, instead of fighting in Sinjar and protecting our community.' There was chaos and not just a verbal but a physical fight between these two groups. Only after the arrival of several police cars and many police officers, was the film director, Mehmet Aktas, able to show the film. But the disruption, disagreement and shouting continued during and after the film. The mobs were almost all men and young men. The voices against these mobs were mainly women's. While men were protecting the traditional laws and were critical of anyone who questioned those rules, women wanted to be at the forefront and pushed for change.

According to the accounts of several women who managed to escape, ISIS members tried to take away the razor blades which many captive Yezidi Kurds were using to cut their own wrists and kill themselves, because they were afraid that they were not going to be accepted by their family and community even if they managed to escape from ISIS. One of these young Yezidi women was the famous Nadia Murad. Her mother and six brothers were killed by ISIS, and she was forced into sexual slavery when she was still in high school. However, she managed to survive the sexual and emotional violence and escaped from ISIS. Later she was awarded the Nobel Peace Prize because of her brave resistance, not only to ISIS, but also her own community, and for challenging the patriarchal tradition and fighting for gender equality. Whereas the majority of Yezidi Kurdish women who survived refused to be identified or go public to talk about the ISIS atrocities, Murad bravely advocated helping survivors. She was not afraid to talk to journalists, to be photographed and lobbied internationally so that the world could recognise the genocide against Yezidi Kurds. She wrote in *The New York Times* on 10 February 2018:

> I was one of thousands of Yazidi women kidnapped by the Islamic State and sold into slavery. I endured rape, torture and humiliation at the hands of multiple militants before I escaped. I was relatively lucky; many Yazidis went through worse than I did and for much longer. Many are still missing.

She was not alone in telling the world about the brutality of ISIS, but unique in trying to push for change in Yezidi society's patriarchal traditions and the recognition of women's rights internationally at the same time. Several Kurdish women militias explained that some of their members and even guerrilla leaders went to the representatives of Yezidi communities in the Sinjar Mountains, to their leading members in diasporas, and most importantly to the families of the captive women and girls in order to change their perception of honour and to welcome their women if and when they escaped from ISIS. They were also supported by some progressive male and most Yezidi women activists. The pressure from the international community and media also played an important role. Finally, after these collaborative pressures, in April 2019, for the first time in history, the spiritual leadership of the Yezidi community decided that the children of captive women and girls who were born to an Islamic State father, usually as the result of rape, should be welcomed by society and their families. The members of the Kurdish women's movement and activists were happy with this decision. However, shortly afterwards the decision was radically changed: these same children were no longer accepted because of the strict rules of the Yezidi faith, and also the anger from the conservative members of society. The captive women were only given the chance to return after abandoning their children. Yezidi belief doesn't recognise a child as Yezidi unless both parents are Yezidi. Karim Sulaiman, a spokesman for the Yezidi Supreme Spiritual Council supported the reverse decision of the religious authority during his interview with *The Washington Post* on 30 July 2019: 'To make special examples in this case would be to whitewash the result of the Yezidi genocide . . . in this case, religion and society just cannot accept them.'

Mothers of these children were left with two options: to leave their children behind; or to live outside the community as a non-Yezidi person. In order to save their children, some women claimed that they had got pregnant by a Yezidi man during their captivity. While almost all Yezidi men captured by ISIS were killed, some teenage Yezidi boys remained alive but were forced to convert to Islam. Other women, who did not hide the fact that their children were fathered by an ISIS man, were supported by their families and allowed to bring their children into the community. Shortly afterwards, however, attitudes changed and these families were described as people without honour. Such families and young mothers were not left much choice but to give their baby or small child away. Some women, who did not want to give up their children, refused to return their families. Some stayed in northern Syria, where the Rojava autonomous administration provided shelter; others even stayed married to their captors.

I managed to talk to two captive women in Germany; one was active within the community, the other stayed married to her Sunni Muslim husband, father of her child. More than 1,000 Yezidi women and children were accepted by the German government after the recent crimes. Germany has been a country where the majority of Yezidi Kurds live outside their homeland, the Sinjar region. While both women could not find the words to describe their time of captivity under Islamic State rule and continuous rape, they were clearly surprised by the level of conservatism within their own community, especially after such genocide. The former captive and new activist, Rojin, said:

> Our religious leaders stated that our girls and women, who were captured brutally by a barbaric terrorist group, are honourable members of our community. They should not be ashamed. They claimed that 'these women and girls are more holy than us because of what they went through and their brave actions for survival is something of an important example for us'.

However, she was also very openly critical of her own society and religious leaders. According to Rojin, as the world glorified the Kurdish women's movement without focusing on the reality, Yezidi community and religious leaders have also exaggerated and held them as 'holy persons' without welcoming their children, demonstrating the whole societal conservatism and inequality. The other woman, Ferah, who stayed married to her elderly Sunni husband and become one of his multiple wives, shared her journey:

> I was captive for a year. I cannot describe the horror of rape. Some days, multiple people were visiting us and forcing us. Rape and violence were regular and normal events. When I was told that a man, elderly Sunni man from Germany wanted to pay a good money and take me as his fourth wife to Germany, I accepted straight away. Nothing was going to be worse than what I was facing. I knew that I would not be accepted by my family and community even if I escaped from the brutality anyway. I met him. He was respected by ISIS members. He took me to Germany. I have a child now. He is not bad man. Sometimes he tells me that he paid huge money, around 10,000 euros for me and I should be grateful to him. This is not nice. I feel like a slave, a piece of meat, but I don't want to leave him now. I don't have a place to go if I leave him. Our Yezidi community here, in Germany, is as conservative as the one in Sinjar.

Both Yezidi women explained separately that, the 'honour' code does not only exist among Yezidi Kurds in the Sinjar Mountains, but it is also very strong in the diaspora. I also observed another case where a different Yezidi woman, mother of four children, was sold for 200,000 euros in Berlin. This case was brought to the Kurdish court but was dismissed because her family did not want to pursue it and the unofficial Kurdish Berlin court judge was told to drop the case.

Both captive women, Rojin and Ferah, repeatedly mentioned that when they were attacked by ISIS, their own Arab, Turkmen and some Sunni Kurdish neighbours helped ISIS and gave them detailed information about Yezidi families, young, unmarried women and young boys. Some of them were sold several times and buyers were even selling them on to another person. There was a modern sex-slave market during and after the war. Rojin shared her experience: 'We were betrayed by almost everybody. First, by our own Sunni neighbours. They co-operated with ISIS and gave information about us. Second, the Iraqi government and forces who were there to protect us, did not do much to help. Third, the international community did not take any action in the beginning and let us be slaughtered. Many of our women are still in the hands of people who sell them as a commodity.' Rojin went on: 'Only a small number of Kurdish guerrillas, mainly women, defended us. Some of our families had old-style Russian Kalashnikov guns, and they used them for defence. Together they sacrificed themselves to avoid the total annihilation of the Yezidi community.'

Kurdish forces in Syria, the People's Protection Units (YPG), pushed ISIS out of Kobane in January 2015. The Kobane victory was the beginning of the end of the Islamic State. Many Peshmerga forces in Iraqi Kurdistan also waged war against Islamic State and lost thousands of their members. In addition, the Peshmerga forces helped Kurdish forces in Syria and local militias inside Iraq to win battles against the Islamic State. Kurds in Iraq and Syria were also helped by the international coalitions, led by the United States and the United Kingdom, which provided the air power, modern weapons, technical support and training.[9] However, on the ground, thousands of Kurdish troops, around 35 per cent of them – 15,000 fighters were women – took part in the actual battles against ISIS first, and then against Turkey in Syria, and many of them lost their lives between 2014 and 2020. On many occasions, the YPJ and the Kurdish women's army carried out independent operations. Hundreds of these women were battling in Kobane against ISIS and played an important role in the creation of Rojava's autonomy.[10] Many surviving young Yezidi Kurdish girls, who looked up to Kurdish women fighters in Syria and Turkey, later also took arms, joined local militias and took action for the liberation of their villages, towns and cities from ISIS.

Increasing numbers of female fighters, women politicians, activists, associations and their independent women's courts have strengthened the power of women's associations and self-determination as part of the Kurdish movement. Kurdish activist and academic, Dilar Dirik wrote in *Al Jazeera* on 29 October 2014: 'No matter how fascinating it is – from an orientalist perspective – to discover a women's revolution among Kurds, my generation grew up recognising women fighters as a natural element of our identity.' Maybe the world was hearing about the role of the Kurdish women's movement for the first time and preferred to glorify it without giving much

[9] Thornton 2015.
[10] See, Del Re 2015; Tax 2016.

attention to the politics of these powerful women, however many decades of struggle lay behind that power. This last action against ISIS, and changing at some level the local 'honour' code, was not the only battle that Kurdish women had. It was just the most recent one.

Kurdish Women's Struggle

The idea of 'democratic confederacies' and 'gender equality' have been two important faces of Kurdish politics over recent decades, both introduced and supported by Öcalan since the early 2000s. The claim has been to change the societal form of historic injustices, and give back women's rights which have been taken away for a long time by the religious supporters of a patriarchal society. The shift from nationalism to democratic confederalism and the claim that democratic autonomy can exist within the borders of the existing nation state, has opened a space for the Kurdish women's movement to institutionalise a new type of power structure, to extend its domestic authority to society and create full equality within the movement.

Historically, older women in particular enjoyed respect and authority within the family circle and society and took part in some decision-making jointly with the men. However, young and newly married women have been oppressed, deprived of their individual, sexual, social, educational, economical and legal rights and expected to be servants not just to male members of the family but to the older women too. Most women were not even be allowed to marry the man they love. There were mainly arranged marriages, which is still common among some Kurds in Iraq, Turkey, Syria and Iran. The only way for women to marry the man of their choice was to be abducted by that man and then the family would usually agree with the marriage as long as the abductor paid compensation, but this abduction could also lead to a blood feud between families. Even if the woman was abducted against her will, and if she was raped during that abduction, in most cases she would still be blamed, not welcomed by her family and in some cases she might even be killed by her own family, as discussed above in the example of Du'a Khalil Aswad's case. This is not just limited to Kurdish society in Iraq, but also happens in Turkey, Syria and Kurdish diaspora communities in Europe.[11]

---

[11] See, Belge 2008 and 2011; Tas 2016d.

When we look at the historical background of Kurdish society, the practice of different religions, social developments and the reality of the Kurdish region, to be occupied and ruled by different nation states and their centralised governments has put women in a weak position. When the authority of the state and religion deal only with men, then women usually lose their power, if they have any, and become passive actors in society. The nation states in the Middle East have oppressed both the identity of Kurds and also women almost equally. Gulistan, a Kurdish active guerrilla and one of the leading diaspora organisers, explained in Germany in September 2017:

> My mother was very upset when I was born because I was not a boy. She would not fully be accepted as a 'proper' women and mother if she did not give birth to several boys. In our village, everybody wanted to have a boy even though they have many boys already. To have boys meant to have important power against their enemies and also economically it was important as they could earn and bring money into house. For these reasons, I always wanted to be a boy. They were the strongest ones. They had the freedom to do whatever they like to do. They were in charge of everything and made all the decisions. They were the ones who were giving life and taking our life and I wanted to be one of them. I didn't want to be like my mum who married in her very early teens, gave birth to eight children and worked all the time, day and night. She was a very active slave for all of us, especially for my brothers and father. No, I wanted to be like a man and take part in a man's world. This was one of the important reasons I joined the Kurdish movement.

Rozerin, another Kurdish women, former guerrilla and acting as an unofficial Kurdish Court judge in Diyarbakır, shared her feelings of love and hate towards her father when she was a young girl:

> My father was a macho man. He walked differently than most men in our village. He had a serious and angry face all the time. He never showed any emotion to anybody aside from anger. He never said to anybody, including my mum and siblings, that he loved them. He would put his jacket over his shoulder, always without his arms in it. He always had one of the most beautiful, fancy rosaries in his hand. He held his cigarette in a very manly way and he always had a cigarette between his lips. He always had a gun and one which could easily be seen in his waistband. His head always was held high

and his every word was an order and definite. He did not negotiate anything with anybody. When he said something, it had to be done urgently. When my brothers did something silly, he would get angry with them and say, 'Don't act like a girl, be like a man' (*kiz gibi davranma, erkek gibi ol*). My mother was totally the opposite of my father. I wanted to be like my father. It was not only my love for him, but it was necessary for me to love him and be like him, as I believed during those times that such feelings and actions could help me to survive under such a masculine power. I loved him as much as I hated him.

During the last four decades not just Kurds in general but most importantly young Kurdish women have been fighting for their real identity and equal position in society, and also within the Kurdish movement. After a long and continuous battle, Kurdish women, who historically, like many other women around the world, carry the burden, have gained some power, not just at the political level, but have pushed for societal change involving full gender equality. Of course, this development, a revolution with women's emancipation at its heart, has not been a very easy process.

The Kurdish movement, from the start, was a mainly male-dominated movement. After the 1990s, when the conflict was no longer only between the Kurdish guerrilla and Turkish state forces, but also between Turkish and Kurdish societies in general, then the number of women within the movement as fighters increased. Especially when the state intensified hostilities and institutionalised the discrimination against Kurdish people, their lands and Kurdish students, a huge number of young men and women, especially university students, joined the PKK, and the number of women was no longer small but was made up a substantial percentage. The PKK's third congress between 25 and 30 October 1986,[12] was an important meeting for discussing the role of women within the party for the first time. However, the discussion

---

[12] Between 1978 and 2020, the PKK officially organised eleven congresses and six conferences where the new structure, policies and aims were discussed and important decisions were taken. This does not include small meetings, especially foundation meetings between 1976 and 1978 in Ankara. The PKK's first and also the foundation congress was organised between 26 and 27 November 1978 in Fis village, Lice, Diyarbakır. Twenty-three delegates attended this first congress, during which it was agreed that Kurdish tribal leaders, especially those who had a close relationship with the state, were to be the main enemies and target for the movement. It was the congress of cleaning the field and the internal enemies before any war

was mainly around 'the question of women and family' and women's roles within the family. After the 1990s the discussion moved from motherhood to 'the question of men and women' within the party. The discussion of 'the gender issue within society' had to wait until after 1995. The equality between

against the Turkish state forces. However, the party name, PKK, was not decided by this first congress, it was decided on 5 April 1979 by the centre committee meeting. The second congress took place between 22 and 25 August 1982 in Beka Valley in Lebanon, where the movement carried out its early training. During this congress, the military and political wings were created and the decision to return to Kurdistan (Kurdish region in south-east Turkey) and prepare to start operations against the Turkish state was made. The fourth congress between 26 and 31 December 1990 and was important as a way of spreading the Kurdish movement and resistance to all Kurdish towns and cities, and most importantly to create liberated cities and towns. This congress took place in a Kurdish region in Turkey, Haftanin, and was organised without the presence of Öcalan. It is described as 'the Congress of Guerrilla'. The fifth congress was organised between 8 and 27 January 1995 in Haftanin. The membership of the PKK was increased with the aim of war against Turkish state. The sixth congress took place between 12 January and 18 February 1999. It was the time when Öcalan was under pressure by the Turkish state and could not find a safe country. The congress started under the active leadership of Öcalan, but he was arrested on 15 February, before the final meeting of the congress. In the same year, in May 1999, the Kurdistan National Congress (*Kongra Netewiya Kurdistan* – KNK) was created, which aimed not just to focus on Kurdish regions in Turkey but the whole of Kurdistan within the borders of Iraq, Syria, Iran and Turkey. The PKK organised its seventh congress, without Öcalan, between 1 and 23 January 2000, with the aim of creating a 'Democratic Republic' in the Middle East. Between 4 and 10 April 2002, during the eighth congress, the PKK changed its name into KADEK – Kurdistan Freedom and Democratic Congress (*Kongreya Azadiya Demokrasiya Kurdistan*). However, just three years later, during the ninth congress between 28 March and 4 April 2005, the name of the PKK would be reused after the new names were widely rejected by the Kurdish people. The ninth congress also decided the new symbols of the PKK and the co-chair system, which was to introduce full gender equality. The same year, on 17 May 2005, the Unity of Kurdistan Communities (KCK - *Koma Ciwakên Kurdistan*) was created and become an umbrella organisation of the movements and parties connected with the PKK in Syria, Iraq, Turkey and Iran. The representatives were selected from different parts of Kurdistan. The tenth congress took place between 21 and 30 August 2008. After the suggestion from Öcalan, the previous congress decision of the 'co-chair' system was replaced with 'the Party Coordination'. The PKK's last, eleventh congress was organised during the peace talks with Turkey, between 5 and 13 September 2013. A new approach and constitutions were accepted, according to a summary of Öcalan's books, 'Manifesto of Democratic Society' and 'Defending a Nation'. The number of the centre committee was increased to fifty-five during this congress.

men and women, and the acceptance of the co-chair system only became a main topic during the PKK's ninth congress, which was organised in 2005, between 28 March and 4 April.

Leyla Zana's election in 1991 was an important symbolic development for the Kurdish women's movement. But real participation and gender equality has taken longer to achieve than Zana's election. Kurdish women were not given equal rights straight away by their male comrades when part of the armed forces, nor at a local and national political level.

Kurdish women joined the Kurdish guerrilla movement for different reasons. While many of them had a dream of creating an egalitarian Kurdistan, some others tried to escape from their village, town or city and oppression from their own family, school or workplace. Others had romantic ideas of being part of the revolution when it happens. Some preferred the mystical side of the Kurdish mountains to their regular lives. However, not many have found what they dreamed of. In a short time, they faced another state-type authoritarian rule, structure and discipline. The romanticism was replaced with real-life challenges. Those who had dreamed of freedom, love and adventure lost their life in a short time during the battles or had to wait decades for any equal rights. Some of them had to adopt even more conservative values and strict dress codes in the early years. For example, female guerrillas were forced to wear headscarves by the male-dominated Kurdish movement itself until the early 1990s. The movement did not want any conflict with the conservative part of the society, and maintained that society was not ready to see women not covering their heads. This rule did not change easily and the headscarf was replaced with a military style of head covering, but only for women. Even during the summer heat, women were not allowed to have short sleeves or to roll up the long sleeves of their thick uniforms. Most of the former and active male and female guerrillas who were willing to talk agreed that there were some harsher rules and laws for women. Another important issue was love. It was not possible, at least for women. Women were imprisoned, punished and even killed if they had an intimate relationship. They were seen as 'a dangerous evil' 'who can bring down man'. Zozan, one of PKK's long-term active guerrilla and cadre trainers, who was in Germany for the transnational activity and training of the members, explained in September 2017:

I was born in a village belonging to Idil, but between Idil and Cizre, in 1974. My family is a big family with a great influence. A family that did not integrate with the state throughout its history. A family coming from a culture of resistance. A family with many Kurdish enemies who especially have a connection with the state. But lastly my family is a feudal family. In this family, there was always resistance, always introducing themselves with their Kurdish identity. We have grown up with this culture. And the result of this culture and my female identity, which had to resist every aspect of life – not just against the state but also against my family and its feudal culture – was to lead me to join the movement in 1990. Our family members were arrested and tortured during and after the 1980 military coup in Turkey. In the late 80s, when the spirit of the Kurdish movement reached my family, they agreed to join the Kurdish resistance. Our family was especially influenced by the young guerrillas of the Kurdish movement who come to our village. Not just my family, many nearby villagers were also influenced by the movement and started supporting them. The influenced families were also convincing other families and extending the support network. I was supported strongly by my family, especially my mum, when I decided to join the movement. They prepared my luggage for the journey. My mother made me special socks for the difficult mountain conditions. She baked her special bread for me. They were proud of me. Many other families showed increased respect towards my family after I joined the active fight. But some other villages informed the state and they continued to arrest and torture members of my family. After long training, I took responsibility and joined the movement's activities in Botan, Behdine, Qandil, Maxmur Camp, Rojava and Europe. Of course, it was not easy for a woman to be a militant in the early years. The movement was new and had to establish tough state-like conditions. Some of our friends were punished heavily for small mistakes. My first ten years were very difficult. On several occasions I was hugely disappointed. My birthday is 28 July, and I joined the movement on 12 July. I have been celebrating 12 July as my birthday since 2001, after, as a women member, we were welcomed and respected by our male comrades. My role now is to establish a women's academy in Kurdistan and also in Europe and to increase women's equality not just within the party, but within society as well.

In the 1990s the number of women within the movement increased, but they experienced different treatment under different local military leaders. Some local commanders were taking decisions without the knowledge of the central authority. If you were lucky enough to have a more tolerant and understanding male leader – most group leaders during 1990s were male – then you could have more equal rights. Otherwise, you could suffer a lot. After a while, especially after 1996, women asked for more authority, responsibility and even a separate branch, but their wishes were not taken into account. Spring 1998 was the first time there was an order directly from Öcalan for women members to create a group made up of sixty or seventy women to go to Semdinli district (a Kurdish town in Turkey), to organise a women's military branch and take action against the Turkish military independently from male leadership. When the women formed this group and arrived in their planned town, a very short time after their arrival, and before any real militarily confrontation with Turkish forces, one of the male deputy leaders from the central command, without Öcalan's orders, asked the group to drop their plan and return to the main camp immediately. Öcalan was in Damascus during that time and did not know much about his deputy's new orders. The leader of the women's group refused to obey the order unless instructions came from Öcalan directly. The male leadership again ordered them to return to the camp otherwise they would be punished. The women did not only refuse, they also turned off their communication with the deputy leadership and continued to ignore their orders unless Öcalan ordered them directly. After this disobedience from the women's branch, the male deputy leader sent seventy to eighty male guerrillas during the night to ambush the female guerrillas' guard. Their weapons were seized, they were all arrested and made to surrender like enemy soldiers, lined up one after another, and taken to the main camp directly as prisoners. The members of the women's groups, especially the leaders were punished. First, all of them were sent to separate places as prisoners for days without much contact with the rest of guerrillas. Later, they were given the task of looking after twelve to fifteen cows which were taken by the guerrillas from nearby villages. The anger and revenge of male leaders continued against 'disobedient' women leaders. They were punished and were sent to difficult and dangerous locations to fight. One of them told me: 'We were sent to be killed. It was an illegal, wild justice, which Kurdish women have already experienced at the hands of their father, husband, state, but now by our own movement. That was our kind of death penalty because we didn't obey the deputy's decision, even though that decision went against that of the leader, Öcalan.' Another former female guerrilla of that group explained that, 'Öcalan was informed later and even though he did not like to be countermanded, he could not do much for two reasons: first, his authority was not fully followed by some other male leaders and local commanders, and very often decisions were taken without his authority; second, there was pressure from Turkey against his presence in Syria and he was focusing on this danger which was threatening his life and also the future of the movement.'

Zozan, active guerrilla and cadre trainer, also shared one of her experiences, which shows that she wasn't the only successful female member to face difficulties, especially during the 1990s:

We had increasing numbers of female fighters but our teachers, trainers and leaders were male. We were asked and forced to cook for male guerrillas instead of taking part in the active fighting. We were given logistic roles. We were closing some roads, creating barriers for the state forces to enter but were not trusted to take part in the active fighting very much. Some of our male commanders were not even socialising or eating with us, or talking to us. Women were not to be trusted and thought to give information away too easily. Because of this, they did not give us full information when they sent us on military operations. I reminded my commanders several times that we were all there to fight for our national liberation. We were all equal and, if necessary, would die for our aims. I myself faced gender discrimination within the military and within the political movement countless times. When we had any success, this was oppressed or ignored by some men. Women's success was not always welcome. I have been a very successful military leader, but some of my male comrades did not like it. For example, during one specifically risky battle, our male military commander deliberately posted my female battalion and myself to a very dangerous location. It was very clear from the beginning that the enemies were close by and that we were going to be in danger. We were purposely sent to there to be killed. It was a deliberate plan against me and my team. The local commander was not happy about my success and feared that I would become his commander in the future. We were forced to go without sufficient weapons and information. We lost three of our fighters, and only managed to survive by luck. When those of us who survived returned, my military commander told me: 'I wish you were dead.' These attitudes might have decreased since then, but there is still some level of resentment and resistance against successful female fighters and leaders.

The number of women and their successes were not just increasing within the movement, but their mothers, sisters and close relatives took part in large street protests, organised demonstrations, creating awareness of the state oppression in Turkey and beyond. However, it is not always easy for active female guerrillas to feel comfortable talking in a critical way, even about past actions. Only after several meetings did they give more detailed information. The former guerrillas who left the movement for different reasons – from ideological and political shifts to preferring a different lifestyle, intimacy, family or education – talk openly. The accounts of many former and active female guerrillas clarified that there was no proper justice and many contradictory and discriminatory decisions were taken before and after the arrest of Öcalan. There was not much institutional structure or proper organisation. The war, active combat, resistance and to be in the mountains was regarded as a real man's job for a long time. Women were seen as weak. They could only be assistants to men, preparing their food while men fight. This attitude had given men absolute power for a long time. An active female PKK guerrilla, Beriwan, explained in October 2017:

> In the early years of my time with the movement, first we [women] had to forget about our identity as women, which was weak and belonged to domestic life. We had to become more masculine, be like a man to be part of a man's world. The war was designed according to men's perspective and needs. For example, the design of our toilets was only for use by men. The jokes and the stories of the war are usually very sexist and for the desire of men. But later our female identity became more important. Our leaders started to see women as tougher, strong and loyal fighters and the movement wanted us to become women again, the ones which we had to kill to be part of the movement in the first place. Everything was so confusing.

After Öcalan's arrest, aside from many other difficulties and pressures, some books were banned from the movement's library reading list and members had to give away some of their books. The writings of Omer Khayyam, Sartre and Erich Froom were among the 'most dangerous' books which were thought by the leadership to have a possible effect on the individual's sexuality and increase their desire for freedom. These books were also thought to encourage liberal critical voices, especially after the unexpected arrest of

Öcalan, and the central authority did not want this to happen during such turbulent times.

Gulten Kisanak also confirmed that they had to fight at every stage to secure women's rights and full equality, because of societal and political barriers.[13] Kisanak's own life reflects the development of the Kurdish women's movement. She is the opposite of Leyla Zana. She does not come from a well-known Kurdish family or a dominant Sunni background. She comes from a Kurdish Alevi background, which is doubly discriminated against in Turkey, ethnically as well as religiously. When she was a young university student, she took part in many political demonstrations against the military junta in 1980. She was sent to prison for her political activism. She faced torture which was also a very common process during and after the 1980s. She was kept in a dog kennel for days because of speaking Kurdish, and not Turkish. When she come out of prison, she worked as a journalist for years and continued her political activism. She worked as much as any active Kurdish man for the movement, but for a long time she had to wait to be recognised, to be given a leading role. She become the Mayor of Diyarbakır in 2014, but just two years later, in 2016, she was arrested again and has been in prison ever since. I managed to get to know her well during my field research, when I was stuck in Sur during the curfew in September 2015. Even during that time of heavy conflict, she organised a seminar for women's rights and equality. I was participating and observed that hundreds of women attended, while at the same time violent clashes were taking place on the other side of the city of Diyarbakır. She is a person with strong political principles of gender equality, who believes women can work as hard as men do, at any job, including that of firefighter, which is very unusual in the context of the Middle East. During her time in office, she often organised public seminars and conferences for gender equality. She told me that empiricial-based scientific knowledge and a human-rights-based morality would close all the loopholes created in society and repair the damage between the genders, as well as different ethnic, religious and language groups.

[13] The full interview with Gulten Kisanak, 'Kurdish women's battle continues against state and patriarchy' was published by *Open Democracy*, available at <https://www.opendemocracy.net/nadje-al-ali-latif-tas-g-ltan-ki-anak/kurdish-women-s-battle-continues-against-state-and-patriarchy-> (last accessed 12 October 2018). See, Al-Ali and Tas 2016a.

The main victory of Kurdish women was not only against the state preventing Kurds from being assimilated; it was also against patriarchal men and society. One of the Kurdish female politicians in Diyarbakır told me: 'Patriarchy and autocratic nation states have similar mindsets, similar souls and similar aims. Both are based on inequality and the imposition of hegemony and one single identity. Both approaches are very selfish and do not want to share power and positions equally.' The Kurdish women's movement has managed to transform Kurdish patriarchal men as well as the patriarchal mind set of the Turkish state. While they were doing this, men and the Turkish state did not simply welcome them and let them have equal rights. According to many of my interviewees, it was not easy. There was huge resistance from men and the state, and this resistance still continues at different levels and in different forms. Autocratic states and men wanted to preserve their old ways, but in the end they had to accept at least some level of women's rights. Former co-Mayor of Diyarbakır, Firat Anli has acknowledged that this battle still continues, but he also believes that the Kurdish women's movement is strong enough to keep on fighting against the patriarchal society and state. Anli stated:

> This is the main reason why the Turkish state is afraid of Kurdish women more than men. They know that Kurdish women have pushed to change their patriarchal Kurdish men, and they are not going to give up the fight for their identity and equal rights against the state's patriarchal, discriminative approach. Kurdish women have been an important identity carrier for Kurds. Without Kurdish women, their fight and beliefs, Kurds could have easily been assimilated under other hegemonic approaches and identities.

Leading Kurdish female guerrillas, such as Sakine Cansiz, who was one of the founder members of the PKK, were important figures who opened the way for supporting gender equality and justice among the Kurdish movement. It was no surprise that the Kurdish women's court in Berlin, and many other court rooms and venues, including Kurdish politicians' and activists' rooms in Turkey and northern Syria (Rojava) have been decorated with photos and murals of Sakine Cansiz and her colleagues. Sakine Cansiz was assassinated in Paris on 9 January 2013. She told me in December 2012, just weeks before her assassination, when in Berlin organising a demonstration in support of a prisoners' hunger strike in Turkey:

> If you ask me what my main purpose for Kurdish society has been during my more than three decades of struggle and fight, I would say two main things: to bring justice to women, and to create an equal, fair, alternative justice for Kurdish people. I never believe in prison. I hate prison. Prison is not just in prison; prison is everywhere today. Many people have made their own prison, especially under the capitalist and authoritarian systems, without recognising they are in prison. I thought my father's house, our town and the state I was living under was a prison for me, and I escaped from them all and rejected them all. When I was in a Turkish prison, I felt sorry for some guards; they had to act like animals against us for their salary and to please the autocratic regime. Many our friends are on hunger strike now at the prison, against such people and their conditions. I am not going to create something for others which I don't believe for myself. There are many ways to make people behave better. Sometimes make them get re-educated or read a book. This also can be a harsh punishment if they have never read a book in their life. Our people are the judges of our system. They are able to elect and reject their own judges.

The existence and success of Kurdish female fighters and female politicians in very difficult war conditions has changed some men's attitudes to the role of women. Many Kurdish women lost their lives during combat and become martyrs (*shahid*). In the past, especially before the 2000s, this had been regarded as an honour only associated with men. Many women have faced torture in Turkish prisons,[14] and this treatment has not only been reserved solely for the guerrillas; many Kurdish female students, activists, artists, journalists, politicians and mothers of these groups have also suffered the same fate. Women do not just fight inequality outside prison; they also continue their struggle in prison against security guards and state forces. A female Kurdish artist, Zehra Dogan, was imprisoned after the 2015 conflicts because of her critical writings and photo-realist paintings of the state actions. She had to continue her work secretly, using the back of letters, or on bedcovers using women's menstrual blood and food as these were only available resource

---

[14] For torture in the Diyarbakır military prison, see Zeydanlioglu 2009.

for her painting. She was not even allowed to have paper, pen and paints for her work. Gulten Kisanak explained in September 2015:

> My own life story has followed the development of the Kurdish women's movement. In the 1980s, I was imprisoned in Diyarbakır prison. This had notoriously brutal conditions, with torture and killings. To be Kurdish, to be a woman and to be leftist tripled the difficulties for me. I was kept in a dog kennel for six months because I refused to say 'I am not a Kurd but a Turk.' Our older women friends, our mothers' age were tortured because they could not speak Turkish. I still have signs of torture from those days on my body. This prison was a place for me to question everything about humanity.

During the earliest times of Kurdish political parties such as HEP and DEP, and also during the first establishment of HADEP, there was not a single female representative at the city and town level. After that, two or three women were symbolically included, but this was not at all meaningful. Society was different in those days; when there was any political occasion or event, Kurdish male representatives were asked to bring their wives and children as well – but this inclusivity was also the beginning of the Kurdish women's movement. Women had just started questioning. Gulten Kisanak continued:

> The 1990s were especially difficult for the Kurdish movement. The state was oppressive and applied considerable pressure. Women experienced those difficulties and paid a huge price. Women organised and led many demonstrations against the state brutality in villages and towns. Many of our female and male friends were arrested, tortured and killed. They had to defend themselves during their trials. They read and researched about their rights. Women not only learnt about Kurdish rights and freedoms, but as women who were simultaneously oppressed by the state and by society, they recognised their rights, their equality with men, and their freedom. This was an important element of the enlightenment of Kurdish women.

The PKK's indoctrination and education has also played an important role, and both on a theoretical and practical level the role of and respect for women in society has increased. The initiative of mothers who lost their children, husbands, brothers, sons and daughters, brought the silent majority, including housewives, into the political arena. Kurdish women's organisations and activities were not just in the cities, but also in smaller towns and villages. In addition to their daily political activities, such as taking part in demonstrations, preparing petitions and helping those in need, these women continued to carry the heavy burden of family and social responsibilities. Their peaceful activism and rejection of all types of violence, while still facing police brutality, has increased women's power not just among the Kurdish society, but also invoked sympathy from some Turkish feminists and leftists. Turkish feminism's strong connection with and support from the Kemalist authoritarianism was challenged by the Kurdish women's approach. The state feminism's long decades of silence and blindness against state oppression was as problematic as the authoritarian state itself. The Kurdish women's new active political stance meant that the women's issues and Kurdish issues became equally as important as each other; both issues became international, gained support from international left-wing groups and even some right-wing political movements.

During the difficult times of the 1990s, some autonomous women's organisations were established. In 1996, the Kurdish movement created a separate women's millitary branch to help with demands from female combatants.[15] Women were already making up almost 30 per cent of the Kurdish guerrilla movement.[16] Increasing female participation in the fight against Turkey helped the development of the system of female political representatives. In 1999, for the first time, three Kurdish women were elected as local mayors. This number more than tripled in 2004 and the Kurdish movement had fourteen female mayors. Most importantly, the co-chairing was also started unofficially in 2004 by the Kurdish political movement. However, women were pressured by their male co-chairs to postpone their wishes and they were perceived as assistants for a while. After 2007, women became more visible and powerful. The 2007 elections were revolutionary for both Kurdish and Turkish women: eight out of twenty-six Kurdish MPs were women.[17] Women became more confident as co-chairs and men had to accept them as equals.

[15] Al-Ali and Tas 2018c.
[16] Ozcan 1999.
[17] See, Çağlayan 2011; Al-Ali and Tas 2016a, 2018b and 2018c.

According to Gulten Kisanak, 'the aim was to put new bricks on top of the existing ones and so to move forward women's issues'. Gulten Kisanak, Ayla Akat and many other Kurdish female politicians and activists also acknowledged that the 40 per cent quota for women had been part of their party policy since 2002. There was a huge barrier for this to come about in practice and the hardest battle with their male comrades was to get the implementation of a women's quota and equality on who was going to decide about women's candidates. In the end, women won the battle and nominated their own candidates but it was not easy. A Kurdish female political activist, Sara, stated:

> Women are very aware of the situation that some men are really opposed to gender equality, while other men have internalised the idea that 'If the leader says it is right, then it must be right.' There are differences between generations . . . Some men are still not willing to follow party rules. Many Kurdish women believe that Kurdish men and the Turkish state have the same attitude towards women. Both have power. If we do not disrupt this power then men will be authoritarian like the state.

While many women pushed for change, especially Öcalan's role, his new ideas of gender equality and contribution cannot be underestimated.[18] Many Kurdish female and male politicians and activists expressed the opinion that if it was left to Kurdish men alone, they were not going to make these changes easily. Still there are many barriers. Gulten Kisanak pointed another important problem:

> Sometimes, there is a risk of ignoring your identity as a woman. So, for instance, if you go to a mosque, they say, you are welcome, because you are the mayor. But I do not want to forget my identity as a woman. I would like to be welcomed as a woman. This is a crucial point in our struggle and if individuals give in to the temptation of privilege linked to status, we will lose our struggle. Individual women will succeed but not women collectively. Women have to resist falling into the trap of acting like men.

Gender inclusion in the early years and pushing for gender equality meant that the Kurdish movement found it more difficult to get support from

[18] See, Öcalan 2009b, 2011b, 2013 and 2015; Tax 2016; Al-Ali and Tas 2016a and 2016b.

traditional patriarchal society in a short time in comparison with other religious or jihadist movements. Firat Anli, lawyer and a former co-Mayor of Diyarbakır, explained that if the Kurdish movement's strategy was constructed according to a radical religious belief, then they could have had societal support and reached their nationalist aims in a very short time. A Kurdish female activist and politician, Elif, who took part in the peace process and sat at the table with Öcalan between 2013 and 2015 in prison explained:

> During the peace negotiations and debates at the prison, I was very comfortable. Of course, in the beginning you are a little reluctant because you don't know the atmosphere but Mr Öcalan was very comforting in this aspect. Even the welcoming/greetings in the beginning were very different. Mr Öcalan was congratulating the women's movement and said that we were an element in the process of finding a solution. That's why we were there. But from the state side this was not expressed. During the debates, state representatives never asked the women representative about their opinions. We were invisible for them even when we were sitting in front of them. They were negotiating with men and we were silenced when we tried to say something, whereas Mr Öcalan repeatedly asked, 'What do the women have to say?', 'Did the women's movement debate this already?'

Many of my Kurdish interviewees believed that to have modernist and leftist ideology and to organise people according to their needs for an equal ethnic and gender identity, within a changing society, is much more difficult. Without exploiting religious ideologies, the role of the mosque and the power of imams, it is not easy to start a revolution in the Middle East. Many conservative and nationalist Kurdish people who I interviewed also criticised the PKK and Öcalan because of their gender approach and for postponing the national cause for that reason. Many of them claimed that it is not their business to support modernist, leftist, socialist ideology which focuses on the rights of women and the class struggle. They wanted the Kurdish movement to focus only on the national identity and the creation of an independent Kurdistan. For them nationalist needs are the most important and should come before everything else. They believe this approach would help produce a Kurdish independent state. Then, after that, they suggested, the Kurdish movement could focus on other things, including gender equality. This strong national-ist ideology exists among many Kurds, and the continuation of authoritarian state violence helps this approach to gain power.

Many Kurdish politicians and activists agree that in the early 2000s the creation of a Women's Commission by the Kurds was part of a regular pro-cess. Like other commissions, this was more about PR than any real attempt at public engagement. It was not truly supportive of women's rights. After this first regular attempt, the Women's Commission was split into different branches. Of course, even these symbolic developments were not supported by the conservative, dogmatic members of the movement, and also the rep-resentatives of the authoritarian state. It was not just about dealing with men and the traditional Kurdish society. State law was also very supportive of the old traditions and inequalities and continued to erect specific barriers against gender equality. These barriers have increased under Erdoğan's authoritarian regime, so that, for example, if a man who raped a woman then marries her, he escapes imprisonment. Once again, the state laws are designed for authori-tarian and criminal men's needs.

When violence takes place against women by men, then those men are protected in many different ways by the state. This puts up a huge barrier to any real theoretical or practical development of gender equality. It is nothing new that the authoritarian nation state and patriarchy think and act in the same way. They are mutually interdependent. They want women to continue to do all necessary work at home, regardless of their roles outside the home. Of course, this ideology is not interested in women standing up for their own rights, inside and outside the home. This puts a special pressure on those women who have active and important roles outside home. For example, some of the wives of Kurdish male politicians come to Kurdish courts and complain about their violent husbands. Or at political demonstrations or seminars, they whisper threats to their husbands that they will complain to the court about their unacceptable behaviour at home. I have observed that some of these men take an important role in the Kurdish movement. The cases I watched showed that some of these men, in public, loudly support gender equality, but not at home, where some of them still enjoy their patri-archal lifestyle and behaviour. For this reason, the Kurdish political move-ment in Turkey and diaspora introduced a new approach. They started only to appoint people who demonstrate a commitment to gender equality both in public and at home and who pass a gender test when they apply to become a leader of an association, a mayor or MP.

After four decades of the development of the Kurdish women's movement, there are still many barriers which need to be challenged and removed. For example, polygamy has declined but has still not totally disappeared. In Kurdish traditional society, men usually have polygamous marriages. The Kurdish movement made very clear that any man who has two or more wives cannot take any official role or position with them. There was, and still is, huge resistance against this decision. Of course, some individual cases are extremely complicated. There is a real issue if a man feels forced to divorce one of his wives so that he can take an active part in Kurdish politics.

The Kurdish women's movement in Rojava (northern Syria) and Iraqi Kurdistan, especially during the Kobane and Sinjar Mountain resistance, made themselves known to the whole world. The YPJ (Women's Protection Units), itself is an outcome of the Kurdish political movement in the Middle East.[19] After some success of the women's movement in Turkey, Rojava, Iraqi Kurdistan and the diaspora, it has become routine for all official posts and at all levels to be filled by both a woman and a man. In this way, the Kurdish movement ensures 50-50 representation. But as with other Kurdish movement gender policies, there has been some resistance to this. Some of the leading members of the movement believed that 'the man should be the official and obvious co-chair while the women should be unofficial and symbolic'. Several men and also conservative women with important positions within the movement told me that 'men can be better leaders . . . Women may be nice but they are not well suited to leadership . . . Kurdish society is traditionalist and not yet ready for radical changes . . . At least at a funeral, women should cover their hair and stay separate from men.' All these criticisms and barriers are gently presented, but they betray strongly held patriarchal views and decrease the chance for full gender equality in the future.

Many Kurdish politicians, activists and community members, admitted that they were not expecting the co-chair system to be such a success. But it has changed the Kurdish and Turkish political tradition in some very

[19] In der Maur et al. 2015; Knapp et al. 2016; Tax 2016.

surprising ways. The June 2015 general election saw important successes for women at parliamentary level. The large number of women who were elected for the Kurdish-led HDP made a huge difference in the number of women in the Turkish parliament. The Turkish authoritarian regime was not happy about the success of Kurds, especially Kurdish women. After only a short time, intensive and extensive state violence erupted against all Kurdish political development. All this violence directly affected the results of the subsequent general election. A lot fewer women were elected in that election.

In recent years, Kurdish women have been seen as the 'most' dangerous Kurds by the Turkish political elite and some societal elements. It is not just Kurdish men but also Turkish politicians who feel threatened by the increasing power of Kurdish women. However, the Kurdish women have to be twice or even three times better than their male counterparts if they are to reach the same position. Firat Anli acknowledge this fact: 'That is how politics is designed unequally in our region. When a woman works hard and has some success then it is common for there to be many attempts to disgrace her. I believe that the full and equal participation of women in political and societal life will add much value. I hope women gain more power. I am ready and willing to transfer some of my own responsibilities to my female colleagues.'

It is also important to argue that the numbers do not represent real equality even if they are 50-50 per cent. The valuable and meaningful development of gender and societal equality is more important than achieving the statistical target of equal quota measurement. According to Goodhart's Law,[20] 'When a measure becomes a target, it ceases to be a good measure.'[21] In other words, when a political ideology sets a specific goal, the focus only turns to these aspects and all other equally important elements are usually ignored or put aside. When the target number is achieved, this is usually submitted as a 'great success'. The quantity ratio success might not represent the real societal facts. In contrast, as discussed in Chapter 1 with the example of the Cunning Figures, the institutional numbers of equal male and female candidates does not always represent

[20] Goodhart 1981.
[21] Strathern 1997.

any real signs of development. This specific-ratio focus may even have a negative effect by blocking any criticism for meaningful change.

Societal changes are more important than any target number for female representatives. The majority of Kurdish towns, cities, neighbourhoods and diasporic organisations have pushed for inclusion of gender equality at all levels. Some liberal critical Kurds believe that this is more important than to have a few seats more or less in the parliament. Early age or forced marriages and violence against women are still common.[22] Kurdish women in particular have faced extra hardship due to the continuous armed conflicts in the Middle East.[23] After the 2015 conflicts, when the Turkish authoritarian regime had replaced most of the Kurdish elected mayors with the state trustees, the first action of these trustees was to shut down centres for the protection of women's rights across south-east Turkey. Such centres were created by Kurdish-elected mayors for 'women and child victims of domestic violence, and promoted their engagement in social and political life'.[24] Ayla Akat explained in September 2015: 'Every month between twenty and thirty women are killed in Turkey. State violence is an important contributor to violence within families. Men embody the authoritarian attitude and physical violence of the state. Our male comrades are also representing the power of the state.'

Many of my interviews highlighted the correlation between the state violence and violence against women and the continuation of gender inequality. Firat Anli, as a lawyer and former co-Mayor of Diyarbakır shared his observations in September 2015: 'When men use violence at home against women, then those men are protected in many different ways by the state. This puts a huge barrier to any real theoretical or practical development of gender equality. The authoritarian nation state and patriarchy think and act in the same way. They are mutually interdependent.' Ayla Akat echoed what Anli said: 'We know that the state is very patriarchal. Seventy to eighty per cent of the Turkish and Kurdish population is very conservative.' Firat Anli concluded: 'We cannot claim that we are in a perfect position with gender equality yet and have come to a level from which we cannot go back. The danger still

---

[22] Tas 2016d; Ali 2015.

[23] Arat 2012; Al-Ali and Tas 2017.

[24] OHCHR 2017: 16.

continues. I have been part of the Kurdish political movement for a long time, since a very young age. I have seen a time when there was not a single female representative among us. Now we have many but the societal problems are almost the same as when I started my political career.' The Kurdish political movement may open a way for Kurdish women to have some level of equality with men, to move away from religious, tribal and societal pressure and control, to become politicians, guerrilla fighters, diplomats, and mayors, but under the movement's new code, some of them have found it difficult to enjoy their individuality and femininity, and to love and to be loved.

New Code of Gendered Relationship

Close friendship between male-male, male-female and female-female members is facing another important challenge within Kurdish movement, not just among the guerrilla fighters but also within the political and activist movement as well. Instead of friendship, which is seen to have some sexual or emotional motivation, comradeship is encouraged and supported. Comradeship conveys neutrality, and the shared aim of forming enemies and sacrificing lives. When two friends come close and share some private time together, talking at some distance from others, this is seen to be dangerous. Friends in such contexts are quickly questioned about their motives, and usually named and shamed if they don't take warnings seriously. A former female guerrilla, and current political activist in Diyarbakır, Zilan, claimed in May 2015:

> All comrades should be open and very close to each other. They cannot be part of a small group. Coupling, especially, is not permitted in the guerrilla movement. A very close relationship between two friends means that something is not right. It could be some flirtation, sexual relationship or plans to betray the movement. All these are not good for our movement.

Creating a new ethical, moral and political structure for the relationship between the same and different genders means establishing new grounds for the societal and judicial codes and limiting the freedom of choice between same and different sexes. The former leader of HDP, Selahattin Demirtaş, who has been imprisoned since 4 November 2016, admitted just a few days before his arrest during our meeting in London on 1 November 2016: 'Social conservatism and taboos around sexuality continue, and we need to address them in the future. However, while we are struggling with acute conflict and violence by the state, it is impossible to focus on this issue. Many of our women colleagues who have been trying to address the issue of sexuality have been arrested.'

While the relationship between two males is still not seen 'as a problem of homosexuality' or 'sexual relationship between men', as Foucault argues, it is still seen part of friendship in Kurdish and many other Middle Eastern contexts. However, for Foucault, 'The disappearance of friendship as a social relation and the fact that homosexuality was declared a social, political, and medical problem are part of the same process.'[25] Within the Kurdish movement, close friendships between men may not still be seen as a 'problem of homosexuality', but more about the betrayal of the movement. One of my interviewees, a female activist called Rosa, stated in Berlin in July 2017: 'It is not right if two men come very close, laugh very loudly, whisper something to each other, and walk away together from the group. I don't approve of such girly and homosexual attitudes.'

While male-female friendships are almost always seen to be on the grounds of sexual interest, or a plan to move away from the movement altogether, close friendships between females are also seen 'odd' or 'lesbian', which again has some sexual connotation and puts their close friendship into question. While such atomic relationships are labelled as a 'bad' or 'not acceptable'; instead, 'brotherhood of man', 'sisterhood of woman', and 'comradeship' are supported. While the first two categories aim to help organise a large gender group and platonic family relations without any sexual thought and desire, the third one is used as an umbrella term which includes everybody.

This controlling of individual relationships is not something which has just been invented naively by the Kurdish movement, but is part of the power-building, institution-building and state-making project. The creation of the modern nation state, the institutions of states and the management of these institutions has become more important than the individual's self-action and freedom. Sacrificing identity, body and mind for the nation and

---

[25] Foucault 1997: 171.

sovereignty is seen more important. Paul Rabinow, who edited Foucault's works on ethics, argued:

> The army, bureaucracy, administration, universities, schools, and so on – in the modern senses of these words – cannot function with such intense friendships. I think there can be seen a very strong attempt in all these institutions to diminish or minimize the affectional relations. I think this is particularly important in schools. When they started grade schools with hundreds of young boys, one of the problems was how to prevent them not only from having sex, of course, but also from developing friendships.[26]

An individual's feelings and friendships not just with another person, but also with their family are questioned and undermined with this new structure. The individual's attitudes to love or close relations with their family are questioned and seen as a weakness. Male are teased, bullied and told they 'miss being around their mother's knee – being tied to their mother's apron strings', 'act like a bourgeois child', or that they are 'not good enough to be a man', 'not brave enough', 'chocolate boy – softie'. Women members of the movement who may have close relationships with their family or who put their family first are also judged. They are considered 'to miss being a housewife', 'to have a small world', 'to have slavery attitude', to be 'mentally and physically weak', 'a production of the capitalist world', 'a bourgeois girl', 'a Barbie girl', 'a make-up girl'. Some real-life examples are helpful as a way of clarifying these societal codes.

The first example is Lamia Baksi (Doctor Cihan). She was a young girl who had just graduated from medical school and become a doctor in Sweden, but preferred to join the Kurdish movement in the mid-1980s. She and some of her friends, who were also educated, had different views and did not hesitate to speak out. She, together with another fifteen young and educated members, were allegedly executed in 1987 by the PKK's death squad. One of the main reasons for her execution was that she was seen to have pitiful bourgeois values and had not given up her lifestyle and habits and so created a bad example for others. Her brother, Lutfi Baksi, who become the leader of an opposition Kurdish party, the Participant and Democracy Party (KADEP), explained on 7 April 2013: 'Lamia was a doctor. We received the news of her death from the PKK publication Serxabun in 1991. All the young people who were killed

---

[26] Foucault 1997: 170–1.

at that time were educated, smart and questioning like Lamia. We still do not know the location of her grave. The PKK later self-criticised and gave her honour back, but we do politics, we don't have a blood feud with the PKK. They also understood their mistakes and have been critical of their actions.'

The second example is an elected Kurdish MP. In 2011, he had already submitted a statement to the official court filing for a divorce, when he was photographed with another woman in the Turkish tourist resort, Bodrum. Because he was viewed as having an affair, not following the movement's new gender and moral codes, despite having filed for a divorce, he was excluded from the BDP, Kurdish Political Party, for a year and not allowed to take part in any political organisation. His salary as MP was also paid directly to his wife as a punishment by the party. He fully divorced on 2 December 2011, but the societal punishment, gossip and rumours continued for years.

On the streets of his own hometown, Batman, where he was originally elected as MP, posters showing photographs of him and his new partner in swimsuits on the beach and drinking alcohol were hung on the walls around the city. The MP reacted to the news, gossip and also photographic attacks against him by stating that it was a friendly meeting and the alcohol belonged to their friends. He was desperate to stop this societal criminalisation, but he could not save his position with the party, and he could not also stop this active and passive naming and shaming punishment. In August 2012, he married the women with whom he was photographed. Even this life change did not stop the passive and active rumours. Years after, the MP went to his hometown where some of his old friends, Kurdish politicians, were arrested. Turkish and Kurdish words were written on the posters of him and his new wife again, stating 'While *hevals* (comrades) go to jail, [the MP] enters the city.' His personal life, choices and freedom were claimed to be 'very bad practice' by the several party members I interviewed. People who follow similar patterns were told 'It is an MP's practice' but not the 'party practice'. The phrase of 'practice' is usually used by Öcalan during his meetings with his lawyer as a way of using self-criticism for the sake of the movement. A Kurdish alternative court judge commented on this case in Diyarbakır, in May 2015:

> Our society, especially men, know that we will act in favour of women. The best punishment is to name and shame, and we frequently use this method.

This is the main defence we have created for women. It used to be the other way around. When a woman was raped in the past, she was also punished by her family. They thought that she would bring shame to the home. Now we are naming and shaming men. We are creating justice and making laws. We don't believe in prison as a punishment, but we have a re-education camp for people who don't follow our rules. We also transfer the salaries of the husband to their wife when they behave badly, use violence or do not commit to their relationship properly.

This example shows that the aim of creating gender equality may create another inequality and that justice may turn into social policing and new injustices. According to a male politician from Diyarbakır, in May 2015, 'If a woman doesn't like somebody and creates false stories about them, if these women are dogmatic believers of the movement, then the accused are guilty even if they prove that they are not.'

While these members who sacrifice their time, energy and life for the Kurdish cause are seen as a bad example, they are also described as 'brave', 'hero', 'warrior', 'leader quality', 'life giving', 'beautiful', 'handsome', 'young' and as 'living forever'. The Kurdish movement has celebrated the life of several 'brave' men and women since the birth of the PKK. One of these examples is Arin Mirkan (Dilar Gencxemis). On 5 October 2014, during the Kobane resistance, in a Kurdish town in northern Syria, Arin, a member of the Kurdish female army wing (YPJ) sacrificed her life, killed many ISIS members and closed an important gate for ISIS. As a result of the almost hand-to-hand fighting, Arkin's sacrifice has become a new symbol of the Kurdish movement in Syria, Turkey, Iraq, Iran and the diaspora. Information about her braveness circulated widely – locally and internationally. Such international news outlets as the *Daily Telegraph*, CNN International, *The Economist*, *The Guardian* made space to report her bravery. Almost all Kurdish news outlets wrote several articles about her, and featured her as one of the most important figures in the successful liberation of Kobane and northern Syria. Several Kurdish news outlets, such as *Ozgur Politika* and *Kurdistan 24*, stated in their different articles about Mirkan: 'Comrade Arin's action is the resistance of all our YPG and YPJ fighters . . . All YPG and YPJ fighters will be Arin, if necessary . . . Arin's response showed that Kurdish women have not had the last word.' There are and continue to be, countless news articles, films, posters and books about the female fighters who fought and died for the Kurdish movement and women's revolution.[27]

Death is usually chosen over life in the nationalistic view: those who sacrifice their lives are celebrated more than those who live and enjoy their lives. Those who are seen as 'heroes' have their posters, pictures, any writings and actions circulated widely, and are regarded as 'good', 'pure', 'full' examples of those who bring success. The people who are seen to be part of the first group are labelled during group meetings, training seminars and even small friendly discussions as 'bad', 'weak', 'contagious', 'dangerous' and 'shameful' examples who may create a danger for the movement. If the individuals who are described as part of the first group are still members of the active guerrilla movement, they are usually separated from the rest, isolated for a time until they are seen as 'strong', 'full', 'clean' members. If these individuals are part of the different local organisations and communities which have a direct connection with the movement, they are usually not trusted, not included in activities and not elected for important positions, such as Kurdish court judge. They have to work hard, refocus and join re-education programmes to show that they have put the movement first and then they may be welcomed and seen as equal members. Such taboos and divisions are used by different institutions and even modern nation states. Two opposing descriptions, 'bad' and 'heroes', are used almost equally. They represent different feelings, but one cannot exist without the other. They are two sides of the same coin and there is a strong connection, almost an intimate relationship between them. As William Robertson Smith stated:

> Alongside of taboos that exactly correspond to rules of holiness, protecting the inviolability of idols and sanctuaries, priests and chiefs, and generally of all persons and things pertaining to the gods and their worship, we find another kind of taboo which in the Semitic field has its parallel in rules of uncleanliness. Women after child-birth, men who have touched a dead body and so forth are temporarily taboo and separated from human society, just as the same persons are unclean in Semitic religion. In these cases the person under taboo is not regarded as holy, for he [or women] is separated from approach to the sanctuary as well as from contact with men [or women]. . . .

---

[27] See for example, Fourest 2019.

In most savage societies no sharp line seems to be drawn between the two kinds of taboo just indicated, and even in more advanced nations the notions of holiness and uncleanliness often touch.[28]

'Disgust and horror are one thing and respect another', Durkheim writes.[29] Within this structure not just 'homosexuals' or 'lesbians' but all genders are imprisoned and forced into a new structured and coded relationship. Within this code, which are the elements of the state type of authority and institution building, there are a few aims. First, while intimate personal relationships are limited, instead an obedient and loyal relationship with the state and feelings of intimacy with the power holder is supported. Second, nationality and the state are seen as more important and a greater love than any intimate relationship one person may have for another and their family members. The message is very clear, the institutions are more important than a lover or your family, and you should sacrifice your life for this new 'love' now. Third, a new gender regime is introduced, which helps the new group identity. This is also the process of eradicating the current ideals of masculinity and feminity. Fourth, love of death is more important than love of life, especially during times of conflict and war, and a brave death is more a cause for celebration than a simple, regular life. Fifth, love of unity is to be encouraged. If a member wants to love someone deeply then they have their leader to love; individuals are not worthy of such love. This ensures love for and dependency on the movement.

Not only friendships, but the customs and traditions of relationships are also re-established. Creating a new form of fear and respect is not just helping to re-identify the new shared customs of gender relations, but also establishes the power and the tolerance of the new authority. The new rituals with shared and communised emotions help the movement to reaffirm and strengthen its unity and to act together physically and emotionally if there is any attack against the group or its leader. Individuality is replaced by the group and family is replaced by the nation. When one member of the group dies during a battle or political struggle then this loss is seen as the loss of every individual within the movement, and also within the nation in general. The new music,

---

[28] Smith 1889: 152–3.
[29] Durkheim 2008: 305.

films, books, paintings, language, flags, dress codes, etc. do not only help the establishment of the new gender and group identity, but it also to create and maintain the unity of the movement and nation. This emotional drive is very important for the Kurds, who do not have any safety net yet and face losses almost daily. Joseph de Rivera states that:

> Customary apparel, bodily marks, and language, evoke mutual sympathy and security, while strangers arouse suspicion, fear, and dislike. Failure to dress appropriately by a member is viewed with contempt so that one is ashamed to do so . . . Laws, probably beginning as taboos placed around what is regarded as sacred, evoke fear, disgust, and horror, and are later extended to antisocial behaviour . . . In fact, all of the 'recognition' emotions that may be used in building and maintaining the social self, both other-directed emotions such as admiration, respect, contempt, horror, and the corresponding self-directed emotions of pride, dignity, shame, and guilt are used to maintain the collective identity of the group.[30]

Norms are established for people to follow and they are not expected to overstep these limitations. Institutions, including the institutionalisation of gender identities, the societal unity, governmentality, authority, tax, policing and conflict management cannot function without these socially constructed rules. Richards and Swanger argue that 'Every day people follow customary norms and make customary calculations in socially constructed realities they regard as natural realities; every day many of the standard customs people routinely follow are part and parcel of a war system.'[31] While the Kurdish movement has shown some important developments and pushed to change society, it has also borrowed and constitutionalised some customary norms when it comes to individual sexuality and freedom.

The Politics of *Jineology*

In December 2017, I was allowed to spend the whole day observing a *jineology* meeting, and the election of members of the Kurdish women's court in Berlin. After several years of intensive fieldwork, which allowed me to establish

[30] Rivera 2014: 218, and 1977.
[31] Richards and Swanger 2009: 66.

relations and gain trust amongst community activists, I was allowed to observe as the only man amongst more than fifty female participants. There were mixed-age groups; the youngest were about 18 and the oldest were in their seventies. There were different dress codes, with most women wearing regular and modest outfits and several in traditional dresses and plain coloured headscarves. There was no hip or local Berlin streetwear. The four walls of the meeting room were covered in flags, symbols and painted images of the martyrs, with a black and white painting of a young Sakine Cansiz in a prominent position, to portray that martyrs always live for a long time and remain young in the heart of others. The only living person among the paintings was Öcalan, the imprisoned Kurdish leader. The meeting started with a minute's silence to show respect for the Kurdish martyrs, and it was chaired by two women in their thirties. One of them was the representative of Kurdish women in Germany, the other was the local Berlin representative. However, the German representative was the leading one. The main chairwoman started giving information, in Turkish, about me first and said, 'We have an academician here today. He is doing research about our movement and would like to follow our meeting today. We know him and trust him. Do you have any questions or objections for him to following this meeting?' After this introduction, most heads turned to me and I become the centre of attention. I was sitting towards the back and was able to see almost everyone. She also said, 'He will take a few photos of us but your faces won't be visible. Do you have any objections to this?' Thankfully, there were no objections and I was allowed to stay and take some photos. The second chairwoman started providing the results of their yearly report, their achievements, the problems they had faced and the work of different branches. The discussion about their activities in 2017 continued for hours. Later the elections of different branches took place; from mosque representatives to women's court judges, family representatives to financial and youth representatives. The aim of *jineology* was discussed in more detail. Women were told to develop themselves and their close networks. Different questions from attendees were answered by the chairwomen. The mosque representative, who was wearing a colourful Kurdish headscarf, was the most active and raised many questions. Later, she come to me and asked several questions about my research and also my opinion on their meeting and work. The representative of Syrian Kurds and the former captive and new activist, Rojin, were also more talkative, using only Kurdish in their communication. There were several women who were over 60 years old, but they were not as active and talkative as the young ones. One of them had been selected as a Kurdish court judge but she was not attending most court meetings when I was present. I asked her later about her limited activities, and she said: 'I am doing it for voluntary purposes. I have health problems and I live a bit far away. I trust our male comrades and their decisions.'

Jineology is described by the Kurdish movement as a 'women's science'. It is claimed to be an alternative to, and wider version of, Western-style limited feminism. When we look at the terminology of *jineology*, *jine* means 'woman' (in Kurdish), *oloji* (ology) means a subject of study. One of the main aims of *jineology* is to create a new women's movement for an equal, democratic modern society and to move beyond national, ethnic and racial identity and limitations. For this aim, increasing research, discussion and study around gender equality is seen as an important tool to help empower women's roles in every part of society. The movement gives women societal, scientific and military education and training to defend themselves against their enemies – including patriarchal traditions and family-based violence – during times of peace as well as war. This approach has influenced the new structure of Kurdish institution and community building. According to this approach, for example, a woman's account is seen as 'fact' and 'true', and men have to prove that they are not guilty. It is believed that killing current ideals of masculinity will open a way for women's freedom. The Western feminist approach is seen as a product of capitalism, and is believed by many Kurdish activists and politicians to increase the problem of the slavery of women rather than giving them their freedom. It is claimed that 'the focus on sexuality and sexual freedom in modern society is a side effect of capitalism'. Within *jineology* the 'gender test' has become an important process of the Kurdish movement and almost every male member needs to take and pass this test before taking up any position.

The above description of *jineology* needs to be unpicked. Some claims deserve critical engagement. I would like to start from the last issue of the gender test. Interestingly, women receive blanket exemption from the test and are assumed to have an innate knowledge of gender equality, which reflects the sometimes imbalanced, rash and PR-focused solutions. One of the main issues about gender inequality has been discussed in detail and it is clear from our discussion, especially throughout this chapter, that the problem of gender inequality does not just come from men. Women have also been part of the engineering of this repressive masculine and patriarchal tradition. Not just the current 'masculinity' but also 'femininity' needs to be challenged and changed for an equal and free gender structure. The accounts of many interviewees showed that there are many homophobic women as well as men. 'Manly like a man', 'a strong', 'masculine man is attractive', was mentioned by many interviewees, including active guerrillas, female politicians and chairs of the *jineology* meeting in Berlin. One may rightly ask why only male members have to take part in this 'gender test' and improve their gender understanding, while many women contribute to gender inequality and hold stereotypical views.

Another claim of *jineoloji* is that 'killing current ideals of masculinity will open a way for women's freedom'. If this is important for the success of *jineoloji* and gender equality, then one can ask why so many women set themselves on fire, in protest, when Öcalan (a male leader) was arrested on 15 February 1999. Several of these women died or had severe burns. It raises the question of why not a single woman or man even attempted similar protests when Sakine Cansiz (a female founder of the PKK) and her female colleagues were assassinated in the centre of Paris on 9 January 2013. In addition, while there have been several campaigns in Turkey and the diaspora for the freedom of male leaders Abdullah Öcalan and Selahattin Demirtaş, even then the women's movement did not focus on the freedom of thousands of Kurdish women in prison, such as Gulten Kisanak (former co-Mayor of Diyarbakır) and Figen Yuksekdag (former co-President of HDP). Furthermore, while we hear and learn of almost all the writings, books and any actions of imprisoned male leaders, the writings and books of the female leaders in prison or female guerrilla fighters in the mountains are not at the top of the agenda in discussions by the Kurdish women's movement. For example, a female columnist, Mehves Evin, wrote in a Kurdish right-wing newspaper, *Artigercek*, on 31 March 2020, about the coronavirus situation and prison conditions in Turkey. She reminded the authoritarian Turkish government about the UN's warning of the conditions for political prisoners, and not granting discriminative amnesty which would exclude them. She focused on three male political prisoners: Osman Kavala, Selahattin Demirtaş and Ahmed Altan. However, she did not even mention a single female prisoner, including Diyarbakır former Co-mayor and MP Gultan Kisanak, former MP Sebahat Tuncel and many other very well-known female political prisoners. On 1 April 2020, Kisanak's daughter, Evin, wrote: 'I have only one criticism on this article . . . It is only about three men. I don't know how to deal with those female prisoners not being visible. I don't know what more to say.' I wrote to her about her criticism and asked further questions. I also requested permission to use her case openly in my writing. She was right that the problem of the current femininity exists equally alongside that of masculinity and both may need to be challenged and changed for an equal gender approach. Gender inequality is a joint collaboration of the state, society, traditions, religion, intellectuals, men and women. All of them contribute almost equally to the continuity of this centuries-long issue.

Jineology's approach of taking women's accounts as factual truth is also problematic. When someone's account, without any fact or evidence, is accepted as truth then how can an equal society, as opposed to authoritarianism, be created? It will only replace one inequality with another. I have witnessed the problem of this approach throughout my own observations during the Kurdish alternative court process in Turkey and also in different parts of the diaspora. There have been some cases where, for example, a woman accuses her male colleague, boss, teacher, friend, ex-husband or ex-boyfriend for revenge or other reasons, but not for the sexual enforcement as claimed. Because any claims connected to sex are punished harshly and difficult to prove, it is easy to accuse somebody in this way. Some cases were dismissed by the Kurdish courts later, but such naming and shaming can be very harmful for the accused. Being proven innocent is not of much interest to the gossipers and local or social media who act as societal guardians, in comparison to claiming someone is guilty when they are innocent. I have observed that members of the *jineology* movement in Turkey, Germany and the UK take part in the unofficial Kurdish court process as judges, and make important decisions about marriage, divorce, violence in and outside of the household, inheritance, petty and even honour crimes, etc. Some of them later admitted during our interviews that the woman's account as 'actual and factual' creates some real problems and is 'misused'. However, they also defended the fact that some of these injustices can be said to count towards men's historical domination of injustices against women. The main chair of the *jineology* meeting in Berlin told me: 'As a representative of the Kurdish women's movement in Europe and someone who has been an active fighter in Syria and Turkey, I don't agree that women's accounts should always be accepted as true. This is open to abuse and will damage the trust in our cause. But capitalism has created a monstrous man and sometimes we have to take side of the women even if we know that they are in the wrong.'

The members of the *jinelogy* movement also believe that the focus on individual sexuality and sexual freedom is a side effect of capitalism. If this claim is true, then one can ask if there was not any oppression against women, men or LGBTQ, and their sexual freedom before capitalism. Did all these problems start with capitalism, or is there no oppression under the current 'non-capitalist', socialist countries and regimes, including Kurdish alternative governmental practices (radical democracy) in Rojava, Turkey and Iraq? We have already discussed the fact that sex without marriage is still taboo and not welcomed by the Kurdish movement, and some members were punished for this.

To sum up, gender has been an especially important subject, a very 'useful category' according to Joan W. Scott,[32] for the Kurdish movement in the Middle East in the last two decades. The findings of this research shows that there is a strong connection between the approach of the Kurdish women's movement, *jineology* and Kurdish nationalism despite some Kurdish women's critical thinking. It is an important platform to help the Kurdish national cause and the development of alternative state-building, as well as some development of women's rights. Gender politics have helped the Kurdish movement to become more international, gain more support and differentiate themselves from the rest of the Middle Eastern politics and practices. Gender approach has also taken real power from the state-centric liberal approach of some feminists who had been talking and writing about Kurds and for Kurdish women without any real methodological, ethnographic and linguistic engagement, but rather with pity, in the manner of a big sister or even a nun. Instead, Kurdish women started talking and writing about themselves,

[32] Scott 1986, 2008 and 2018; Butler and Weed 2011.

organising their own seminars and conferences, creating their own independent branches and collaborating with an international, progressive feminist approach. Instead of being guided by the ideal of the state-centric feminist, the Kurdish women's movement has taken the lead and created some new examples and approaches for other Middle Eastern liberal and authoritarian feminist movements. As Scott writes, 'Gender is a primary way of signifying relationships of power. It might be better to say gender is a primary field within which or by means of which power is articulated.'[33] When we look at how the Kurdish new gender approach has been produced, organised and practised, then we can also see that there are some new moral and ideological codes and limitations for individual freedom which can also create institutionalised rules, judgements and punishments. The next chapter will focus on how alternative justice is practised and how it affects the new gender rights and alternative state-building.

Figure 4.1 An elderly Kurdish women who spent most of her life fighting for Kurdish rights and wishes to see an independent Kurdistan before her death. Photo taken in September 2017, in Cologne. (Author's fieldwork image)

[33] Scott 1986: 1069.

Figure 4.2 Protest organised by Kurdish women activists in Berlin against the state and men's violence against Kurdish women, December 2017. (Author's fieldwork image)

Figure 4.3 A former mayor of Diyarbakır, Gulten Kisanak, who has been in prison since October 2016, speaking during a women's conference which she organised during the heavy conflict in Diyarbakır in September 2015. (Author's fieldwork image)

Figure 4.4 Kurdish women elect their representatives, including women's judges. The author was allowed to take part of this 'women only' meeting in Berlin, December 2017. (Author's fieldwork image)

Figure 4.5 Kurdish artist Zehra Dogan's painting symbolises how Kurdish women went against traditional religious and patriarchal rule and carried the dead body of a woman to the graveyard themselves, without men's involvement. (Written image rights have been secured from the artist, Zehra Dogan)

Figure 4.6 The author met with Yezidi refuges who escaped from ISIS brutality. They show from their recordings how ISIS murdered their relatives and religious leader. (Author's fieldwork image)

Figure 4.7 A young Yezidi girl who escaped from ISIS, at a refugee camp in Greece, July 2016.

5

PARALLEL JUSTICE AND ALTERNATIVE GOVERNMENTALITY

When I was appointed a position in this city by the government, my family and I were very upset. We did not want to come to here. I even considered quitting so not to come here. We are from the western part of Turkey. We thought it would be very dangerous for us, and the Kurdish people would not be like the people we know. You know! We had our presumptions and thoughts. It has been four years that we have lived here. Actually, people are nice and very hospitable – more so than even our neighbours in the Aegean region [western part of Turkey]. They don't create any problems for us at all; we hardly have any interaction with the people. My colleagues in the western part of Turkey have to deal with hundreds, even thousands, of cases each year, but our court rooms here are empty. Don't get me wrong, probably the people here have thousands of issues, fights, business and family conflicts but they don't come to us. If the police don't arrest and bring the Kurdish political people and activists, the courts here would have no cases. People are hospitable but they don't trust us. They always keep their distance. Even my barber and people in my regular tea shop would not tell me much. They are usually very talkative with each other but when I enter, the silence starts. I think we have deeply lost connection. The division is huge. As state judges, here we are not in charge. They don't even allow us to enable peace between them. They don't trust our peace and judgement. We don't have any power over their daily lives. We don't know what is going on. We have parallel lives. Nobody tells us anything even for the criminal cases. I feel powerless and useless. In this region, we are just making our own judgements mostly without witnesses or evidences, but just according to police reports. (A Turkish judge, Diyarbakır, May 2015)

To demonstrate and find answers for the concerns of these Turkish judges, this chapter engages with the development of the Kurdish court and justice system in Turkey, and the transformation from the militiary court to the people's court. The formation of a new society and governmentality, and how Kurdish judges have practised and negotiated prevailing power relations within the Kurdish political movement before and after the arrest of Öcalan are important in the process of taking power from an existing state and building a new one. By the end of this chapter, we will have a clearer understanding of where all these Kurdish cases are going.

Authoritarian states lose the power of judgement. The practice and development of Kurdish courts and judiciary represents the face of the Kurdish movement and alternative governmentality. This was not something which happened overnight, but the injustices of the state against Kurdish people had already disconnected them from the state system. The people had used different methods before, including calling upon tribal and family elders, and imams, as mediators. For this reason, there were many powerful, influential leaders, families and imams in almost every area. After the PKK-led Kurdish movement started in the 1980s, families went to PKK members for some important cases and asked them to be mediators. It was an important power gap and it did not take the Kurdish movement long to discover and make connections with society in this way.

The elimination of the power of tribal leaders, influential families and imams was secured in three ways. First, some of them surrendered their power to the Kurdish movement, accepted its authority and passed on any cases if and when they received them. Second, some powerful elites and tribes collaborated with the Kurdish movement directly and sought legitimacy from the movement to carry out what they were already doing, but had to agree to pay regular taxes and report all their actions and developments. Third, some families, tribes, well-known figures and elites refused to follow any orders from the movement. They continued their old-style hegemony over people and became very close to the state. They worked and collaborated with the state, passing on information about the Kurdish movement, and in return they received additional security, support and funding. While in the 1980s and 1990s the third way was very strong, after 2000 the first and second way were followed by the people and the Kurdish movement started to institutionalise its judicial system and spread to almost every city, town and village in the Kurdish regions.

The judiciary is one of the main arenas where the alternative sovereignty is established and also seized, not just by powerful local elites, but also the state. It is almost the only service that the PKK-led Kurdish movement has provided in the last four decades, while the people have given almost everything they have to the movement, including their lives, for its success. The judiciary and the courts are where the Kurdish movement is able to observe and control each and every individual and group, as well as the economy, investments and taxes. It is also able to establish authority by the use of punishment and violence, and to grant amnesty.

It is also the one of the areas where the movement makes a strong connection with the local youth. Young boys and girls who do not engage in active guerrilla warfare, but work for local militias, implement all court decisions and collect taxes for the movement. These responsibilities give them power, not just over local families and tribes, but also against the state police. Aside from implementing the court decisions and collecting taxes, they have the right to defend their local neighbourhood. They organise meetings, take business initiatives, become involved in active daily propaganda, 'educate' local neighbourhoods according to the ideology of the party, and promote and defend Kurdish politics, rights, culture, language and symbols. They also take military action and back up active guerrilla forces, as we saw after the 2015 conflict in Kurdish cities and towns in Turkey. These young people and their local supporters are some of the most important servants of the Kurdish movement and active Kurdish nationalism. They are the hand, eyes, ears, legs and heart of the movement. Some of them become local judges, mayors and politicians and go on to become decision-makers for the movement. Most of the young people and their supporters are aware of this and there is collaboration as well as competition between them. They can see a future for themselves. Even though the path is rocky, dangerous and often leads them to an early death, it still has more opportunities than the official state would offer them.

The local community and parallel institution structures are the basic foundations of the Kurdish movement and state-building process. The development of institutions and the judiciary is an ongoing and evolving process. While Kurdish justice seized state power for the functionality of the new system and created a new attitude and sovereignty, it also faced and brought new challenges. Aside from Rojava (northern Syria), Maxmur Refugee Camp[1] and the Sinjar Mountains (Iraqi Kurdistan), there is not much 'safe' space from the state security for Kurdish institution building to be carried out openly. Most Kurdish court practices and judicial activities in Turkey operate invisibly and secretly. These institutions are not just limited within Turkey, the Kurdish diaspora also introduced its own system and selected its own alternative judges, as I discussed in detail in my previous book.[2]

Aside from my previous research on the London Kurdish community, I was not only following the conflict and alternative process in Kurdish cities in Turkey (Mardin, Diyarbakır, Kars, Istanbul), but also in the diaspora, especially Germany. I participated in and directly observed the general and women's court processes. While the Kurdish community in the UK finds a pluralistic environment and some level of tolerance from the state to carry out its activities openly, including Kurdish court processes, and even has some level of connection or interaction with the state forces and institutions,[3] the Kurdish community in Germany is not much different than Turkey when it comes to alternative court practices. The community representatives and judges of the informal court do not try to fully take on the role of the state in the UK because of the state's tolerant approach towards diverse communities. They transfer some cases, especially criminal, to the state when necessary. However, these self-limitations in the power of the community do not occur in Turkey or Germany.

In Turkey and also in Germany, the community has to deal with almost all conflicts secretly, including criminal cases, passing sentence without informing or having any connection with the state. For example, the London Kurdish court files are stored at their community centre, not hidden like guns or diamonds, but the community approach is different when they live under centralistic or authoritarian rules and oppression. In June 2019, the head of the Kurdish court in Germany described the way they deal with cases in Germany:

> I am only sharing these files with you. I know you well and I know about your research. You have gained our respect. But you should also know that even

[1] Yilmaz 2016.
[2] Tas 2016d.
[3] Tas 2016d.

most of our members don't know where we put these files. The German state representatives and their attitudes towards our communities are not much different than the Turkish state. If they see these files, I will go to jail for a long time. I don't commit any crime here. I resolve people's conflicts when they ask me to do so. They come here. But the state sees this as a big crime, and these files can be used as the evidence of crime which the state would claim against us. We hide these like guns or diamonds. If we know that there will be a search by the state police, we will burn these files but nothing else. These files show how many cases we have dealt with in the last seven years. All the details are there. The information about different parties and our judges' signatures are there. The fines and compensation we have decided for each case is there. Our annual report is there. You should know that you are holding, looking at and reading our most valuable papers.

While Germany claims to be a federal state and Turkey claims to have strong local governments, still the mentality of governmentality and functionality of these two states is very centralistic and they have similar institutional attitudes towards some minorities. Their approaches may allow Germans and Turks to follow some practices differently and to have a degree of societal self-regulation in different corners of the country, but this does not mean it welcomes and tolerates diversity,[4] including pluralistic approaches as we can see in the example of the UK.

While the Kurdish political movement creates its own courts, and practises its own laws, it also intervenes in some community cases at the state legal courts. For example, in September 2017 a Kurdish man was on trial in a state court in Berlin for brutally murdering his wife, in what appeared to be an honour-based killing. While the official German court proceedings took place, Kurdish women were staging protests in front of the state court and also within the Kurdish community centre where regular community court proceedings were held. The women prevented some men from their own community from stepping forward as witnesses in defence of the man. However, despite the women's efforts some still stood as supportive witnesses for the murderer and claimed that his wife had provoked the attack, which reduced his punishment, and he was only sentenced for nine years. This episode is

[4] See, Viellechner 2020.

an example of the important role of alternative justice mechanisms not only within the community, but also the actions taken which affect the results of the cases within the state court as well.

Alternative justice – the creation, practice, implementation, control and monopoly of power – is an important tool for community building and the creation of an alternative sovereignty. While the main approach of the local alternative court does not make everybody happy, it makes nobody unhappy. Everybody is somewhere in between, trying to find a compromise. This has increased respect for the movement and brought them more cases. All types of conflicts and disagreements are dealt with by the local Kurdish courts, including criminal, family, inheritance, social, marriage and divorce cases. This is important evidence of the establishment of the parallel authority. The state is almost paralysed in that sense. When the state loses such cases and the courts are unable to deal with the conflict resolution; the authority, legitimacy and power of the state can be limited or destroyed and another power holder takes over. Judicial power means having the power to collect taxes, to provide security, and to influence and shape people's daily lives and attitudes.

The Kurdish movement sees itself as the representative of the whole Kurdish public and claims to have a right to pass judgement against people but again for the will of the people. The structure of the judgement, punishment and level of fines vary from region to region, group to group and member to member. However, there are some basic rules that cannot be challenged and should be followed by all members, and these are the foundation of Kurdish basic law. From the beginning of the movement, between 1980 and 2000, the party members based their judgement on the ideology of the party and the Kurdish people. These two foundations have been the main moral grounds and regulators of people's lives – the political, legal and moral stand of the Kurdish authority. Everyone can be free and equal as long as they recognise and respect these two basic rules. Later, especially after 2000, gender equality and respect for diversity (for those who recognise the authority of the party) were included as the third and fourth main grounds for the judgement. The party symbols and Öcalan as the founding leader have constituted other important codes, values, moral and ethical grounds which cannot be challenged by members. Rules are imposed and justified, and societal reasoning and public order is carried out under these codified values. The people who don't follow and support these basic ground rules are seen as enemies or traitors.

After these immutable and unchallenged basic rules, the process of judgement can be different. For example, a case can more easily be resolved by a moderate member of the party with a peaceful agreement for both sides. However, a similar case, especially one dealt with by dogmatic and conservative members of the party, often takes a harsher approach and one or both sides may be heavily punished. Different methods and actions by members have affected people's relationship with the movement. While some people become more critical, leave their village or town for a big city, and collaborate with the state forces or alternative power holders, other members increase their support and connection with the movement. Members' understanding of local people, their culture and relations plays an important role. For that reason, while the Kurdish movement has not allowed any member who would become dominant to stay in one place for a long time, it has also made sure that judges are generally from a particular area when they move their local representative members around. The system is similar to that of state governors or the military; they keep moving and transferring, and one member doesn't usually remain in one role and in one region for more than three years. The aim is to avoid increasing the power of any one member and creating the risk of them becoming local lords. A similar rule applies to Kurdish mayors and MPs; they are rotated after one or two terms maximum.

Justice before 2000

The Kurdish movement's legal processes and practices are not very different from many established state processes. While the Kurdish movement was constructed with the notion of having a centralistic and authoritarian structure, almost like the Turkish and German state structure, there was some flexibility allowed for local commanders, leading guerrillas, politicians, community representatives and judges. They had legitimate power from the central authority. Aside from carrying out active military operations against state apparatus and institutions, they observed communities, carried out ideological and military training, collected taxes, increased membership, cut people's relations with the state, established alternative institutions, created large local militias to run these institutions, dealt with the local complaints and conflicts, created local and mobile fast-track courts, made orders and implemented their judgements. They were also advised to make independent decisions, to take the initiative for all these actions when urgently needed. However, they were also obliged to inform the central command for their each and every action, and to provide written reports for their superiors. Most of the time peaceful, balanced settlements were reached, including gaining membership. For example, if a family could not provide a member, then they had to help in another way; to pay a fine or to work as local counsellors, activists, judges or with a militia.

The early version, especially between 1980 and 2000, meant that there were several aims of the alternative judiciary practice. The first, especially for mild and harmless cases, was mainly to help resolve local problems quickly, cheaply and in a balanced way without much delay or conflict, as a way of creating some 'fairness' against the state system, and also to establish the power of the movement locally. The second, for authority, power and societal morally based cases, was to introduce retributive justice[5] to punish those who commit wrongful acts according to the codes of the movement, and for them to be punished disproportionately as a way to establish the authority of the movement. In particular, those found guilty of state collaboration by acting as spies or traitors, stealing the movement's money, or leaving the movement, paid the highest price with their lives. Such labelling and moral grounds for protecting Kurdishness, defending Kurdish identity and fighting to create a Kurdish state, created enough justification in the eyes of the local Kurdish public.

This justification was increasing in Kurdish regions and succeeded in creating fear and establishing power over local influential families and tribes by collecting taxes from them and making them agents of the movement. In the first two decades, especially, harsh punishments were inflicted as a way to make people obey and respect the Kurdish movement. To spread fear and authority in this way was very important as it weakened the existing power holders and made them obey the order of the movement. Even for some major crimes there was a way for some people, especially if they were the

---

[5] For detailed discussion of retributive justice, see Hart 1968; Murphy 1973 and 2007; Shafer-Landau 1996 and 2000; Moore 1997; Duff 2001; Christopher 2002; Golash 2005; Zaibert 2006; Boonin 2008; Husak 2010; White 2011; Tomlin 2014.

members of large tribes, to avoid heavy punishment by paying hefty fines, allowing one of their young family members to join the movement, and making a public apology and accepting the authority of the movement. The main approach of the PKK-led Kurdish movement with the use of threats or heavy punishment was to win the support of Kurdish society at large, especially big tribal families. If heavy punishment was going to make one of these big families the enemy instead of members of the movement, then the movement preferred heavy fines and spared lives. However, the Kurdish movement did not hesitate to punish even big tribal families, such as Bucak and Suleymancilar, when they refused to obey the orders of the movement.

The Anatomy of Power and Justice

In September 1992, an important case was heard in Kars, an eastern city of Turkey. The case was a good example of the relations of the state and the Kurdish movement with the local people, the Kurdish movement's early court process and judgement, and the battle for power between the state and the Kurdish movement. I visited several villages and towns in Kars between 2013 and 2016, and interviewed some fifteen people specifically about this case and the anatomy of the conflict between the state and Kurdish movement in this region.

Kars is one of the multinational, multifaith border cities,[6] like Mardin, whose boundaries change very often. It is a diversely populated city, where many towns and villages are occupied by Kurds, but some other towns and villages belong to Turkish people. It is a very cold, mountainous area and most of the villages and towns are covered with snow for more than four months a year. It is this aspect which was the main subject of Orhan Pamuk's book, *Snow*. Pamuk's investigative and anthropologically rich novel also observes that the city centre was divided between multiple ethnic and religious identities. Churches, mosques and medreses were built side by side. Currently only mosques are well looked after and while many new ones are built, others have

---

[6] Including Turkey, Kars has borders with five countries; Georgia, Armenia, Iran and Nakhichevan. However, because of the increasing security problem and the development of the Kurdish movement, the city was divided into three new cities (Kars, Ardahan and Igdir) as a way to manage security easily and quickly.

become dilapidated. The city was part of the Russian Empire between 1877 and 1921, and the Turkish state has treated it as a border place which they may lose one day, and so they have seen no point in making any investment. For this reason, one of the most historically rich places, the medieval city of Ani, has not been restored but left to its destiny, and has become a ghost city.[7] Protecting the cultural heritage, identity and rights of others is seen as 'insulting' to the Turkish nation or government institutions.[8] Some towns and villages of Kars where predominantly Turkish people live received some basic social and economic investment in the form of roads, a water system, factories, schools, telephone and TV connections after the 1950s. However, Kurdish towns and villages had to wait until the middle of the 1980s to receive these basic services. In Kars alone, hundreds of Kurdish villages only received some basic state services – roads, electricity, telephone connection, a water system, schools, even mosques – after the Kurdish movement, the PKK, started controlling some of these towns and villages and became virtually the only authority. The PKK-led Kurdish movement started its organisation in 1978, but increased its fight against Turkish state forces after 1984.

The period between 1978 and 1984 can be described as a time of preparation when the Kurdish movement initially established its authority against local Kurdish tribal leaders and some powerful families. People stopped obeying the rules of tribal families and started to follow the orders of the local Kurdish guerrilla forces. This unification of local power and authority was important for mounting a real challenge to the authority of the state. The tribal leaders and powerful families were in co-operation with the state in

---

[7] See, Watenpaugh 2014.

[8] Article 301 Turkish Penal Code (updated 8 May 2008), protects the Turkish nation, Turkish Republic and its institutions and organs of the state from any criticism. Even the updated and 'modernised' version of the article opened a way for political criminalisation and the authority for the justice minister to decide the crime and criminal person. See, the European Court of Human Rights' judgement of *Taner Akcam v. Turkey*, application no. 27520/07 (25 October 2011). Under the previous version of this article, a well-known Armenian-Turkish journalist, Hrant Dink, who was killed by a nationalist Turk, was tried for his writing which was claimed to insult Turkishness. Orhan Pamuk, the Nobel laureate, also faced prosecution for saying, '30,000 Kurds and one million Ottoman Armenians were killed in Turkey.' See also, Algan 2008; Gocek 2008 and 2015; Dixon 2010; Adar 2018.

the name of Kurdish people and oppressing people in the name of the state. However, once these families lost power over the people it meant that the state also lost power and control. The state had to act directly to regain its authority. Since there were no proper roads to thousands of villages in the Kurdish regions, the state had to build them in order to access every village, and this was done in a short period of time.[9] The main purpose of building of these new roads was not for the local people but for the state to move around its modern weapons and vehicles. The roads were followed by local military checkpoints, which were created in mountainous areas, between different towns and villages, for observing the local people and their relations with the Kurdish guerrillas.

Electricity was another important requirement for these checkpoints. Hundreds of villages in Kars alone for the first time saw electricity coming to their area. During the first sixty years of the Turkish Republic, between 1923 and 1983, electricity was supplied to only 24,400 villages, mostly in the western part of Turkey. However, between 1983 and 1987, in just four years, 33,800 villages were supplied with electricity.[10] The main purpose was again not for the people, but for the checkpoints. Indirectly, however, people also benefited. Telephones were brought for these checkpoints and one telephone line was installed at the house of the head of the village (*muhtar*), as a way to inform the state of any important matters arising from their village. They were forced to be state spies and if they refused to comply then they faced 'support of terrorism' charges.

After roads, electricity and telephone lines, the schools arrived. It was not for the modern education of the children but mainly indoctrination of Kurdish children according to state policies. School was also seen as very important for the fast assimilation and Turkification of Kurds by the authoritarian regime. For the first time, compulsory education was introduced for all children between 6 and 11 years old. Mobile primary education was introduced to some small villages which could not have school or teachers because of geographical or security reasons. Not only was education compulsory, but so was the dress code – black uniform (*önlük*). Everybody had

---

[9] See, Official Newspaper 1987; DPT 1992.
[10] See, Official Newspaper 1987.

to wear it. By the mid-1980s, the colour of uniform changed to blue but the educational structure and aims did not change, and represented the visibility of the authoritarian and militarised state. Even if the security forces were not around, the people would see the power of the state from these uniforms. Every morning, children had to line up in the playground to swear that they were ready to sacrifice themselves for the Turkish state, that they loved Ataturk and were ready to be his soldiers, and that everybody should be proud to be a Turk.[11]

Many Kurdish families refused to send their children to school at first. However, some were forced, but then they hesitated to send their daughters. The assimilation of women meant losing everything for the Kurds and it was seen as the main threat to their cultural and linguistic existence. Meanwhile the state, with the help of the media, created continuous propaganda that the local people were against the education of girls. The state was also aware of the importance placed on the role of women and cared about the assimilation of women more than their right to education. While many feminist movements in Turkey looked down on the Kurdish community and criticised the resistance of families to girls' education, they hardly criticised the state's assimilative policies.

TV was another important vehicle for state propaganda and indoctrination. Almost every Kurdish village, especially the muhtar's house, had a TV connected. TV was also used for distance learning and education purposes and what children learned at school was usually repeated on television, with the information being presented as the only truth, even if it was not the case. Kurdish people were learning from the village schools, from Turkish teachers and also TV that they were no longer Kurds but Turks. Before the state's strident voice arrived, many Kurdish people looked forward to the 4 p.m. 'Radio Yerevan' news. The Kurdish broadcasting of Armenia's Radio Yerevan was on almost all day in many Kurdish houses around the cities of Kars, Agri and Van for decades. It did not only provide the news, but also entertainment, Kurdish music and stories – it was an important platform for Kurdish artist and singers. It was a form of cultural, linguistic medicine and therapy

---

[11] See, DPT 1989; Olur 1994; Çakır 1999; Ataman 2002; Erdem 2005; Kaya 2009; Yildirim et al. 2018.

for many Kurds, especially when Kurdish was forbidden by the Turkish state. Because of Radio Yerevan, the Kurdish language of older people was very rich and eloquent. On 27 April 2020, the Turkish and Kurdish news outlet, *Bianet*, stated:

> The Kurdish broadcasting of Armenia's Radio Yerevan has very much affected the generation of the time and the ones coming after. Especially in Turkey, where even speaking Kurdish was forbidden, people, with their limited means, would turn on their radios and listen to the news, stories and songs broadcast by Radio Yerevan. Hundreds of artists performed their works [during the 'Kurdish hour'] on the radio.

However, with the new Turkish schooling and TV, Kurds were disconnected from Radio Yerevan and the Kurdish language was almost lost in that region. The state introduced these new methods as 'bringing civilisation to our people'.[12]

As has happened many times before and since, Turkish liberals and feminists strongly supported the state monopolisation of perceptions which did not result in any progress or education but only killed culture, folk music and stories. It would not be wrong to claim that Kurds have different generations of knowledge; one with those who grew up with Radio Yerevan, who are rich in literature and stories that have influenced their creativity, and another with those who have grown up with state radio, education and TV, and who do not have much knowledge of literature and the stories of Kurds, but have gained many slogans. This clash between slogans and stories has affected the Kurdish movement.

The schools and TV were followed by mosques and state imams as a way to stop people following the Kurdish movement, and instead to be loyal to the state. Imams and mosque gatherings have played a crucial role in informing people that the Kurdish movement 'is not Muslim, but a communist,

---

[12] Official Newspaper 1987. The official newspaper explained: 'We are introducing civilisation to our people. Our villager, who knows nothing but his own village and lifestyle, will see through the window of this colourful television a world where other people walk on asphalt roads, live in houses with water fountains and toilets, and he will want to see the same in his village.'

godless (*Allahsiz*) movement'. While there were 42,744 mosques in 1971, ten years later, in 1981, this had increased to 47,645. However, this number jumped to 62,947 in just seven years, in 1988. These numbers represent only the mosques which belonged to Turkey's Religious Affairs Department (*Diyanet*) and do not include the mosques run by different religious groups which also worked with the state and for the state. The 32 per cent increase in seven years was huge compared with the previous decade. These additional new mosques were mainly built in Kurdish areas, especially in villages and small towns. While the village and small-town populations have decreased 4 per cent during the same period, the 32 per cent increase in the number of mosques is interesting. Many Kurds saw the Islamisation of the state after the 1980s. The state used re-Islamisation as a weapon to scupper the Kurdish movement and their plan to create an independent state. Kars was one of the cities where there was a tremendous increase in mosques (in total 788) considering the size of the population.[13]

However, not only Kars, but thousands of villages in Kurdish regions received all these developments after 1980. The Kurdish movement, with its fight against the state, indirectly helped people to have some basic necessities, even if this was not the aim of the state. Before 1984, patients needing emergency care died without seeing a doctor, women gave birth at home without the help of a professional midwife, and many died of curable illnesses. Without roads to towns or cities, which could take hours or days to reach on foot, patients had to be transported on the back of horses or donkeys.

The state had a presence in many Kurdish towns and villages only after the PKK came into existence. Thousands of villages in Kurdish regions, and hundreds in Kars alone, faced all these developments in the space of a few years, one after another in quick succession. They would see different branches of the state authorities during the day, but once evening arrived, the Kurdish movement took charge and moved into the central village, visiting different houses, for ideological and political reasons or for food, equipment and to collect taxes. They started dealing with the problems of the village or town and were aware of all weddings, deaths, economic progress, the members of

[13] See, Yucekok 1971; Sanalan 1973; Vergin 1985; Akşit 1986; Saylan 1987; Ozcan 1990 and 1994; Ayata 1991; Yavuz 2003.

each and every household and conflicts between people. People would compete with each other to host guerrillas and it became a privilege to have the members of the Kurdish movement as guests. Some people would use this power against any other families they may be in conflict with.

Despite roads, electricity, telephones, schools and the power of imams, the state could not be fully in charge, and especially could not control the power of the Kurdish movement over people during the evenings. Many young locals also started joining the movement. The state was collecting information on every young male and female in the Kurdish regions from their informers. Some of the young people who were planning to join the movement but had hesitated, or had not yet made the decision, were arrested or killed by the state forces.[14] After such developments, local people not only supported the movement ideologically and ethnically, but more importantly emotionally as well. To give any information and help the state meant to kill their loved one, their daughter, son, husband, brother or sister. The Kurdish movement was aware of this and always left some of their local guerrillas as a link between the movement and the local people. This would later encourage the people to support the movement, and make them a viable power against the state.

The state was also desperate to divide and rule villages as a way to take control. They introduced new tactics to support one family against another in return for some financial and security benefits. They forced families to use weapons and to work as village guards for the state, especially during the night. Kurdish village guards have been used for decades by the state for operations against Kurdish guerrillas. They were deliberately put on the front line where they could intercept the guerrillas as a way of preventing the death of state armed forces and also creating the possibility that some local people could be killed by the Kurdish movement which would result in anger against the movement. This worked for the state in many places where people who

---

[14] In the last four decades, since the 1980s, people have faced human rights abuse on an almost daily basis. The right to life was under threat, extrajudicial executions were almost routine and torture was systematic. Successive Turkish governments have seen a military solution and punishment as the only way to deal with the conflict with Kurds. The Kurdish movement, PKK, is also responsible for brutal assaults on innocent people during the same period. For example, 2,932 people were killed in 1992 alone, and in 1994, this number increased to 4,041. See, TIHR 1994, 2000 and 2014.

had lost a member of their family as a village guard started openly supporting the state against the Kurdish movement. In other places, even though people could not refuse to become village guards as they would face prison under 'supporting terrorism laws', they accepted the state's offer, became village guards, received salaries, but turned a blind eye when the Kurdish movement came to their villages. Some of them even collaborated secretly with guerrillas against the state, while others committed crimes against the state forces in the absence of any guerrillas, as a way of claiming that there was a conflict so that the state would continue to pay their monthly salaries and give them weapons and support.

The Death of a Turkish Man

The case described below took place in one of these villages, a village which experienced all the above developments from the mid-1980s. I won't name the village or the people, in order to protect them from any future punishment from the state and/or the Kurdish movement.

Most people in this village, like many other Kurdish villages, were closely related and from one or two families. However, the third generation of villagers was divided into two rival groups. While one side supported the state and agreed to be village guards, the other side was against state authority and supported the Kurdish movement. Marriages usually took place between the families of the village and also nearby villages. However, after 1984 when the roads, telephone connection, electricity, schools, mosques and imams arrived, there were also marriages between village women and western Turkish men.[15]

---

[15] My ethnographical findings and cases argued go against the discussions and findings submitted by Gunduz-Hosgor and Smith (2002). They claimed that 'most Turkish-Kurdish inter-marriage takes place between Kurdish males and Turkish females and that both Turks and Kurds intermarry more in the large cities and in regions where their own group is small. With regard to education, the highest intermarriage tendencies are found among Turks with a low educational level and among Kurds with a high educational level. This finding is in line with social exchange theory.' This is a very superficial generalisation and an example of how research based on the official state data can be misleading and and result in false assumptions. The claim that 'Kurdish females had little access to the outside world' indicates clearly that without any real ethnographical data, an argument based on official statistics creates problems. Aside from the case I discuss here in detail, another dozen cases from just one village show that there was an increase in marriages between educated Turkish men and less

Many Turkish politicians, including former presidents and prime ministers such as Turgut Ozal, Suleyman Demirel, Tansu Ciller, Ahmet Davutoglu and also the current President Erdoğan, believed that intermarriage between Turks and Kurds, especially between Turkish men and Kurdish women, would replace antagonism with kinship and resolve the Turkish-Kurdish conflict. I was told by interviewees that a large number of Turkish men, many of them well educated and well off, travelled to their villages between 1980 and the 2000s to find a first or often second wife. This was also part of the state-proposed solution for the assimilation of Kurds into Turkishness, to encourage men from western Turkey to marry Kurdish women.

The assimilation of women was seen the assimilation of all Kurds, since women were seen as the main carriers of Kurdish language and tradition. However, they were also a barrier to this assimilation. They started to join the Kurdish movement as fighters, which made it much more difficult for the state to deal with Kurdish questions. After women became guerrillas, to support the Kurdish movement become an honour because women were seen as the representatives of the family's honour. If women can fight for Kurdish rights and independence, then men who still collaborate with the state are shamed and seen as criminals. For this reason, the local state authorities have played a pivotal role in supporting intermarriage between Turks and Kurds since they believe that if young Kurdish girls marry western Turkish men for a 'better' life instead of joining the Kurdish movement, it will change the whole society. Instead of joining the movement, people could follow their daughters and move to towns and cities for a better life, and instead of 'hating Turks' they could become 'one family', and 'create a bond' with Turks.

The following is an example of this. A Kurdish man from the village, who was working in Istanbul as a seasonal worker and looking after his family with his earnings, was asked to help his Turkish boss in Istanbul in 1992. His boss wanted to marry a young Kurdish woman. He was already married and had

educated Kurdish women. Emine Erdoğan, wife of the current Turkish president, and Semra Ozal, wife of Turgut Ozal, the former prime minister and president of Turkey between 1983 and 1993, are just two examples. Within political, economic and intellectual elites alone this can be observed very easily. According to research carried out by Konda in 2008, titled 'Kurtler ve Kurt Sorunu – Kurds and Kurdish Problem', 3.7 per cent of Turks and Kurds are intermarried; in other words, around 2 million 600 thousand of them have kinship.

children, but he also wanted to have a Kurdish connection and family. He told the Kurdish man, whom I interviewed in 2014, 'There are of course good Kurds. You are one of them. I like you. I want Turks and Kurds to become one family and live together. I would like to marry a nice Kurdish woman. I would be happy to pay. Would you like to introduce me to some candidates?' The Kurdish man was aware that the Turkish man was already married, but he also knew that this had become the norm and that other men from western Turkey had taken a young Kurdish woman as a first or second wife. He offered to help. They travelled to Kars together from Istanbul. It was a long journey, around a 24-hour drive. The Turkish man was driving his new BMW car – a wealthy image was important for him and would help him to find a suitable candidate quickly. He also took some cash with him as a way to pay for a bride.

They arrived around noon and stayed in the Kurdish man's father's house that evening to rest. The following day, after breakfast, they went to visit a family in a nearby village. There was a young widow whose guerrilla husband had been killed a year earlier. The family of the young woman was informed a little in advance and they agreed to the marriage, but the woman did not want it. Her family were also afraid of their dead son-in-law's family and did not put much pressure on their daughter. The two men did not stay very long there. After an hour they left and drove back to the Kurdish man's village where they visited a family with a young, single daughter. The visit lasted two hours, and they agreed to visit again the following day for dinner. The Turkish man did not have much time as he wanted to return to Istanbul for his work, so they made two visits on their second day. They were back at the Kurdish man's father's house in the late afternoon. The Kurdish man was married, had three children and was living just a few hundred metres away from his father's house, but he preferred to take his guest to his father's house. They had afternoon tea and ate a light snack.

It was still early, just after 5 p.m., when most villagers were giving their animals their last feed and sending them to their stables. They usually have their dinner after that. Most females of the household were out tending to the livestock, as well as preparing dinner. Most males were sitting with their guests. The main door suddenly flew open and two guerrillas entered like a whirlwind, with their heavy guns. Everyone panicked. It was too early for the guerrillas' normal visiting time. The Kurdish man's father stood up and welcomed them. The guerrillas knew him, but angrily pushed him aside. The women and children from outside came in to see what was going on. Some children were crying from the shock. The guerrillas ordered everybody outside, including children, women and the elderly. Some young men of the family were very angry, but could not do much. There were five guerrillas; two were inside and three of them were outside, barricading the entrance to the house. All of them were holding big guns. Later, the family members noticed that some guerrillas were also guarding the entrance and exit of the village road. The group was led by two guerrillas who were mostly talking and giving orders, Misto and Omer, who were very well known and had been helped by the villagers for years.

They took the Turkish man and the Kurdish man who had brought him to village and separated them from the rest of the group. They walked in the direction of the Kurdish man's house, which was the last one at the end of the village, pushing and punching the two men until they arrived. The Kurdish man's wife and children were ordered to leave the house and to walk to his father-in-law's house. The two men were begging for their lives.

The father of Kurdish man was begging them for forgiveness if they had done something wrong. The Kurdish man's wife was crying and also pleading with them. She refused to leave until they freed her husband and their guest. The guerrillas and the leader were seemingly deaf and not listening to anything. There was a wooden power-line pylon close to the Kurdish man's house and they took both men there. Misto, the lead guerrilla shouted angrily, 'You are both going to be judged now in the name of Kurdish people, in front of the public and revolutionary court.'

One of the young men, a relative of the Kurdish man, went up the hill secretly to ask some soldiers for help. They were just a kilometre away from the village and could easily see everything from their barracks at the top of the hill. It took him just ten minutes to reach the soldiers, even though it was a steep hill. He said to them, 'Please help, a few guerrillas are in our village, as you can see from here. They are very angry. We don't know why but they might kill our relatives and our Turkish guest.' However, the soldiers refused to come down to the village at that time. It was around 6 p.m. They replied, 'We can't do much. It's dangerous for us to come down there. We are just ten soldiers here and we don't want to risk our lives.' The young man was screaming and begging for help. He asked them to call for help from the town which was just twenty-five kilometres away. The soldiers responded, 'This time we can't do anything, nor can any soldiers from the next town. We will come to village tomorrow morning, when there is daylight.' And they sent the young man back to village without any help.

The lead guerrilla, Misto, stated the reason for their anger: 'You will both be punished. Why are you forcing a Kurdish woman to marry a Turkish man?' Now everybody understood the reason for their anger and violence. The father of the Kurdish man increased his pleading, knelt down and kissed their shoes, begging them to forgive his son and their guest. He promised them the guest would leave immediately. He offered his life and to pay a heavy fine instead. They were not listening. Misto said, 'It is not your fault but your son and this man are guilty. They will be punished in the name of Kurdish people and set as an example so that similar actions aren't repeated.' The old man and Kurdish man's wife did not want to give up. After almost an hour of continuous begging from the father of the Kurdish man, his wife and crying children, the two main guerrillas, Misto and Omer had a discussion between themselves. The guerrilla leader, Misto, turned to the old man and the Kurdish man's wife and said, 'We have reached our verdict. We have often eaten your food. You have been good to us. This is a serious crime that your son has committed. He should not have brought this Turkish man here, encouraging him to marry a Kurdish woman, especially the wife of a guerrilla who lost his life for all of you. We will forgive your son now, take him away and all of you go back to your house. But we will punish this Turkish man. We will burn your son's house with everything inside for his punishment, but we will spare his life. If you stay a minute more, we will also kill your son and punish your family as well. Go now.' One member of the family who was present at that moment told me about their relations with guerrillas before that incident:

> My family were very polite and helpful to the guerrillas for a long time. My grandad was feeding them almost every evening before feeding us. My father and grandfather were spending what little money we had in the town to get whatever the guerrillas wanted before our own needs. It was firstly out of fear, and then we supported them and respected them. There had been no sign of the state in our village before. We never saw doctors, nurses or postmen. From

time to time, especially during summer and in the daytime, military vehicles were passing through our village after the appearance of the guerrillas in our area. Soon after, the state built a small military look-out station at the top of our village, where they based ten to fifteen personnel most of the time. They weren't just watching our village but around forty other villages nearby. The station was in a place where we used to hunt partridges or rabbits during the winter. After the look-out station was built, the state was the hunter and we were its prey. But this was only during the daytime. In the evening, the state, personnel and station usually shut their doors to people. It was the time for the PKK's guerrilla to come to our village, to question anybody who had a close relationship with the state.

The father of the Kurdish man followed the orders of the guerrilla leader and sent all his family members inside his house, including his son. The old man was still resisting and not giving up, hoping to save the Turkish man's life as well. The Turkish man was also begging for his life and apologising for his mistake of trying to buy a Kurdish woman as a second wife. His hands were behind his back and had been handcuffed to the power-line pylon. He was wearing a white shirt; he had left his jacket at the old man's house. The guerrilla leaders asked about his car keys and he showed his pocket. They took the car keys from his pocket. He offered them money and his car and promised to pay more fines if they would let him go. He told them he had money with him, some in the pocket of his jacket and some in a small bag inside the car.

They did not show any mercy. Misto, the head guerrilla, announced their judgement and final words: 'You believe that the Kurds and Kurdish women are for sale. You think you can buy us with your dirty, colonised money. I will show you now that you are mistaken.' After this last statement, the Turkish man was shot many times. His whole body was full of bullets, slouched against the pylon with his head on one side. His white shirt had turned red with his blood. The shooting could be heard from every part of the village and also from the military station. After this, they went to set fire to the Kurdish man's house. He had stables next to his house with a lot of livestock inside. Everything was on fire. One of the guerrillas opened the door of the stables and the animals all ran away without any injuries. Then, they went to the Turkish man's car. The lead guerrilla opened the door, took out the bag with the money and gave it to the Kurdish man's father. He told the old man: 'Take this money and give it to this Turkish man's family when they come. We are not here for his money. Tell them why we punished him – we don't want them to think that we punished him because of his money.' After that they set the car on fire. Now, the car, house and everything around was burning.

The fire was very visible. The Turkish man's body was about fifty metres away from the fire. I asked one of the witnesses of that evening what she remembered about the event. She said:

> I was able to see almost everything. The things I will never forget are the smell of the house burning and the explosion of the car. Our village houses used to be burned by the state forces, but this time guerrillas burned our house as a punishment. The state burned our houses and forced us to move away from our land because they assumed we were supporting the guerrillas. The guerrillas also burned our house this time, thinking that we were supporting the state and helping a Turk. I am also still very angry with the Turkish man who expected to buy a Kurdish woman easily, but this should not have been justification for his death. I am still having nightmares about that evening and I am haunted by the voice of the Turkish man begging for his life.

I also talked to the Kurdish man, who explained:

> We were not doing anything wrong. I think my boss was a nice man. I worked for him for a long time. He wanted to marry a Kurdish woman. He was ready to pay for this marriage. What was wrong with that? I was just introducing him to a few people and we did not force anybody. We thought the guerrillas were like family to us and would not hurt us. We knew the leader of the group and had hosted him as our guest many times. It was a night of horror. They killed my friend. They burned my house without any mercy. They burned his car. I did not care much about the house even though it was newly built and we had everything, including what little savings we have, inside. But my father, whom they usually respected a lot, was desperate to save my Turkish friend's life. But they set the public court there, made a decision very quickly and punished innocent people. My Turkish friend did not understand what was going on. He was speechless from shock and shaking all over. It was a cold September evening, but he was sweating. He was crying and begging for his life. We all begged for his life. I wish they had killed me instead. He was offering them money, his car or anything in return for his life. They were not

listening to anybody. It was a horrible, unforgettable night. I left that village and took my family to town and never went back again.

People were afraid to go too close, until late the following morning. The father of the Kurdish man was the only person who was outside, staying close by the body of the Turkish man, not letting any dogs come near all night. The state soldiers arrived only after 10 a.m. the following morning. They claimed that the phone line had been cut by the guerrillas before they come to the village and for that reason the station could not call for help. They understood that the soldiers from the station could not help and put their own lives at risk. They collected the body of the Turkish man, and also put his burnt car onto a military carrier vehicle. All his other belongings, jacket and money were taken by the soldiers. They also arrested the Kurdish man, telling his family it was just for questioning, and they left the village very quickly. They released the Kurdish man a day later.

One of the heads of the guerrilla group, Omer, would be killed in the following months during clashes with state forces around the city of Agri. A year later, the main leader, Misto, was bitten by a snake and died in a town close to Kars. Many guerrillas were dying young, but many new young members were also joining. The guerrilla members were changing, rules and Kurdish justice was developing but the power of the Kurdish movement was just expanding and deepening. The presence of the state, physically and emotionally, was diminishing in most Kurdish villages, even though it was claiming to have won the war. The state was not even able to stop a case which was happening just a kilometre away, and was powerlessly watching. In the early years, the PKK's public court and processes were mobile and fast. Not all cases ended with the death penalty. The fear of punishment was like the wind and spread very quickly. One case could deter a hundred villagers from having a Turkish man in their house for any reason. There was societal disconnection and divide, and there was no longer much intermarriage. The aim of the PKK had been achieved.

Justice after 2004

After the arrest of Öcalan by the Turkish intelligence service in Kenya, in February 1999, the Kurdish movement was in a serious crisis and divisions occurred. After a few years of chaos, the Kurdish movement began to establish a new structure and politics and strengthened its unity. New institution- and state-building processes took place. The Kurdish movement moved from retribution to distribution justice after 2000. Each local authority was given the power and support to establish and develop its own local court and justice system. Since then, the selection of judges and the court process has been separated from the guerrillas' daily activities and battles. However, the local process still has to follow the party's structure and authority. There are members of the movement who are in a position to inform on all processes to their superiors, but they don't take part in any of them actively and directly if it is not necessary. These 'super' powerful representatives usually work as agents of the Kurdish movement, and they mostly get their information from the councils and judges who are publicly known, locally and respected people. They then report all the information regularly to their superiors, the central authority. These representatives are not from their local working area and are only appointed for a limited time before they are moved on to another place. With this rotational positioning, the movement makes sure that the member doesn't get too involved with the local culture and traditions and their role and responsibility to the central authority continues. During my field research, I identified four different categories of members at the local level who take part in the process of justice and other institution building.

1. *Party officers or representatives*: These co-members, one man and one woman, are appointed for 1–3 years by the movement. They stay in a particular local area for a fixed time and are usually moved around after they complete their term. They work as governors for the Kurdish movement.
2. *Permanent members*: These are mainly loyal, committed local party members and supporters. Local youths and their supervisors are part of this group. They continue their role and responsibilities as long as their commitment, loyalty and 'good' reputation continues. There are business people, teachers, activists, lawyers, drivers and cooks among them. They organise most of the local activities, taking part in education and indoctrination programmes. Kurdish judges, local militias and most local politicians are selected from this group.
3. *Temporary members*: These are also could be youths, business people, activists, lawyers, different service and technical people, who are not direct members of the movement and do not follow their activities day to day,

but they support and take action when they are needed and invited. Like the first two groups, these are also ideologically committed and support the Kurdish nation state, identity, culture and language but they don't want to be very visible members. There are two reasons for this: (1) they are afraid to be blacklisted by the state; (2) the movement also encourages these people to keep their distance so as not to create an environment in which all its members could be targeted or arrested by the state. If the state arrests and imprisons permanent members then some of these temporary members step up and take on the role of the permanent members.

4. *Sympathetic members*: These are mainly members of the public who take voluntary roles from time to time, including taking part in demonstrations, lending their property or space for the movement's activities, ideologically supporting and contributing to the movement and paying regular tax. This group has close connections with the judges, brings their own conflicts or inform of any conflicts in their apartments or neighbourhood to the movement's local branch.

I was told by several members of the Kurdish movement that one of the aims of the process based on elected judges is to take a lesson from previous mistakes and actions. Aside from building a possible Kurdistan state institution, making good connections with the people, reaching diverse groups, following local values, institutionalising the process of judiciary and increasing people's respect and trust have been important reasons for the new judiciary system. The election of council members and the selection of judges is important as a way to keep gender, ethnic and religious equality and representation. The purpose is to widen societal inclusion, to encourage historically neglected groups to support the movement, and to extend the authority and power of the movement beyond close members and supporters. Gender representation and quota is also another factor when deciding who is going to be a judge. The local council members are elected by members of the community for two- and four-year terms depending on the need of the locals and individual circumstances. But not all members are elected. Around 40 per cent of council members are appointed by the central authority for a similar term. The council members elect board members and create different committees (such as a women's committee, mosque committee, economic committee, justice committee, local youth committee). The executive power of each local council should be shared between a male and female as a co-president system and the local council high committee should have at least six members, including co-presidents. Each board, including the justice, also should have co-spokespersons and have enough numbers of male and female representatives for their activities. These boards and their works are observed by the high committee as well as the party's local representative. The local councils and different branches should always follow the principle of the party's code and conduct.

The local high committee organises their own agenda, releases statements and decides about the organisation of any meetings, publications and media. They have regular meetings but are also obliged to meet outside the regular arrangement if and when it is necessary. They have an obligation to implement their agenda on time, monitor all activities of their boards and inform the central authority. Aside from the selection of judges, it also approves members for its local security process. These security officers are usually taken from local militias and members of the youth organisation, recruited 'voluntarily', but they are organised, commanded and ordered by the party's local military representative who also works closely with the party's local political representative. As well as dealing with direct or indirect conflict with the state and helping the main guerrilla forces, the local armed security forces implement all local decisions which are made by the local councils and boards, and protect the properties and lives of local people. Article 67 of the Social Contract of the Democratic Federalism of Northern Syria,[16] which can also be described as the constitution of the PKK-led Kurdish movement, states that:

> The democratic justice system solves the problems related to justice and social rights through peoples' participation and self-organisation. The vision of justice is based on the moral principles of the democratic society. It aims at building a society which adopts a democratic approach and vision and ecology that believes in the freedom of women and societal life and organises itself on the basis of democratic society. Justice is served through social participation and the organisation of democratically formed local units.

[16] The Social Contract of the Democratic Federalism of Northern Syria was established on 29 December 2016.

The justice system has also different boards and branches: justice offices, investigation committees, reconciliation committees, women's justice council and general justice council. All these branches and their members are elected by the general councils. The methods and work of these boards are different but they are interlinked and inform each other. A Kurdish mayor stated in September 2016:

> A democratic state has an equal law for all and an equal justice. Has this been served by the state we live in? No! Then Kurds have to create their own system. Justice offices are in every part of our regions now. We have a huge demand from our people. We even had to open one of the justice offices at our municipality building. Apart from other things, my colleagues and I are serving justice to our people. Many municipalities which are run by Kurdish mayors have to respond to this demand.

According to the needs of local people, every district, town and city has its own justice office, which is the equivalent of a local court, and receives all kinds of complaints. These offices can be placed at the community centre, local party office or one of the rooms of the Kurdish-led, political-party-run mayor's building. Justice council meetings, court processes and decisions take place at these offices. The members work voluntarily and are selected from respected, socially accepted and trusted members of the councils.

After any complaints or applications, the members of the investigation committee make a detailed search and investigation of the case, collect evidence, talk with different sides, reveal the crimes or conflict, and help judges to make decisions. The members of the investigation committee are also members of the local de facto security forces, who have an almost similar role and responsibility to the state police.

The reconciliation committee works closely with different neighbourhoods, and is committed to solving conflicts in as early a stage as possible. If they are needed, even during the night, they take the initiative and go to the place or people in dispute, to talk to them directly. They are supported and escorted by the local militia and security forces if necessary.

Women's courts have been very successful and effective especially for limiting violence against women, stopping early-age marriages and increasing the equality and role of women within society and the movement. The women's council deals with a variety of issues, especially for those who don't want to discuss their cases in front of a general, mixed court, or who prefer the involvement of female councils (judges). Crime, especially honour crimes against women and men, is on the increase. The female councils aim to eliminate this kind of violence. For example, 35-year-old Semsiye Alak had a love affair in Mardin in December 2002 with 55-year-old Halil Acilga. It was an 'honour' case. Both Halil and Semsiye were stabbed and stoned to death by Semsiye's brothers and father. She was four months pregnant at the time. Halil was killed on the spot. His throat was cut after he had been knifed and stoned. Semsiye's baby died as a result of her knife injuries. Semsiye struggled to survive for a further six months, but she died in May 2003. Her family did not accept her body. Several Kurdish women's organisations and activists explained, 'We could not save her from her family, but we took responsibility for her body and buried her with respect.'

In 2015, there was another similar case in the same region. The Kurdish women's organisation got information in advance this time and managed to stop the crime. They contacted the family first not to take any action against their daughter. They also contacted the local militias and sent a few of them to the women's family to talk to her elders. The family were afraid of militias. Strong persistence from the members of the women's organisation stopped the family from putting their daughter in danger. However, the women's organisation did not trust the family and did not want to take any risk, so they asked the local Kurdish mayor for help, to provide a safe place for the woman to stay away from her family. Her life was saved. The state was not involved during any of these processes.

In different parts of the Middle East, North Africa and Asia, it is the family and community who decide if women should live or die if their behaviour is seen as 'unacceptable' according to their family. Not just patriarchal and criminally minded men, but even many women have normalised violence or have been forced to accept violence as normal. Without women facing and fighting against this normalisation it would not be possible to change the minds of society and the authorities. The role of the Kurdish movement, women fighters and also the creation of women's councils have influenced many families and stopped them from punishing their women. As a result of such a development, young men and women have also become more outspoken and are pushing for change. In May 2015, a member of the women's council in Mardin told me:

We managed to destroy the power of the state in our region. It was the main power behind our families' patriarchal system. We are now dealing with our families and their understanding of honour. To beat families is harder than to beat the state but we are almost there.

In September 2015, a member of Kurdish women's movement explained in Diyarbakır:

Honour crime is not seen as 'honour crime' but it is seen as crimes of love or of passion in the western part of Turkey. There is discrimination in relation to crimes in Turkey as well. This stigmatisation has also affected society. There are some women who come to us, but many of them do not. We try to go to different villages and towns to spread our education and to include many women and children. We use local languages and talk to them directly. We want them to be aware of their options. Kurdish courts and our militias exist to protect them. We have individual and also family meetings. We get a lot of support from the young members of families. They are also part of the Kurdish movement and pushing for change.

The general justice councils are made up of male and female members from different social and ethnic backgrounds. They work as judges and they supervise and organise work between different branches. They also help to build the alternative judiciary system, arrange co-ordination and collaboration between different local justice offices, and provide regular reports to their superiors and the central authority. The justice system, the court, the committee members and especially judges represent the social face and reputation of the Kurdish movement. When they face a problem and receive a complaint, they contact the most appropriate and closest local group that can influence the parties and resolve the case quickly. The response time in which they act is very important for preventing any further escalation of crimes. The role of the state is very limited and most people refuse to inform and involve it. When the local courts take part in this kind of mediation then the process itself becomes an educational experience for those involved. The aim is for the educational process and programmes to cause them to change their attitude, to recognise the problem and to make peace.

The number of judges also varies from region to region, but there are usually between five to eight for an averagely populated city. While sometimes one judge deals with a small and easy case alone (under supervision and monitored by one of the local area representatives), at other times at least three judges take a role for a complicated and difficult case. The immunity of members of councils and judges are guaranteed when they serve justice and they are not held accountable for their decisions and judgments by the local people. The local area representatives and judges are supported, their security is guaranteed and their social justice decisions are implemented by the local militias. However, judges are judged and their decisions are also challenged by the movement's high justice council. Article 68 of the Social Contract explains the principle of social justice:

> (1) Social justice is considered a basis for the organisation and self-protection of society. It depends on solving social problems related to justice in the villages, neighborhoods and district communities. It solves problems by means of dialogue, negotiation and mutual consent. (2) Actions which harm social life and environment are considered a crime. When a crime is committed, victims have the opportunity to defend their rights. Society shall have the right to assess the damage, criticise and give suggestions, and participate in decision-making. (3) Punishments shall aim to rehabilitate guilty people, force them to repair any damage which they created, develop awareness, and correctly include them in social life. (4) Regarding the problems related to peoples, groups and social segments, they shall have the right to form justice mechanisms and develop special solution methods provided that they do not contradict the social contract or basic human rights. (5) Regarding issues related to the general interest and security of all people and groups, they are settled in justice systems which represent the whole society. (6) Special female organisations and equal representation of women are essential for justice and its institutional activities. Women-related decisions are dealt with by female justice systems.

The central authority decided that economic self-support is the main criteria of these local councils and social justice. Any additional money, donations and income from fines are usually transferred to the central authority. The regular reports of all activities are one of the main responsibilities of co-presidents. This is the one of the indicators of the institutionalisation of the work. The aim is to create a state-style system. The problem with this self-support is that in some local councils judges may push people to pay high fines or involuntary donations, especially for business and criminal cases. Aside from increasing tensions and damaging trust, it can also increase nepotism and a culture of bribery, creating new injustices and favouritism. I have observed that the central authority is aware of some of these problems and for that reason their local area representatives observe the judges very closely, inform the central authority regularly and dismiss judges if they think it necessary.

If one side takes their case to the Kurdish court, especially in Kurdish regions, there is not much option for the other side to refuse to go to court, or not to accept the judgement made by the court. It is a state-like system in that someone cannot just dismiss any call or judgement from the state, but has an obligation to follow the structure and obey decisions. The Kurdish court has similar powers and processes. If there is an application against an individual then they will follow or to be forced to follow the process and the outcome of the process.

The documented filed evidence shows that formal written applications from individuals are still limited, especially during processes with people in the Kurdish regions of Turkey.[17] The aim is not to create any direct evidence that state forces could find and then use to punish individuals. The details of the cases and processes are deliberately untraceable. The complaint is usually oral, the process is usually oral and the decision is made orally and is told directly to the parties in person or by phone. One or a few members usually visit the location of the case, which can be a house, community centre, mayor's office or an arranged place outside the inhabited areas. They invite the parties concerned, to listen to their complaints and to make decisions there, face to face. The parties are usually given some weeks or months to pay if it is a fine, or are just made to shake hands and promise not to have any further conflicts if the crime is minor.

---

[17] In the diaspora, the written and signed document is used for the application of the process and also the final agreement between parties. See, Tas 2016d.

The documenting process usually takes place when the local commanders report to their superiors. In this report, they give information about the number of cases, the kind of cases and processes, and the results they have achieved in their local areas. It is also documented who followed and who did not follow their decisions, what kind of cases were resolved easily, and what kind of cases need to be dealt with by the central authority. Particularly if there is a conflict between powerful tribes who support the movement but have a dispute with each other, they can be dealt with by the central authority. They provide detailed information about how much money they collect as fines, donations, taxes or support from local people. The report gives information about the people's relations with the movement, highlights who has a close connection with the state and possibly works as a 'state agent', but who also supports the movement despite all difficulties, torture and harassment from the state. The information about the local activists, politicians, journalist, new militias and fighters are important parts of the report. Operations against state forces, their successes and losses are usually detailed. The need for military, medical and educational equipment, and the transfer and training of some new members is submitted as part of their routine report. This detailed information means that all activities and processes are documented, but only the actual members and the central authority have access to these written records, not the local people or judges.

Different Kurdish Laws for Different Cases

While most cases are left to the selected judges to deal with under the supervision of the representative of the central authority, other family, business, criminal, religious and ethnic-related cases that are dealt with by local judges and councils have to follow the directive of the central authority fully. The cases are reviewed and treated differently. I have categorised the structure and divisions of these cases below, according to my direct observations of different Kurdish cases and courts:

Family law: The movement's high committee does not get involved in many cases related to family matters and leaves the main decisions to the local community judges. This approach is followed for several reasons. First, the central authority and its militias do not want to be part of any family conflicts which could affect their reputation, as has happened in the past. Second, they want to keep the problem local and let local administration have some level of power. Third, they want the inclusion and knowledge of local, societal and family values, which differ from area to area. However, there is still the issue of inheritance, which is the catalyst for many family feuds. Most wealth and assets are registered in the man's name, usually the head of the household; it can be the father or older brother but not the women. Many women still do not feel comfortable to ask for full equality and their share. This is not just a problem for Kurdish women locally, but the problem of women in Turkey and the Middle East in general. Many local Kurdish women, activists and even a female lawyer said: 'How can I ask for this? Society would name and shame me if I asked for any inheritance from my family.' The Kurdish movement in general and judges specifically have not pushed much for this equality. I have seen their soft approach on inheritance matters during their processes. The aim is to resolve one problem at a time and 'honour crime' is seen as the most urgent and important family problem. One of the Kurdish judges in Diyarbakır stated in June 2016:

> We are dying every day. Many women are killed. Our first job is to keep society, especially women, alive, and to secure their right to live. After that we will create equal living conditions for them, including inheritance. Without life, nobody cares about inheritance. We need society's help to stop honour crimes and we cannot push all changes in one go. Most families, even modern ones, follow the old traditions when it comes to inheritance.

When it comes to inheritance, even the most educated families find it difficult to consider equal shares. A female activist from Diyarbakır stated in September 2015:

> I have tried to ask my family for an equal share but it is not easy for me even to initiate this subject. Most families don't take women's questions seriously. They respond to them with a joke and say 'Yeh yeh, maybe, if you are a good girl.' What does 'a good girl' mean? This 'good girl' mockery is not applicable for boys. What society says about us affects most decisions here. All unwritten societal codes and rules control and command us. The religion, state and even Kurdish movement are supportive of these old societal rules.

Another well-educated teacher, with a master's degree, said in Diyarbakır, in September 2015:

> I have had similar difficulties with my family. Our inheritance was not going to be shared equally between the male and female family members, even though we are a well-educated family and most of our family members live in Istanbul, Germany and the UK. Especially my father, who lives in Germany, played an important role in advocating in favour of my equal share. The other males and my mother in particular still don't like this. They call my dad a 'soft man', 'too liberal', 'not masculine enough'. For them, a strong man is someone who follows traditions. My mum has been very angry with me, telling me that I have brought shame to the family by taking the family wealth away from my brothers, to an alien husband.

The Kurdish women's movement and some local judges push for strict punishment when it comes to violence, divorce and the rights of the wife and children. The salary of the husband may be transferred to the wife as a form of punishment. For the implementation of some decisions, guerrillas and local militias play an important role. There are some cases when people do not want to follow the decisions made by the local elected judges. In these cases, the PKK take over the role and use enforcement and make sure that the rules are followed. They resolve the conflict much more easily and quickly than the local elected judges, because they have guns and more power.

Criminal law: Kurdish central authority and local militias have full authority and monopoly of power over these kinds of cases. The administrative processes of cases are dealt with by local judges, the parties in conflict are invited for the meetings, but the party's high committee and local area representatives are directly involved, resolve, punish and administer justice. However, the elected judges are usually present and the preparation of these cases will be left to local judges in the future, when the autonomy or independence of Kurdistan is recognised. Currently, this does not happen for several reasons. First, the movement wants to show that they have the monopoly on violence and punishment. Second, at a local level people know each other and might have close relationships with both parties and the trust of local judges may be less, which may affect their authority. Third, a case might escalate and turn into a blood feud if it is left to local judges alone. Fourth, the resolution may take longer if the local judges take the initiative alone. Fifth, these cases involve high levels of compensation, changing the living places of some parties and even imprisonment. These kinds of decisions and punishments cannot be made and carried out by the local authority. Heavy punishments, including fines, compensation, re-education and imprisonment, can only be effective if imposed by the strong central authority which is more independent than local judges. Sixth, even though the local judges are (s)elected by the local people, their decided punishments may not be followed fully, which may then damage the authority of the party and leadership. For example, a man was killed in a revenge crime in the city of Van in 2015. There was already an arrangement between two families. The family which had committed the crime gave their 13-year-old daughter to the other family. This was one of the conditions of the peace. The Kurdish militias from Diyarbakır, which is 364 kilometres away from Van, heard about the case. They sent a few of their members to Van. They took the 13-year-old girl from the other family to a Kurdish women's refugee centre in Diyarbakır and settled the conflict with compensation. However, both families were punished with heavy fines for their actions. They were also informed that if any further crimes or forced marriages take place, they would receive harsher punishment.

Business law: If the cases are small and only concern the immediate family, and if there are no criminal factors, fights, injuries or deaths involved, then the central authority allows such conflicts to be resolved quickly by the local judges. However, if the value of the conflict is high, has some criminal aspect and is between different families or tribes, then the central authority follows these cases very closely. It is briefed at every step by judges and local area representatives and makes the final decision. These cases generate the highest revenue and involve large donations from both parties, as well as fines, so it is important that they are monitored and considered carefully.

Religious power and Kurdish justice: These are related to marriage, divorce, business agreements and activities within and between different individuals or religious groups which may have specific religious codes, laws and conditions involved. The Kurdish movement's different local religious authorities, branches and mosques take action and help (s)elected judges for some cases. For example, if the case concerns Yezidi marriages, the Kurdish movement makes sure that the Yezidi high authority and mediation system is involved in the conflict and helps to resolve it quickly. This approach is followed for several reasons. First, most of these cases are family cases and local family values and sensitivities are taken into consideration. As mentioned in the above family law section, the movement encourages the local different religious groups to take responsibility for these cases. Second, in this way, the movement keeps its authority and power over individuals, religious groups and different communities and shows that it can also delegate when necessary. I was told by one of the Kurdish women judges in Diyarbakır in May 2015 that they are aware that there is some conflict of interest between the approach of the religious groups and the approach of Kurdish women's organisations. She continued:

> Religion is important. We can no longer let it be used by the state and different religious organisations to influence our people and take them away from us. We made some mistakes in the past by dismissing religious groups. Some of them have also joined our movement and we need to respect their approach even if we don't fully agree. We know that many families are influenced by different religious groups. Our councils and judges co-operate with the different religious groups and their leaders. Their involvement is important. Religious leaders can stop some families from carrying out a crime against a 'guilty' member of the family. To involve them is also part of the process of changing and modernising them. If we exclude them, then they cannot know about our structure and laws. Our militias observe them all the time, more than the police do.

These practices in the Kurdish regions show that the Kurdish movement doesn't follow strict secular rules as it does in some parts of the diaspora.[18] It sometimes sacrifices the priorities of the Kurdish women's organisations for the sake of the religious group, to dissipate any tension and also to expand and increase its popularity and power within these religious groups. This also shows that while the Kurdish movement's power increases and more and more

---

[18] See, Tas 2016d.

groups join, their earlier leftish secular approach decreases. The movement and its de facto institutions take a more conservative and moderate stance.

Four Types of Believers and their Judgements

From my field research and the perspective of the people I interviewed, I observed the level of plurality of views among Kurdish people in general. However, I have also noticed different views and perspectives among Kurdish people who have a close connection, membership or show their strong support and solidarity for the PKK-led movement. Not all supporters have the same views and feelings. There is some collective thinking, such as aiming for a Kurdish nation state, but there is a lot of tension between different groups of members. In regard to how different individuals and groups react to the approaches of the Kurdish movement, I have identified four different types of behaviour and reactions. These are (1) dogmatic (2) passive (3) moderate and (4) liberal critical followers. The first type in particular, dogmatic members, needs further explanation. These descriptions may not only be specific to Kurds and their relationship with PKK politics and policies, but also to many other similar groups of supporters.

Dogmatic believers: These are totally committed and it is not possible for them to tolerate any criticism towards the leader or movement. Their fundamentalist stance does not even accept any light criticism supported by clear evidence. They may go further to protect the leader (Öcalan) from the leader himself, to protect the party (PKK) again from the party (PKK), and will not even accept any criticism from the leader against his own leadership and the movement's actions. Even if they hear any direct self-criticism from the leader and movement, they are unwilling to justify it. The original approach, codes and rules which were introduced by the movement are accepted without any criticism by these believers.

Dogmatic believers may isolate anyone who doesn't follow these rules, including the actual fighters of the movement. The sexual preferences of individuals are often discussed as a weakness and individuals who are seen as liberal are usually blamed for not following the party codes and not living accordingly. Cancelling culture is one of the main weapons of these kind of believers. Rumours and fabricated stories are used to ostracise individuals who do not think, dress or socialise as they do. Political group meetings, demonstrations, social media, conferences and even some academic networks and collaborations are used for this group's personal needs and aims. They thrust critical and innovative thinkers out of social and professional circles, not just from social media or online networks but also in the real world. They establish and use a social death penalty for others, and the social massacre of others has become this group's only aim and practice. These are not just members of the guerrilla or militia movement, but there are many community members, activists, lawyers, teachers and academics amongst them.

In my last twelve years of field research on Kurds, I have directly observed many such cases, but one case which deserves mentioning here is an example of these dogmatic believers. The case took place just after a Kurdish conference was held in the UK. I had a conversation with two Kurdish 'academics' about some of the presentations and ideas at the conference. I talked about my research on Kurds, mentioned the PKK's previous actions, crimes against civilians and Kurdish people, the process after Öcalan's arrest in 1999, the limitation of individual sexual freedom, and Öcalan's criticism of the early PKK period. They became very angry and the male academic turned to me and said, 'Are you a Turkish agent? These kinds of things are not true and only claimed by Turkish state agents. Show me proof that the PKK killed any civilians, their own members or a Kurdish person.' Other female Kurdish academics supported the first one's defensive approach and questioned my Kurdishness and their friendship with me. I was totally shocked that these two 'academics', who were very close friends with each other, who had already completed their PhD on Kurds, deeply believed that the PKK did not kill any Kurds, civilians or their former members. My thoughts were seen as 'too liberal' and likened to the 'state's approach'. I was told and they followed up by email later that I should respect and listen to what they say because they finished their PhD before me and their work 'exceeds' my own achievements. I kept giving different examples, such as the death of PKK's former senior representatives Hikmet Fidan in Diyarbakır on 6 July 2005, and Gani Yilmaz and Sabri Tori in Iraqi Kurdistan on 11 February 2006. I also gave several examples of the deaths of civilians, imams and teachers at the hands of the PKK, but it was not possible to convince them.

These two academics hadn't completed any ethnographical field research on Kurds, and used only secondary sources for their research or any arguments they had. They were part of the second generation of migrants in the diaspora. Their families came from a city where the Kurdish movement was not very active and never in control. They and their families had not faced any day-to-day conflicts between the state forces and PKK. They were hearing and seeing things from a great distance. Growing up in a small family circle in the diaspora, close to dogmatic members of the movement, shaped their understanding and is reflected in their work and attitudes. Their anger towards the Turkish state, governments and society also did not help them to look at the issue from a critical, academic perspective. On the contrary, this anger has made them act aggressively towards any criticism. I kept mentioning that even the PKK and Öcalan himself would disagree with them, and that spreading fear and increasing respect and loyalty among their members by the use of harsh methods was one of the most important characteristics of this kind of organisation, which desires a state-like power and structure. For example, one of the PKK's former leaders, Nizamettin Tas, talked to the Turkish *Sabah* newspaper, on 27 August 2013, during the peace talks between the Turkish government and PKK:

> The PKK aimed for the complete annihilation of a family who were critical of them. They ordered: 'Destroy it completely so that no guerrilla should be able to leave from the party, to come down from the mountain, nor fight against the PKK' . . . The PKK also later announced that it had pardoned those who left the party after the congress. It was announced that executions against its own members in the past had stopped and the movement wanted to turn over a new leaf. However, the internal executions continue . . . We wanted to set up an alternative Kurdish party in the past, but as soon as it was established, they shot not only Hikmet Fidan and Gani Yilmaz, but eight friends . . . In a period when the war ceased and peace started, the PKK's attacks against its former members and critics continued . . . The only person to stop these executions in the PKK is Abdullah Öcalan.

Hikmet Fidan was one of the representatives of the opposition wing. He was also the former deputy chairman of the Kurdish People's Democracy Party (HADEP). On the morning of 6 July 2005, in the narrow streets of the Baglar district of Diyarbakır, he was killed with a single bullet to his neck. Several former PKK guerrillas explained during our interviews that hundreds of people were sentenced to death by the PKK's revolutionary courts (*Devrim*

Mahkemeleri) and the sentences were carried out. Especially during the 1980s and 1990s, when the PKK was establishing and increasing its power not just against the Turkish state, but also against different powerful local tribes and groups, they established alternative courts and prisons around different camps and cities in and outside the border of Turkey.

To be accused of being a 'state agent' was enough for the revolutionary court to make a decision in favour of execution. These types of accusations are often used by critics on different platforms and in discussions. If anyone has different views or criticises any of the movement's actions towards one of the dogmatic believers, the first accusation they receive is that they are a 'state agent'.

Making people scared of the movement and creating continuous fear is one of the most effective ways of establishing authority and gaining power, as discussed earlier in this chapter with the case of the Turkish man planning to marry a Kurdish woman. Learning from the main reason for the failure of the previous Kurdish movements, which was that they were not widely supported by the local Kurdish people, the PKK made use of propaganda, force or fear to ensure that local Kurdish people took part in the movement and supported it unconditionally. I was told by some active and former guerrilla members that without this method their destiny would not have been much different from the previous Kurdish revolts and movements. Civilian victimisation and the politics around this have not just been used by the PKK against the state but also by the state against the Kurdish movement.[19]

The PKK managed to spread fear in every corner of Kurdish cities, towns and villages. Fear became a cloud over Kurdish regions, not just because of the state but the PKK too. With the help of fear, the PKK managed to break Kurdish people's relations with the state and different tribes, benefited from intertribal conflict, and increased the numbers of its fighters and its economic income. Some families, who could not afford to pay taxes, agreed that one of their family members could join the movement. These families were then feared and gained status in their neighbourhoods. While families who provided guerrillas were arrested and tortured by the state, at the same time they increased their power over and respect from other Kurdish families who had

[19] See, Belge 2016.

not provided wealth or fighters to the movement. The fear made the movement a new refugee centre for many Kurds.

The movement with its large number of supporters managed to shut down large cities. It punished individuals, families and whole villages or tribes if they disobeyed any of its orders. It made sure that Kurdish people followed the PKK's rules and laws and paid their share. In this way, they also cut Kurdish people's connections or any relationship with the state. The state was made the enemy for each and every Kurd. The disconnection with the state also made the PKK the only option for the people – it made them fear the movement, and then gain respect through the fear. Many active and former guerrillas, activists and Kurdish politicians explained that without this fear, people could easily give away information of some benefit to the state about the members' activities. Because the state had been spreading fear and using violence against Kurdish people for a long time, the PKK's members visited almost every neighbourhood and household, advertising their ruthlessness with examples and making it very clear that if people collaborated with the state, they would be enforcing harsher punishments than those of the state. The movement thought that male members with their 'authoritative' voices and harsh punishments could act more ruthlessly than women, and this was important for creating fear in a short period of time. This was one of the main reasons why female members were left at the camps cooking, washing the dishes and doing laundry work while they were part of the movement between the 1980s and 1990s. There was such a strong mindset on gender roles and positionality which requires time to overcome.

There was a gender stereotype that 'men could create fear easily by their actions and that people could obey and follow the word of men but not women'.[20] The state has also followed this approach and usually sends male governors to Kurdish areas. The Kurdish movement channelled the fear with a real example as did the state. As we discussed from example cases, the PKK didn't hesitate to punish even innocent people in order to establish its authority. For example, the PKK later apologised for killing an innocent imam,

[20] See the studies carried out by Sanbonmatsu 2003; Hansen and Laura 2007; Holman et al. 2011. See also specifically the early gender condition with the PKK, by one of its leading members, Cansiz 2018.

Salih Bildik, in 1989. He was shot dead after rumours that he was in contact with the state and causing trouble for guerrillas, which was understood later not to be true. Salih Bildik's relationship with the state was limited to his official duties as imam. Another example took place in 1998, in the village of Bate within Beytussebap township, where the PKK guerrillas killed ten village guards, who had been forced into their roles by the state, but who had not caused any disruption nor did they have any direct conflict with the PKK. The event was later investigated by the PKK's justice committee and it was found to be a 'wrong and unjust practice', and an apology was made to the families of the victims.

Most dogmatic members would not accept these very clear incidents, which have even been accepted by the PKK itself. Dogmatic believers are not only male, there are many females among them who claim that the Kurdish movement has had gender 'equality' from the beginning and reject the fact that the women's role was limited to 'making tea and serving men' in the early days. Some female guerrillas, two former and one still active, explained during our focus group discussion in Diyarbakır, in May 2015:

> A few strong women and some critical male members refused to accept the women's role of making tea and serving men. Women also wanted to take part in active fighting. They wanted to be part of the decision-making process. In the end, women reached all these goals but only after struggling for decades and the sacrifice of many lives. It took decades for dogmatic believers to lose some power. These people are still among us and refuse to change their opinions. Many of them have similar attitudes, but they lost the support of the leader, Öcalan, after 2000. Their existence and domination create a risk for gender equality and many other important rights will be at risk if they occupy the party again, or if something happens to Öcalan.

The continuous economic, cultural, linguistic and political deprivation of Kurds by the state has increased the number of dogmatic believers who justify all PKK's actions. They are against the development of gender and minority rights within the movement. The anger toward the state has also increased the public support for these dogmatic members and their actions. Dogmatic believers helped to justify any action of the movement for the movement, more than would ever have been expected. For dogmatic believers, there should be no criticism until the movement creates a unitary power, establishes its authority and creates an independent Kurdistan. One of my interviewees said in Diyarbakır, in May 2015:

> The state is our enemy. I would not even accept any of their positive steps, of which there are none. However, the PKK is ours. We, all Kurds, are the children of the PKK. Sometimes it is good if a father gives a few slaps to a child. Otherwise, how can you discipline a child, how can you keep a family united and moving in one direction together?

Similar justifications were made by several other interviewees. They believe that without some fear and punishment, it would not be possible to keep people focused on unity. Since his arrest, Öcalan has accepted and written about some harsh and wrong decisions, including executions which were carried out by the PKK's local members and commanders during the 1980s and 1990s.[21] He explained even in 1992, during one of his interviews with the famous Turkish journalist Mehmet Ali Birand, that he had already got rid of the old, nationalistic Öcalan and embraced the 'peace' which would allow Kurds, Turks, Arabs, Persians, men and women to live together peacefully and equally. A decade later, Öcalan himself ordered the establishment of a 'Truth and Reconciliation Commission'[22] on 14 January 2004 when he met with his lawyer on Imrali Island where he has been imprisoned. His aim was that the leading Kurdish institutions and communities should create such a commission which was to investigate any war crimes committed by both the PKK and Turkish state security forces. Öcalan told his lawyers, one of whom I interviewed, a member of Diyarbakır Bar Association, in 2015:

> Democracy does not develop without a justice and truth commission. Without the establishment of the Commission, dirty war, decades of hidden things don't come to light. The requirement of mutual trials is important for a real peace. Unilateral, one-sided trials can only create injustice. We are not against real justice, international courts and trials. Four thousand Kurdish villages

---

[21] See also, Öcalan and Kucuk 1993; Öcalan 2000; Yildiz 2001; Yilmaz 2014.
[22] The commission is also called '*Koma Komalên Kurdistan* – KKK' (Kurdish), '*Hakikat ve Adalet Komisyonu*' (Turkish).

were burned and so many innocent people were killed. We agree, there was a dirty war and we played our part in this. A Truth and Justice Commission must be created. All crimes and injustices, including ours, will remain hidden if not. This is very important.

Öcalan's order was put into practice in 2006. After the establishment of the 'Truth and Reconciliation Commission', the PKK accepted the killing of an imam and ten village guards, who were also Kurds, and made an apology for their crimes against civilians. While I was given many similar examples from the field of how the PKK made apologies for some of its previous actions, it was not possible to change or convince these two 'academics' and similar members' minds, and attempting to do so only fuelled their anger. Dogmatic believers do not change their minds easily, even when they are provided with facts and examples.

Passive believers: This group has almost the same views as the dogmatic believers but they don't openly declare their position easily. They might accept some mistakes or wrongs done in the past without criticism. While the first group claims that there is no dirt, this group brushes the dirt under the carpet. They try not to say much. They keep quiet until they find their safe environment. It may take a few meetings or discussions with members of this group before they show their uncritical position towards the movement and strong judgement against people with different views. Their dark and accusing tone may be heard when they have many fellow supporters and people with similar views around them. For example, in a first meeting in response to criticism of the movement's gender perspective, taboos on sexuality or individual freedoms, they would say: 'I don't know much. I don't like to talk about these subjects.' However, after second or third meetings, they would cite different quotes from Öcalan's writings, books or talks, mainly exaggerated or wrongly cited, and claim that 'While the rest of the women in the world have almost no rights, the PKK has introduced full gender equality for all.' They would not accept any opposing ideas, and claim that 'feminists and liberals don't understand the Kurdish movement'. The main source of their information is usually Öcalan's books or any book or work suggested by Öcalan. Like the first group, people who reject the approaches and opinions

of this group, can be discredited and attacked by public naming and shaming. They spread gossip and create false rumours about these individuals, and
make sure that they are not welcome in any institution of the movement.
In this passive but effective way, the will and desire of different individuals
becomes the main reason to be punished. The main aim is the annihilation of
individuality and the creation of one uniform persona.

Some of the Kurdish movement's new approaches may be helpful for
women and may allow for quicker solutions to their needs; however, it also
presents the risk of new injustices and punishment without facts or evidence,
according to fabricated stories, whispering campaigns and claims. I observed
that some members of these groups have taken on important roles in the
community, and without saying much to the individual or group concerned,
have then made important cases against them when they have left the court
room or discussion table.

The passive believers' decisions and approaches affect many other innocent
people and create other injustices. For example, if a woman lives according
to her own choices, but not this group's or the movement's, then the gossip
about her 'looseness', 'flirtatiousness', 'wildness', 'promiscuity', 'being a prostitute or libertine', 'not trustworthy' and 'incapable of participating in the life
of the community' is widely circulated. If a man is the subject of gossip, then
labels such as 'not trustworthy', 'selfish', 'not decent', 'arrogant', 'being incapable of participating in the life of the community', 'being bourgeois', 'liberal
life style', 'flirtatious', 'promiscuous', 'having many girlfriends', 'bad practice',
or 'state spy' are used and circulated. Such naming and shaming is the main
punishment used by the movement and their members against uncommitted
members, critics or people who have a different way of life. These behaviours and societal criminalisation are similar to the authoritarian supporter's
attacks on their political opponents and critics, as discussed in Chapter 1.

I have observed from the alternative court judgements, the approaches of
several activists and academics, and also the descriptions of regular community members, that not many people will feel strong enough to support a case
against the dogmatic or passive believer. When the members of these groups
claim something without proof, the rest are ready to believe so as not to get
into any trouble. This creates a new injustice in that the power and privilege
of some groups is more than others, whether you are male or female. Group

membership creates a new gender condition and having or not having that membership creates a new injustice and the possibility of group or community lynching.

Moderate believers: These are the people who are less extreme, welcome different views and find a common ground for the representation of wider audiences. They position themselves somewhere in the middle of polarised and conflicted camps that have dogmatic, passive, nationalistic, religious, radical right, radical left, liberal and very critical voices. The moderate position is never easy. They are not much liked by different groups and the majority of the public, and can be targeted by all sides and groups. Moderates try to not be labelled by dogmatic and passive believers as 'inadequate members', but they also make an effort to adopt important points from liberal critical voices and update their policies and rules. The ideological gap, the different gender and policy approaches and continuous conflict between the critical liberal voices and dogmatic believers open a gate for the moderates to take the lead position of management. In recent years, most Kurdish judges, heads of different institutions, branches and community leaders have been elected from this group. Their mediation-based solutions are not just critical of the patriarchal system, but are also helping to develop democratic institutions where the people may find an equal solution and are not judged according to their group membership, ethnicity, colour, gender or lifestyle but evidence and facts. Aggressive and exclusive nationalism and monopolistic group identity is also not much voiced by this group. People's different sexual, ethnic, racial, religious and ideological identities are not discussed, nor do they shape the outcome of the cases or activities as is common among the first two groups of dogmatic and passive believers. Firat Anli, former co-Mayor of Diyarbakır explained in September 2015 the difficulty of taking a moderate perspective:

> If our strategy was constructed according to jihadist and dogmatic ways and their solutions then we could have had societal support and reached our nationalist aims in a very short time. To have modernist, moderate and leftist ideology and to organise people according to their needs for ethnic and gender identity, within a changing society, is much more difficult. Without exploiting religious ideologies, the role of the mosque and the power of

imams, it is not easy to make a revolution in the Middle East. We have faced much criticism from our own people and community members because of the modern and challenging approaches we have chosen. Some Kurds have criticised Mr Öcalan because of these approaches. Even now, some of our members have been questioning whether it is our business to support modernist, leftist and socialist ideology and the rights and needs of women and poor people. They want us to focus first on the national identity of Kurdistan. For them nationalist needs are the most important and should come before everything else. They believe this approach would help produce a Kurdish independence. Then, after that, they suggest we could focus on other things, including gender equality. This strong nationalist, dogmatic ideology exists among many Kurds and the continuation of state violence helps this approach to gain power. But the Kurdish political movement has chosen to follow a different way, even if it is more difficult. Our aim is to change societal, ethnic, religious, gender and geographical inequalities. To do this, many risks need to be taken. In the long term, other Middle Eastern societies will benefit from our hard, moderate and pluralistic work.

The advantage of moderates is that they are to be able to talk to different camps, to see different points of view and to compare and test the right information or direction.[23] They are the meeting point. However, one of the problems with moderate believers is that they try to make all sides happy, which is usually not possible and not right. It may also slow down the process and block any meaningful changes. One former guerrilla, who later become a Kurdish activist told me in Istanbul, in 2016: 'I am a moderate, but a critical one. When you are a true moderate believer and wary of making strong statements then you don't resolve any problem in a meaningful way, but just keep all sides happy. I know that it is not possible to please everyone. I listen to different sides first, then I show my critical perspective.'

Liberal critical believers: This group does not believe the official line and follows a very sceptical approach. Their detailed engagement, analysing every detail and questioning what they hear and see creates tension within the group. They don't compromise easily and ask for radical changes. There is

[23] See, Carr 2019.

continuous conflict between this group and the first two, the dogmatic and passive believers. Whereas the first two groups prefer to support even acts of injustice by the group to keep the status quo and retaliate against any criticism towards the movement, liberal voices engage with every action, protest against injustices, and refuse to stay silent or compromise. While they acknowledge the positive side of the movement, they are also not afraid to speak out. They believe this is healthier for a strong group and any possibility of creating an independent Kurdistan, rather than to blindly follow 'like sheep' as do the first two groups, which is seen as the main reason for the failure. However, their positionality and critical voices are not much welcomed by the rigid political structure. Especially when hearing the arguments for gender equality and freedom, we can observe the clash of different believers. One of the liberal voices, a former guerrilla and also the head of the women's organisation in Diyarbakır told me in May 2018, in Berlin:

> I started this fight to change the whole society and its taboos. After thirty years of active service, I witnessed only brick walls from some of our own members. The individual's life, actions and freedom is questioned by some who happily lend their mind to any ideology and push others to do the same. Sexuality is not to be enjoyed or even talked about. When we bring up this subject our dogmatic members start questioning our comradeship. The passive members usually giggle without saying much in one-to-one meetings, but they also support dogmatic believers. They think we should postpone our sexuality for the success of the movement. I always question these narrow-minded, patriarchal approaches. I can fight for my rights, our national cause and also enjoy my freedom at the same time. My sexual freedom is one of my most important rights. This clash of freedom forced me to leave the active guerrilla life.

To sum up, Kurdish alternative courts and judiciary systems have played an important role in the development of Kurdish state institutions and power over its people. The state's power and legitimacy has been limited with the help of a parallel judiciary. The quality, equality and fairness of judgements and court processes have changed and have been modernised at some level, but the development continues. I have directly observed hundreds of Kurdish court cases in different geographical areas for over a decade, and witnessed the different judgements on similar cases by dogmatic, passive, moderate and liberal judges and community leaders. I have widely observed equal, fair and affordable justice by many Kurdish judges, but I have also noticed some injustices. The actions of some parallel court judges and community leaders are for personal gain and nepotistic relations, which slows down the development of fair and equal justice in some locations. Moderate and liberal voices are particularly important for a better, equal and fair justice system. They do not only create balanced, well-developed gender equality and fair platforms for all, but also prevent the movement from being captured by dogmatic and intolerant groups.

CONCLUSION

Justice is the backbone of any power, authority or state. If and when justice serves an authority and becomes injustice, not only small communities or states, but even empires cannot survive for long. Without studying and understanding societal and political authoritarianism and injustice in the Middle East, it would not be possible to understand the main reasons for the multiple and continuous conflicts and often changing borders. At times when the judiciary ceases to be independent from government structures and their political aims, when uncertainty, violence and fear become commonplace, we often witness the end of existing nation states and their institutions. In the context of authoritarian regimes, the aspirations of ethnic and religious minorities frequently conflict with the prevailing identities and forms of governmentality within existing nation states. Demands and aspirations for alternative governmentality and justice become important mainly when the existing political and legal systems are plagued with inequalities, corruption and the discrimination against ethnic, religious and/or political minorities. In these contexts, state power tends to be challenged.

Kurdish battles against authoritarian states in the Middle East are nothing new, and have already moved beyond the fourth generation. Using insurgency tactics against oppressive state regimes, Kurds have achieved some significant political and military victories, often against much bigger powers. They have gained rights, lands, more autonomy step by step, bringing down authoritarian state regimes in ongoing efforts to build their own state(s) one by one. Kurds in Iraq brought down Saddam Hussein's regime and gained a state-type autonomy after more than half a century of continuous fighting. Kurds in Syria have created their self-autonomous rule after sixty years of silent resistance. Kurds in Turkey are pushing the Turkish state to the edge after a century of revolts and uprisings, and more than forty years of active, local, national and transnational fights. Kurds in Iran have also been following in their brothers' footsteps since WW2. Kurds in general have so far rejected any religious fundamentalism, and followed the doctrine of democratic autonomy, justice and gender equality, which are welcomed by the Western and modern world. All this has come at a price: decades-long struggles and resistance, many lives lost, and more new challenging questions to be resolved.

In this book, I have tried to draw out the implications of my arguments for theorising alternative governmentality from the perspective of Kurdish state-building, equal justice, gendered participation in political transitions, and attempts to circumvent centralised and authoritarian state power and discriminatory legislation. I have underlined the problems with and for authoritarian regimes, the ways in which alternative politics, internal and international mobilisation and courts have been created and instrumentalised to serve competing political agendas and new power structures. The new gender roles and norms have also emerged as key to an alternative governmentality. The empirical case study of Kurdish political mobilisation has contributed to the wider conceptual understandings of the intersections between alternative justice, new forms of political power, and attempts to address gender-based inequalities, as well as the challenges of creating alternative forms of governmentality amongst minorities.

Authoritarianism and alternative politics do not only occur between newly born or dying powers and states, but also incestuously within and during the life cycles of regimes and states. Societies are complex, transform and manage to survive longer, but states fall when they fail to represent all the people within their realm. The state and its institutions may look strong and solid, but in reality, they are very weak and fragile entities. The state looks to be leading everything, but this is not the case when it faces real crisis and challenges. In a similar way to abused internal organs, which eventually will be the cause of death, or diseases when the body attacks itself and the outcome, again, is fatal. The birth and death of the state is as natural as the birth and death of different species and human beings. Sometimes a little trigger, like a virus, can be the unrelated tipping point, which is enough to kill the state.

There are good, healthy states, but there are many fragile and unhealthy states too. While healthy states address and overcome challenges, transform themselves accordingly and serve their people equally, unhealthy states become blinded by power seeking, serve specific individuals and often face regime changes, serious conflict and eventual downfall. When states become violent, ruthless and discriminative, they decline more quickly. Like a mafia gang leader, they face their own death after violence against others, in acts of increasingly evident nihilism. Historically, the numbers and names of the dead states or even once very powerful empires are too many to recall. In just the last century we had dozens of these examples; the British Empire, Ottoman Empire, Austrian-Hungary Empire, and the Soviet Union are just a few which were once claiming eternal power. There are many other state structures that have been reformed, fragmented and divided, resulting in endless conflict in places such as Iraq, Libya, Sudan, Syria, Afghanistan, Congo and Yemen. There are some others who are on the verge of transformation or collapse, including Turkey, Iran and, by some accounts, Brazil.

There is real need for change if unhealthy states are to be transformed or returned to health. Recognising diversity and serving equally at all levels is vital, as is creating a power balance rather than continuously changing rules and laws for certain people, increasing the quality of social justice, limiting the power of the central authority, greater recognition of regional autonomy, trusting the people, limiting a leader's time in office and not allowing the constitution to be changed for the extension of specific people and groups. Of course, these things are not easy and there is always the risk of power-hungry individuals and populist autocrats. While history has shown us that there is not a single authoritarian regime which has brought peace and prosperity to its people, internally and globally, people do not learn from these past examples, experiences and abuses of autocracy. Most who have experienced a military dictator or oppressive elected dictator in the past have made similar problematic choices again and again.

Accounts from different people and my direct observations in Turkey and more widely in the Middle East have shown that the legal and moral regulations of the nation and individuals are not equal. The goal of the official judicial system, for example, is no longer concerned with peace or justice, but only with serving the needs of autocrats. While some nations are treated as masters over the rest, 'the others' – people without a nation or minorities – are treated like pariahs. Their movements are restricted and their exposure to other people is limited as if they were contagious. This is seen as 'normal' justice for them. Those who question this unhealthy autocratic authority and would like to change the state and its institutions are seen as 'cowards', 'terrorists' or 'separatists'. This has not just been unique to Turkey's regime, but it has been the foundation of most authoritarian governmentalities in the past and present.

As this study has argued and shown from the Kurdish case studies, authoritarianism and being the enemy of minority groups are interconnected. While mafia bosses and criminals are considered the real protectors of the state, innocent members of minority groups are attacked and killed (il)legally by the forces of the autocratic regime. To be born into a minority group may be enough of a reason for someone to be discriminated against for a lifetime, even if such individuals disguise or hide their identity and voluntarily assimilate under a hegemonic identity, as we have seen from many individual Kurdish examples. One of the only predictable things about an authoritarian regime is their unpredictability. Power corrupts most rulers, but in the case of authoritarian rulers absolute corruption is not just limited to the rulers, but extends to society as well. There are similarities between viruses and autocratic regimes. Both spread very fast and corrupt and limit the life and space of people. Both of them are very costly to eradicate and take a long time to disappear.

So many majoritarian-fixated people, allow a dictator to slip in and damage the entire fabric of their nation. However, authoritarianism is not only based on one 'crazy' autocrat and their style. It is a collective and inter(nationally) linked process. It is an institutional development which may need to be crafted step by step by a few authoritarian like-minded leaders. One such leader might want to create an authoritarian regime but not have enough time or support, or might not be knowledgeable or competent enough. However, as a start they usually normalise abnormal things and open the way for a regime change. They damage democratic institutions to produce and normalise the language of intolerance, divide society sharply, and, importantly, create a circle of beneficiaries. These fundamental changes and the people who support them will ease the way for the next authoritarian-minded leader, who will be not easily beaten or removed. Each autocrat takes off a brick from democratic institutions until a large hole is created which normalises and establishes the authoritarian mindset, power and governmentality. The heart of a regime, interestingly though, is not its autocratic leader but the society and its followers who can survive until they find another populist leader with the same traits and myths to become their new hero. Most authoritarian regimes and autocrats have important similarities when it comes to their propaganda, rhetoric, policies and institutional structures.

Autocrats keep selling impossible dreams to their audiences and make sure that the people under their rule forget their existing conditions and struggles and continue to be part of the autocrat's self-fabricated, monstrous dreams. These include intolerance and the creation of conspiracy theories against minorities. These fictionalised, fixated and repeated claims are the main engines of an autocrat's tactics to stay in power for as long as possible. Evidence-based truths and democratic equal values are attacked, delegitimised, disenfranchised, and replaced by these shared but imaginary and false claims. While the truth can be difficult to accept, falsehoods are believed faster than the coming of daylight. Knowledge and science are continuously delegitimised by power seekers. Demagogues drag large sections of society behind them with nepotistic promises. People of different ages, education and race, including workers, the poor and the middle-class, desperately want to escape reality and be offered hope, and it does not matter if what they hear is lies.

When authoritarian leaders are accorded a 'godlike' level of unaccountable authority, power and impunity, it doesn't take long for their followers, who are ready to join in the destruction of the lives of others for their own happiness, to become a protective wall around them. It does not matter how empty the hopes and lies are, people don't care to think much about it. The moment they may recognise the truth could be the moment they have to sacrifice their loved ones, when it is already too late. Even then, many will still not face reality, and try to find some reason to blame anybody but themselves or the populist tyrants who put them in that situation.

Autocrats steal the truth, recalibrate reality and fine-tune it to suit their purpose and to play their own song. At the same time, they project their own venom, deflect their own corruption and call all those who insist on the truth 'liars'. With the increase of nationalism, populist liars no longer need churches or mosques to put in the time to convince people by getting them to read religious textbooks. People do not need to be convinced, nor want to read books or search for the truth anymore. Instead they look at the flags and huge messiah-style images of autocrats all around them, ubiquitous in the media, which encourage such self-serving showmanship. No one can avoid seeing them, not only on important boulevards, but also on almost every corner of every road, in houses and apartments, on every TV screen and anchorperson's chest badge, at any sports event or celebration, even on any daily soap opera. These banners can be seen across the sky, on the sea, on the back of the bus they are following, on the ambulance that comes to their rescue, in the shop, in the barber's, in the first aid kit. Even the church and mosque did not have that power. These simple banners and images of autocrats are now more powerful than any godly book. If someone manhandles them, they can be executed, and people will celebrate their death and congratulate the person who killed them. This new power has become greater than any promise of new technology, scientific advances, ecological recovery or a new and long life.

Millions of autocrat-lovers circulate fallacious messages repeatedly, which gradually erodes the real truth from the public sphere. The most shocking thing is how many people are ready to buy lies so easily and believe anything their leader says, but accept nothing from those critical of autocrats even when supported with real facts. Autocrat followers become trapped in their beliefs, and at the same time the autocrats become trapped in the things which their society believes. Society can create autocrats as well as populist autocrats can change the direction of society.

Seeking cover and gaining an easy advantage is widespread among autocrat followers. This creates an animal aggression against others for fear of losing their easily earned benefits. People believe their leader is the best, most hard-working person, who tells only the truth. They believe that their country is the best, their military is the strongest, their land is the richest and that their leaders only make them greater. They believe that anyone outside their circle is envious of them. They believe that those who do not share their beliefs are their enemies. What their leader says becomes the only truth for them. They are almost drugged or hypnotised by their religion, beliefs and leaders. As Voltaire wrote, in his 1765 essay, 'Those who can make you believe absurdities can make you commit atrocities.'

The wealth of autocrats and their narrow circles is mainly based on the wealth of others which is seized and stolen. The laws they create also protect them by legalising, regulating and normalising their wrongdoings. Legal, political and economic control ensures the success and continuation of the power of autocrats. Autocrats do not compete with anyone: the law is what they decide. And this becomes the order of the day for their militant followers. When the resulting injustice reaches a certain level, people who ask questions are labelled as 'traitors', and are usually imprisoned, forced out or even murdered.

Real intellectuals search for a better, brighter future and a cure for existing and possible problems. They do not serve individuals or regimes but the truth, the whole of society, and nature. However, autocrats hate factual, progressive, diverse knowledge and real intellectuals. They need fictionalised alternative knowledge, and there are armies of 'intellectuals' who are desperate for protection and to gain some advantages, status and wealth, without any real, scientific production. They purposely produce such fictional mono knowledge for the benefit of autocrats and their regimes. When brutalism is supported, and false information is created in the name of 'intellectualism' then the darkness takes over more quickly than expected. The aim of this repetitive and fictional knowledge is to polish and shine the autocrat's extra egocentric attitude, strengthen their discriminative policies, and increase their internal and international influence. Authoritarian journalists, social media supporters and academics are not much different than the autocrats themselves, and can be even worse. The intellectuals who work for autocrats theorise and justify how their leader is skilfully serving the people, without acknowledging that certain groups are discriminated against for the sake of others. Many other silent groups deny that any crimes are committed by their leaders and enjoy nepotistic relationships and benefits.

Autocrats and their regimes do not act independently from society, which is strangled by authoritarian and populist politics. The political system and governors are similarly choked by the mentality of a majoritarian crowd. If the autocrats disappear, it does not mean that the problem goes away. It stays within society and the institutions and may easily be replaced with similar-minded people or structures. The regime may continue until it and its supporters, the society of dictators, are challenged and changed radically.

Autocratic societies are as guilty as their leaders. Many members of society are involved in criminal activity; they monopolise certain goods for their own needs and exclude others from trade or various positions. A silent and silenced society fuels the actions of autocrats. Some people collaborate due to fear, others to receive benefits, or they are really convinced by 'the system'. They do not feel guilty or raise their voices even when they see discrimination and criminal acts taking place in front of their eyes. Instead, they stay silent or become angry with the critics of autocrats, rather than the autocrats themselves. As a result, crimes become routine, normalised, and collective actions. In many autocratic societies, if you throw a needle into the air, it is more likely to land on an autocrat supporter who has collaborated with and benefited from the system, rather than dropping to the ground.

Oppression and state violence is directly connected to the quality of the justice system. When the state and its justice system serve personal interests rather than the diverse public needs, then lawlessness takes over and violence becomes routine. Limiting and controlling the power of the courts is important for establishing an iron fist. The court, especially a constitutional court, is an important place for autocrats to justify all their actions and shape the system according to their needs. There is no 'independent' court or 'justice' under authoritarian rules. Hardly any legal and court actions, especially against political opponents and critical voices, are impartial or autonomous, but almost fully biased, theatrical and staged. Until 2010, the Turkish legal system had some level of autonomy; it was not perfect, but it was at least giving some breathing space to minorities and oppressed groups. However, after the dramatic changes in the Turkish constitution, almost all legal institutions of the state lost their autonomy and in effect become a button on a remote control under the authoritarian regime. The courts and laws became very useful tools if and when they were needed. If one of Trump's false claims had been supported by the US high court, it would not have been possible to remove him from office. This shows that the US court system still maintains its own constitutional and democratic power and autonomy, and was not allowed to be occupied fully by an authoritarian-minded leader and his fabricated allegations. However, under Trump's administration more than 300 judges for different high courts, all of them white and with a similar mentality to Trump, were appointed. This created real damage to the political and judicial system, which could easily be made worse by another authoritarian-minded person if the whole political system, including the courts, is not repaired from the harm caused by Trump's presidency.

When the judiciary loses its power and becomes a tool in the hands of the ruler rather than a central independent organ of the state, justice loses its normality and legitimacy. The security and continuity of the regime becomes the only purpose of the state and judiciary when things start to go wrong. Unequal laws are created to bolster the authoritarian regime, and do not generally help all individuals equally. Especially for authoritarian regimes, justice is no longer a weapon of the weak, but it is used by autocrats against any opposition. Since the beginning of the Turkish Republic, internal and external enemies have always been created, even if they did not exist. The underlying idea of this security threat has been the basic rule of any legal and political education and practices. The notion of always having enemies and putting territorial integrity and security before all other factors, especially justice, in the end creates an enemy even if there was none before. Excessive concentration of state powers puts territorial integrity into question even if the nation was safe before the autocrats arrived.

It has become almost normal for authoritarian regimes and their institutions to sign international agreements claiming to protect the lives and basic human rights of others, but instead they act with great evil. This evil and greed does not just destroy the fabric of the society, but also destroys nature and the climate. This makes international institutions and their agreements meaningless if/when they do not act against such regimes by enforcing and honouring laws and agreements which are in place to protect the lives of others. Universal moral values and the respect for and protection of the life of others who are different are undermined.

Current international laws are mostly not structured to protect the individual, but primarily benefit the state. Individual lives are not as important as state sovereignty, even when the state openly commits crimes. Recently, for example, Turkey, Myanmar and Hungary, have not respected the rights of their minorities – Kurds, Rohingya and Romani – who suffer under these authoritarian regimes without any meaningful protection.

In the same way that a muted society is not impartial, the international community also remaining silent or claiming to be impartial during conflicts between oppressors and the oppressed is not impartiality, it is clearly taking sides, especially when silence loudly supports the oppressors. When a country, institution or corporation uses unnecessary force, legitimises and institutionalises discrimination and crimes by law and openly acts accordingly, then there is an instinctive right of all individuals to organise and join the resistance against such injust institutions, corporations and regimes. Without a strong voice of opposition silence serves only to create and strengthen an autocratic and chaotic state. It would not be right to stay silent and let that institution, corporation or regime continue to exist, allowing it to spread like wildfire to create more destruction. Any additional time means more crimes, discrimination and possible ethnic, racial, religious and political cleansing by such unscrupulous and self-serving authorities.

The fight for freedom, fair laws and justice, and the right to live and live meaningfully is becoming a necessity when one or all basic living conditions are damaged or threatened. The pursuit of freedom and living safely are basic human rights, but have become a threat to authoritarian regimes. These regimes create a privileged lifestyle for a small group, but reserve prison-type conditions, oppression and deprivation for the rest. There will be hardly any strong opposition left to stand against these regimes if swift action is not taken. They are very successful in dividing any opposition into the smallest pieces, with the help of their monopolised media, intellectuals, the police, economic circles, the army and the judiciary. They benefit from continuous conflict and sow the seeds of new conflicts between different ethnic, religious and political groups.

Under an authoritarian regime, people's lives become fraught, miserable and unbearable, and this is representative of the societal life lived under a repressive regime. The life of the people mirrors the life of the regime in which they live. The heavy and oppressive presence of the autocrat is felt everywhere. Society becomes paralysed and starts to die slowly and painfully, as if from carbon monoxide poisoning, without recognising their shortness of breath and suffocation.

When people's needs are not met, then it is not possible to gain their trust and keep the security and integrity of the state and society intact anymore. People have limited tolerance for injustice, however. For the authoritarian regime, left or right, this does not change as long as the minority groups do not defend their own identity, resist and change the political system radically. As Hannah Arendt stated,[1] if a Jew is attacked because of their Jewish

---

[1] Arendt 1992.

identity, they should defend themselves as Jews. If a group or individual who has been attacked doesn't defend themselves with their real identity, they will remain concealed and their freedom will be limited. It is not a crime but it is a duty to stop the danger of authoritarianism if one does not want to be enslaved. As previously mentioned, how we mobilise to find a cure for a pandemic virus and rush to destroy it before it creates great damage, is not that much different from an authoritarian dictatorship. This also creates huge danger, not just locally against opposition groups, but also globally.

Most wars take place for political and economic reasons – internally or internationally – seizing the land and wealth of others for the benefit of a specific group. Most wars are 'unjust' as Walzer argues, but as he also suggests, there are 'just' wars too, implying a right to intervene in order to stop evil actions and chronic conflicts.[2] The right of states, as well as individuals, are limited by international laws and humanitarian moral values especially. If and when the rights of the state and the rights of individuals clash, then it should be the innocent human life that needs to be protected. The state is not a living organism, it can be replaced and transformed easily.

As discussed in detail in Chapter 1, under dictatorship regimes many more people are killed by their own governments than any enemy country. In the twentieth century alone, more than 128 million people were deliberately killed by their own regimes.[3] There have been important studies suggesting that the world powers should take action to intervene if there is the possibility of preventing further violence and rescuing the oppressed.[4] If Hitler had been stopped in the mid-1930s, if Saddam Hussein had been stopped in the early 1980s, if Assad had been stopped in the early 2000s, we would not have suffered such extreme human catastrophes. Their trails of destruction did not just affect their own people, though even that was enough reason to stop them, but they created global disasters. In addition to the deaths, hundreds of millions of people were displaced and have become refugees.

To be born into an authoritarian regime or in a country which has a long history of oppression does not mean that there is no possibility for change. The support from local people, even if not the majority of them, is essential.

[2] Walzer 2006.
[3] See, Rummel 1994; Meister 2010.
[4] See, Walzer 1994 and 2004; Miller 2007; Gross 2008; Evans 2009; Fassin and Pandolfi 2010; Fassin 2011a; De Lauri 2018 and 2019.

Without creating a strong power balance, limiting the rulers' power by creating different power actors and mechanisms, including independently elected semi-autonomous local authorities, strong autonomous regions, collecting local taxes and setting up independent courts, then it remains easy for any ruler to be corrupted and not to respect any rules and laws, but to create their own.

Fighting against injustice is nothing new or unique to Kurds. Injustices are suffered by great people as well as small powerless ethnic, religious and racial groups; from Socrates to Walter Benjamin; from Mevlana to Mandela; Jews, Irish, Kurds and black people. Today not many people remember those who were responsible and who felt no shame for their discrimination and injustices, but many people know the name of Socrates, Benjamin, Mevlana and Mandela, and the story of the Jews, Irish, Kurds and black people. History has shown us that if individuals and groups refuse to be enslaved by oppressive systems, then they will fight to the end for justice, truth and equality and create their own institutions and societies based on equal and fair values, as is often seen after the defeat of authoritarian regimes.

Without historical reparation and restitution, justice, equality and peace cannot be maintained. If the protection of the individual as well as the welfare of the community is not guaranteed and even if the discussion of this is not permitted, then it is not be possible to talk about the basic notions of justice and liberty. Otherwise, a few legal changes here and there would be easily reversed by a different government, who would like to play a populist card for their own success. As history has shown many times, for dictators and authoritarian regimes, the presence of constitutions and their legal principles cannot alone be a guarantee. Laws have often been changed by autocrats for the needs of autocrats. Habitually, in quick succession, they change the things which they changed before.[5]

---

[5] For example, under Erdoğan's rule Turkey signed the Istanbul agreement in 2011 as a way of promising to protect women's rights, promote gender equality and fight violence against women. The Council of Europe accord of 'Convention of Preventing and Combating Violence against Women and Domestic Violence' was signed in Istanbul a decade ago. However, after monopolising power, Erdoğan ended Turkey's involvement with a human rights treaty on 20 March 2021, in order to please his Islamist supporters and silencing dissenting voices. Even though Erdoğan's single sentence withdrawal from the treaty was against article 90 of the Turkish constitution, this is another important example of autocrats considering themselves to be above the rules and constitutions and of their orders becoming the law.

The 'Kurdish Question in the Middle East'

Kurds have a long history and a stable presenceI in the Middle East. However, the nations around them are very transient, unstable and aggressive and this creates a difficult life for Kurds. Kurdish people in the Middle East are among the main victims of the new type of authoritarian nationalism and aberrations of democracy. The ongoing crisis in the Middle East is not just a problem for Kurds or neighbouring states to deal with and resolve, but also for the modern nation states. The problems in the Middle East are evidently multiple and need multiple formulas for a peaceful resolution. Without acknowledgement of these problems, the Kurdish problem itself cannot be resolved.

The Kurdish case studies analysed in this book show that Turkey and many other Middle Eastern authoritarian regimes share a phobia of Kurds. This is not just limited to the political elites, but has deep societal roots. This mental blockage has shaped the Middle East over the last century and has obstructed the way for bringing peace internally and internationally. It has also formed the Turkish political structure and state foundation, which has allowed the innate national authoritarian culture to take over. This started from the time of the late Ottoman Empire, was sharpened by the Kemalist regime, and become a lethal weapon under the Erdoğan regime. In order to understand and stabilise this authoritarian governmental power in Turkey, it is not enough to know the instruments of suppression, especially where the needs of Kurds are positively and negatively tied to the interests and needs of the government in power. The authoritarian government does not just repress and punish, but it also persuades at the same time.

Most prisoners in Turkey are Kurds, and most of the prisoners are there for their political opinions and asking for their equal rights. Put simply, when a Kurd opens their mouth or writes a short sentence of simple criticism against the authoritarian regime, they are punished with a long prison sentence. Criticism of the state is described as 'terrorism' by laws which give a free hand to autocrats to put anybody behind bars or create a prison type of environment for all. Prisons are more or less created for the Kurds. The main purpose of the imprisonment of political activists and critics is to dehumanise them. There are often amnesties for different criminals, including murderers and rapists, but these rarely include Kurdish political prisoners. There is not much room left for Kurds to live a normal life – only to resist. The case of the

Kurds in the Middle East is an important example of a necessary and strong resistance against authoritarianism.

It is clear that some form of resistance is necessary for transforming the rule of the authoritarian state, or breaking up the state, especially if it does not serve the nation but only autocrats and their supporters. While Kurds have resisted and revolted for decades in the hope of achieving one of these outcomes, the authoritarian state structure in the Middle East has been opposing both options, the existing states do not want any change and do not want to let the Kurds establish their own authority. It is inevitable that this war will continue until the establishment of a proper pluralistic state or states where political, judicial and economic equality is guaranteed, and society is fully open to the transformation necessary to support these crucial elements rather than the wishes of autocrats.

As discussed in detail and from different perspectives in Chapters 2, 3 and 5, there is no such thing as a good Kurd for the Turkish and Middle Eastern authoritarian governments, but there may be useful Kurds who can be utilised for the purposes of government policies and actions against others. People are asked to give up their identity, native language and culture to please the regime. If people do this, then the receiving, dominant authority asks for more and more. This includes sacrificing their lives for the war against their own people, which gives more power and wealth to the autocrats. The more people give, the more autocrats and their regimes ask from them. While people's obligations become greater, the regime's responsibilities become smaller, until nothing remains for the people to give, including their lives.

Not only the power of the judiciary, but also parliament has been disabled in Turkey and both have become less powerful under the authoritarian regime. As the Reichstag building fire in 1933 gave full control to Hitler's regime, so the Kurdish youth movement's digging of trenches in August 2015 and the so-called military coup in Turkey on 16 July 2016 also destroyed whatever power the Turkish parliament had, and transferred all power to the autocrat. Erdoğan also used these incidents to seize power and stated after the coup attempt in July 2016 that it was a gift from God. Interestingly, Hitler also saw the fire of the Reichstag building as 'a God-given signal'.[6]

---

[6] Notably, the former US authoritarian-minded president, Donald Trump, also stated that his catching of the Covid-19 virus, just weeks before the November 2020 presidential election, was 'a blessing from God'.

For a real, meaningful change, alternative politics and practices need to be introduced for plural, competing power structures and democratic institutions. As Michael Walzer argues, 'We need movements of resistance, and we need citizen activists who remember the old labour union imperative: Organize!'[7] Judicial independence and the balance of power are the most important foundations of plural democracy and freedom. Without controlling the judiciary, it would not be possible to establish or continue an autocratic regime. The laws and courts are the supplying arteries of political power, therefore it is no surprise that autocrats first prioritise taking and controlling this kind of power. Equally, autocrats without power over the judiciary are dysfunctional and their own veins bleed dry. Active resistance creates a political philosophy and moral belief that the ruler should adopt such a culture to convince others, work closely, compromise when it is necessary and required and step down when their time is up, according to fair laws and unchangeable constitutions.

As discussed throughout this book, in the case of Kurds, de facto alternative governmentality, local councils and the judiciary are usually established in parallel and in a matrix structure over the territory and population where at the same time the authoritarian state has 'full sovereignty' rights according to its laws. The case of Kurds and Turks shows that this contested sovereignty has deepened the ethnoterritorial conflict between two nations and it is heading for full division if authoritarianism continues and the human rights of Kurdish people continue to be threatened as brutally as they are now.

While Kurdish alternative governmentalities are very new and developing, with their own challenges and obstacles, there are not many options for Kurds but to establish their alternative institutions, create international allies and become stronger in the Middle East in order to survive. After securing autonomy in Iraq, Kurds for the first time won a big battle against powerful ISIS and its supporters in Kobane, Syria. This victory has been one of the most important battles in Kurdish history and a significant advance on their road to an independent Kurdistan. Kurdish youths digging trenches and conducting a city war against Turkish military forces may have been physically suppressed, but the mental and physical divisions between Turkish and

---

[7] Walzer 2019: xvi.

Kurdish society have increased to an almost irreparable and irreversible level. The latest state oppression by military forces, as well as the threat of imprisonment, has increased the number of Kurdish people and groups joining the Kurdish movement forces, and disobeying the authoritarian state rules and laws. It has also in parallel increased the establishment of local de facto councils and courts. A rising number of local taxes are now paid to the Kurdish movement instead of the state. Authoritarian state power has become almost non-existent, even though the state military, police and judges appear to be in charge, they are mainly confined to their barracks, increasingly in fear of the Kurdish people around them.

In this book, I have argued that alternative politics is essential for the construction of alternative forms of governmentality when faced with abusive and oppressive regimes. Such alternative structures tend to evolve into de facto parallel state-making processes. The politics of alternative justice is to use alternative judicial and political processes for the purpose of limiting, changing and balancing current social and economic oppressive power bases and mechanisms, but also influencing and creating new forms of sovereignty and political power. Kurds in the Middle East have created their own parallel justice institutions and military power as a means of forging an alternative sovereignty and gaining political control. The creation of independent institutions, including autonomous courts, within current state borders, is not just taking place in every city, town and village of the Kurdish regions, but in big metropolitan areas such as Istanbul, and also transnationally in Berlin and London. For Kurds, as many other stateless minorities, transnational mobilisation and links are significant factors in the development of new forms of governmentality, linking diaspora communities with populations back home.

The wider Kurdish Political Movement, inspired by the Kurdistan Workers Party (PKK), has focused on establishing a system of what has been coined 'democratic confederalism'. The aim of democratic confederalism is to provide a democratic and egalitarian framework for its people, including ethnic, religious and linguistic minorities, to have greater autonomy and to be able to organise their daily lives freely. Although the movement claims that democratic confederalism replaces earlier aspirations for an independent nation state, my ethnographic accounts show that the Kurdish political movement is engaging in parallel state-making through creating new institutions, mechanisms and processes, and extending their judicial, economic and local military sphere. Providing justice and addressing and challenging existing social inequalities, including those pertaining to gender, are important mechanisms for alternative politics and governmentality. The spheres or domains of governmentality and justice cannot be separated, and one is justification or preparation for the other.

While this book develops a critique of existing authoritarian governmentalities, it illustrates that justice and power are simultaneously localised and transnational. This book shows that parallel governmentality captures and effectively restricts the power of autocratic regimes at both the local and transnational levels, and this new power configuration affects national politics and international relations directly. While this may not be enough to achieve a quick solution or to challenge authoritarian regimes or states in the short term, it definitely limits the period of dominance of such regimes or states. Foucault and other scholars allow us to see how the state combines, arranges and fixes existing relations of power, which are then codified, consolidated and institutionalised for the governmentalisation of the state. However, in this book I have critically engaged the existing writings of Foucault and others on governmentality which do not recognise alternative and/or parallel power and governmentality structures within any given state. Alternative governmentality and its institutions exist largely independently of the state, particularly in relation to justice and political representation, by subsidising, policing and securing its respective population. The book has also challenged the traditional theory of international relations with its focus on the nation state's unitary sovereignty and shows how alternative governmentality can affect and be applied to almost all aspects of social life and international relations.

Max Weber claimed that the state has the 'monopoly on violence' (*Gewaltmonopol des Staates*) and monopoly on the legitimate use of physical force within its territory. However, this book has argued that the Weberian notion has its limits too. People who are continuously treated unjustly by the state take back their right to use violence for their own defence and protection. This right is normally given up by the people for the sake of a democratic and equal state. Within parallel governmentality and a new de facto state structure, as the book illustrates in the case of Kurds, a centralised state can be challenged with the use of force or violence and this power is used by alternative power holders locally, in a de facto way, as we have seen from the Kurdish youth and guerrilla movement.

Kurdish groups have been controlling their land and border in Iraq since 1991, and also in Syria since the conflict there started in 2011. They created parallel de facto states which aim to give equal space to different ethnic and religious minorities. Especially in Syria, the Kurdish autonomous state aims to create gender equality by creating a co-chair leadership, one man and one woman, and these are implemented and practised in almost all their institutions. In secured zones, such as north-east Syria, even under continuous conflict and oppression, the Kurdish movement has managed to educate children in their mother tongue, spoken the Kurdish language freely on the streets, and taught children their own history, rather than the state's concocted version. This has created a real threat to the authoritarian Turkish regime, which fears that Kurds in Turkey may achieve similar rights and practices. These are the reasons why the Turkish authoritarian regime is so brutal in its suppression of Kurdish people inside and outside Turkey.

As the book discussed in detail, specifically in Chapter 4, women's freedom and equality have been articulated as a core principle of alternative politics, and the Kurdish political movement's thesis of radical democracy by Kurdish leaders. Given the centrality of gender-based equality and justice within the aim of radical democracy, as claimed by the wider Kurdish political movement in Turkey and Syria, this study has paid particular attention to the ways in which gender-based justice is put into practice, or not, as the case may be. The findings of the research demonstrate that there is an important gap between rhetoric and everyday practices, when we look into Kurdish gender-based norms, real-life practices and justice. The way that Kurdish men and women who have been critical of the respective patriarchal states and their authoritarian attitudes and practices have also reproduced prevailing gender norms and relations while creating and engaging in alternative justice and political systems is somewhat alarming.

The different attitudes of members of the Kurdish movement, such as dogmatic, passive, moderate and liberal, as discussed in detail in Chapters 4 and 5, show that there are new codes, barriers and limitations for an individual's life and freedom. Personal, sexual and life choices have been controlled, disciplined, policed and sidelined, especially by the dogmatic members of the Kurdish movement. Cancel culture is one of the main weapons of dogmatic believers. Rumours and fabricated stories are used for the successful ostracism of individuals who don't think, dress, or socialise like them. They thrust critical and innovative thinkers out of social and professional circles, not just from social media or online networks, but also in the real world too. They establish and convict a social death penalty for others, and the social massacre of others become this group's only aim. These are not only members of the guerrilla or militia movement, there are many community members, activists, lawyers, teachers and academicians amongst them. Very interestingly, while these members appear to argue against state authoritarianism, they display a similar authoritarian mentality on a local and individual level.

As discussed in Chapter 5, the Kurdish alternative court and justice system is still being developed and has some limitations and injustices. However, the problem of the judiciary is not only the case for the Kurdish movement, which has no state or state institutions, but also for many modern states and so-called well-established institutions which often commit injustices. While most so-called Western democratic countries still have statues of slave traders or their previous ruthless leaders in central squares, and continue to celebrate them as heroes, there are similar-minded people in the Middle East who commit injustices and want to be recognised as heroes and have their statues erected.

While recognising the diversity and heterogeneity of Kurdish political ideology and mobilisation, it has also been a surprise to me that when there is no judicial, political and economic validity and equality for Kurds within the existing state model, some Kurds still show their love for their oppressors and even sacrifice their lives for the continuity of the existing authoritarian states, while these same states fail to accommodate them. The approach of these Kurds reminds me of the Roman poet Ovid's famous description: 'I am dragged along by a strange new force. Desire and reason are pulling in different directions. I see the right way and approve it, but follow the wrong.' Losing their identity has almost become an addiction for some Kurds, however, their children will continue to rebel and lose their lives for the wrong choices and short-sightedness of their father and mother.

The Kurdish movement fights against capitalism, imperialism, authoritarianism and patriarchy at the same time, and claims to transform its own society and as well as the societies of Turks, Arabs and Persians. However, this is not an easy process and it is also very problematic as it means assimilating all Middle Eastern societies and politics into one new uniformed ideology. It would be another type of domination and risks endangering the existing diversity, a risk which the Kurdish movement claims to fight against. This is not yet practical for a group which has not fully transformed their own society, and has not even established an independent space for its own people. Without economic, military and political powers, international allies and a territory of their own, this only gives false hope to a nation that has continuously sacrificed many of its people's lives. This will raise unrealistic hopes, which, as Bismarck once stated, only create large appetites but with false teeth. This would mean that Kurds would not only be betrayed by others, but also by their own political leaders who force them to have unrealistic expectations which would bring nothing but loss for Kurds.

The Kurdish movements are still in search of a political and national identity. Once they claimed to be aiming to create a socialist state. Then, after 2000, they moved on to the idea of democratic autonomy, which was seen as the right direction for themselves and the other Middle Eastern societies. However, since 2015, after a failing peace process with Turkey and increasing conflict in Syria, they have tried to make a Kurdish connection with the Neolithic times, searching for a strong historical stance. This shows that the Kurdish political movement still does not have a clear vision for driving their nation into the future, but continues to search for an imaginative identity and politics. Without restoring diversity and rebuilding the nations' identities and culture, homology only damages the balance and harmony of peace and creativity.

Kurds must also learn to ignore their fear of statelessness and their proclivity for indulging in victimhood. Kurds are not a minority group; they should recognise their role in the wider Middle East as a large and established nation. Once the attitude of victimisation turns into victory and celebration, then Kurds and many other similar nations will start along the road of success and peace. The constant feeling of being an outsider without friends and support only keeps one as an outsider who is easily alienated. Like individuals, nations also decide and forge their own destiny. Celebration of the past is important for a successful and better future. Past and present are needed for the creation of a common memory of a nation. However, to live too much in the past and present only blocks the future. Kurdish leadership needs to focus on something beyond the current conflicted time and space and prepare their people for new knowledge, regeneration and a better future.

If the current status quo continues, the state and societal ideology will stay ultra-nationalist and authoritarian in the Middle East, and the Kurdish issue and conflict will continue to be like a transnational cancer that nobody can hope to cure. Without finding a peaceful solution for the Kurds, the authoritarianism in the Middle East will be replaced, but will not cease.

For alternative politics and pluralistic democracy to rise, then authoritarianism must fall. Democracy and authoritarianism cannot coexist. There are several different options for Kurds and other nations in the Middle East for a better, peaceful and democratic future. First, regional autonomy without larger nation states, so some kind of asymmetrical political arrangement may be necessary for Kurds and other similar nations to finally end the conflict in the Middle East. Second, limiting the power of the central state, as has happened within the context of the EU, giving more power to local authorities and greater devolution for different ethnic groups. Middle Eastern 'big' states, including Turkey and Iran, then have to be ready to accept such regional autonomy and cannot claim to be rigidly centralised and authoritarian political entities. If one of the two options above succeeds, then a third possible option, but the most difficult, is for Kurds no longer to ask for one central Kurdish state, but a few strong autonomous or federal Kurdish states within a large and federative Middle Eastern Union.

REFERENCES

Abbas, Tahir (2016). *Contemporary Turkey in Conflict: Ethnicity, Islam and Politics*. Edinburgh: Edinburgh University Press.

Abbas, Tahir and Ismail Hakki Yigit (2014). 'Perspectives on Ethno-National Conflict among Kurdish Families with Members in the PKK', *Terrorism and Political Violence*, pp.1–19.

Abdulla, Namo (2016). 'How ISIL advanced Kurdish nationalism', *Turkish Policy Quarterly*, 14: 89–97.

Abu-Lughod, Lila (2005). *Dramas of Nationhood: The Politics of Television in Egypt*. Chicago: University of Chicago Press.

Adamson, Fiona (2019). 'Non-state authoritarianism and diaspora politics', *Global Networks, a Journal of Transnational Affairs*, 20(1): 150–69.

Adar, Sinem (2018). 'Emotions and Nationalism: Armenian Genocide as Case Study', *Sociological Forum*, 33(3): 735–56.

Adar, Sinem and Yektan Turkyilmaz (2019). 'Turkey: the post-election brawl – a regime at a crossroads', *Open Democracy* (30 April 2019).

Agamben, Giorgio (1998). *Homo Sacer: Sovereign Power and Bare Life*. Stanford, CA: Stanford University Press.

Ahmad, Feroz (2003). 'The Kemalist Era, 1919–1938', in *Turkey: The Quest for Identity*, ed. Feroz Ahmad. Oxford: Oneworld, pp. 75–94.

Ahmad, Feroz (1993). *The Making of Modern Turkey*. London: Routledge.

Akcali, Emel (2016). *Neoliberal Governmentality and the Future of the State in the Middle East and North Africa*. Basingstoke: Palgrave Macmillan.

Akcura, Belma (2010). *The Kurdish Movie of the State: Reports about the Kurds from 1925 to 2007*. Erbil: Mukriyani Publisher.

Akkaya, A. Hamdi and Joost Jongerden (2012). 'Reassembling the Political: The PKK and the project of Radical Democracy', *European Journal of Turkish Studies*, 14.

Akkaya, A. Hamdi and Joost Jongerden (2013). 'Confederalism and autonomy in Turkey: The Kurdistan Workers' Party and the reinvention of democracy', in *The Kurdish Question in Turkey*. London: Routledge, pp. 86–204.

Akşit, Bahattin (1986). 'Imam-Hatip and Other Secondary Schools in the Context of Political and Cultural Modernization of Turkey', *Journal of Human Sciences*, 5(1): 25–41.

Ali, Othman (1997). 'The Kurds and the Lausanne Peace Negotiations, 1922–23', *Middle Eastern Studies*, 33(3): 521–34.

Al-Ali, Nadje and Nicola Pratt (2011). 'Between Nationalism and Women's Rights: The Kurdish Women's Movement in Iraq', *Middle East Journal of Culture and Communication*, 4(3): 339–55.

Al-Ali, Nadje and Latif Tas (2016a). 'Kurdish women's battle continues against state and patriarchy, says first female co-mayor of Diyarbakır', *Open Democracy* (12 August 2016).

Al-Ali, Nadje and Latif Tas (2016b). 'Kurds and Turks are at the edge of a cliff', *Open Democracy* (2 November 2016).

Al-Ali, Nadje, and Latif Tas (2017). '"War Is like a Blanket": Feminist Convergences in Kurdish and Turkish Women's Rights Activism for Peace', *Journal of Middle East Women's Studies*, 13(3): 354–75.

Al-Ali, Nadje, and Latif Tas (2018a). 'Reconsidering Nationalism and Feminism: The Kurdish Political Movement in Turkey', *Nations and Nationalism*, 24(2): 453–73.

Al-Ali, Nadje, and Latif Tas (2018b). 'Clashes, Collaborations & Convergences: Evolving Relations of Turkish and Kurdish feminists', *The Journal of Balkan and Near Eastern Studies*, 21(3): 304–18.

Al-Ali, Nadje, and Latif Tas (2018c). 'Dialectics of Struggle: Challenges to the Kurdish Women's Movement', *LSE Middle East Centre: Social Movement and Popular Mobilisation in the MENA*, 22.

Al-Dahdah, Edouard and C. Corduneanu-Huci (2016). *Rules on Paper, Rules in Practice: Enforcing Laws and Policies in the Middle East and North Africa*. World Bank.

Algan, Bulent (2008). 'The Brand New Version of Article 301 of Turkish Penal Code and the Future of Freedom of Expression Cases in Turkey', *German Law Journal*, 9(12): 2237–51.

Ali, Sirvan Kamil (2015). 'Domestic Violence Encountered among Kurdish Women', *Journal of Education and Practice*, 6(3): 27–33.

Allen, Robert C. (ed.) (2002). *To Be Continued . . .: Soap Operas around the World*. London: Routledge.

Allsopp, Harriet and W. van Wilgenburg (2019). *The Kurds of Northern Syria: Governance, Diversity and Conflicts*. London: I. B. Tauris.

Altinay, Ayşegül (2004). *The Myth of the Military-Nation: Militarism, Gender, and Education in Turkey*. New York: Palgrave.

Amnesty International (2007). 'Iraq: "Honour Killing" of teenage girl condemned as abhorrent', *Amnesty International UK Press Releases* (2 May 2007).

Amnesty International (2016a). 'Turkey: End abusive operations under indefinite curfews', *Amnesty International Report* (21 January 2016).

Amnesty International (2016b). 'Turkey: Detention of academics intensifies crackdown on freedom of expression', *Amnesty International Report* (15 January 2016).

Amnesty International (2016c). 'Annual Report – Turkey 2015/2016', *Amnesty International Report* (24 February 2016).

Amrane-Minne, Danièle Djamila (1999). 'Women and Politics in Algeria from the War of Independence to Our Day', *Research in African Literatures*, 30(3): 62–77.

Amrane-Minne, Danièle Djamila (2007). 'Women at War: The Representation of Women in The Battle of Algiers', *Interventions: The Journal of Postcolonial Studies* 9(3): 340–9.

Anderson, Perry (2008). 'Kemalism', *London Review of Books*, 30(17).

Andreas, P. and T. Snyder (eds) (2000). *The Wall Around the West: State Borders and Immigration Controls in North America and Europe*. Lanham, MD: Rowman & Littlefield.

Aras, Bulent and Yasin Duman (2014). 'The Kurdish Peace Process and Presidential Election in Turkey', *Report for the Global Europe Program, Woodrow Wilson International Center*.

Arat, Yesim (2010). 'Religion, Politics and Gender Equality in Turkey: implications of a democratic paradox?', *Third World Quarterly*, 31(6): 869–84.

Arat, Zehra F. K. (2012). 'Women', in *The Routledge Handbook of Modern Turkey*, ed. Metin Heper and Sabri Sayari. Abingdon: Routledge, pp. 259–69.

Arendt, Hannah (1951). *The Origins of Totalitarianism*. New York: Schocken Books.

Arendt, Hannah (1958). *The Human Conditions*. Chicago: University of Chicago Press.

Arendt, Hannah (1964). 'Personal Responsibility Under Dictatorship', *The Listener*, 6: 185–7.

Arendt, Hannah (1971). 'Thinking and Moral Considerations', *Social Research*, 38: 417–46.

Arendt, Hannah (1992). *Eichmann in Jerusalem. A Report on the Banality of Evil.* London: Penguin Books.

Arsan, Esra and Yasemin Yıldırım (2014). 'Reflections of neo-Ottomanist discourse in Turkish news media: The case of the magnificent century', *Journal of Applied Journalism & Media Studies* 3(3): 315–34.

Aslan, Senem (2014). *Nation-Building in Turkey and Morocco: Governing Kurdish and Berber Dissent.* Cambridge: Cambridge University Press.

Ataman, Muhittin (2002). 'Özal leadership and restructuring of Turkish ethnic policy in the 1980s', *Middle Eastern Studies*, 38(4): 123–42.

Ataturk, M. Kemal (1997). *Atatürk'ün Söylev ve Demeçleri, Cilt II (1906–1938).* Ankara: Atatürk Araştırma Merkezi Yayını.

Avedian, Vahagn, (2012). 'State Identity, Continuity, and Responsibility: The Ottoman Empire, the Republic of Turkey and the Armenian Genocide', *The European Journal of International Law*, 23(3): 797–820.

Ayata, Sencer (1991). 'Traditional Sufi Orders on the Periphery', in *Islam in Modem Turkey*, ed. Richard Tapper. London: I. B. Tauris.

Aydin, Delal (2005). *Mobilizing the Kurds in Turkey: Newroz as a Myth.* MA Thesis, the Middle East Technical University.

Aydin, Zülküf (1986). *Underdevelopment and Rural Structures in Southeastern Turkey: The Household Economy in Gisgis and Kalhana.* London: Ithaca Press.

Aydin-Duzgit, Senem, Daniela Huber, Meltem Muftuler-Bac, E. Fuat Keyman, Michael Schwarz and Nathalie Tocci (2015). *Global Turkey in Europe III: Democracy, Trade, and the Kurdish Questions in Turkey-EU Relations.* Rome: Edizioni Nuova Culture.

Aytar, Osman (1992). *Hamidiye alaylarindan köy koruculuguna.* Istanbul: Medya Günesi.

Bachvarova, Mira (2013). 'Non-domination's role in the theorizing of global justice', *Journal of Global Ethics*, 9(2): 173–85.

Balci, Ali (2015). 'The Kurdish movement's EU policy in Turkey: An analysis of a dissident ethnic bloc's foreign policy', *Ethnicities*, 15(1): 72–91.

Ballard, Roger (1994). *Desh Pardesh: The South Asian Presence in Britain.* London: C. Hurst & Co.

Ballard, Roger (2005). 'Coalitions of Reciprocity and the Maintenance of Financial Integrity within Informal Value Transmission Systems: the operational dynamics of contemporary Hawala networks', *Journal of Banking Regulation* 6(4): 319–52.

Ballard, Roger (2014). 'Hawala and Hundi Vehicles for the long-distance transmission of value', in *Routledge Handbook of the South Asian Diaspora*, ed. Joya Chatterji and David Washbrook. Abingdon: Routledge, pp. 53–64.

Bargu, Banu (ed.) (2019). *Turkey's Necropolitical Laboratory: Democracy, Violence and Resistance*. Edinburgh: Edinburgh University Press.

Barry, Kim (2006). 'Home and away: The construction of citizenship in an emigration context', *NYU Law Review*, 81(1): 11–59.

Baser, Bahar (2015). *Diasporas and Homeland Conflicts: A Comparative Perspective*. Farnham: Ashgate.

Bauman, Zygmunt (2004). *Wasted Lives: Modernity and its Outcasts*. Cambridge: Polity Press.

Beisner, Robert L. (1968). 'Twelve Against Empire: The Anti-Imperialists, 1898–1900', *Science and Society*, 33(3): 371–4.

Belge, Ceren (2008). *Whose Law? Clans, Honor Killings, and State-Minority Relations in Turkey and Israel*. Unpublished PhD thesis, University of Washington.

Belge, Ceren (2011). 'State Building and the Limits of Legibility: Kinship Networks and Kurdish Resistance in Turkey', *International Journal of Middle East Studies*, 43(1): 95–114.

Belge, Ceren (2016). 'Civilian Victimization and the Politics of Information in the Kurdish Conflict in Turkey.' *World Politics*, 68(2): 275–306.

Benakay, Madina A. (2016). *The 'Badass' Female Fighters: Media Representations of Kurdish Women in Kobane*. MA thesis, Istanbul Bilgi University.

Benjamin, Walter (1978). 'Critique of Violence', in *Reflections: Essays, Aphorisms and Autobiographical Writings*, ed. P. Demetz. New York: Harcourt Brace Javanovich Inc.

Berberoglu, Enis (1998). *Kod adi Yüksekova. Susurluk, Ankara, Bodrum, Yüksekova fay hatti*. Istanbul: Milliyet.

Besikci, Ismail (1990). *Bilim, resmi ideoloji, devlet, demokrasi ve Kürt sorunu (Science, official ideology, state, democracy and the Kurdish question)*. Istanbul: Alan.

Besikci, Ismail (1992a). *Dogu Anadolu'nun Düzeni: Sosyo-ekonomik ve Etnik Temeller (The order of East Anatolia: Socio-economic and ethnic basis)*. Ankara: Yurt Kitap.

Besikci, Ismail (1992b). *PKK üzerine düsünceler: özgürlügün bedeli (Thoughts on the PKK: The Price of Freedom)*. Istanbul: Melsa.

Besikci, Ismail (2015). *International Colony Kurdistan Paperback*. London: Gomidas Institute.

Bieber, Florian (2018). 'Patterns of competitive authoritarianism in the Western Balkans', *East European Politics*, 34(3): 337–54.

Bilici, Mücahit (2017). *Kürt Hamal: Türk İslamı ve Kürt Sorunu*. Istanbul: Avesta.

Boas, Franz [1932] (2017). *Anthropology and Modern Life*. Abingdon: Routledge.

Bochenska, Joanna (ed.) (2018). *Rediscovering Kurdistan's Cultures and Identities: The Call of the Cricket*. Cham: Palgrave Macmillan.

Bohman, James (2004). 'Republican Cosmopolitanism', *The Journal of Political Philosophy*, 12(3): 336–52.

Bolton, John (2020). *The Room Where It Happened*. New York, London: Simon & Schuster.

Bookchin, Murray (1996). *The Philosophy of Social Ecology: Essays on Dialectical Naturalism*. Montreal: Black Rose Books.

Bookchin, Murray (2005). *The Ecology of Freedom: The Emergence and Dissolution of Hierarchy*. Oakland, CA: AK Press.

Bookchin, Murray (2015). *The Next Revolution: Popular Assemblies and the Promise of Direct Democracy*. New York: Verso Books.

Boonin, David (2008). *The Problem of Punishment*. New York: Cambridge University Press.

Boratav, Korkut (1998). *Economic History of Turkey, 1908–1985*. Istanbul: Real Publisher.

Bozarslan, M. Emin (2002). *Doğu'nun Sorunları*. Istanbul: Avesta.

Bozarslan, Hamit (2012). 'Between integration, autonomization and radicalization. Hamit Bozarslan on the Kurdish Movement and the Turkish Left: Interview by Marlies Casier and Olivier Grojean', *European Journal of Turkish Studies*, 14: 1–20.

Bozarslan, Hamit (2014). 'The Kurds and Middle Eastern "State of Violence": the 1980s and 2010s', *Kurdish Studies Journal*, 2(1): 4–13.

Bozarslan, Hamit (2017). 'When the Present Sends Back to the Past: Reading the Kurdish Issue in the 2010s', *Middle East Critique*, 27(1): 7–24.

Brands, Hal and Charles Edel (2019). *The Lessons of Tragedy: Statecraft and World Order*. New Haven, CT: Yale University Press.

Bratich, Jack Z., Jeremy Packer and Cameron McCarthy (eds) (2003). *Foucault, Cultural Studies, and Governmentality*. Albany: State University of New York Press.

Bröckling, Ulrich, Susanne Krasmann and Thomas Lemke (eds) (2011). *Governmentality: Current Issues and Future Challenges*. New York: Routledge.

Brownlee, Jason (2007). *Authoritarianism in an Age of Democratization*. Cambridge: Cambridge University Press.

Bunce, Valerie J. and Sharon L. Wolchik (2010). 'Defeating Dictators: Electoral Change and Stability in Competitive Authoritarian Regimes', *World Politics*, 62(1): 43–86.

Burak, Begum (2011). 'The Role of the Military in Turkish Politics: To Guard Whom and From What?', *European Journal of Economic and Political Studies*, 4(1): 143–69.

Burç, Rosa (2019). 'One state, one nation, one flag – one gender? HDP as a challenger of the Turkish nation state and its gendered perspective', *Journal of Balkan and Near Eastern Studies*, 21(3): 319–34.

Burchell, Graham, Colin Gordon and Peter Miller (eds) (1991). *The Foucault Effect: Studies in Governmentality*. Chicago: University of Chicago Press.

Burckhardt, Jacob (1943). *Force and Freedom*. New York: Pantheon Books.

Busse, Jan (2017). *Deconstructing the Dynamics of World-Societal Order: The Power of Governmentality in Palestine*. Abingdon: Routledge.

Butler, Judith and Elizabeth Weed (eds) (2011). *The Question of Gender: Joan W. Scott's Critical Feminism*. Bloomington and Indianapolis: Indiana University Press.

Çağlayan, Handan (2007). *Analar, Yoldaslar, Tanricalar: Kurt Hareketinde ve Kadin Kimliginin Olusumu* (*Mother, Comrades, and Goddesses: Women in the Kurdish Movement and the Formation of Women's Identity*). Istanbul: Iletisim Yayinlari.

Çağlayan, Handan (2011). 'Bir Kota Örneği Olarak Demokratik Toplum Partisinde 40% Kadın Kotası', in *İsmail Beşikçi*, ed. B. Ünlü and O. Değer. Istanbul: İletişim.

Çaha, Omer (2011). 'The Kurdish women's movement: A third-wave feminism within the Turkish context', *Turkish Studies*, 12(3): 435–49.

Çakır, T. (1999). *Cumhuriyet'in Yetmiş Beşinci Yılında Türk Milli Eğitiminde İlköğretim*. Unpublished Master's thesis. Sakarya Üniversitesi Sosyal Bilimler Enstitüsü, Sakarya.

Camus, Albert (1991). *The Plague*. New York: Vintage Books.

Cansiz, Sakine (2018). *Sara: My Whole Life Was a Struggle, the Memoirs of a Kurdish Revolutionary*. Exeter: Pluto Press.

Cappelli, Mary Louisa (2018). 'Toward enacting a Zapatista feminist agenda somewhere in *la Selva Lacondona*: We are all Marias?', *Cogent Arts & Humanities*, 5(1).

Carr, Richard (2019). *March of the Moderates*. London: Bloomsbury.

Casier Marlies (2010). 'Designated Terrorists: The Kurdistan Workers' Party and its Struggle to (Re)Gain Political Legitimacy', *Mediterranean Politics*, 15(3): 393–413.

Casier, Marlies and Joost Jongerden (eds) (2010). *Nationalisms and Politics in Turkey: Political Islam, Kemalism and the Kurdish Issue*. Abingdon: Routledge.

Cayir, Kenan (2015). 'Citizenship, nationality and minorities in Turkey's textbooks: from politics of non-recognition to "difference multiculturalism"', *Comparative Education*, 51(4): 519–36.

Cederman, Lars-Erik, Andreas Wimmer and Brian Mim (2010). 'Why Do Ethnic Groups Rebel? New Data and Analysis', *World Politics*, 62(1): 87–119.

Cetin, Berfin Emre (2014). 'The "politicization" of Turkish television dramas', *International Journal of Communication*, 8(2): 2462–83.

Cetin, Berfin Emre (2015). *The Paramilitary Hero on Turkish Television: A Case Study on Valley of the Wolves*. Newcastle upon Tyne: Cambridge Scholars Publishing.

Cevik, Senem B. (2019). 'Turkish historical television series: public broadcasting of neo-Ottoman illusion', *Southeast European and Black Sea Studies*, 19(2): 227–42.

Chakrabati, Pratik (2013). *Medicine & Empire: 1600–1960*. Basingstoke: Palgrave Macmillan.

Chandler, David and Oliver Richmond (2015). 'Contesting postliberalism: governmentality or emancipation?', *Journal of International Relations and Development*, 18(1): 1–24.

Christofis, Nikos (2019). 'The state of the Kurds in Erdogan's "new" Turkey', *Journal of Balkan and Near Eastern Studies*, 21(3): 251–9.

Christopher, Russell L. (2002). 'Deterring Retributivism: The Injustice of "Just" Punishment', *Northwestern University Law Review*, 96: 843–976.

Chyet, Michael L. (1991). *And a Thornbush Sprang Up Between Them: Studies on Mem u Zin, a Kurdish Romance*. PhD thesis, University of California, Berkeley.

Cianetti, Licia, James Dawson and Seán Hanley (2018). 'Rethinking "democratic backsliding" in Central and Eastern Europe – looking beyond Hungary and Poland', *East European Politics*, 34(3): 243–56.

Cicek, Cuma (2017). *The Kurds of Turkey: National, Religious and Economic Identities*. London: I. B. Tauris.

Ciçekli, Bülent (2003). 'Turkish citizenship policy since 1980', *Immigration, Asylum and Nationality Law*, 17(3): 179–91.

Clark, Colin, Dee Matthew and Vicki Burns (2018). 'Power, privilege and justice: intersectionality as human rights?', *The International Journal of Human Rights*, 22(1): 108–26.

Cohen, David (1995). *Law, Violence, and Community in Classical Athens*. Cambridge: Cambridge University Press.

Cohen, Jean L. and Andrew Arato (1994). *Civil Society and Political Theory*. Cambridge, MA: The MIT Press.

Cubukcu, Ayca (2018). *For the Love of Humanity: The World Tribunal on Iraq*. Philadelphia: University of Pennsylvania Press.

Cooper, Craig (ed.) (2007). *Politics of Orality*. Leiden and Boston: Brill.

Çürükkaya, Selim (1996). *Apo'nun ayetleri/Beyrut Günlügü* (*Apo's Verses/Beirut Diary*), Istanbul: Doz Yayınları.

Dag, Veysi (2021). *The Voices of Marginalised: The Self-narratives of Kurdish Refugees in Europe*. Unpublished manuscript.

Darici, Haydar (2013). '"Adults see politics as a game": Politics of Kurdish Children in Urban Turkey', *The Journal of Middle East Studies*, 45: 775–90.

De Genova, Nicholas and Nathalie Peutz (eds) (2010). *The Deportation Regime: Sovereignty, Space, and the Freedom of Movement*. Durham, NC: Duke University Press.

De Lauri, Antonio (2014). 'Bourgeois Knowledge', *Allegra Lab*.

De Lauri, Antonio (2018). 'Humanitarian militarism and the production of humanity', *Social Anthropology*, 27(1): 84–99.

De Lauri, Antonio (2019). 'A Critique of the Humanitarian (B)order of Things', *Journal of Identity and Migration Studies*, 13(2): 148–66.

Dean, Mitchell (1999). *Governmentality: Power and Rule in Modern Society*. London: Sage.

Del Re, Emanuela C. (2015). 'Female Combatants in the Syrian Conflict, in the Fight against or with the IS and in the Peace Process', in *Female Combatants in Conflict and Peace: Challenging Gender in Violence and Post-Conflict*, ed. Seema Shekhawat. New York: Palgrave Macmillan, pp. 84–97.

Diamond, Larry Jay (2002). 'Thinking About Hybrid Regimes', *Journal of Democracy*, 13(2): 21–35.

Dinc, Pinar (2020). 'The Kurdish Movement and the Democratic Federation of Northern Syria: An Alternative to the (Nation-)State Model?', *Journal of Balkan and Near Eastern Studies*, 22(1): 47–67.

Diner, Cagla and Sule Toktas (2010). 'Waves of feminism in Turkey: Kemalist, Islamist and Kurdish women's movements in an era of globalisation', *Journal of Balkan and Near Eastern Studies*, 12(1): 41–57.

Dixon, Jennifer M. (2010). 'Defending the Nation? Maintaining Turkey's Narrative of the Armenian Genocide', *South European Society and Politics*, 15(3): 467–85.

Donabed, Sargon (2016). *Reforging a Forgotten History: Iraq and the Assyrians in the Twentieth Century*. Edinburgh: Edinburgh University Press.

Dorronsoro, Gilles (2005). 'The autonomy of the political field. The resources of the Deputies of Diyarbakır (Turkey): 1920–2002', *European Journal of Turkish Studies*, 3.

DPT (1989). *DPT Altıncı Beş Yıllık Kalkınma Planı 1990–1994: Yayin No 2174*. Ankara: Devlet Planlama Teşkilatı Yayınları.

DPT (1992). *Karayollu Ulastirmasi: VI Bes Yillik Kalkinma Plani OIK Raporu*. Ankara: T.C. Basbakanlik Devlet Planlama Teskilati.

Duff, R. A. (2001). *Punishment, Communication, and Community*, New York: Oxford University Press.

Durkheim, Emile (2008). *The Elementary Forms of Religious Life*. Oxford: Oxford University Press.

Dursun, Habip (2013). *Jin Dergisi'nde Kürt Milliyetçiliği (Kurdish Nationalism in Women's Magazines)*. Unpublished Master's thesis, Atılım University, Ankara.

Duruiz, Deniz (2020). 'Seasonal farm workers: Pitiful victims or Kurdish laborers demanding equality', in *The Turkish question*, ed. Heinrich Böll Stiftung – Turkey Representation. Istanbul: Heinrich Böll Stiftung, pp. 32–7.

Düzgün, Meral (2016). 'Jineology: The Kurdish Women's Movement', *Journal of Middle East Women's Studies*, 12(2): 284–7.

Dyer, Owen (2020). 'Covid-19: Turkey cracks down on doctors who doubt official figures.' *British Medical Journal* (BMJ), 29 September, <https://www.bmj.com/content/370/bmj.m3787> (last accessed 25 June 2021).

Easterly, William (2013). *The Tyranny of Experts: Economics, Dictators and the Forgotten Rights of the Poor*. Philadelphia: Basic Books.

Eber, Christine and Christine Kovic (2003). *Women of Chiapas: Making History in Times of Struggle and Hope*. New York: Routledge.

Einstein, Albert (1954a). *A Letter to Erik Gutkind*. Princeton.

Einstein, Albert (1954b). *Ideas and Opinions*. New York: Bonanza Books.

Ensaroglu, Yilmaz (2013). 'Turkey's Kurdish Question and the Peace Process', *Insight Turkey*, 15(2): 7–17.

Ercanbrack, Jonathan (2015). *The Transformation of Islamic Law in Global Financial Markets*. Cambridge: Cambridge University Press.

Erdem, Ali Riza (2005). 'İlköğretimimizin Gelişimi ve Bugün Gelinen Nokta', *Üniversite ve Toplum Dergisi*, 5(2): 75–86.

Ergil, Dogu (2000). 'The Kurdish Question in Turkey', *The Journal of Democracy*, 11(3): 122–35.

Ergil, Dogu (2020). 'Turkey's Turkish identity question', in *The Turkish Question*, by Heinrich Böll Stiftung – Turkey Representation. Istanbul: Heinrich Böll Stiftung.

Eriksen, Thomas H. (1995). *Small Places, Large Issues: An Introduction to Social and Cultural Anthropology*. London: Pluto Press.

Erkaya, Yusuf (2015). *Corruption, Bribery and Nepotism: The Case of Turkey*. London: Lambert Academic Publishing.

Ersanlı-Behar, B. (1992). *İktidar ve Tarih: Türkiye'de Resmi Tarih Tezinin Oluşumu, 1929–1937*. İstanbul: Afa yayınları.

Esen, Berk and Sebnem Gumuscu (2016). 'Rising Competitive Authoritarianism in Turkey', *Third World Quarterly*, 37(9): 1581–1606.

Evans, Gareth (2009). *The Responsibility to Protect: Ending Mass Atrocity Crimes Once and for All*. Washington, DC: Brookings Institution.

Ezrow, Natasha M. and Erica Frantz (2011). *Dictators and Dictatorships: Understanding Authoritarian Regimes and Their Leaders*. Continuum International Publishing Group.

Fanon, Frantz (1963) *The Wretched of the Earth*. New York: Grove Press.

Fassin, Didier (2001). 'The Biopolitics of Otherness: Undocumented Foreigners and Racial Discrimination in French Public Debate', *Anthropological Today*, 17(1): 3–7.

Fassin, Diddier (2007). *When Bodies Remember: Experiences and Politics of AIDS in South Africa*. Berkeley: University of California Press.

Fassin, Didier (2009). 'Another Politics of Life is Possible', *Theory, Culture & Society*, 26(5): 44–60.

Fassin, Didier (2011a). *Humanitarian Reason. A Moral History of the Present*. Berkeley: University of California Press.

Fassin, Didier (2011b). 'Policing Borders, Producing Boundaries: The Governmentality of Immigration in Dark Times', *Annual Review of Anthropology*, 40: 213–26.

Fassin, Didier (2017). 'The endurance of critique', *Anthropological Theory*, 17(1): 4–29.

Fassin, Didier and Mariella Pandolfi (eds) 2010. *Contemporary States of Emergency: The Politics of Military and Humanitarian Interventions*. Cambridge: Zone Books.

Feldman, Ilana and Miriam Ticktin (eds) (2010). *In the Name of Humanity: The Government of Threat and Care*. Durham, NC: Duke University Press.

Ferejohn, John E. (2002). 'Judicializing Politics, Politicizing Law', *Law & Contemporary Problems*, 65(3): 41–68.

Filali-Ansary, Abdou and Sekeena K. Ahmed (eds) (2009). *The Challenge of Pluralism: Paradigms from Muslim Contexts*. Edinburgh: Edinburgh University Press.

Fish, M. Steven (2002). 'Islam and Authoritarianism', *World Politics*, 55(1): 4–37.

Forensic Architecture (2019). 'CGI scene reconstruction opens new leads in Kurdish activist killing', *Open Democracy* (8 February 2019).

Foucault, Michel (1972). *The Archaeology of Knowledge*. New York: Pantheon.

Foucault, Michel (1978). *The History of Sexuality*. New York: Vintage Books.

Foucault, Michel (1988). 'Truth, Power, Self: an interview with Michel Foucault', in *Technologies of the Self: A Seminar with Michel Foucault*, ed. Luther H. Martin, Huck Gutman and Patrick H. Hutton. Amherst: University of Massachusetts Press, pp. 9–15.

Foucault, Michel (1991). 'Governmentality', in *The Foucault Effect: Studies in Governmentality*, ed. Graham Burchell, Colin Gordon and Peter Miller. Chicago: University of Chicago Press.

Foucault, Michel (1997). *Ethics: Subjectivity and Truth*. New York: The New Press.

Foucault, Michel (2000a). 'The subject and power', in *Essential Works of Foucault 1954–1984*, ed. James D. Faubion. New York: The New Press.

Foucault, Michel (2000b). 'Confronting Governments: Human Rights', in *Essential Works of Foucault 1954–1984*, ed. James D. Faubion. New York: The New Press.

Foucault, Michel (2000c). 'Governmentality', in *Essential Works of Foucault 1954–1984*, ed. James D. Faubion. New York: The New Press, pp. 201–22.

Foucault, Michel (2000d). 'Truth and Power', in *Essential Works of Michel Foucault, 1954–1984*, ed. James D. Faubion. New York: The New Press.

Foucault, Michel (2003). 'Preface to The History of Sexuality, Volume Two', in *The Essential Foucault*, ed. Paul Rabinow and Nikolas Rose. New York: The New Press.

Foucault, Michel (2007). *Security. Territory, Population. Lectures at the Collège de France, 1977–1978*. Basingstoke: Palgrave Macmillan.

Foucault, Michel (2008). *The Birth of Biopolitics: Lectures at the Collège de France, 1978–1979*. Basingstoke: Palgrave.

Foucault, Michel and Colin Gordon (1980). *Power and Knowledge: Selected Interviews and Other Writings, 1972–1977*. New York and London: Harvester Wheatsheaf.

Foucault, Michel, Arnold I. Davidson and Graham Burchell (2008). *The Birth of Biopolitics: Lectures at the Collège de France, 1978–1979*. Basingstoke and New York: Palgrave Macmillan.

Fourest, Caroline (dir.) (2019). *Soeurs d'Armes (Sisters in Arms)*, film.

Freedom House (2018). 'Freedom in the World 2018: The Annual Survey of Political Rights & Civil Liberties', <https://freedomhouse.org/sites/default/files/2020-02/FreedomintheWorld2018COMPLETEBOOK_0.pdf> (last accessed 23 June 2021).

Freedom House (2019). 'Freedom in the World 2019: Democracy in Retreat', <https://freedomhouse.org/report/freedom-world/2019/democracy-retreat> (last accessed 23 June 2021).

French, Peter A. (2011). *War and Moral Dissonance*. Cambridge: Cambridge University Press.

Friedrich, Carl Joachim and Zbigniew K. Brzezinski (1956). *Totalitarian Dictatorship and Autocracy*. Cambridge, MA: Harvard University Press.

Gal, Susan (1995). 'Language and the "Arts of Resistance"', *Cultural Anthropology*, 10(3): 407–24.

Galanter, Mark (1981). 'Justice in Many Rooms: Courts, Private Ordering, and Indigenous Law', *Journal of Legal Pluralism and Unofficial Law*, 19: 56–72.

Galip, Ozlem B. (2015). *Imagining Kurdistan: Identity, Culture and Society*. London and New York: I. B. Tauris.

Gandhi, Jennifer (2008). *Political Institutions under Dictatorship*. Cambridge: Cambridge University Press.

Garret, Laurie (1994). *The Coming Plague: Newly Emerging Diseases in a World out of Balance*. London: Penguin Books.

Garrett, Laurie (2001). *Betrayal of Trust: The Collapse of Global Public Health*. New York: Hyperion Books.

Gellately, Robert and Ben Kiernan (eds) (2003). *The Specter of Genocide: Mass Murder in Historical Perspective*. New York: Cambridge University Press.

Ghalib, Sabah Abdullah (2011). *The Emergence of Kurdism with Special Reference to the Three Kurdish Emirates within the Ottoman Empire 1800–1850*. Unpublished PhD thesis, University of Exeter.

Glover, Jonathan (2000). *Humanity: A Moral History of the Twentieth Century*. New Haven, CT: Yale University Press.

Gocek, Fatma Muge (2008). 'Through a Glass Darkly: Consequences of a Politicized Past in Contemporary Turkey', *Annals of the American Academy of Political and Social Science*, 61(7), 88–106.

Gocek, Fatma Muge (2015). *Denial of Violence: Ottoman Past, Turkish Present, and Collective Violence against the Armenians, 1789–2009*. Oxford: Oxford University Press.

Gokalp, Deniz (2007). *Beyond Ethnopolitical Contention: The State, Citizenship and Violence in the "New" Kurdish Question in Turkey*. PhD Dissertation, The University of Texas.

Gokalp, Ziya (1992). *Kürt asiretleri hakkinda sosyolojik tetkikler*. Istanbul: Sosyal Yayinlar.

Gokcen, Sabiha (1996). *Ataturk'le Bir Omur*. Istanbul: Altin Kitaplar.

Goktas, Hidir (2007). 'Interview: Turkish Kurds want democracy not state says MP', *Reuters* (Online, 3 August 2007).

Golash, Deirdre (2005). *The Case against Punishment: Retribution, Crime Prevention, and the Law*. New York: New York University Press.

Goodhart, Charles (1981). 'Problems of Monetary Management: The UK experience', in *Inflation, Depression, and Economic Policy in the West*, ed. Anthony S. Courakis. New Jersey: Barnes & Noble Books, pp. 111–46.

Gordon, Colin (1991). 'Governmental rationality: an introduction', in *The Foucault Effect: Studies in Governmentality*, ed. Graham Burchell, Colin Gordon and Peter Miller. Chicago: University of Chicago Press.

Gourlay, William (2017). 'Oppression, Solidarity, Resistance: The Forging of Kurdish Identity in Turkey', *Ethnopolitics*, 17(2): 130–46.

Gourlay, William (2020). *The Kurds in Erdoğan's Turkey: Balancing Identity, Resistance and Citizenship*. Edinburgh: Edinburgh University Press.

Gözaydın, İstar B. (2008). 'Diyanet and Politics', *The Muslim World*, 98: 216–27.

Graeber, David (2011). *Dept: The First 5,000 Years*. New York: Melville House.

Greenhouse, Carol J. (2019). '"This Is Not Normal": Are Social Facts Finished?', *American Anthropologist*, 121(1): 167–70.

Gross, Michael L. (2008). 'Is There a Duty to Die for Humanity?: Humanitarian Intervention, Military Service and Political Obligation', *Public Affairs Quarterly*, 22(3): 213–29.

Gunduz-Hosgor, Ayse and Jeroen Smits (2002). 'Intermarriage between Turks and Kurds in Contemporary Turkey: Inter-ethnic relations in an urbanizing environment', *European Sociological Review*, 18(4): 417–32.

Gunter, Michael (2004). 'The Kurdish Question in Perspective', *World Affair*, 166(4): 197–205.

Gunter, Michael (2013). 'The Turkish-Kurdish Peace Process', *Georgetown Journal of International Affairs*, 14(1): 101–11.

Gurses, Mehmet (2015). 'Is Islam a cure for ethnic conflict? Evidence from Turkey', *Politics and Religion*, 8(1): 135–54.

Gurses, Mehmet (2018). *Anatomy of a Civil War: Sociopolitical Impacts of the Kurdish Conflict in Turkey*. Ann Arbor: University of Michigan Press.

Habermas, Jurgen (1994). 'Human Rights and Popular Sovereignty: The Liberal and Republican Versions', *Ratio Juris*, 7(1): 1–13.

Hanioglu, Sukru (2001). *Preparation for a Revolution: The Young Turks (1902–1908)*. New York and Oxford: Oxford University Press.

Hansen, Susan B. and Laura Wills Otero (2007). 'A Woman for President? Gender and Leadership Traits Before and After 9/11', *Journal of Women, Politics & Policy*, 28(1): 35–60.

Hansen, Thomas Blom and Finn Stepputat (eds) (2005). *Sovereign Bodies: Citizens, Migrants, and States in the Postcolonial World*. Princeton: Princeton University Press.

Hanson, Gordon H. and Antonio Spilimbergo (1999). 'Illegal Immigration, border enforcement and relative wages.' *American Economic Review*, 89(5): 1337–57.

Harris, Edward M. (2007). 'The Rule of Law in Athenian Democracy. Reflections on the Judicial Oath', *Ethics & Politics*, IX(1): 55–74.

Harris, Edward M. (2013). *The Rule of Law in Action in Democratic Athens*. Oxford: Oxford University Press.

Hart, H. L. A. (1968). *Punishment and Responsibility*. Oxford: Oxford University Press.

Hashim, Ahmed (2013). *When Counterinsurgency Wins: Sri Lanka's Defeat of the Tamil Tigers*. Philadelphia: University of Pennsylvania Press.

Hawke, Jason (2011). *Writing Authority: Elite Competition and Written Law in Early Greece*. DeKalb: Northern Illinois University Press.

Hegel, G. W. F. [1820] (1991). *The Philosophy of Rights*. Cambridge: Cambridge University Press.

Heper, Metin (2007). *State and Kurds in Turkey: The Questions of Assimilation. Tradition in Turkey*. London: Palgrave Macmillan.

Heper, Metin (2010). 'The Ottoman Legacy and Turkish Politics', *Journal of International Affairs*, 54(1): 63–82.

Heper, Metin and Sabri Sayari (eds) (2012). *The Routledge Handbook of Modern Turkey*. Abingdon: Routledge.

Herbert, Roy (1987). 'Chernobyl disaster: how the Soviet Union's cover story was blown', *New Scientist* (23 April 1987).

Ho, Karen and Jillian R. Cavanaugh (2019). 'What happened to Social Facts?', *American Anthropologist*, 121(1): 160–7.

Hobbes, Thomas (1985). *Leviathan*. London: Penguin Books.

Hobbes, Thomas (1991). *Man and Citizen*. Indianapolis: Hackett Publishing Company.

Holden, Livia (ed.) (2014). *Legal Pluralism and Governance in South Asia and Diasporas*. Abingdon: Routledge.

Holman, Mirya R., Jennifer L. Merolla, Elizabeth J. Zechmeister (2011). 'Sex, Stereotypes, and Security: A Study of the Effects of Terrorist Threat on Assessments of Female Leadership', *Journal of Women, Politics & Policy*, 32(3): 173–92.

Home Office (2020). 'Country Policy and Information Note Turkey: Peoples' Democratic Party (HDP)', Version 4.0 report published by *British Home Office* (March 2020).

Human Rights Watch (2017). 'Turkey: Academics on Trial for Signing Petition, 'Terrorist Propaganda' Charge Stifles Free Speech', 5 December, <https://www.hrw.org/news/2017/12/05/turkey-academics-trial-signing-petition> (last accessed 24 June 2021).

Human Rights Watch (2018). 'Turkey: Government Targeting Academics Dismissals, Prosecutions Create Campus Climate of Fear', 14 May, <https://www.hrw.org/news/2018/05/14/turkey-government-targeting-academics> (last accessed 24 June 2021).

Human Rights Watch (2020). 'Turkey: Kurdish Mayors' Removal Violates Voters' Rights: End Politically Motivated Arrests and Trials', 7 February, <https://www.hrw.org/news/2020/02/07/turkey-kurdish-mayors-removal-violates-voters-rights> *Human Rights Watch Website* (last accessed 24 June 2021).

Huntington, Samuel P. (1968). *Political Order in Changing Societies*. New Haven, CT: Yale University Press.

Hür, Ayse (2012). 'Tarih Defteri', *Taraf* (22 January 2012).

Husak, D. (2010). *The Philosophy of Criminal Law: Selected Essays*. New York: Oxford University Press.

Ibn Khaldun (1989). *The Muqaddimah: An Introduction to History*. Princeton: Princeton University Press.

Ibrahim, Ferhad and Gulistan Gurbey (eds) (2000). *The Kurdish Conflict in Turkey: Obstacles and Chances for Peace and Democracy*. New York: St. Martin's Press.

ICJ (2016). 'Turkey: the Judicial System in Peril', *International Commission of Jurists (ICJ)*, Geneva, Switzerland.

Ignatieff, Michael (ed.) (2001). *Human Rights as Politics and Idolatry*. Princeton: Princeton University Press.

In der Maur, Reneé et al. (eds.) 2015. *Stateless Democracy: With the Kurdish Women's Movement*. Amsterdam: New World Academy.

Irving, David (1996). *Goebbels: Mastermind of the Third Reich*. London: Focal Point Publications.

Jensehaugen, Helge (2016). 'Filling the void': Turkish settlement in Northern Cyprus, 1974–1980', *Settler Colonial Studies*, 7(3): 354–71.

Jerven, Morten (2013). *Poor Numbers: How We are Misled by African Development Statistics and What to Do about It*. Ithaca and London: Cornell University Press.

Johansson, Thomas and Philip Lalander (2012). 'Doing resistance – youth and changing theories of resistance', *Journal of Youth Studies*, 15(8): 1078–88.

Jongerden, Joost (2017). 'Looking beyond the state: transitional justice and the Kurdish issue in Turkey', *Ethnic and Racial Studies*, 41(4).

Jongerden, Joost (2019). 'Conquering the state and subordinating society under AKP rule: a Kurdish perspective on the development of a new autocracy in Turkey', *Journal of Balkan and Near Eastern Studies*, 21(3): 260–73.

Jongerden, Joost and Ahmet Hamdi Akkaya (2011). 'Born from the Left: The Making of the PKK', in *Nationalism and Politics in Turkey: Political Islam, Kemalism and the Kurdish Issue*, ed. Marlies Casier and Joost Jongerden. New York: Routledge.

Jwaideh, Wadie (2006). *Kurdish National Movement: Its Origins and Development*. New York: Syracuse University Press.

Kakutani, Michiko (2018). *The Death of Truth: Notes on Falsehood in the Age of Trump*. New York: Tim Duggan Books.

Kandiyoti, Deniz (ed.) (1991). *Women, Islam and the State*. London: Palgrave Macmillan.

Kandiyoti, Deniz, Nadje Al-Ali and Kathryn Spellman (2019). *Gender, Governance and Islam*. Edinburgh: Edinburgh University Press.

Karáth, Kata (2020). 'Covid-19: Hungary's pandemic response may have been worse than the virus', *British Medical Journal (BMJ)*, 4 November, <https://www.bmj.com/content/371/bmj.m4153> (last accessed 24 June 2021).

Karpat, Kemal (1982). 'Millets and Nationality: The Roots of the Incongruity of Nation and State in the Post Ottoman Era', in Benjamin Braude and Bernard Lewis (eds), *Christians and Jews in the Ottoman Empire: The Functioning of a Plural Society*. New York and London: Holmes & Meier Publishers, pp. 141–67.

Karpat, Kemal (2001). *The Politicization of Islam: Reconstructing Identity, State, Faith, and Community in the Late Ottoman State*. Oxford and New York: Oxford University Press.

Kasaba, Reşat (2004). 'Do States Always Favor Stasis? Changing Status of Tribes in the Ottoman Empire', in Joel Migdal (ed.), *Boundaries and Belonging*. Cambridge: Cambridge University Press, pp. 27–48.

Kaur, Raminder and dyuti a (2020). 'Reclaiming the sublime. The (un)making of the people's constitution in India', *HAU: Journal of Ethnographic Theory* 10(3): 716–25.

Kaya, Ayhan (2014). 'Islamisation of Turkey under the AKP Rule: Empowering Family, Faith and Charity', *South European Society and Politics*, 20(1): 47–69.

Kaya, Nurcan (2009). *Forgotten or Assimilated? Minorities in the Education System of Turkey*. Minority Right Group (MRG) International Report.

Keane, Webb (2015). *Ethical Life: Its Natural and Social Histories*. Princeton. Princeton University Press.

Keles, Janroj Y. (2015). *Media, Diaspora and Conflict: Nationalism and Identity amongst Kurdish and Turkish Migrants in Europe*. London and New York: I. B. Tauris.

Kelly, Mark G. E. (2014). *Foucault and Politics: A Critical Introduction*. Edinburgh: Edinburgh University Press.

Kelly, Michael (ed.) (1994). *Critique and Power: Recasting the Foucault/Habermas Debate*. Cambridge, MA: The MIT Press.

Keyman, E. Fuat (2007). 'Modernity, Secularism and Islam: The Case of Turkey', *Theory, Culture & Society* 24: 215–34.

Kim, Jim Yong, Joyce V. Millen, Alec Irwin and John Gershman (eds) (2001). *Dying for Growth: Global Inequalities and the Health of the Poor*. Monroe, ME: Common Courage Press.

King, L. W. (2005). *The Code of Hammurabi*. New Haven: Yale University Press.

Kirdis, Esen (2019). *The Rise of Islamic Political Movements and Parties: Morocco, Turkey and Jordan*. Edinburgh: Edinburgh University Press.

Kirisci, Kemal (1998). 'Turkey'. *Internally Displaced People: A Global Survey*, ed. Janie Hampton. London: Earthscan Publications Ltd.

Klein, Hilary (2015). *Compañeras: Zapatista Women's Stories*. New York: A Seven Stories Press.

Knapp, Michael, Anja Flach and Ercan Ayboğa (2016). *Revolution in Rojava. Democratic Autonomy and Women's Liberation in Syrian Kurdistan*. London: Pluto Press.

Kokal, Kalindi (2019). *Local Self-Regulation in India*. Abingdon: Routledge.

Kötter, Matthias, Tilmann J. Röder, Gunnar Folke Schuppert and Rüdiger Wolfrum (2015). *Non-State Justice Institutions and the Law: Decision-Making at the Interface of Tradition, Religion and the State*. London: Palgrave Macmillan.

Koukoudakis, George (2017). 'Authoritarianism in Turkey: From "Kemalist" to "Erdoganism" via Democratic Reforms and Economic Development', *Romanian Journal of History and International Studies*, 4(1): 63–101.

Krohn-Hansen, Christian and Knut G. Nustad (2005). *State Formation: Anthropological Perspectives*. London: Pluto Press.

Kurt, Mehmet (2017). *Kurdish Hizbullah in Turkey: Islamism, Violence and the State*. London: Pluto Press.

Kurt, Mehmet (2019). '"My Muslim Kurdish brother": colonial rule and Islamist governmentality in the Kurdish region of Turkey', *Journal of Balkan and Near Eastern Studies*, 21(3): 350–65.

Kuru, Ahmet T. (2009). *Secularism and State Policies toward Religion. The United States, France, and Turkey*. Cambridge: Cambridge University Press.

Laborde, Cecile (2008). *Critical Republicanism*. Oxford: Oxford University Press.

Laborde, Cecile (2010). 'Republicanism and Global Justice: A Sketch', *European Journal of Political Theory*, 9(1): 48–69.

Lanni, Adriaan (2006). *Law and Justice in the Courts of Classical Athens*. Cambridge: Cambridge University Press.

Lavinas, Lena (2013). '21st Century Welfare', *New Left Review*, 84: 5–40.

Lavinas, Lena (2017). *The Takeover of Social Policy by Financialization: The Brazilian Paradox*. New York: Palgrave Macmillan.

Leblang, David (2017). 'Harnessing the diaspora: dual citizenship, migrant return remittances', *Comparative Political Studies*, 50(1): 75–101.

Leezenberg, Michiel (2016). 'The ambiguities of democratic autonomy: The Kurdish movement in Turkey and Rojava', *South European and Black Sea Studies*, 16(4): 671–90.

Leon, David and Gill Walt (eds) (2001). *Poverty, Inequality, and Health*. Oxford: Oxford University Press.

Levitsky, Steven and Lucan Way (2010). *Competitive Authoritarianism: Hybrid Regimes After the Cold War*. Cambridge: Cambridge University Press.

Levitsky, Steven and Lucan Way (2020). 'The New Competitive Authoritarianism', *Journal of Democracy*, 31(1): 51–65.

Levitsky, Steven, Lucan Way and Brent Kallmer (2020). 'A Conversation on Competitive Authoritarianism', *Journal of Democracy* (11 February 2020).

Linz, Juan J. (2000). *Totalitarian and Authoritarian Regimes*. London: Lynne Rienner.

Linz, Juan J. and Alfred Stepan (1996). *Problems of Democratic Transition and Consolidation: Southern Europe, South America, and Post-Communist Europe*. Baltimore: The Johns Hopkins University Press.

Locke, John (1947). *Two Treatises of Government*. New York: Hafner Press.

Locke, John (2010). *Letter on Toleration*. Indianapolis: Liberty Fund.

Lockman, Zachary (2009). *Contending Visions of the Middle East: The History and Politics of Orientalism*. Cambridge: Cambridge University Press.

Luhrmann, Anna and Staffan L. Lindberg (2019). 'A third wave of autocratization is here: what is new about it?', *Democratization*, 26(7): 1095–1113.

Lundy, Patricia and Mark McGovern (2008). 'Whose Justice? Rethinking Transitional Justice from the Bottom Up', *The Journal of Law and Society*, 35(2): 265–92.

McCormick, John and Mairi MacInnes (eds) (1962). *Versions of Censorship*. London: Routledge.

McDowall, David (2004) *A Modern History of the Kurds*. London and New York: I. B. Tauris.

Maimbo, Samuel Munzele (2003). *The Money Exchange Dealers of Kabul: A Study of the Hawala System in Afghanistan*. World Bank Working Paper No. 13. Washington, DC: World Bank.

Mankekar, Purnima (1999). *Screening Culture, Viewing Politics: An Ethnography of Television, Womanhood, and Nation in Postcolonial India*. Durham, NC and London: Duke University Press.

Marcus, Aliza (2017). *Blood and Belief. The PKK and The Kurdish Fight for Independence*. New York and London: New York University Press.

Markell, Patchen (2008). 'The Insufficiency of Non-domination', *Political Theory*, 36(1): 9–36.

Martin, Biddy (1988). 'Feminism, criticism and Foucault', in *Feminism and Foucault: Reflections on Resistance*, ed. Irene Diamond and Lee Quinby. Boston: Northeastern University Press.

Martire, Jacope (2017). *A Foucauldian Interpretation of Modern Law: From Sovereignty to Normalisation and Beyond*. Edinburgh: Edinburgh University Press.

Marx, Karl (1978). 'The German ideology', *The Marx–Engels Reader*, ed. Robert C. Tucker. New York: W. W. Norton, pp. 146–200.

Meister, Robert (2010). *After Evil: A Politics of Human Rights*. New York: Colombia University Press.

Menski, Werner 2006). *Comparative Law in a Global Context: The Legal Systems of Asia and Africa*. Cambridge: Cambridge University Press.

Menski, Werner (2011). 'Flying kites in a global sky: New models of jurisprudence', *Socio-Legal Review*, 7: 1–22.

Migdal, Joel S. (2001). *State in Society: Studying how States and Societies Transform and Constitute One Another*. Cambridge: Cambridge University Press.

Mill, John Stuart (1975). *On Liberty*. New York: W. W. Norton.

Mill, John Stuart (1977). *The Collected Works of John Stuart Mill, Vol. XVIII*. Toronto: University of Toronto Press.

Miller, David (2007). *National Responsibility and Global Justice*. Oxford, Oxford University Press.

Mills, C. Wright (1956). *The Power Elite*. Oxford: Oxford University Press.

Milosz, Czeslaw (1955). *The Captive Mind*. New York: Vintage Books.

Montesquieu, Baron de [1748] (2001). *The Spirit of Laws*. Kitchener, ON: Batoche Books.

Moore, B. (1966). *Social Origins of Dictatorship and Democracy: Lord and Peasant in the Making of the Modern World*. Boston: Beacon.

Moore, S. Falk (1973). 'Law and Social Change: The Semi-autonomous Social Field as an Appropriate Subject of Study', *Law & Society Review*, 7(4): 719–46.

Moore, Michael S. (1997). *Placing Blame: A Theory of Criminal Law*. Oxford: Oxford University Press.

Morlino, Leonardo (2006). '"Good" and "bad" democracies: how to conduct research into the quality of democracy', *Journal of Communist Studies and Transition Politics.* 20(1): 5–27.

Murad, Nadia (2017). *The Last Girl: My Story of Captivity, and My Fight Against the Islamic State.* New York: Tim Duggan Books.

Murphy, Jeffrie G. (1973). 'Marxism and Retribution', *Philosophy and Public Affairs,* 2: 217–43.

Murphy, Jeffrie G. (2007). 'Legal Moralism and Retribution Revisited', *Criminal Law and Philosophy,* 1: 5–20.

Nagel, Thomas (1975). *The Possibility of Altruism.* Oxford: Clarendon Press.

Nash, Patrick S. (2017). 'Sharia in England: The Marriage Law Solution', *Oxford Journal of Law and Religion,* 6(3): 523–43.

Natanel, Katherine (2016). *Sustaining Conflict Apathy and Domination in Israel-Palestine.* Oakland: University of California Press.

Navaro-Yashin, Yael (2002). *Faces of the State: Secularism and Public Life in Turkey.* Princeton: Princeton University Press.

Neiburg, Fredrico and Omar Riberio Thomaz (2020). 'Ethnographic views of Brazil's (new) authoritarian Right', *HAU: Journal of Ethnographic Theory* 10(1): 7–11.

Nelson, Alondra (2020). 'Society after Pandemic', *Social Science Research Council (SSRC),* 23 April 2020.

Nerney, Gayne (1985). 'Hobbes: The Twofold Grounding of Civil Philosophy', *History of Philosophy Quarterly,* 2(4): 395–409.

Nietzsche, Friedrich (2007). *'On the Genealogy of Morality' and Other Writings.* Cambridge: Cambridge University Press.

Nimni, Ephraim and Elcin Aktoprak (eds) (2018). *Democratic Representation in Plurinational States: The Kurds in Turkey.* London and New York: Palgrave Macmillan.

Nozick, Robert (1974). *Anarchy, State, and Utopia.* New York: Basic Books.

Öcalan, Abdullah (1999). *Declaration on the Democratic Solution of the Kurdish Question.* Neuss: International Initiative.

Öcalan, Abdullah (2000). *Gerçeğin Dili ve Eylemi.* Istanbul: Aram Yayınları.

Öcalan, Abdullah (2009a). *War and Peace in Kurdistan. Perspectives for a Political Solution of the Kurdish Question.* Cologne: International Initiative-Mesopotamian Publishers.

Öcalan, Abdullah (2009b). *Özgürlük Sosyolojisi* (Sociology of Freedom). İstanbul: Aram.

Öcalan, Abdullah (2011a) *The Road Map to Democratization of Turkey and Solution to the Kurdish Question.* Cologne: International Initiative.

Öcalan, Abdullah (2011b). *Democratic Confederalism*. London: Transmedia.

Öcalan, Abdullah (2013). *Liberating Life: Women's Revolution*. Cologne: International Initiative-Mesopotamian Publishers.

Öcalan, Abdullah (2015). *Manifesto for a Democratic Civilization. Volume 1, Civilization. The Age of Masked Gods and Disguised Kings*. Cologne: International Initiative-New Compass.

Öcalan, Abdullah (2016). *Democratic Nation*. Cologne: International Initiative-Mesopotamian Publishers.

Öcalan, Abdullah (2017a). *The Political Thought of Abdullah Öcalan. Kurdistan, Woman's Revolution and Democratic Confederalism*. London: Pluto Press.

Öcalan, Abdullah (2017b). *Manifesto for a Democratic Civilization. Volume 2, Civilization. The Age of Unmasked Gods and Naked Kings*. Cologne: International Initiative-New Compass.

Öcalan, Abdullah and Yalcin Kucuk (1993). *Kürt bahçesinde sözleşi*. Istanbul: Başak Yayınları.

Official Newspaper (1987). *T.C. Resmi Gazete Kodu: 311287*. Ankara.

OHCHR (2016a). '"They come to destroy": ISIS crimes against Yazidis', *United Nations Human Rights Office of the High Commissioner* (15 June 2016).

OHCHR (2016b). 'Turkey: Zeid concerned by actions of security forces and clampdown on media', *United Nations Human Rights Office of the High Commissioner* (1 February 2016).

OHCHR (2017). 'Report on the human rights situation in South-East Turkey: July 2015 to December 2016', *United Nations Human Rights Office of the High Commissioner* (February 2017).

Öktem, Kerem (2004). 'Incorporating the time and space of the ethnic "other": nationalism and space in Southeast Turkey in the nineteenth and twentieth centuries', *Nations and Nationalism*, 10(4): 559–78.

Öktem, Kerem (2008) 'The Nation's Imprint: Demographic Engineering and the Change of Toponymes in Republican Turkey', *European Journal of Turkish Studies*, 7.

Olson, Mancur (1993). 'Dictatorship, Democracy, and Development', *American Political Science Review*, 87(3): 567–76.

Olson, Robert (1989). *The Emergence of Kurdish Nationalism and the Sheikh Said Rebellion, 1880–1925*. Austin: University of Texas Press.

Olson, Robert (1996). *The Kurdish Nationalist Movement in the 1990s: Its impact on Turkey and the Middle East*. Lexington: The University Press of Kentucky.

Olur, N. (1994). *Türkiye Eğitiminde Çağdaşlaşma*. Unpublished PhD thesis. Marmara Üniversitesi Türkiyat Araştırmaları Enstitüsü, İstanbul.

O'Malley, Pat (2004). *Risk, Uncertainty and Government*. London: Routledge.

Onis, Ziya (2015). 'Monopolising the Centre: The AKP and the Uncertain Path of Turkish Democracy', *The International Spectator*, 50(2): 22–41.

Ophir, Adi (2005). *The Order of Evils: Toward an Ontology of Morals*. Cambridge: Zone.

Ottaway, Marina (2003). *Democracy Challenged: The Rise of Semi-Authoritarianism*. Washington, DC: Carnegie Endowment for International Peace.

Özbudun, Ergun (2014). 'AKP at the Crossroads: Erdogan's Majoritarian Drift', *South European Society and Politics*, 19(2): 155–67.

Özbudun, Ergun (2015). 'Turkey's Judiciary and the Drift Toward Competitive Authoritarianism', *The International Spectator*, 50(2): 42–55.

Ozcan, Nihat A. (1999). *PKK (Kurdistan Workers' Party): History, Ideology and Method* [*PKK (Kürdistan İşçi Partisi) Tarihi, İdeolojisi, Yöntemi*]. Ankara: ASAM.

Özcan, Ali Kemal (2006). *Turkey's Kurds: A Theoretical Analysis of the PKK and Abdullah Öcalan*. London and Abingdon: Routledge.

Ozcan, Yusuf Z. (1990). 'Ülkemizdeki Cami Sayıları Üzerine Sayısal Bir İnceleme', *Journal of Islamic Research*, 4(1): 5–20.

Ozcan, Yusuf Z. (1994). 'Mosques in Turkey: A Quantitate Analysis', *Intellectual Discourse*, 2(1): 19–40.

Ozel, Mehmet (2000). *2000'li Yillara Girerken Turk Ordusu (Turkish Millitary into the 2000s)*. Ankara: The Director for Fine and Arts in the Ministry of Culture and Ankara Chamber of Commerce.

Oznur, Fatih (2009). *Ataturk'un Kurtleri: Vaat Edilmis Topraklarin Hikayesi*. Istanbul: Karakutu.

Ozoglu, Hakan (2001). 'Nationalism and Kurdish Notables in the Late Ottoman and Early Republican Era', *International Journal of Middle East Studies*, 33(3): 343–409.

Ozoglu, Hakan (2004). *Kurdish Notables and the Ottoman State: Evolving Identities, Competing Loyalties, and Shifting Boundaries*. Albany: New York University Press.

Öztürk, Ahmet Erdi (2016). 'Turkey's Diyanet under AKP Rule: From Protector to Imposer of State Ideology?', *Southeast European and Black Sea Studies* 16: 619–35.

Özyürek, Ezra, Gaye Özpınar and Emrah Altindis (eds) (2018). *Authoritarianism and Resistance in Turkey: Conversations on Democratic and Social Challenges*. Cham: Springer

Pamuk, Şevket (2019). *Uneven Centuries: Economic Development in Turkey Since 1820*. Princeton: Princeton University Press.

Pankhurst, Donna (2008). *Gendered Peace: Women's Struggle for Post-War Justice and Reconciliation*. New York: Routledge.

Parla, Taha (1992). *Kemalist Tek-Parti Ideolojisi ve CHP'nin Alti Ok's*. Istanbul: Iletisim.

Passas, Nikos (1999). 'Informal Value Transfer system and Criminal Organizations: A Study into So-called Underground Bankers Networks', SSRN, 14 December 1999.

Pavičić-Ivelja, K. (2016). 'The Rojava Revolution: Women's Liberation as an Answer to the Kurdish Question', *West Croatian History Journal*, 11: 131–48.

PEN International (2016). 'Turkey: Arrest of Academics is an unacceptable violation of freedom of expression', PEN International (15 January 2016).

Peters, Michael A., A. C. Besley, Mark Olssen, Susanne Weber (2009). *Governmentality Studies in Education*. Rotterdam: Sense Publishers.

Pettit, Philip (1997). *Republicanism: A Theory of Freedom and Government*. Oxford: Clarendon Press.

Pettit, Philip (2001). *A Theory of Freedom: From the Psychology to the Politics of Agency*. Oxford: Oxford University Press.

Phelp, M. Lizabeth (2014). 'Doppelgangers of the State: Private Security and Transferable Legitimacy', *Politics and Policy*, 42(6): 824–49.

Philips, David L. (2015). *The Kurdish Spring: A New Map of the Middle East*. New Brunswick, NJ: Transaction Publishers.

Pistor, Katharina (2019). *How the Law Creates Wealth and Inequality*. Princeton: Princeton University Press.

Plato (1906). *The Republic of Plato*. London: E. P. Dutton & Co.

Plattner, Marc F. (2015). 'Is Democracy in Decline?', *Journal of Democracy*, 26(1): 5–10.

Polat, Necati (2016). *Regime Change in Contemporary Turkey: Politics, Rights, Mimesis*. Edinburgh: Edinburgh University Press.

Porto, Mauro (2011). 'Telenovelas and representations of national identity in Brazil', *Media, Culture & Society*, 33(1): 53–69.

Power, Samantha (2002). *'A Problem From Hell': America and the Age of Genocide*. New York: Basic Books.

Prince, J. Dyneley (1904). 'Review: The Code of Hammurabi', *The American Journal of Theology*, 8 (3): 601–9.

Przeworski, Adam, Michael E. Alvarez, José Antonio Cheibub and Fernando Limongi (2000). *Democracy and Development: Political Institutions and Well-Being in the World, 1950–1990*. Cambridge: Cambridge University Press.

Rabinow, Paul (ed.) (1997). *Michael Foucault/Ethics: Subjectivity and Truth*. New York: The New Press.

Raby, Rebecca (2005). 'What is Resistance?', *Journal of Youth Studies*, 8(2): 151–71.

Rajagopal, Arvind (2001). *Politics after Television: Religious Nationalism and the Reshaping of the Indian Public*. Cambridge: Cambridge University Press.

Ramji, Rubina (2005). 'From Navy Seals to The Siege: Getting to Know the Muslim Terrorist, Hollywood Style', *Journal of Religion & Film*, 9(2).

Ranharter, Katherine and Gareth Stansfield (2016). 'Acknowledging the Suffering Caused by State-Mandated Sexual Violence and Crimes: An Assessment of the Iraqi Hight Tribunal', *The Journal of Middle Eastern Studies*, 52(1): 27–45.

Rawls, John (1997). 'The Idea of Public Reason Revisited', *The University of Chicago Law Review*, 64(3): 765–807.

Rawls, John (1999). *The Law of Peoples with 'The Idea of Public Reason Revisited'*. Cambridge, MA: Harvard University Press.

Rawls, John (2001). *Justice as Fairness: A Restatement*. Cambridge, MA: Harvard University Press.

Richards, Howard and Joanna Swanger (2009). 'Culture Change: A Practical Method with a Theoretical Basis', in *Handbook on Building Cultures of Peace*, ed. Joseph de Rivera. New York: Springer.

Rieff, David (ed.) (2005). *At the Point of a Gun: Democratic Dreams and Armed Intervention*. New York: Simon and Schuster.

Rivera, Joseph de (1977). *A Structured Theory of the Emotion*. New York: International Universities Press.

Rivera, Joseph de (2014). 'Emotion and the formation of social identities', in *Collective Emotions*, ed. Christian von Scheve and Mikko Salmela. Oxford: Oxford University Press, pp. 217–30.

Romano, David (2006). *The Kurdish Nationalist Movement, Opportunity, Mobilization and Identity*. Cambridge: Cambridge University Press.

Rohe, Mathias (2019). *Paralleljustiz*. Baden-Wurttemberg: Ministerium der Justiz und fur Europa.

Rohloff, Caroline (2012). 'Reality and Representation of Algerian Women: The Complex Dynamic of Heroines and Repressed Women', *Honors Projects*. Paper 6, <https://digitalcommons.iwu.edu/french_honproj/6/> (last accessed 26 June 2021).

Rose, Nikolas (1999). *Powers of Freedom: Reframing Political Thought*. Cambridge: Cambridge University Press.

Rudi, Axel (2018). 'The PKK's Newroz: Death and Moving Towards Freedom for Kurdistan', *Zanj: The Journal of Critical Global South Studies*, 2(1): 92–114.

Rudolph, C. (2006). *National Security and Immigration: Explaining Policy Development in the United States and Western Europe since 1945*. Stanford, CA: Stanford University Press.

Rueschemeyer, Dietrich, Evelyne Huber Stephens and John D. Stephens (1992). *Capitalist Development and Democracy*. Chicago: University of Chicago Press.

Rugman, Jonathan (1996). *Ataturk's Children: Turkey and the Kurds*. London: Cassel.

Rumelili, Bahar and Didem Cakmakli (2017). 'Civic Participation and Citizenship in Turkey: A Comparative Study of Five Cities', *South European Society and Politics*, 22(3): 365–84.

Rummel, Rudolph J. (1994). *Death by Governments*. Abingdon: Routledge.

Saeed, Seevan (2014). *The Kurdish National Movement in Turkey: From the PKK to the KCK*. Unpublished PhD thesis, University of Exeter.

Saeed, Seevan (2019). 'The dilemma of the Kurdish struggle in Turkey', *Journal of Balkan and Near Eastern Studies*, 21(3): 274–85.

Safrastian, Arshak (1948). *Kurds and Kurdistan*. London: The Harvill Press.

Sahin, Osman (1995). *Firat'in sirtindaki kan: Bucaklar*. Istanbul: Kaynak.

Sahin-Mencutek, Zeynep (2016). 'Strong in the Movement, Strong in the Party: Kurdish Women's Representation in Political Parties of Turkey', *Political Studies*, 64: 470–87.

Said, Edward (1993). *Culture and Imperialism*. London: Vintage.

Said, Edward (1995). *Orientalism: Western Conceptions of the Orient*. London: Penguin.

Said, Edward (1997). *Covering Islam. How the Media and the Experts Determine how We See the Rest of the World*. New York: Random House.

Salamandra, Christa (2005). 'Television and the ethnographic endeavour: The case of Syrian drama', *Transnational Broadcasting Studies*, 14: 1–22.

Sanalan, Timucin (1973). *Kalkinmada Oncelikli Yorelerin Tespiti ve Bu Yorelerdeki Tesvik Tedbirleri*. Ankara: T. C. Basbakanlik Devlet Planlama Yayinlari.

Sanbonmatsu, Kira (2003). 'Political Knowledge and Gender Stereotypes', *American Politics Quarterly*, 31(6): 575–94.

Sarigil, Zeki (2010). 'Curbing Kurdish ethno-nationalism in Turkey: an empirical assessment of pro-Islamic and socio-economic approaches', *Ethnic and Racial Studies*, 33(3): 533–53.

Sarigil, Zeki and Ekrem Karakoc (2016). 'Who wants secession? The determinants of secessionist attitudes among Turkey's Kurds', *Nations and Nationalism*, 22(2): 325–46.

Saylan, Gencay (1987). *İslamiyet ve Siyaset: Türkiye Örneği*. Ankara: V. Yayınlan.

Scarciglia, Roberto and Werner F. Menski (2018). *Normative Pluralism and Religious Diversity: Challenges and Methodological Approaches*. Alphen aan den Rijn: Wolters Kluwer and CEDAM.

Schedler, Andreas (ed.) (2006). *Electoral Authoritarianism: The Dynamics of Unfree Competition*. Boulder, CO: Lynne Rienner Publishers.

Scheppele, Kim Lane (2018). 'Autocratic Legalism', *The University of Chicago Law Review*, 85(2): 545–84.

Schmidinger, Thomas (2018). *Rojava: Revolution, War and the Future of Syria's Kurds*. London: Pluto Press.

Schumpeter, Joseph A. (1943). *Capitalism, Socialism and Democracy*. London: Allen & Unwin.

Scott, James C. (1985). *Weapons of the Weak: Everyday Forms of Peasant Resistance*. New Haven, CT: Yale University Press.

Scott, James C. (1990). *Domination and the Arts of Resistance; Hidden Transcripts*. New Haven, CT: Yale University Press.

Scott, Joan W. (1986). 'Gender: A Useful Category of Historical Analysis', *The American Historical Review*, 91(5): 1053–75.

Scott, Joan W. (2008). 'AHR Forum: Unanswered Questions', *American Historical Review*, 113: 1422–30.

Scott, Joan W. (2009). 'Knowledge, Power and Academic Freedom', *Social Research*, 76(2): 451–80.

Scott, Joan W. (2018). *Gender and the politics of history. 30th Anniversary edition*. New York: Colombia University Press.

Scott, Joan W. (2019). *Knowledge, Power and Academic Freedom*. New York: Colombia University Press.

Sezgin, Yuksel (2014). *Human Rights under State-Enforced Religious Family Laws in Israel, Egypt and India*. Cambridge: Cambridge University Press.

Shafer-Landau, Russ (1996). 'The Failure of Retributivism', *Philosophical Studies*, 82: 289–316.

Shafer-Landau, Russ (2000). 'Retributivism and Desert', *Pacific Philosophical Quarterly*, 81: 189–214.

Shah, Prakash, Marie-Claire Foblets and Mathias Rohe (2014). *Family, Religion and Law: Cultural Encounters in Europe*. Farnham: Ashgate.

Shapiro, Michael J. and Hayward R. Alker (1996). *Challenging Boundaries: Global Flows, Territorial Identities*. Minneapolis: University of Minnesota Press.

Sharp, Joanne P., Paul Routledge, Chris Philo and Ronan Paddison (eds) (2000). *Entanglements of Power: Geographies of Domination/Resistance*. London: Routledge.

Shen-Bayt, Fiona (2018). 'Strategies of Repression: Judicial and Extrajudicial Methods of Autocratic Survival.' *World Politics*, 70(3): 321–57.

Simon, Jonathan (1994). 'Between Power and Knowledge: Habermas, Foucault, and the Future of Legal Studies', *Law & Society Review*, 28(4): 947–61.

Skolnick, Jerome (1966). *Justice without Trial: Law Enforcement in Democratic Society*. New York: John Wiley & Sons.

Smith, Adam (1759). *Theory of Moral Sentiment*. London: A. Millar.

Smith, Adam (1999). *The Wealth of Nations, Books I-III*. London: Penguin Books.

Smith, Anthony D. (1999). *The Ethnic Origins of Nations*. Oxford: Basil Blackwell.

Smith, Linda Tuhiwai (2008). *Decolonizing Methodologies: Research and Indigenous Peoples*. London and New York: Zed Books.

Smith, W. Robertson (1889). *Lectures on the Religion of the Semites*. London: A & C Black.

Solanki, Gopika (2011). *Adjudication in Religious Family Laws: Cultural Accommodation, Legal Pluralism and Gender Equality in India*. New Delhi: Cambridge University Press.

Somer, Murat (2016). 'Understanding Turkey's democratic breakdown: old vs. new and indigenous vs. global authoritarianism', *Southeast European and Black Sea Studies*, 16(4): 481–503.

Speed, Shannon, R. Aída Hernández Castillo and Lynn M. Stephen (eds) (2006). *Dissident Women: Gender and Cultural Politics in Chiapas*. Austin: University of Texas Press.

Strathern, Marilyn (1997). 'Improving Ratings: Audit in the British University System', *European Review*, 5(3): 305–21.

Svolik, Milan (2008). 'Authoritarian Reversals and Democratic Consolidation', *American Political Science Review*, 102(02): 153–68.

Szmolka, Inmaculada (ed.) (2017). *Political Change in the Middle East and North Africa: After the Arab Spring*. Edinburgh: Edinburgh University Press.

Tait, Gordon (2000). *Youth, Sex and Government*. Peter Lang Publishing.

Tank, Pinar (2005). 'The effects of the Iraq war on the Kurdish issue in Turkey', *Conflict, Security and Development*, 5(1): 69–86.

Tas, Latif (2014). 'The Myth of the Ottoman Millet System: Its Treatment of Kurds and a Discussion of Territorial and Non-Territorial Autonomy', *International Journal on Minority and Group Rights*, 21(4): 497–526.

Tas, Latif (2015). 'What kind of peace? The case of the Turkish and Kurdish peace process', *Open Democracy* (9 July 2015).

Tas, Latif (2016a). 'How International Law Impacts on Statelessness and Citizenship: the case of Kurdish nationalism, conflict and peace', *Cambridge Journal of Law in Context*, 12(1): 41–82.

Tas, Latif (2016b). 'Peace Making or State Breaking: The Turkish-Kurdish Peace Processes and the Role of Diasporas', *International Journal of Review of Social Studies (RoSS)*, 3(1): 25–66.

Tas, Latif (2016c). 'Stateless Kurds and their multiple diaspora', The International Migration Institute (IMI), University of Oxford, Working Papers 126.

Tas, Latif (2016d). *Legal Pluralism: Dispute Resolution and the Kurdish Peace Committee*. Abingdon: Routledge.

Tas, Latif (2019). 'Regimes of Evil: colonization continues', *Open Democracy* (24 October 2019).

Tax, Meredith (2016). *A Road Unforeseen: Women Fight the Islamic State*. New York: Bellevue Literary Press.

Tazzioli, Martina (2014). *Spaces of Governmentality: Autonomous Migration and the Arab Uprisings*. Lanham, MD: Rowman & Littlefield.

Tekdemir, Omer (2018). 'The reappearance of Kurdish Muslims in Turkey: the articulation of religious identity in a national narrative', *British Journal of Middle Eastern Studies*, 45(4): 589–606.

Tekdemir, Omer (2019). 'Left-wing populism within horizontal and vertical politics: the case of Kurdish-led radical democracy in agonistic pluralism', *Journal of Balkan and Near Eastern Studies*, 21(3): 335–49.

Teorell, Jan (2010). *Determinants of Democratization: Explaining Regime Change in the World, 1972–2006*. Cambridge: Cambridge University Press.

Tezcur, Güneş M. (2009). Kurdish Nationalism and Identity in Turkey: A Conceptual Reinterpretation. *European Journal of Turkish Studies*.

Tezcur, Guneş M. (2013). 'Prospects for Resolution of the Kurdish Question: A Realist Perspective', *Insight Turkey*, 15(2).

Tezcur, Güneş M. (2014). 'Violence and nationalist mobilization: the onset of the Kurdish insurgency in Turkey', *The Journal of Nationalism and Ethnicity*, 43(2): 248–66.

Thornton, Rod (2015). 'Problems with the Kurds as proxies against Islamic State: insights from the siege of Kobane.' *Small Wars & Insurgencies*, 26(6): 865–85.

Tibi, Bassam (2014). *Political Islam, World Politics and Europe: From Jihadist to Institutional Islamism*. Abingdon: Routledge.

TIHR (1994). *Turkiye Insan Haklari Raporu*. Ankara: Turkiye Insan Haklari Yayinlari.

TIHR (2000). *Turkiye Insan Haklari Raporu*. Ankara: Turkiye Insan Haklari Yayinlari.

TIHR (2014). *Turkiye Insan Haklari Raporu*. Ankara: Turkiye Insan Haklari Yayinlari.

TİHV (2017). '16 Ağustos 2015'ten Bugüne 2 Yılda İlan Edilen Sokağa Çıkma Yasakları', *Türkiye İnsan Hakları Vakfı* (TIHV) (17 August 2017).

TİHV (2018). '16 Ağustos 2015 – 1 Haziran 2018 Tarihleri Arasında İlan Edilen Sokağa Çıkma Yasakları', *Türkiye İnsan Hakları Vakfı* (TIHV) (1 June 2018).

Tilly, Charles (1977). *From Mobilisation to Revolution*. Center for Research on Social Organization (CRSO) Working Paper, University of Michigan.

Tilly, Charles (1985). 'War making and state making as organized crime', in *Bringing the State Back*, ed. Peter B. Evans, Dietrich Rueschemeyer and Theda Skocpol. Cambridge: Cambridge University Press.

Toktamış, Kumru F. (2019). '(Im)possibility of negotiating peace: 2005–2015 peace/reconciliation talks between the Turkish government and Kurdish politicians', *Journal of Balkan and Near Eastern Studies*, 21(3): 286–303.

Tomlin, Patrick (2014). 'Retributivists! The Harm Principle Is Not for You!', *Ethics*, 124: 272–98.

Toros, Taha (1939). *Atatürk'ün Adana Seyahatleri*. Adana: Seyhan Basımevi.

Tugal, Cihan (2009). *Passive Revolution: Absorbing the Islamic Challenge to Capitalism*. Stanford, CA: Stanford University Press.

Tunc, Asli (2018). 'All is flux: A hybrid media approach to macro-analysis of the Turkish media', *Middle East Critique* 27(2): 141–59.

Turam, Berna (ed.) (2012). *Secular State and Religious Society: Two Forces in Play in Turkey*. New York: Palgrave Macmillan.

Turshen, Meredith (2002). 'Algerian Women in the Liberation Struggle and the Civil War: From Active Participants to Passive Victims?', *Social Research*, 69(3): 889–911.

Ungor, Ugur (2011). *The Making of Modern Turkey: Nation and State in Eastern Anatolia, 1913–1950*. Oxford: Oxford University Press.

Uzun A (2005). 'Economic Etatism and Market Economy Culture During One-Party Era', *The Market Magazine*, 14.

Van Bruinessen, Martin (1992). *Agha, Shaikh and State: The Social and Political Structure of Kurdistan*. London and New York: Zed Books.

Van Bruinessen, Martin (2000). *Kurdish Ethno-Nationalism versus Nation-Building States: Collected Articles*. Istanbul: The Isis Press.

Van Bruinessen, Martin (2002). 'Kurds, states and tribes', in *Tribes and Power: Nationalism and Ethnicity in the Middle East*, ed. Faleh A. Jabar and Hosham Dawod. London: Saqi, pp. 165–83.

Varisco, Daniel M. (2007). *Reading Orientalism: Said and the Unsaid*. Seattle: University of Washington Press.

Vatansever, Asli (2020). *At the Margin of Academia: Exile, Precariousness, and Subjectivity*. Leiden: Brill.

Vergin. N. (1985) 'Toplumsal Değişme ve Dinsellikte Artış.' *Toplum ve Bilim*, 29/30: 9–28.

Viellechner, Lars (2020). '"Friendliness" Towards Others: How the German Constitution Deals with Legal Pluralism', in *Debating Legal Pluralism and Constitutionalism: New Trajectories for Legal Theory in the Global Age*, ed. Guillaume Tusseau. Cham: Springer, pp. 189–228.

Wahman, Michael, Jan Teorell and Axel Hadenius (2013). 'Authoritarian regime types revisited: updated data in comparative perspective', *Contemporary Politics*, 19(1): 19–34.

Waldinger, Roger and David Fitzgerald (2004). 'Transnationalism in question', *American Journal of Sociology*, 109(5): 1177–95.

Wallerstein, Immanuel (1976). *The Modern World System*. New York: Academic Press.

Watenpaugh, Heghnar Z. (2014). 'Preserving the Medieval City of Ani: Cultural Heritage between Contest and Reconciliation', *Journal of the Society of Architectural Historians*, 73(4): 528–55.

Walzer, Michael (1983). *Spheres of Justice*. Oxford: Blackwell.

Walzer, Michael (1994). *Thick and Thin: Moral Argument at Home and Abroad*. Notre Dame, IN: University of Notre Dame Press.

Walzer, Michael (2004). 'The Duty to Rescue,' in *Arguing About War*. New Haven, CT: Yale University Press.

Walzer, Michael (2006). *Just and Unjust Wars: A Moral Argument with Historical Illustrations*. New York: Basic Books

Walzer, Michael (2019). *Political Action: A Practical Guide to Movement Politics*. New York: New York Review Books.

Watts, Nicole F. (2009). 'Re-Considering State-Society Dynamics in Turkey's Kurdish Southeast', *European Journal of Turkish Studies*, 10.

Weber, Max (1927). *General Economic History*. London: Allen & Unwin.

Weber, Max (1958). *The Protestant Ethic and the Spirit of Capitalism*. New York: Scribner's.

Weber, Max (1974). *On Universities: The Power of the State and the Dignity of the Academic Calling in Imperial Germany*. Chicago: University of Chicago Press.

Weber, Max (2014). *Economy and Society*. Oakland: University of California Press.

Weber, Max (2015). *Rationalism and Modern Society*. Basingstoke: Palgrave Macmillan.

Weir, Lorna (2008). 'The Concept of Truth Regime', *The Canadian Journal of Sociology*, 33(2): 367–89.

Weitz, Eric D. (2003). *A Century of Genocide: Utopias of Race and Nation*. Princeton: Princeton University Press.

White, Jenny (2013). *Muslim nationalism and the new Turks*. Princeton: Princeton University Press.

White, Mark D. (ed.) (2011). *Retributivism: Essays on Theory and Policy*. New York: Oxford University Press.

White, Paul (2000). *Primitive Rebels or Revolutionary Modernizers? The Kurdish Nationalism Movement in Turkey*. London: Zed Books.

Whyte, Jessica (2012). 'Human rights: confronting governments? Michel Foucault and the right to intervene', in *New Critical Legal Thinking: Law and the Political*, ed. Matthew Stone, Illan Rua Wall and Costas Douzinas. Abingdon: Routledge, pp. 11–31.

Williams, Christopher (1993). 'Who are "street children?"? A hierarchy of street use and appropriate responses', *Child Abuse & Neglect*, 17: 831–41.

Wright, Joseph (2008). 'Do Authoritarian Institutions Constrain? How Legislatures Affect Economic Growth and Investment', *American Journal of Political Science*, 52(2): 322–43.

Wright, Joseph and Abel Escribà-Folch (2012). 'Authoritarian Institutions and Regime Survival: Transitions to Democracy and Subsequent Autocracy', *British Journal of Political Science*, 42(2): 283–309.

Yadirgi, Veli (2017). *The Political Economy of the Kurds of Turkey: From the Ottoman Empire to the Turkish Republic*. Cambridge: Cambridge University Press.

Yalcin-Heckmann, Lâle (1991). *Tribe and Kinship among the Kurds*. Frankfurt am Main: Peter Lang.

Yanikdag, Yucel (2014). *Healing the Nation: Prisoners of War, Medicine and Nationalism in Turkey, 1914–1939*. Edinburgh: Edinburgh University Press.

Yavuz, M. Hakan (2003). *Islamic Political Identity in Turkey*. Oxford: Oxford University Press.

Yavuz, M. Hakan and A. E. Öztürk (2019). 'Turkish secularism and Islam under the reign of Erdoğan', *Southeast European and Black Sea Studies*, 19(1): 1–9.

Yegen, Mesut (1996). 'The Turkish state discourse and the exclusion of Kurdish identity', *Middle Eastern Studies*, 32(2): 216–29.

Yegen, Mesut (2007). 'Turkish nationalism and the Kurdish question', *Ethnic and Racial Studies*, 30(1): 119–51.

Yegen, Mesut (2016). 'The Turkish Left and the Kurdish Question', *Journal of Balkan and Near Eastern Studies*, 18(2): 157–76.

Yildiz, Ahmet (2001). *Ne Mutlu Turkum Diyebilene: Turk Ulusal Kimliginin Etno-Sekuler Sinirlari (1999–1938)*. Istanbul: Iletisim.

Yildiz, Hasan (2001). *Muhatapsız Savaş Muhatapsız Barış*. Istanbul: Doz.

Yilmaz, Arzu (2016). *Artus'tan Maxmur'a Kurt Multeciler ve Kimligin Yeniden Insasi*. Istanbul: Iletisim Yayinlari.

Yilmaz, Aytekin (2014). *Yoldaşını Öldürmek*. Istanbul: Iletisim.

Yilmaz, Ihsan and Galib Bashirov (2018). 'The AKP after 15 years: emergence of Erdoganism in Turkey', *Third World Quarterly*, 39(9): 1812–30.

Yildirim, M. C., N. Beltekin and T. T. Oral (2018). 'Increasing school attendance and schooling rates for girls: Persuasion process', *Journal of Oriental Scientific Research*, 10(2): 783–804.

Yucekok, A. E (1971). *Türkiye'de Örgütlenmiş Dinin Sosyo-Ekonomik Tabanı (1946–1968)*. Ankara: SBF Yayinlari.

Yüksel, Metin (2006). 'The Encounter of Kurdish Women with Nationalism in Turkey', *The Journal of Middle Eastern Studies* 42(5): 777–802.

Yuval-Davis, Nira (2003). 'Nationalist Projects and Gender Relations', *Croatian Journal of Ethnology and Folklore Research*, 40(1): 9–35.

Yuval-Davis, Nira (1997). *Gender and Nation*. London: Sage Publications.

Yuval-Davis, Nira and Floya Anthias (1989). *Woman-Nation-State*. London: Palgrave Macmillan.

Zaibert, L. (2006). *Punishment and Retribution*. Burlington: Ashgate.

Zakaria, F. (1997). 'The Rise of Illiberal Democracy', *Foreign Affairs*, 76: 22–43.

Zartman, I. William (2017). 'States, boundaries and sovereignty in the Middle East: unsteady but unchanging', *International Affairs*, 93(4): 937–48.

Zeydanlioglu, Welat (2009). 'Torture and Turkification in the Diyarbakır Military Prison', in *Rights, Citizenship and Torture: Perspectives on Evil, Law and the State*, ed. Welat Zeydanlioglu and John T. Parry. Oxford: Inter-Disciplinary Press, pp. 73–92.

Zihnioglu, Yaprak (2003). *Kadinsiz Inkilap: Nezihe MUhittin, Kadinlar Halk Fikrasi, Kadin Birligi*. Istanbul: Metis.

Zürcher, Erik Jan (2010). *Young Turk Legacy and Nation Building: From the Ottoman Empire to Atatürk's Turkey*. London: I. B. Tauris.

INDEX

Note: **bold** indicates illustrations